# In Praise of *Knowledge Representation and Reasoning*

*This book clearly and concisely distills decades of work in AI on representing information in an efficient and general manner. The information is valuable not only for AI researchers, but also for people working on logical databases, XML, and the semantic web: read this book, and avoid reinventing the wheel!*

**Henry Kautz, University of Washington**

*Brachman and Levesque describe better than I have seen elsewhere, the range of formalisms between full first order logic at its most expressive and formalisms that compromise expressiveness for computation speed. Theirs are the most even-handed explanations I have seen.*

**John McCarthy, Stanford University**

*This textbook makes teaching my KR course much easier. It provides a solid foundation and starting point for further studies. While it does not (and cannot) cover all the topics that I tackle in an advanced course on KR, it provides the basics and the background assumptions behind KR research. Together with current research literature, it is the perfect choice for a graduate KR course.*

**Bernhard Nebel, University of Freiburg**

*This is a superb, clearly written, comprehensive overview of nearly all the major issues, ideas, and techniques of this important branch of artificial intelligence, written by two of the masters of the field. The examples are well chosen, and the explanations are illuminating.*

*Thank you for giving me this opportunity to review and praise a book that has sorely been needed by the KRR community.*

**William J. Rapaport, State University of New York at Buffalo**

*A concise and lucid exposition of the major topics in knowledge representation, from two of the leading authorities in the field. It provides a thorough grounding, a wide variety of useful examples and exercises, and some thought-provoking new ideas for the expert reader.*

**Stuart Russell, UC Berkeley**

*No other text provides a clearer introduction to the use of logic in knowledge representation, reasoning, and planning, while also covering the essential ideas underlying practical methodologies such as production systems, description logic-based systems, and Bayesian networks.*

**Lenhart Schubert, University of Rochester**

*Brachman and Levesque have laid much of the foundations of the field of knowledge representation and reasoning. This textbook provides a lucid and comprehensive introduction to the field. It is written with the same clarity and gift for exposition as their many research publications. The text will become an invaluable resource for students and researchers alike.*

**Bart Selman, Cornell University**

*KR&R is known as "core AI" for a reason — it embodies some of the most basic conceptualizations and technical approaches in the field. And no researchers are more qualified to provide an in-depth introduction to the area than Brachman and Levesque, who have been at the forefront of KR&R for two decades. The book is clearly written, and is intelligently comprehensive. This is the definitive book on KR&R, and it is long overdue.*

**Yoav Shoham, Stanford University**

# KNOWLEDGE REPRESENTATION AND REASONING

# About the Authors

**Ron Brachman** has been doing influential work in knowledge representation since the time of his Ph.D. thesis at Harvard in 1977, the result of which was the KL-ONE system, which initiated the entire line of research on description logics. For the majority of his career he served in research management at AT&T, first at Bell Labs and then at AT&T Labs, where he was Communications Services Research Vice President, and where he built one of the premier research groups in the world in Artificial Intelligence. He is a Founding Fellow of the American Association for Artificial Intelligence (AAAI), and also a Fellow of the Association for Computing Machinery (ACM). He is currently President of the AAAI. He served as Secretary-Treasurer of the International Joint Conferences on Artificial Intelligence (IJCAI) for nine years. With more than 60 technical publications in knowledge representation and related areas to his credit, he has led a number of important knowledge representation systems efforts, including the CLASSIC project at AT&T, which resulted in a commercially deployed system that processed more than $5 billion worth of equipment orders. Brachman is currently Director of the Information Processing Technology Office at the U.S. Defense Advanced Research Projects Agency (DARPA), where he is leading a new national-scale initiative in cognitive systems.

**Hector Levesque** has been teaching knowledge representation and reasoning at the University of Toronto since joining the faculty there in 1984. He has published over 60 research papers in the area, including three that have won best-paper awards. He has also co-authored a book on the logic of knowledge bases and the widely used TELL–ASK interface that he pioneered in his Ph.D. thesis. He and his collaborators have initiated important new lines of research on a number of topics, including implicit and explicit belief, vivid reasoning, new methods for satisfiability, and cognitive robotics. In 1985, he became the first non-American to receive the Computers and Thought Award given by IJCAI. He was the recipient of an E.W.R. Steacie Memorial Fellowship from the Natural Sciences and Engineering Research Council of Canada for 1990–1991. He was also a Fellow of the Canadian Institute for Advanced Research from 1984 to 1995, and is a Founding Fellow of the AAAI. He was elected to the Executive Council of the AAAI, and is on the editorial board of five journals. In 2001, Levesque was the Conference Chair of the IJCAI-01 conference, and is currently Past President of the IJCAI Board of Trustees.

Brachman and Levesque have been working together on knowledge representation and reasoning for more than 25 years. In their early collaborations at BBN and Schlumberger, they produced widely read work on key issues in the field, as well as several well-known knowledge representation systems, including KL-ONE, KRYPTON, and KANDOR. They presented a tutorial on knowledge representation at the International Joint Conference on Artificial Intelligence in 1983. In 1984, they coauthored a prize-winning paper at the National Conference on Artificial Intelligence that is generally regarded as the impetus for an explosion of work in description logics and which inspired many new research efforts on the tractability of knowledge representation systems, including hundreds of research papers. The following year, they edited a popular collection, *Readings in Knowledge Representation*, the first text in the area. With Ray Reiter, they founded and chaired the international conferences on Principles of Knowledge Representation and Reasoning in 1989; these conferences continue on to this day. Since 1992, they have worked together on the course in knowledge representation at the University of Toronto that is the basis for this book.

# KNOWLEDGE REPRESENTATION AND REASONING

Ronald J. Brachman

Hector J. Levesque

with a contribution by Maurice Pagnucco

AMSTERDAM • BOSTON • HEIDELBERG • LONDON
NEW YORK • OXFORD • PARIS • SAN DIEGO
SAN FRANCISCO • SINGAPORE • SYDNEY • TOKYO

Morgan Kaufmann is an imprint of Elsevier

ELSEVIER

MORGAN KAUFMANN PUBLISHERS

Senior Editor: Denise E. M. Penrose
Publishing Services Manager: Andre Cuello
Production Manager: Brandy Palacios
Production Management: Graphic World Publishing Services
Editorial Assistant: Valerie Witte
Design Manager: Cate Barr
Cover Design: Dick Hannus, Hannus Design Associates
Cover Image: "Trout River Hills 6: The Storm Passing", 1999, Oil on board, 80" × 31¾".
            Private Collection. Copyright Christopher Pratt
Text Design: Graphic World Publishing Services
Composition: Cepha Imaging Pvt. Ltd.
Technical Illustration: Graphic World Publishing Services
Copyeditor: Graphic World Publishing Services
Proofreader: Graphic World Publishing Services
Indexer: Graphic World Publishing Services
Printer: Maple Press
Cover Printer: Phoenix Color

Morgan Kaufmann Publishers is an Imprint of Elsevier
500 Sansome Street, Suite 400, San Francisco, CA 94111

*This book is printed on acid-free paper.*

Library of Congress Cataloging-in-Publication Data

Brachman, Ronald J., 1949-
    Knowledge representation and reasoning / Ronald J. Brachman, Hector J. Levesque.
      p. cm.
    Includes bibliographical references and index.
    ISBN: 1-55860-932-6
      1. Knowledge representation (Information theory) 2. Reasoning. I. Levesque, Hector J.,
    1951- II. Title.

    Q387.B73 2003
    006.3′32′—dc22

                                                                            2004046573

For information on all Morgan Kaufmann publications,
visit our website at www.mkp.com

Printed in the United States of America
04 05 06 07 5 4 3 2 1

*To Gwen, Rebecca, and Lauren; and Pat, Michelle, and Marc
— because a reasoning mind still needs a loving heart.*

# ■ Contents

## 9    Structured Descriptions                                    155

## 10    Inheritance                                               187

# ■ PREFACE

■

■

Knowledge representation and reasoning is the area of Artificial Intelligence (AI) concerned with how knowledge can be represented symbolically and manipulated in an automated way by reasoning programs. More informally, it is the part of AI that is concerned with thinking, and how thinking contributes to intelligent behavior.

There are, of course, many ways to approach the topic of intelligence and intelligent behavior: We can, for example, look at the neuroscience, the psychology, the evolution, and even the philosophy of the concepts involved. What does knowledge representation have to offer here? As a field of study it suggests an approach to understanding intelligent behavior that is radically different from the others. Instead of asking us to study humans or other animals very carefully (their biology, their nervous systems, their psychology, their sociology, their evolution, or whatever), it argues that what we need to study is *what humans know*. It is taken as a given that what allows humans to behave intelligently is that they know a lot of things about a lot of things and are able to apply this knowledge as appropriate to adapt to their environment and achieve their goals. So in the field of knowledge representation and reasoning we focus on the knowledge, not on the knower. We ask what *any* agent—human, animal, electronic, mechanical—would need to know to behave intelligently, and what sorts of computational mechanisms might allow its knowledge to be made available to the agent as required.

This book is the text for an introductory course in this area of research.

## REPRESENTATION AND REASONING TOGETHER

The easiest book to have written might have been one that simply surveyed the representation languages and reasoning systems currently popular with researchers pushing the frontiers of the field. Instead, we have taken a definite philosophical stance about what we believe matters in the research, and then looked at the key concepts involved from this perspective. What has made the field both intellectually exciting and relevant to practice, in our opinion, is the *interplay between representation and reasoning*. It is not enough, in other words, to write down what needs to be known in some formal representation language; nor is it enough to develop reasoning procedures that are effective for various tasks. Although both of these are honorable enterprises, knowledge representation and reasoning is best understood as the study of how knowledge can at the same time be represented as comprehensively as possible *and* be reasoned with as effectively as possible.

There is a tradeoff between these two concerns, which is an implicit theme throughout the book and one that becomes explicit in the final chapter. Although we start with first-order logic as our representation language and logical entailment as the specification for reasoning, this is just the starting point, and a somewhat simplistic one at that. In subsequent chapters we wander from this starting point, looking at various representation languages and reasoning schemes with different intuitions and emphases. In some cases, the reasoning procedure may be less than ideal; in other cases, it might be the representation language. In still other cases, we wander far enough from the starting point that it is hard to even see the logic involved. However, in all cases, we take as fundamental the impact that needing to reason with knowledge structures has on the form and scope of the languages used to represent a system's knowledge.

## OUR APPROACH

We believe that it is the job of an introductory course (and an introductory textbook) to lay a solid foundation, enabling students to understand in a deep and intuitive way novel work that they may subsequently encounter and putting them in a position to tackle their own later research. This foundation does not depend on current systems or the approaches of specific researchers. Fundamental concepts like knowledge bases, implicit belief, mechanized inference using sound deductive methods, control of reasoning, nonmonotonic and probabilistic extensions to inference, and the formal and precise representation of actions and plans are so basic to the understanding of AI that we believe that the right approach is to teach them in a way that parallels the teaching of elementary physics or economics. This is the approach that we have taken here. We start with very basic assumptions of the knowledge representation enterprise and build on them with simplified but pedagogically digestible descriptions of mechanisms and "laws." This will ultimately leave the student grounded in all of the important basic concepts and fully prepared to study and understand current and advanced work in the field.

This book takes a strong stand on this. We have taken it as our goal to cover most of the key principles underlying work in knowledge representation and reasoning in a way that is, above all else, accessible to the student, and in a sequence that allows later concepts to regularly build directly on earlier ones. In other words, pedagogical clarity and the importance of the material were our prime drivers. For well more than ten years we have taught this material to early graduate students and some fourth-year undergraduates, and in that time we have tried to pay close attention to what best prepared the students to jump directly from our course into the active research literature. Over the years we have tuned and refined the material to match the needs and feedback of the students; we believe that this has resulted in a very successful one-semester course, and one that is unique in its focus on core principles and fundamental mechanisms without being slanted toward our own technical work or interests of the week. Based on our experience with the course, we approached the construction of the book in a top-down way: We first outlined the most important topics in what we felt was the ideal sequence, and then worked to determine the appropriate relative weight (i.e., chapter length) of each set of concepts in the overall book. As we wrote, we worked hard to stay within the structure and bounds that we had initially set, despite the frequent temptation to just keep writing about certain topics. We will have to leave it to you, our reader, to judge, but we feel that the relative emphases and scope of the chapters are important contributions to the value of the book.

Perhaps it would have been nice to have written the comprehensive and up-to-the-minute book that might have become the "bible" of the field, and we may someday tilt at that windmill. But that is not the book we set out to write. By adhering to the approach outlined here, we have created something that fits very well in a one-semester course on the principles and mechanisms that underlie most of the important work going on in the field. In a moment, we will discuss other courses that could be built on top of this textbook, but we feel that it is important for you to know that the book you hold in your hands is first and foremost about the basics. It is intended to put students and practitioners on a firm enough foundation that they can build substantial later work on top of what they learn here.

## OVERVIEW OF THE BOOK

The text is organized as follows. The first chapter provides an overview and motivation for the area of knowledge representation and reasoning and defines the core concepts on which the rest of the book is built. It also spells out the fundamental relationships between knowledge, representation, and reasoning that underlie the rest of the material in the text. Chapters 2 through 4 are concerned with the basic techniques of knowledge representation using first-order logic in a direct way. These early chapters introduce the notation of first-order logic, show how it can be used to represent commonsense worlds, and cover the key reasoning technique of Resolution theorem-proving. Chapters 5 through 7 are concerned with representing knowledge in a more limited way, so that the reasoning is more amenable to procedural control; among the important concepts covered are rule-based systems. Chapters 8 through 10 deal with a more object-oriented approach to knowledge representation and the taxonomic reasoning that goes with it. Here we delve into the ideas of frame representations and description logics and spend time on the notion of inheritance in hierarchies of concepts. Chapters 11 and 12 deal with reasoning that is uncertain or logically unsound, using defaults and probabilities. Chapters 13 through 15 deal with forms of reasoning that go beyond simply drawing conclusions from what is known, including performing diagnosis and generating plans using knowledge about actions. Finally, Chapter 16 explores the tradeoff mentioned earlier.

Exercises are included at the end of each chapter. These exercises focus on the technical aspects of knowledge representation and reasoning, although it should be possible with this book to consider essay-type questions as well. The exercises tend to be more than just drills, often introducing new ideas or extending those presented in the text. All of them have been student tested. Depending on the students involved, a course instructor may want to emphasize the programming questions and deemphasize the mathematics, or perhaps vice versa.

Each chapter includes a short section of bibliographic notes and citations. Although far from complete, these can serve as entry points into the research literature related to the chapter. As stated, it is one of our main pedagogical goals that students who have mastered the topics of the book should be able to read and understand research papers. In this sense, the book is intended to hold a position somewhere between the general AI textbooks that give an overview of the entire field (but somewhat cursorily) and the technical research papers themselves (which are more appropriately covered in an advanced graduate course, perhaps).

## AN INTRODUCTORY COURSE

The material in this book has been used for the past ten years or so in a one-semester (26 hours) introductory course on knowledge representation and reasoning taught at the University of Toronto. (Drafts of the actual text have only been available to students for the past three years.) This course is typically taken by first-year graduate students in computer science, with a smattering of fourth-year computer science undergraduates as well as occasional graduate students from other departments. The syllabus of the course has evolved over the years, but has converged on the 16 chapters of this book, presented in sequence. Students are assigned four problem sets, from which we have culled the exercises appearing in the book. There are two tests given in class, and no final exam.

In our opinion, going through the entire book in sequence, and especially doing the exercises in each chapter, is the best way to learn the basics of knowledge representation. It takes one-hour lectures to cover most chapters, with the chapters on description logic (9), defaults (11), uncertainty (12), diagnosis (13), action (14), and the tradeoff (16) each requiring an additional hour, and the chapter on Resolution (4) requiring a bit more. This adds up to about 24 total hours; in our course, the remaining two hours have been used for tests.

Even if some of the chapters appear to have less immediate relevance to current AI research—for instance, the chapters on procedural reasoning (6) and inheritance (10)—they introduce concepts that remain interesting and important. Negation as failure, for example, introduced in Chapter 6 on procedural representations, is the source of many other ideas that appear elsewhere in the text. Similarly, we feel that students benefit from having seen defeasible inheritance in Chapter 10 before seeing the more demanding Chapter 11 on default reasoning. Before seeing inheritance, it helps to have seen slots with default values used in commonsense examples in Chapter 8 on frames. Before seeing frames, it helps to have seen procedural representations in a non-object-oriented form in Chapter 6. And so on.

On the other hand, despite the many historical and conceptual connections among the chapters, only a few chapters are absolutely necessary from a technical point of view in order to understand the technical material and do the exercises in later chapters. We can think of these as strong prerequisites. Here is a breakdown:

- Chapter 2 on first-order logic is a strong prerequisite to Chapters 3 on expressing knowledge, 4 on Resolution, 9 on description logic, 11 on default reasoning, and 14 on action;

- Chapter 4 on Resolution is a strong prerequisite to Chapters 5 on Horn logic and 13 on diagnosis;

- Chapter 9 on description logic is a strong prerequisite to Chapter 16 on the tradeoff;

- Chapter 14 on actions is a strong prerequisite to Chapter 15 on planning.

Other than these, any chapter appearing before any other in the sequence can be thought of as "recommended preparation."

## USING PARTS OF THE BOOK

As we have emphasized, this book matches up best with a full-semester course intending to cover the basic foundations in knowledge representation and reasoning. However, we believe that it is possible to meaningfully use parts of the book in a shorter course, or in a course that delves more deeply into one or more sets of issues of current interest.

Here is our recommendation for a course on knowledge representation that takes about two thirds of the time as the full course (roughly 16 classroom hours):

> Chapters 1 (introduction), 2 (first-order logic), 3 (expressing knowledge), 4 (Resolution), 9 (description logic), 11 (default reasoning), 12 (vague representations and probabilistic reasoning), 14 (reasoning about action), and 16 (the tradeoff).

In our opinion, these are the core chapters, and armed with these a student should be able to understand the context at least of research papers in the major subareas of the field.

One possibility for an advanced course in knowledge representation is to cover the core chapters and then supplement them, according to the interests of the students and instructor, with additional chapters from the book and research papers selected by the instructor.

Without attempting to be exhaustive, here are some suggestions for advanced courses that could still use this book to provide the broader picture:

1. *limited reasoning:* add Chapter 5 on Horn logic, and papers on logics of explicit belief, modern description logics, knowledge compilation, and limited rationality;

2. *constraint satisfaction:* add Chapter 5 on Horn logic, and papers on SAT, arc consistency, problems of bounded tree width, and theoretical properties of randomized problems;

3. *answer set programming:* add Chapter 5 on Horn logic, Chapter 6 on procedural representations, and papers on default logic and the varieties of semantics for logic programs;

4. *ontology:* add Chapter 8 on frames, and papers on modern description logics, the CYC project, and the semantic web;

5. *semantic networks:* add Chapter 8 on frames, Chapter 10 on inheritance, and papers on associative reasoning, mental models, meaning representations for natural language, and modern semantic network languages (e.g., Conceptual Graphs, SNePS);

6. *belief revision:* add Chapter 10 on inheritance, and papers on logics of knowledge, the AGM postulates, nonmonotonic reasoning, and knowledge and action;

7. *rule-based systems:* add Chapter 6 on procedural representations, Chapter 7 on production systems, and papers on the SOAR project and case studies of deployed systems;

8. *medical applications:* add Chapter 7 on production systems, Chapter 13 on explanation and diagnosis, and papers on expert systems in medicine, as well as those on model-based diagnosis and treatment prescription;

9. *belief networks:* add papers on reasoning methods based on propagation for special network topologies, approximate reasoning, and expectation maximization (EM);

10. *planning algorithms:* add Chapter 15 on planning, and papers on graph-based planning, SAT-based planning, conditional planning, and decision-theoretic planning;

11. *cognitive robotics:* add Chapter 15 on planning, and papers on the logics of knowledge and action, sensing, and dealing with noise;

12. *agent theory:* add Chapter 15 on planning, and papers on the logics of belief, goals, intentions, and communicative actions.

Finally, it is worth addressing one notable omission. Given the scope of our course, we have chosen not to attempt to cover learning. Learning is a rich and full subfield of AI on its own, and given the wide variety of ways that humans seem to learn (by reading, by being taught, by observing, by trial and error, by mental simulation, etc.), as an area of intellectual pursuit it would easily be worth a semester's introductory course of its own. Our own belief is that it will be very important for the learning community and the knowledge representation community to find significant common ground—after all, ultimately, intelligent systems will need to do both and we would expect significant common foundations for both areas. Perhaps by the time a second edition of this text might be warranted there will be enough to say on this issue to facilitate a new chapter.

## A NOTE TO THE PRACTITIONER

Although it is clear that when we designed this textbook we had most directly in mind the student who was planning to go on to further study or research in AI, we have tried to stay aware of the potential role of this material in the lives of those who are already in the field and are practicing their trade in a more down-to-earth systems- and applications-building way. The complementarity between the more academic side of the field and its more practical side has been an important ingredient in our own technical work, and the ultimate use of this textbook by the more pragmatic community is important to us.

The current textbook is clearly not a self-contained practitioner's "handbook," and there is not an emphasis here on detailed issues of direct practical impact. However, our own experience in building AI systems (and we have built and deployed several with teams of collaborators) has taught us that a deep understanding of the concepts explained in this book is an invaluable part of the practitioner's toolkit. As we have mentioned here, and is clearly emphasized in the text, we believe that the reasoning side of the equation is as important as the representation side, and boils down in the end to the question of building reasoning systems that operate within the time and resource constraints of the applications that need them. Further, as described, we have written the text in a fashion that emphasizes simplicity of description of the mechanisms and the basic generality of the material. As a result, we believe that the understanding of the content here would be of great value to someone building systems in industry or supporting a research or development team in a laboratory or other enterprise. Among the exercises, for example, we include programming tasks that should help practitioners understand the core principles behind almost all of the approaches covered in the text. Also, in almost all cases there are fielded systems based on the technologies treated here, and these are either pointed to in the bibliographic notes or are easily accessible in conference proceedings (e.g., from the Innovative Applications of AI conference, sponsored by AAAI) or on the Internet. There are ways to augment the core material presented in the book to make it even more valuable for practitioners, and we are eager to hear from you with your suggestions for doing that.

## A NOTE TO THE EXPERIENCED RESEARCHER

No single book of this size can be expected to cover all the topics one might think of as essential to the study of knowledge representation, and as we have mentioned, that was never our intention. If you are actively involved in research in the area, there is a good chance that your sub-area is only partly covered here, or perhaps is not covered at all. As we have prepared the material in the book, one comment we have heard from time to time is that it would be "inconceivable" to do a book on knowledge representation without covering topic X (where inevitably the person making the comment happened to work on topic X). Such comments may be justified, but as we have tried to emphasize, our focus was on pedagogically digestible material covering a limited number of core concepts in the field. We chose quite intentionally to limit what we covered.

But even having made that decision, there are of course even further choices that needed to be made. Some of these clearly involved our own personal preferences and research history. When it comes to modeling change, should we focus on belief change or world change? (We chose the latter.) Should we deal with world change in terms of action or time? (The former.) Should it be in a modal or a reified representation language? (The latter—hence Chapter 14.) Other choices were possible.

In other cases, what might appear to be missing material might involve a slight misinterpretation of what we set out to do. This book is not intended to be a text on logic-based AI, for example. Although logic plays an important role in our approach (as explained in Chapter 1), there is significant work on logic that is not essential to knowledge representation. Similarly, this is not a book about ontologies or knowledge-based systems. Although we will define what we mean by a knowledge-based system (again, in Chapter 1) and use this to motivate what follows, the techniques for engineering such systems and developing suitable large-scale ontologies involve a different set of concerns. Nor is the book intended as a text in cognitive science. We do believe that cognitive science should be informed by the considerations raised here and vice versa, but in the end the goals of cognitive science suggest an approach that, despite being broad and interdisciplinary, is still focused on the study of people—the knower, not the knowledge.

Finally, as mentioned earlier, this book is not intended to be a complete overview of the field or of the current state of the art. Those interested in learning about the latest advances will need to look elsewhere. What we have intended to cover are the basic foundational ideas that underlie research in the field. What we lose in immediacy and topicality, we hope to gain in the long run in applicability.

One last caveat: As will be apparent to the expert, we have made many significant simplifications. Each of our chapters presents a simplified and sometimes nonstandard form of representation or reasoning: We introduce logic, of course, but only first-order predicate calculus; we present a definition of Resolution that does not work in all cases; we define production systems, but virtually ignore their implementations; we present description logics, but with a subsumption procedure that has largely been superseded by a different type of method; we define only one sort of preemption in inheritance networks; we present a version of default logic that is known to exhibit anomalies; we omit the circumscription schema and axiom altogether; we present belief networks with only the most rudimentary form of reasoning procedure; we present the situation calculus, but with very strict assumptions about how actions can be represented;

we define planning, but only hint at how planning procedures can be made to run efficiently.

As should now be clear, we have made these simplifications for peda-gogical reasons and to create a course of modest scope and length. It is true, for instance, that we do not use Reiter's original definition of a default extension. What we do present, however, works identically in many cases, and is much easier for students to digest (some of this has been learned through hard experience with our students over the years). Near the end, with the basics in hand, we can then raise the somewhat esoteric exam-ples that are not well-handled by our definition, and suggest Reiter's much more complex version as a way to deal with them.

Having said all of this, comments and corrections on all aspects of the book are most welcome and should be sent to the authors.

# ■ ACKNOWLEDGMENTS

■

■

To quote Crosby, Stills, and Nash (and perhaps date ourselves), "It's been a long time comin'." The impetus for this book goes back to a tutorial on knowledge representation that we presented at the International Joint Conference on Artificial Intelligence in Karlsruhe, in 1983. In the process of preparing that overview of the field and a subsequent collection of readings that grew out of it, we began to see research in the area as primarily an attempt to reconcile two conflicting goals: to represent knowledge (and especially, incomplete knowledge) as generally as possible, and to reason with it in an automated way as efficiently as possible. This was an idea that surfaced in some of our own research papers of the time, but as we came to see it as a commonality across much of the work in the area, we also came to feel that it really needed a great deal more thought, and perhaps even a book, to develop in detail. A lot of plans, a lot of talk, and a lot of stalling intervened, but we finally offered an introductory course on these ideas at the University of Toronto in 1987, and then yearly starting in 1992. As the course matured and we evolved ways to explain the core mechanisms of various representation frameworks in simple terms, the idea of a new introduction to the field took shape. At that stage, what existed were slides for lectures, and subsequently, detailed notes for an ambitious and comprehensive book that would have been about twice the size of the current one. We began writing drafts of chapters on and off around 1994, but it took till the start of the new millennium before we had enough material to hand out to students. The last year or two has been spent fine-tuning the manuscript, weaving elements of the different chapters together, integrating exercises, and ultimately trying to find enough time to put it all together. It seems nothing short of miraculous to us that we've finally managed to do it!

Many people contributed directly and indirectly to bringing this text into existence. We thank our colleagues at Fairchild, Schlumberger, Bell Labs, AT&T Labs, DARPA, CNRI, and the University of Toronto, as well as the institutions themselves, for providing the wonderful intellectual environments and resources to support endeavors of this nature.

We first want to acknowledge our dear colleague and friend, the late Ray Reiter, who inspired and encouraged us year after year. We miss him terribly. His ideas are everywhere in the book. We also thank Maurice

Pagnucco, who agreed to do the bibliographic notes and compile the bibliography for us, and did an extraordinary job in a very short time.

Over the years, many other friends and colleagues contributed, in one way or another, to this project. Ron would like to thank his colleagues from AT&T who contributed so much to his work and the general backdrop of this book, including especially those in the CLASSIC group, namely, Alex Borgida (Rutgers), Deborah McGuinness, Peter Patel-Schneider, and Lori Alperin Resnick. His immediate supporting team of managers and colleagues helped to create the world's best environment for AI research: Bill Aiello, Julia Hirschberg, Larry Jackel, Candy Kamm, Henry Kautz, Michael Kearns, Dave Maher, Fernando Pereira, John Rotondo, and Gregg Vesonder. Ron would also like to give special thanks to Ken Schmidt, who provided so much assistance in his lab at AT&T, and more recently at DARPA. Hector would like to acknowledge Jim Delgrande, Jim des Rivières, Patrick Dymond, Patrick Feehan, and Maurice Pagnucco. Some of them may think that they've had nothing to do with this book, but they'd be wrong. Without their friendship and support there would be no book. He would also like to thank Sebastian Sardiña, Mikhail Soutchanski, and Eugenia Ternovskaia, who served as teaching assistants for the knowledge representation course and helped debug the exercises, and all the members of the Cognitive Robotics group, with a special mention to the external members, Giuseppe de Giacomo, Gerhard Lakemeyer, Yves Lespérance, Fangzhen Lin, Fiora Pirri, and Richard Scherl. Special thanks also to Phil Cohen, Richard Fikes, and David Israel, with whom we both have had such enjoyable and exciting collaborations over many years.

We also need to express our deep gratitude to all of our secretaries and assistants over the lifetime of this enterprise; they were essential in so many ways: Helen Surridge, Kara Witzal, Romaine Abbott, Marion Riley, Mary Jane Utter, and Linda Morris, and Veronica Archibald, Belinda Lobo, and Marina Haloulos.

A number of students and instructors have used drafts of the text over the years and have helped us fix a healthy number of bugs and oversights. Among them, we especially thank Selmer Bringsjord, Shannon Dalmao, Ken Forbus, Peter Kanareitsev, Ioannis Kassios, Gerhard Lakemeyer, Wendy Liu, Phuong The Nguyen, Maurice Pagnucco, Bill Rapaport, Debajyoti Ray, Ray Reiter, Sebastian Sardiña, Richard Scherl, Patricio Simari, and Nina Thiessen. We also wish to acknowledge our esteemed colleagues, Tony Cohn, Jim Delgrande, Henry Kautz, Bernhard Nebel, and Peter Norvig, who reviewed a draft in detail for the publisher and gave us invaluable feedback at many levels. All remaining errors are our fault alone, of course, although in reading this, the reader agrees to accept the current volume as is, with no warranty of correctness expressed or implied. Right.

We would also like to thank Denise Penrose and Valerie Witte and the other staff members at Morgan Kaufmann and Elsevier, as well as Dan Fitzgerald and Seth Reichgott, all of whom provided enormous support and enthusiasm in the development and production of this book. Mike Morgan was also very encouraging and helpful in the early stages, and always treated us better than we felt we deserved. Financial support for this research was gratefully received from the Natural Sciences and Engineering Research Council of Canada, and the Canadian Institute for Advanced Research.

Last, but nowhere near least, we would like to thank our families— Gwen, Rebecca, and Lauren; and Pat, Michelle, and Marc—who heard us talking about doing this book for so long, it became a bit of a family joke. Well guys, joke or not, here it is!

*Ron Brachman and Hector Levesque*
Westfield, New Jersey, and Toronto, Ontario

December 2003

# CHAPTER 1

# INTRODUCTION

■

■

■

Intelligence, as exhibited by people anyway, is surely one of the most complex and mysterious phenomena that we are aware of. One striking aspect of intelligent behavior is that it is clearly conditioned by *knowledge:* for a very wide range of activities, we make decisions about what to do based on what we know (or believe) about the world, effortlessly and unconsciously. Using what we know in this way is so commonplace that we only really pay attention to it when it is not there. When we say that someone has behaved *unintelligently*, like when someone has used a lit match to see if there is any gas in a car's gas tank, what we usually mean is not that there is something that the person did not know, but rather that the person has failed to use what he or she *did* know. We might say, "You weren't thinking!" Indeed, it is *thinking* that is supposed to bring what is relevant in what we know to bear on what we are trying to do.

One definition of Artificial Intelligence (AI) is that it is the study of intelligent behavior achieved through computational means. Knowledge representation and reasoning, then, is that part of AI that is concerned with how an agent uses what it knows in deciding what to do. It is the study of thinking as a computational process. This book is an introduction to that field and in particular, to the symbolic structures it has invented for representing knowledge and to the computational processes it has devised for reasoning with those symbolic structures.

If this book is an introduction to the area, then this chapter is an introduction to the introduction. In it, we will try to address, if only briefly, some significant questions that surround the deep and challenging topics of the field: What exactly do we mean by "knowledge," by "representation," and by "reasoning," and why do we think these concepts are useful for building AI systems? In the end, these are philosophical questions, and thorny ones at that; they bear considerable investigation by those with a more philosophical bent and can be the subject matter of whole careers. But the purpose of this chapter is not to cover in any detail what philosophers, logicians, and computer scientists have said about knowledge over the years; it is rather to glance at some of the main issues involved, and examine their bearings on Artificial Intelligence and the prospect of a machine that could think.

## 1.1   THE KEY CONCEPTS: KNOWLEDGE, REPRESENTATION, AND REASONING

**Knowledge**   What is knowledge? This is a question that has been discussed by philosophers since the ancient Greeks, and it is still not totally demystified. We certainly will not attempt to be done with it here. But to get a rough sense of what knowledge is supposed to be, it is useful to look at how we talk about it informally.

First, observe that when we say something like "John knows that ...," we fill in the blank with a simple declarative sentence. So we might say, "John knows that Mary will come to the party," or "John knows that Abraham Lincoln was assassinated." This suggests that, among other things, knowledge is a relation between a knower, like John, and a *proposition*, that is, the idea expressed by a simple declarative sentence, like "Mary will come to the party."

Part of the mystery surrounding knowledge is due to the nature of propositions. What can we say about them? As far as we are concerned, what matters about propositions is that they are abstract entities that can be true or false, right or wrong.[1] When we say, "John knows that $p$," we can just as well say, "John knows that it is true that $p$." Either way, to say that John knows something is to say that John has formed a judgment of some sort, and has come to realize that the world is one way and not another. In talking about this judgment, we use propositions to classify the two cases.

A similar story can be told about a sentence like "John hopes that Mary will come to the party." The same proposition is involved, but the relationship John has to it is different. Verbs like "knows," "hopes,"

---

[1]Strictly speaking, we might want to say that the *sentences* expressing the proposition are true or false, and that the propositions themselves are either factual or nonfactual. Further, because of linguistic features such as indexicals (that is, words whose referents change with the context in which they are uttered, such as "me" and "yesterday"), we more accurately say that it is actual tokens of sentences or their uses in specific contexts that are true or false, not the sentences themselves.

"regrets," "fears," and "doubts" all denote *propositional attitudes,* relationships between agents and propositions. In all cases, what matters about the proposition is its truth: If John hopes that Mary will come to the party, then John is hoping that the world is one way and not another, as classified by the proposition.

Of course, there are sentences involving knowledge that do not explicitly mention propositions. When we say, "John knows who Mary is taking to the party," or "John knows how to get there," we can at least imagine the implicit propositions: "John knows that Mary is taking so-and-so to the party," or "John knows that to get to the party, you go two blocks past Main Street, turn left, ...," and so on. On the other hand, when we say that John has a skill, as in "John knows how to play piano," or a deep understanding of someone or something, as in "John knows Bill well," it is not so clear that any useful proposition is involved. While this is certainly challenging subject matter, we will have nothing further to say about this latter form of knowledge in this book.

A related notion that we are concerned with, however, is the concept of *belief*. The sentence "John believes that *p*" is clearly related to "John knows that *p*." We use the former when we do not wish to claim that John's judgment about the world is necessarily accurate or held for appropriate reasons. We sometimes use it when we feel that John might not be completely convinced. In fact, we have a full range of propositional attitudes, expressed by sentences like "John is absolutely certain that *p*," "John is confident that *p*," "John is of the opinion that *p*," "John suspects that *p*," and so on, that differ only in the level of conviction they attribute. For now, we will not distinguish among any of them. What matters is that they all share with knowledge a very basic idea: John takes the world to be one way and not another.

**Representation** The concept of *representation* is as philosophically vexing as that of knowledge. Very roughly speaking, representation is a relationship between two domains, where the first is meant to "stand for" or take the place of the second. Usually, the first domain, the representor, is more concrete, immediate, or accessible in some way than the second. For example, a drawing of a milkshake and a hamburger on a sign might stand for a less immediately visible fast food restaurant; the drawing of a circle with a plus below it might stand for the much more abstract concept of womanhood; an elected legislator might stand for his or her constituency.

The type of representor that we will be most concerned with here is the formal *symbol*, that is, a character or group of characters taken from some predetermined alphabet. The digit "7," for example, stands for the number 7, as does the group of letters "VII" and, in other contexts, the words *sept* and *shichi*. As with all representation, it is assumed to be easier to deal with symbols (recognize them, distinguish them from each other, display them, etc.) than with what the symbols represent. In some cases, a word like "John" might stand for something quite concrete; but many words, like "love" or "truth," stand for abstractions.

Of special concern to us is when a group of formal symbols stands for a proposition: "John loves Mary" stands for the proposition that John loves Mary. Again, the symbolic English sentence is fairly concrete: It has distinguishable parts involving the three words, for example, and a recognizable syntax. The proposition, on the other hand, is abstract. It is something like a classification of all the different ways we can imagine the world to be into two groups: those where John loves Mary, and those where he does not.

*Knowledge representation*, then, is the field of study concerned with using formal symbols to represent a collection of propositions believed by some putative agent. As we will see, however, we do not want to insist that these symbols must represent *all* the propositions believed by the agent. There may very well be an infinite number of propositions believed, only a finite number of which are ever represented. It will be the role of *reasoning* to bridge the gap between what is represented and what is believed.

**Reasoning**  So what is reasoning? In general, it is the formal manipulation of the symbols representing a collection of believed propositions to produce representations of new ones. It is here that we use the fact that symbols are more accessible than the propositions they represent: They must be concrete enough that we can manipulate them (move them around, take them apart, copy them, string them together) in such a way as to construct representations of new propositions.

It is useful here to draw an analogy with arithmetic. We can think of binary addition as being a certain formal manipulation: We start with symbols like "1011" and "10," for instance, and end up with "1101." The manipulation in this case is addition, because the final symbol represents the sum of the numbers represented by the initial ones. Reasoning is similar: We might start with the sentences "John loves Mary" and "Mary is coming to the party," and after a certain amount of manipulation produce the sentence, "Someone John loves is coming to the party." We would call this form of reasoning *logical inference* because the final sentence represents a logical conclusion of the propositions represented by the initial ones, as we will discuss later. According to this view (first put forward, incidentally, by the philosopher Gottfried Leibniz in the seventeenth century), reasoning is a form of calculation, not unlike arithmetic, but over symbols standing for propositions rather than numbers.

## 1.2 WHY KNOWLEDGE REPRESENTATION AND REASONING?

Why is knowledge even relevant at all to AI systems? The first answer that comes to mind is that it is sometimes useful to describe the behavior of sufficiently complex systems (human or otherwise) using a vocabulary involving terms like "beliefs," "desires," "goals," "intentions," "hopes," and so on.

Imagine, for example, playing a game of chess against a complex chess-playing program. In looking at one of its moves, we might say to ourselves something like this: "It moved this way because it believed its queen was vulnerable, but still wanted to attack the rook." In terms of how the chess-playing program is actually constructed, we might have said something more like, "It moved this way because evaluation procedure $P$ using static evaluation function $Q$ returned a value of $+7$ after an alpha-beta minimax search to depth 4." The problem is that this second description, although perhaps quite accurate, is at the wrong level of detail, and does not help us determine what chess move we should make in response. Much more useful is to understand the behavior of the program in terms of the immediate goals being pursued relative to its beliefs, long-term intentions, and so on. This is what the philosopher Daniel Dennett calls taking an *intentional stance* toward the chess-playing system.

This is not to say that an intentional stance is always appropriate. We might think of a thermostat, to take a classic example, as "knowing" that the room is too cold and "wanting" to warm it up. But this type of anthropomorphization is typically inappropriate—there is a perfectly workable electrical account of what is going on. Moreover, it can often be quite misleading to describe a system in intentional terms: Using this kind of vocabulary, we could end up fooling ourselves into thinking we are dealing with something much more sophisticated than it actually is.

But there's a more basic question: Is *this* what knowledge representation is all about? Is all the talk about knowledge just that—talk—a stance one may or may not choose to take toward a complex system?

To understand the answer, first observe that the intentional stance says nothing about what is or is not represented symbolically within a system. In the chess-playing program, the board position might be represented symbolically, say, but the goal of getting a knight out early, for instance, may not be. Such a goal might only emerge out of a complex interplay of many different aspects of the program, its evaluation functions, book move library, and so on. Yet we may still choose to describe the system as "having" this goal if this properly explains its behavior.

So what role is played by a symbolic representation? The hypothesis underlying work in knowledge representation is that we will want to construct systems that contain symbolic representations with two important properties. First is that we (from the outside) can understand them as standing for propositions. Second is that the system is designed to behave the way that it does *because* of these symbolic representations. This is what the philosopher Brian Smith calls the *Knowledge Representation Hypothesis:*

> Any mechanically embodied intelligent process will be comprised of structural ingredients that a) we as external observers naturally take to represent a propositional account of the knowledge that the overall process exhibits, and b) independent of such external semantic attribution, play a formal but causal and essential role in engendering the behaviour that manifests that knowledge.

In other words, the Knowledge Representation Hypothesis implies that we will want to construct systems for which the intentional stance is grounded by design in symbolic representations. We will call such systems *knowledge-based systems* and the symbolic representations involved their *knowledge bases* (KBs).

### 1.2.1   Knowledge-Based Systems

To see what a knowledge-based system amounts to, it is helpful to look at two very simple PROLOG programs with identical behavior. Consider the first:

```
printColor(snow)  :- !, write("It's white.").
printColor(grass) :- !, write("It's green.").
printColor(sky)   :- !, write("It's yellow.").
printColor(X)     :- write("Beats me.").
```

Here is an alternate:

```
printColor(X)  :- color(X,Y), !,
       write("It's "), write(Y), write(".").
printColor(X)  :- write("Beats me.").
color(snow,white).
color(sky,yellow).
color(X,Y)  :- madeof(X,Z), color(Z,Y).
madeof(grass,vegetation).
color(vegetation,green).
```

Observe that both programs are able to print out the color of various items (getting the sky wrong, as it turns out). Taking an intentional stance, both might be said to "know" that the color of snow is white. The crucial point, as we will see, however, is that only the second program is designed according to the Knowledge Representation Hypothesis.

Consider the clause `color(snow,white)`, for example. This is a symbolic structure that we can understand as representing the proposition that snow is white, and moreover, we know, by virtue of knowing how the PROLOG interpreter works, that the system prints out the appropriate color of snow precisely *because* it bumps into this clause at just the right time. Remove the clause and the system would no longer do so.

There is no such clause in the first program. The one that comes closest is the first clause of the program, which says what to print when asked about snow. But we would be hard-pressed to say that this clause literally represents a belief, except perhaps a belief about what ought to be printed.

So what makes a system knowledge-based, as far as we are concerned, is not the use of a logical formalism (like PROLOG), or the fact that it is complex enough to merit an intentional description involving knowledge, or the fact that what it believes is true; rather, it is the presence of a knowledge base, a collection of symbolic structures representing what it believes and reasons with during the operation of the system.

Much (though not all) of AI involves building systems that are knowledge-based in this way, that is, systems whose ability derives in part from reasoning over explicitly represented knowledge. So-called expert systems are a very clear case, but we also find KBs in the areas of language understanding, planning, diagnosis, and learning. Many AI systems are also knowledge-based to a somewhat lesser extent—some game-playing and high-level vision systems, for instance. Finally, some AI systems are not knowledge-based at all: Low-level speech, vision, and motor-control systems typically encode what they need to know directly in the programs themselves.

How much of intelligent behavior needs to be knowledge-based in this sense? This remains an open research question. Perhaps the most serious challenge to the Knowledge Representation Hypothesis is the "connectionist" methodology, which attempts to avoid any kind of symbolic representation and reasoning, and instead advocates computing with networks of weighted links between artificial "neurons."

## 1.2.2 Why Knowledge Representation?

An obvious question arises when we start thinking about the two PROLOG programs of the previous section: What advantage, if any, does the knowledge-based one have? Wouldn't it be better to "compile out" the KB and distribute this knowledge to the procedures that need it, as we did in the first program? The performance of the system would certainly be better. It can only slow a system down to have to look up facts in a KB and reason with them at runtime in order to decide what actions to take. Indeed, advocates within AI of what has been called procedural knowledge take pretty much this point of view.

When we think about the various skills we have, such as riding a bicycle or playing a piano, it certainly *feels* like we do not reason about the various actions to take (shifting our weight or moving our fingers); it seems much more like we just know what to do, and do it. In fact, if we try to think about what we are doing, we end up making a mess of it. Perhaps (the argument goes), this applies to most of our activities: making a meal, getting a job, staying alive, and so on.

Of course, when we first learn these skills, the case is not so clear: It seems like we need to think deliberately about what we are doing, even riding a bicycle. The philosopher Hubert Dreyfus first observed this paradox of "expert systems." These systems are claimed to be superior precisely because they are knowledge-based, that is, they reason over explicitly represented knowledge. But novices are the ones who think and reason, claims Dreyfus. Experts do not; they learn to recognize and to react. The difference between a chess master and a chess novice is that the novice needs to figure out what is happening and what to do, but the master just "sees" it. For this reason (among others), Dreyfus believes that the development of knowledge-based systems is completely wrongheaded if it is attempting to duplicate human-level intelligent behavior.

So why even consider knowledge-based systems? Unfortunately, no definitive answer can yet be given. We suspect, however, that the answer will emerge in our desire to build a system that can deal with a set of tasks that is *open-ended*. For any fixed set of tasks it might work to "compile out" what the system needs to know, but if the set of tasks is not determined in advance, the strategy will not work. The ability to make behavior depend on explicitly represented knowledge seems to pay off when we cannot specify in advance how that knowledge will be used.

A good example of this is what happens when we read a book. Suppose we are reading about South American geography. When we find out for the first time that approximately half of the population of Peru lives in the Andes, we are in no position to distribute this piece of knowledge to the various routines that might eventually require it. Instead, it seems pretty clear that we are able to assimilate the fact in declarative form for a very wide variety of potential uses. This is a prototypical case of a knowledge-based approach.

Further, from a system-design point of view, the knowledge-based approach exhibited by the second PROLOG program seems to have a number of desirable features:

- We can add new tasks and easily make them depend on previous knowledge. In our PROLOG program example, we can add the task of enumerating all objects of a given color, or even of painting a picture, by making use of the already specified KB to determine the colors.

- We can extend the existing behavior by adding new beliefs. For example, by adding a clause saying that canaries are yellow, we automatically propagate this information to any routine that needs it.

- We can debug faulty behavior by locating the erroneous beliefs of the system. In the PROLOG example, by changing the clause for the color of the sky, we automatically correct any routine that uses color information.

- We can concisely explain and justify the behavior of the system. Why did the program say that grass was green? It was because it believed that grass is a form of vegetation and that vegetation is green. We are justified in saying "because" here, since if we removed either of the two relevant clauses the behavior would indeed change.

Overall, then, the hallmark of a knowledge-based system is that by design it has the ability to be *told* facts about its world and adjust its behavior correspondingly.

This ability to have some of our actions depend on what we believe is what the cognitive scientist Zenon Pylyshyn has called *cognitive penetrability*. Consider, for example, responding to a fire alarm. The normal response is to get up and leave the building, but we would not do so if we happened to believe that the alarm was being tested. There are any number of ways we might come to this belief, but they all lead to the same effect. Our response to a fire alarm is cognitively penetrable because it is conditioned on what we can be made to believe. On the other hand, something like a blinking reflex as an object approaches your eye does not appear to be cognitively penetrable: Even if you strongly believe the object will not touch you, you still blink.

## 1.2.3  Why Reasoning?

To see the motivation behind reasoning in a knowledge-based system, it suffices to observe that we would like action to depend on what the system *believes* about the world, as opposed to just what the system has *explicitly represented*. In the second PROLOG example, there was no clause representing the belief that the color of grass was green, but we still wanted the system to know this. In general, much of what we expect to put in a KB will involve quite general facts, which will then need to be applied to particular situations.

For example, we might represent the following two facts explicitly:

1. Patient $x$ is allergic to medication $m$.

2. Anyone allergic to medication $m$ is also allergic to medication $m'$.

In trying to decide if it is appropriate to prescribe medication $m'$ for patient $x$, neither represented fact answers the question. Together, however, they paint a picture of a world where $x$ is allergic to $m'$, and this, together with other represented facts about allergies, might be sufficient to rule out the medication. We do not want to condition behavior only on the represented facts that we are able to *retrieve*, like in a database system. The beliefs of the system must go beyond these.

But beyond them to where? There is, as it turns out, a simple answer to this question, but one which, as we will discuss many times in subsequent chapters, is not always practical. The simple answer is that the system should believe $p$ if, according to the beliefs it has represented, the world it is imagining is one where $p$ is true. In the example, facts (1) and (2) are both represented. If we now imagine what the world would be like if (1) and (2) were both true, then this is a world where

3. Patient $x$ is allergic to medication $m'$

is also true, even though this fact is only implicitly represented.

This is the concept of *logical entailment:* We say that the propositions represented by a set of sentences $S$ entail the proposition represented by a sentence $p$ when the truth of $p$ is implicit in the truth of the sentences in $S$. In other words, if the world is such that every element of $S$ comes out true, then $p$ does as well. All that we require to get some notion of entailment is a language with an account of what it means for a sentence to be true or false. As we argued, if our representation language is to represent knowledge at all, it must come with such an account (again, to know $p$ is to take $p$ to be true). So any knowledge representation language, whatever other features it may have, whatever syntactic form it may take, whatever reasoning procedures we may define over it, ought to have a well-defined notion of entailment.

A simple answer to what beliefs a knowledge-based system should exhibit, then, is that it should believe all and only the entailments of what it has explicitly represented. The job of reasoning, then, according to this account, is to compute the entailments of a KB.

What makes this account simplistic is that there are often quite good reasons not to calculate entailments. For one thing, it can be too *difficult* computationally to decide which sentences are entailed by the kind of KB we will want to use. Any procedure that always gives us answers in a reasonable amount of time will occasionally either miss some entailments or return some incorrect answers. In the former case, the reasoning process is said to be *logically incomplete;* in the latter case, the reasoning is said to be *logically unsound.*

But there are also conceptual reasons why we might consider unsound or incomplete reasoning. For example, suppose $p$ is not entailed by a KB, but is a reasonable guess, given what is represented. We might still want to believe that *p* is true. To use a classic example, suppose all I know about an individual Tweety is that she is a bird. I might have a number of facts about birds in the KB, but likely none of them would *entail* that Tweety flies. After all, Tweety might turn out to be an ostrich. Nonetheless, it is a reasonable assumption that Tweety flies. This is logically unsound reasoning since we can imagine a world where everything in the KB is true but where Tweety does not fly.

Alternately, a knowledge-based system might come to believe a collection of facts from various sources that, taken together, cannot all be true. In this case, it would be inappropriate to do logically complete reasoning, because then *every* sentence would be believed: Since there are no worlds where the KB is true, every sentence *p* will be trivially true in all worlds where the KB is true. An incomplete form of reasoning would clearly be more useful here until the contradictions were dealt with, if ever.

Despite all this, it remains the case that the simplistic answer is by far the best starting point for thinking about reasoning, even if we intend to diverge from it. So while it would be a mistake to *identify* reasoning in a knowledge-based system with logically sound and complete inference, it is the right place to begin.

## 1.3 THE ROLE OF LOGIC

The reason *logic* is relevant to knowledge representation and reasoning is simply that, at least according to one view, logic *is* the study of entailment relations—languages, truth conditions, and rules of inference. Not surprisingly, we will borrow heavily from the tools and techniques of formal symbolic logic. Specifically, we will use as our first knowledge representation language a very popular logical language, that of the predicate calculus, or as it is sometimes called, the language of first-order logic (FOL). This language was invented by the philosopher Gottlob Frege at the turn of the twentieth century for the formalization of mathematical inference, but has been co-opted by the AI community for knowledge representation purposes.

It must be stressed, however, that FOL itself is also just a starting point. We will have good reason in what follows to consider subsets and supersets of FOL, as well as knowledge representation languages quite different in form and meaning. Just as we are not committed to understanding reasoning as the computation of entailments, even when we do so we are not committed to any particular language. Indeed, as we shall see, certain representation languages suggest forms of reasoning that go well beyond whatever connections they may have ever had with logic.

Where logic really does pay off from a knowledge representation perspective is at what Allen Newell has called the *knowledge level*.

The idea is that we can understand a knowledge-based system at two different levels (at least). At the knowledge level, we ask questions concerning the representation language and its semantics. At the *symbol level*, on the other hand, we ask questions concerning the computational aspects. There are clearly issues of adequacy at each level. At the knowledge level, we deal with the expressive adequacy of a representation language and the characteristics of its entailment relation, including its intrinsic computational complexity; at the symbol level, we ask questions about the computational architecture and the properties of the data structures and reasoning procedures, including their algorithmic complexity.

The tools of formal symbolic logic seem ideally suited for a knowledge-level analysis of a knowledge-based system. In the next chapter we begin such an analysis using the language of first-order logic, putting aside for now all computational concerns.

## 1.4  BIBLIOGRAPHIC NOTES

Much of the material in this chapter is shared with the first chapter of Levesque and Lakemeyer [244].

The area of knowledge representation and reasoning is one of the most active areas of AI research, dominating many of the general AI conferences, as well as having a conference of its own. Some of the more influential early papers (that is, before 1985) may be found in a collection of readings by Brachman and Levesque [47]. An overview of the field as a whole at about that time is presented by Levesque [240]. For an even earlier view of the state of the art during a time of great progress and intellectual debate, see the *SIGART Newsletter, Special Issue on Knowledge Representation* [50].

Sowa [394] also discusses general aspects of knowledge representation and reasoning and, in particular, how various proposals relate to formal logic and to a specific representation formalism he invented called *conceptual graphs* [392]. Other books devoted to the general topic include those by Davis [86], Ringland and Duce [354], and Reichgelt [338].

Most textbooks on Artificial Intelligence contain material on knowledge representation and reasoning. A general AI textbook by Genesereth and Nilsson [153] emphasizes (first-order) logic and its use in Artificial Intelligence. Some popular textbooks that spend considerable time on knowledge representation include those by Dean et al. [98], Ginsberg [160], Luger [260], Nilsson [311], Poole et al. [332], Rich and Knight [352], Russell and Norvig [359], and Winston [428].

Leibniz was one of the first to see logic as providing a unifying basis for all mathematics and science. For a summary of his views about thinking as a form of calculation, see [118], vol. 3, p. 422. Frege [135] developed propositional logic and introduced the idea of quantification and a notation for expressing logical concepts.

The distinction between knowledge and belief is discussed at length in the philosophical literature. Gettier's article [156] represents one of the landmarks in this area, presenting arguments against the common view of knowledge as true, justified belief. A collection of papers by Pappas and Swain [314] contains responses to Gettier's work.

Dennett's intentional stance is discussed in [102]. The notion of cognitive penetrability is addressed by Pylyshyn [334]. The knowledge representation hypothesis is due to Smith [390]. An alternate opinion on the general question of what constitutes a knowledge representation is expressed by Davis et al. [89]. The original conception of the knowledge level is due to Newell [305]. The knowledge level as applied directly to the knowledge representation and reasoning enterprise was addressed by Levesque [238] and by Brachman et al. [52].

Despite the centrality of knowledge representation and reasoning to AI, there are alternate views. Some authors have claimed that human-level reasoning is not achievable via purely computational means. These include Dreyfus [113], Searle [373, 374], and Penrose [327] (see also the collection by Boden [33]). Others suggest that intelligence derives from computational mechanisms that are not as directly representational as those discussed in this book. Among these are the so-called connectionists, such as Kohonen [220] and Smolensky [391].

## 1.5 EXERCISES

These exercises are all taken from [244].

1. Consider a task requiring knowledge, like baking a cake. Examine a recipe and state what needs to be known to follow the recipe.

2. In considering the distinction between knowledge and belief in this book, we take the view that belief is fundamental and knowledge is simply belief where the outside world happens to be cooperating (the belief is true, is arrived at by appropriate means, is held for the right reasons, and so on). Describe an interpretation of the terms where knowledge is taken to be basic and belief is understood in terms of it.

3. Explain in what sense reacting to a loud noise is and is not cognitively penetrable.

**4.** It has become fashionable to attempt to achieve intelligent behavior in AI systems without using propositional representations. Speculate on what such a system should do when reading a book on South American geography.

**5.** Describe some ways in which the firsthand knowledge we have of some topic goes beyond what we are able to write down in a language. What accounts for our inability to express this knowledge?

# CHAPTER 2

# THE LANGUAGE OF FIRST-ORDER LOGIC

■

■

■

Before any system aspiring to intelligence can even begin to reason, learn, plan, or explain its behavior, it must be able to formulate the ideas involved. You will not be able to learn something about the world around you, for example, if it is beyond you to even express what that thing is. So we need to start with a *language* of some sort, in terms of which knowledge can be formulated. In this chapter, we will examine in detail one specific language that can be used for this purpose: the language of first-order logic. FOL is not the only choice, but is a simple and convenient one to begin with.

## 2.1 INTRODUCTION

What does it mean to "have" a language? Once we have a set of words or a set of symbols of some sort, what more is needed? As far as we are concerned, there are three things:

1. *syntax:* we need to specify which groups of symbols, arranged in what way, are to be considered properly formed. In English, for example, the string of words "the cat my mother loves" is a well-formed noun phrase, but "the my loves mother cat" is not. For knowledge representation, we need to be especially clear about which of the well-formed strings are the *sentences* of the language, since these are what express propositions.

2. *semantics:* we need to specify what the well-formed expressions are supposed to mean. Some well-formed expressions like "the hard-nosed decimal holiday" might not mean anything. For sentences, we need to be clear about what idea about the world is being expressed. Without such an account, we cannot expect to say what believing one of them amounts to.

3. *pragmatics:* we need to specify how the meaningful expressions in the language are to be used. In English, for example, "There is some-one right behind you" could be used as a warning to be careful in some contexts and a request to move in others. For knowledge representation, this involves how we use the meaningful sentences of a representation language as part of a knowledge base from which inferences will be drawn.

These three aspects apply mainly to declarative languages, the sort we use to represent knowledge. Other languages will have other aspects not discussed here, for example, what the words sound like (for spoken languages), or what actions are being called for (for imperative languages).

We now turn our attention to the specification of FOL.

## 2.2   THE SYNTAX

In FOL, there are two sorts of symbols: the *logical* ones and the *nonlogical* ones. Intuitively, the logical symbols are those that have a fixed meaning or use in the language. There are three sorts of logical symbols:

1. *punctuation:* "(", ")", and ".".

2. *connectives:* "¬," "∧," "∨," "∃," "∀," and "=." Note the usual interpretation of these logical symbols: ¬ is logical negation, ∧ is logical conjunction ("and"), ∨ is logical disjunction ("or"), ∃ means "there exists...," ∀ means "for all...," and = is logical equality. ∀ and ∃ are called *quantifiers*.

3. *variables:* an infinite supply of symbols, which we will denote here using $x$, $y$, and $z$, sometimes with subscripts and superscripts.

The nonlogical symbols are those that have an application-dependent meaning or use. In FOL, there are two sorts of nonlogical symbols:

1. *function symbols:* an infinite supply of symbols, which we will write in uncapitalized mixed case, e.g., bestFriend, and which we will

denote more generally using $a$, $b$, $c$, $f$, $g$, and $h$, with subscripts and superscripts.

2. *predicate symbols:* an infinite supply of symbols, which we will write in capitalized mixed case, e.g., OlderThan, and which we will denote more generally using $P$, $Q$, and $R$, with subscripts and superscripts.

One distinguishing feature of nonlogical symbols is that each one is assumed to have an *arity*, that is, a nonnegative integer indicating how many "arguments" it takes. (This number is used in the syntax of the language.) It is assumed that there is an infinite supply of function and predicate symbols of each arity. By convention, $a$, $b$, and $c$ are only used for function symbols of arity 0, which are called *constants*, while $g$ and $h$ are only used for function symbols of nonzero arity. Predicate symbols of arity 0 are sometimes called *propositional symbols*.

If you think of the logical symbols as the reserved keywords of a programming language, then nonlogical symbols are like its identifiers. For example, we might have "Dog" as a predicate symbol of arity 1, "OlderThan" as a predicate symbol of arity 2, "bestFriend" as a function symbol of arity 1, and "johnSmith" as a constant. Note that we are treating "$=$" not as a predicate symbol, but as a special logical symbol (unlike the way that it is handled in some logic textbooks).

There are two types of legal syntactic expressions in FOL: *terms* and *formulas*. Intuitively, a term will be used to refer to something in the world, and a formula will be used to express a proposition. The set of terms of FOL is the least set satisfying these conditions:

- every variable is a term;
- if $t_1, \ldots, t_n$ are terms, and $f$ is a function symbol of arity $n$, then $f(t_1, \ldots, t_n)$ is a term.

The set of formulas of FOL is the least set satisfying these constraints:

- if $t_1, \ldots, t_n$ are terms, and $P$ is a predicate symbol of arity $n$, then $P(t_1, \ldots, t_n)$ is a formula;
- if $t_1$ and $t_2$ are terms, then $t_1 = t_2$ is a formula;
- if $\alpha$ and $\beta$ are formulas, and $x$ is a variable, then $\neg\alpha$, $(\alpha \wedge \beta)$, $(\alpha \vee \beta)$, $\forall x. \, \alpha$, and $\exists x. \, \alpha$ are formulas.

Formulas of the first two types (containing no other simpler formulas) are called *atomic formulas* or *atoms*.

At this point, it is useful to introduce some notational abbreviations and conventions. First of all, we will add or omit matched parentheses and periods freely, and also use square and curly brackets to improve readability. In the case of predicates or function symbols of arity 0, we will usually omit the parentheses since there are no arguments to enclose. We will also sometimes reduce the number of parentheses by assuming that $\wedge$ has higher precedence than $\vee$ (the way $\times$ has higher precedence than $+$).

By the *propositional subset* of FOL, we mean the language with no terms, no quantifiers, and where only propositional symbols are used. So, for example,

$$(P \wedge \neg(Q \vee R)),$$

where $P$, $Q$, and $R$ are propositional symbols, would be a formula in this subset.

We also use the following abbreviations:

- $(\alpha \supset \beta)$ for $(\neg\alpha \vee \beta)$;
- $(\alpha \equiv \beta)$ for $((\alpha \supset \beta) \wedge (\beta \supset \alpha))$.

We also need to discuss the scope of quantifiers. We say that a variable occurrence is *bound* in a formula if it lies within the scope of a quantifier, and *free* otherwise. That is, $x$ appears bound if it appears in a subformula $\forall x. \alpha$ or $\exists x. \alpha$ of the formula. So, for example, in a formula like

$$\forall y. P(x) \wedge \exists x[P(y) \vee Q(x)],$$

the first occurrence of the variable $x$ is free, and the final two occurrences of $x$ are bound; both occurrences of $y$ are bound.[1] If $x$ is a variable, $t$ is a term, and $\alpha$ is a formula, we use the notation $\alpha_t^x$ to stand for the formula that results from replacing all free occurrences of $x$ in $\alpha$ by $t$. If $\vec{x}$ is a sequence of variables, $\vec{c}$ is a sequence of constants of the same length, and $\alpha$ is a formula whose free variables are among those in $\vec{x}$, then $\alpha[\vec{x}]$ means $\alpha$ itself and $\alpha[\vec{c}]$ means $\alpha$ with each free $x_i$ replaced by the corresponding $c_i$.

Finally, a *sentence* of FOL is any formula without free variables. The sentences of FOL are what we use to represent knowledge, and the rest is merely supporting syntactic machinery.

## 2.3   THE SEMANTICS

As noted in Section 2.1, the concern of semantics is to explain what the expressions of a language mean. As far as we are concerned, this involves

---

[1] In some textbooks, the occurrence of the variable just after the quantifier is considered neither free nor bound.

specifying what claim a sentence of FOL makes about the world, so that we can understand what believing it amounts to.

Unfortunately, there is a bit of a problem here. We cannot realistically expect to specify once and for all what a sentence of FOL means, for the simple reason that the nonlogical symbols are used in an application-dependent way. I might use the constant "john" to mean one individual, and you might use it to mean another. So there's no way we can possibly agree on what the sentence "Happy(john)" claims about the world, even if we were to agree on what "Happy" means.

Here is what we can agree to: The sentence "Happy(john)" claims that the individual named by "john" (whoever that might be) has the property named by "Happy" (whatever that might be). In other words, we can agree once and for all on how the meaning of the sentence derives from the interpretation of the nonlogical symbols involved. Of course, what we have in mind for these nonlogical symbols can be quite complex and hard to make precise. For example, our list of nonlogical symbols might include terms like

    DemocraticCountry, IsABetterJudgeOfCharacterThan,
    favoriteIceCreamFlavorOf, puddleOfwater27,

and the like. We should not (and cannot) expect the semantic specification of FOL to tell us precisely what terms like these mean. What we are after, then, is a clear specification of the meaning of sentences *as a function of the interpretation of the predicate and function symbols*.

To get to such a specification, we take the following (simplistic) view of what the world could be like:

1. There are objects in the world.

2. For any predicate $P$ of arity 1, some of the objects will satisfy $P$ and some will not. An *interpretation* of $P$ settles the question, deciding for each object whether it has or does not have the property in question. (Borderline cases are ruled in separate interpretations: In one, it has the property; in another, it does not.) Predicates of other arities are handled similarly. For example, an interpretation of a predicate of arity 3 decides on which triples of objects stand in the corresponding ternary relation. Similarly, a function symbol of arity 3 is interpreted as a mapping from triples of objects to objects.

3. No other aspects of the world matter.

The assumption made in FOL is that this is all you need to say regarding the meaning of the nonlogical symbols, and hence the meaning of all sentences.

For example, we might imagine that there are objects that include people, countries, and flavors of ice cream. The meaning of "Democratic-Country" in some interpretation will be no more and no less than those objects that are countries that we consider to be democratic. We may disagree on which those are, of course, but then we are simply talking about different interpretations. Similarly, the meaning of "favorite-IceCreamFlavorOf" would be a specific mapping from people to flavors of ice cream (and from nonpeople to some other arbitrarily chosen object, say). Note that as far as FOL is concerned, we do not try to say what "DemocraticCountry" means the way a dictionary would, in terms of free elections, representative governments, majority rule, and so on; all we need to say is which objects are and are not democratic countries. This is clearly a simplifying assumption, and other languages would handle the terms differently.

### 2.3.1 Interpretations

Meanings are typically captured by specific interpretations, and we can now be precise about them. An *interpretation* $\Im$ in FOL is a pair $\langle \mathcal{D}, \mathcal{I} \rangle$, where $\mathcal{D}$ is any nonempty set of objects, called the *domain* of the interpretation, and $\mathcal{I}$ is a mapping, called the *interpretation mapping*, from the nonlogical symbols to functions and relations over $\mathcal{D}$, as described later.

It is important to stress that an interpretation need not only involve mathematical objects. $\mathcal{D}$ can be *any* set, including people, garages, numbers, sentences, fairness, unicorns, chunks of peanut butter, situations, and the universe, among other things.

The interpretation mapping $\mathcal{I}$ will assign meaning to the predicate symbols as follows: To every predicate symbol $P$ of arity $n$, $\mathcal{I}[P]$ is an $n$-ary relation over $\mathcal{D}$, that is,

$$\mathcal{I}[P] \subseteq \underbrace{\mathcal{D} \times \cdots \times \mathcal{D}}_{n \text{ times}}.$$

So, for example, consider a unary predicate symbol Dog. Here, $\mathcal{I}[\text{Dog}]$ would be some subset of $\mathcal{D}$, presumably the set of dogs in that interpretation. Similarly, $\mathcal{I}[\text{OlderThan}]$ would be some subset of $\mathcal{D} \times \mathcal{D}$, presumably the set of pairs of objects in $\mathcal{D}$ where the first element of the pair is older than the second.

The interpretation mapping $\mathcal{I}$ will assign meaning to the function symbols as follows: To every function symbol $f$ of arity $n$, $\mathcal{I}[f]$ is an $n$-ary function over $\mathcal{D}$, that is,[2]

$$\mathcal{I}[f] \in [\underbrace{\mathcal{D} \times \cdots \times \mathcal{D}}_{n \text{ times}} \to \mathcal{D}].$$

---

[2]Here and subsequently, mathematical functions are taken to be total.

So, for example, $\mathcal{I}[\text{bestFriend}]$ would be some function $[\mathcal{D} \rightarrow \mathcal{D}]$, presumably the function that maps a person to his or her best friend (and does something reasonable with nonpersons). Similarly, $\mathcal{I}[\text{johnSmith}]$ would be some element of $\mathcal{D}$, presumably somebody called John Smith.

It is sometimes useful to think of the interpretation of predicates in terms of their characteristic functions. In this case, when $P$ is a predicate of arity $n$, we view $\mathcal{I}[P]$ as an $n$-ary function to $\{0, 1\}$:

$$\mathcal{I}[P] \in [\mathcal{D} \times \cdots \times \mathcal{D} \rightarrow \{0, 1\}].$$

The relationship between the two specifications is that a tuple of objects is considered to be in the relation over $\mathcal{D}$ if and only if the characteristic function over those objects has value 1. This characteristic function also allows us to see more clearly how predicates of arity 0 (i.e., the propositional symbols) are handled. In this case, $\mathcal{I}[P]$ will be either 0 or 1. We can think of the first one as meaning "false" and the second "true." For the propositional subset of FOL, then, we can ignore $\mathcal{D}$ completely, and think of an interpretation as simply being a mapping, $\mathcal{I}$, from the propositional symbols to either 0 or 1.

### 2.3.2  Denotation

Given an interpretation $\Im = \langle \mathcal{D}, \mathcal{I} \rangle$, we can specify which elements of $\mathcal{D}$ are denoted by any variable-free term of FOL. For example, to find the object denoted by the term "bestFriend(johnSmith)" in $\Im$, we use $\mathcal{I}$ to get hold of the function denoted by "bestFriend," and then we apply that function to the element of $\mathcal{D}$ denoted by "johnSmith," producing some other element of $\mathcal{D}$. To deal with terms including variables, we also need to start with a *variable assignment* over $\mathcal{D}$, that is, a mapping from the variables of FOL to the elements of $\mathcal{D}$. So if $\mu$ is a variable assignment and $x$ is a variable, $\mu[x]$ will be some element of the domain.

Formally, given an interpretation $\Im$ and a variable assignment $\mu$, the *denotation* of term $t$, written $\|t\|_{\Im,\mu}$, is defined by these rules:

1. if $x$ is a variable, then $\|x\|_{\Im,\mu} = \mu[x]$;

2. if $t_1, \ldots, t_n$ are terms, and $f$ is a function symbol of arity $n$, then

$$\|f(t_1, \ldots, t_n)\|_{\Im,\mu} = \mathcal{F}(d_1, \ldots, d_n)$$

where $\mathcal{F} = \mathcal{I}[f]$, and $d_i = \|t_i\|_{\Im,\mu}$.

Observe that according to these recursive rules, $\|t\|_{\Im,\mu}$ is always an element of $\mathcal{D}$.

### 2.3.3   Satisfaction and Models

Given an interpretation $\mathfrak{I} = \langle \mathcal{D}, \mathcal{I} \rangle$ and the $\| \cdot \|_{\mathfrak{I},\mu}$ relation just defined, we can now specify which sentences of FOL are true and which are false according to this interpretation. For example, "Dog(bestFriend(johnSmith))" is true in $\mathfrak{I}$ if and only if the following holds: If we use $\mathcal{I}$ to get hold of the subset of $\mathcal{D}$ denoted by "Dog" and the object denoted by "bestFriend(johnSmith)," then that object is in the set. To deal with formulas containing free variables, we again use a variable assignment, as shown earlier.

More formally, given an interpretation $\mathfrak{I}$ and variable assignment $\mu$, we say that the formula $\alpha$ is *satisfied* in $\mathfrak{I}$, written $\mathfrak{I}, \mu \models \alpha$, according to these rules:

Assume that $t_1, \ldots, t_n$ are terms, $P$ is a predicate of arity $n$, $\alpha$ and $\beta$ are formulas, and $x$ is a variable.

1. $\mathfrak{I}, \mu \models P(t_1, \ldots, t_n)$ iff $\langle d_1, \ldots, d_n \rangle \in \mathcal{P}$, where $\mathcal{P} = \mathcal{I}[P]$, and $d_i = \|t_i\|_{\mathfrak{I},\mu}$;

2. $\mathfrak{I}, \mu \models t_1 = t_2$ iff $\|t_1\|_{\mathfrak{I},\mu}$ and $\|t_2\|_{\mathfrak{I},\mu}$ are the same element of $\mathcal{D}$;

3. $\mathfrak{I}, \mu \models \neg\alpha$ iff it is not the case that $\mathfrak{I}, \mu \models \alpha$;

4. $\mathfrak{I}, \mu \models (\alpha \wedge \beta)$ iff $\mathfrak{I}, \mu \models \alpha$ and $\mathfrak{I}, \mu \models \beta$;

5. $\mathfrak{I}, \mu \models (\alpha \vee \beta)$ iff $\mathfrak{I}, \mu \models \alpha$ or $\mathfrak{I}, \mu \models \beta$ (or both);

6. $\mathfrak{I}, \mu \models \exists x.\alpha$ iff $\mathfrak{I}, \mu' \models \alpha$, for some variable assignment $\mu'$ that differs from $\mu$ on at most $x$;

7. $\mathfrak{I}, \mu \models \forall x.\alpha$ iff $\mathfrak{I}, \mu' \models \alpha$, for every variable assignment $\mu'$ that differs from $\mu$ on at most $x$.

When the formula $\alpha$ is a sentence, it is easy to see that satisfaction does not depend on the given variable assignment (recall that sentences do not have free variables). In this case, we write $\mathfrak{I} \models \alpha$ and say that $\alpha$ *is true* in the interpretation $\mathfrak{I}$, or that $\alpha$ *is false* otherwise. In the case of the propositional subset of FOL, it is sometimes convenient to write $\mathcal{I}[\alpha] = 1$ or $\mathcal{I}[\alpha] = 0$ according to whether $\mathcal{I} \models \alpha$ or not. We will also use the notation $\mathfrak{I} \models S$, where $S$ is a set of sentences, to mean that all of the sentences in $S$ are true in $\mathfrak{I}$. We say in this case that $\mathfrak{I}$ is a *logical model* of $S$.

## 2.4   THE PRAGMATICS

The semantic rules of interpretation tell us how to understand precisely the meaning of any term or formula of FOL in terms of a domain and an interpretation for the nonlogical symbols over that domain. What is less clear, perhaps, is why anyone interested in knowledge representation should care about this. How are we supposed to use this language to represent knowledge? How is a knowledge-based system supposed to reason about concepts like "DemocraticCountry" or even "Dog" unless it is somehow given the intended interpretation to start with? How could we possibly "give" a system an interpretation, which could involve (perhaps infinite) sets of honest-to-goodness objects like countries or animals?

### 2.4.1  Logical Consequence

To answer these questions, we first turn to the notion of logical consequence. Observe that although the semantic rules of interpretation depend on the interpretation of the nonlogical symbols, there are connections among sentences of FOL that do not depend on the meaning of those symbols.

For example, let $\alpha$ and $\beta$ be any two sentences of FOL, and let $\gamma$ be the sentence $\neg(\beta \wedge \neg\alpha)$. Now suppose that $\Im$ is any interpretation where $\alpha$ is true. Then, by using the earlier rules we can see that $\gamma$ must be also true under this interpretation. This does not depend on how we understand any of the nonlogical symbols in $\alpha$ or $\beta$. As long as $\alpha$ comes out true, $\gamma$ will as well. In a sense, the truth of $\gamma$ is implicit in the truth of $\alpha$. We say in this case that $\gamma$ is a logical consequence of $\alpha$.

More precisely, let $S$ be a set of sentences, and $\alpha$ any sentence. We say that $\alpha$ is a *logical consequence* of $S$, or that $S$ *logically entails* $\alpha$, which we write $S \models \alpha$, if and only if, for *every* interpretation $\Im$, if $\Im \models S$ then $\Im \models \alpha$. In other words, every model of $S$ satisfies $\alpha$. Yet another way of saying this is that there is no interpretation $\Im$ where $\Im \models S \cup \{\neg\alpha\}$. We say in this case that the set $S \cup \{\neg\alpha\}$ is *unsatisfiable*.

As a special case of this definition, we say that a sentence $\alpha$ is logically *valid*, which we write $\models \alpha$, when it is a logical consequence of the empty set. In other words, $\alpha$ is valid if and only if, for every interpretation $\Im$, it is the case that $\Im \models \alpha$ or, in still other words, if and only if the set $\{\neg\alpha\}$ is unsatisfiable.

It is not too hard to see that not only is validity a special case of entailment but entailment when the set is finite also reduces to validity: If $S = \{\alpha_1, \ldots, \alpha_n\}$, then $S \models \alpha$ if and only if the sentence $[(\alpha_1 \wedge \cdots \wedge \alpha_n) \supset \alpha]$ is valid.

### 2.4.2  Why We Care

Now let us reexamine the connection between knowledge-based systems and logical entailment, since this is at the heart of the knowledge representation enterprise.

What we are after is a system that can reason. Given something like the fact that Fido is a dog, it should be able to conclude that Fido is also a mammal, a carnivore, and so on. In other words, we are imagining a system that can be told or learn a sentence like "Dog(fido)" that is true in some user-intended interpretation, and that can then come to believe other sentences true in that interpretation.

A knowledge-based system will not and cannot have access to the interpretation of the nonlogical symbols itself. As we noted, this could involve infinite sets of real objects quite outside the reach of any computer system. So a knowledge-based system will not be able to decide what to believe by using the rules of Section 2.3.3 to evaluate the truth or falsity of sentences in this intended interpretation. Nor can it simply be "given" the set of sentences true in that interpretation as beliefs, because, among other things, there will be an infinite number of such sentences.

However, suppose a set of sentences $S$ entails a sentence $\alpha$. Then we do know that whatever the intended interpretation is, if $S$ happens to be true in that interpretation, then so must be $\alpha$. If the user imagines the world satisfying $S$ according to his or her understanding of the nonlogical symbols, then it satisfies $\alpha$ as well. Other nonentailed sentences may or may not be true, but a knowledge-based system can safely conclude that the entailed ones are. If we tell our system that "Dog(fido)" is true in the intended interpretation, it can safely conclude any other sentence that is logically entailed, such as "¬¬Dog(fido)" and "(Dog(fido) ∨ Happy(john))," without knowing anything else about that interpretation.

But who cares? These conclusions are logically unassailable of course, but not the sort of reasoning we would likely be interested in. In a sense, logical entailment gets us nowhere, since all we are doing is finding sentences that are already implicit in what we were told.

As we said, what we really want is a system that can go from "Dog(fido)" to conclusions like "Mammal(fido)," and on from there to other interesting animal properties. This is no longer logical entailment, however: There are interpretations where "Dog(fido)" is true and "Mammal(fido)" is false. For example, let $\Im = \langle \mathcal{D}, \mathcal{I} \rangle$ be an interpretation where for some dog $d$, $\mathcal{D} = \{d\}$, for every predicate $P$ other than "Dog," $\mathcal{I}[P] = \{\}$, where $\mathcal{I}[\text{Dog}] = \{d\}$, and where for every function symbol $f$, $\mathcal{I}[f](d, \ldots, d) = d$. This is an interpretation where the one and only dog is not a mammal. So the connection between the two sentences is not a strictly logical one.

To get the desired connection between dogs and mammals, we need to include within the set of sentences $S$ a statement connecting the nonlogical symbols involved. In this case, the sentence

$$\forall x. \, \text{Dog}(x) \supset \text{Mammal}(x)$$

should be an element of *S*. With this universal and "Dog(fido)" in *S*, we do get "Mammal(fido)" as a logical consequence. We will examine claims of logical consequence like this in more detail later, but for now note that by including this universal as one of the premises in *S*, we rule out interpretations like the one where the set of dogs is not a subset of the set of mammals. If we then continue to add more and more sentences like this to *S*, we will rule out more and more unintended interpretations, and in the end, logical consequence itself will start to behave much more like "truth in the intended interpretation."

This, then, is the fundamental tenet of knowledge representation:

> Reasoning based on logical consequence only allows safe, logically guaranteed conclusions to be drawn. However, by starting with a rich collection of sentences as given premises, including not only facts about particulars of the intended application but also those expressing connections among the nonlogical symbols involved, the set of entailed conclusions becomes a much richer set, closer to the set of sentences true in the intended interpretation. Calculating these entailments thus becomes more like the form of reasoning we would expect of someone who understood the meaning of the terms involved.

In a sense, this is all there is to knowledge representation and reasoning; the rest is just details.

## 2.5 EXPLICIT AND IMPLICIT BELIEF

The collection of sentences given as premises to be used as the basis for calculating entailments is what we called a *knowledge base* in Chapter 1—in our case, a finite set of sentences in the language of FOL. The role of a knowledge representation system, as discussed before, is to calculate entailments of this KB. We can think of the KB itself as the beliefs of the system that are *explicitly* given, and the entailments of that KB as the beliefs that are only *implicitly* given.

Just because we are imagining a "rich" collection of sentences in the KB, including the intended connections among the nonlogical symbols, we should not be misled into thinking that we have done all the work and there is no real reasoning left to do. As we will see in the following example, it is often nontrivial to move from explicit to implicit beliefs.

### 2.5.1 An Example

Consider the "blocks-world" example illustrated in Figure 2.1. Suppose we have three colored blocks stacked on a table, where the top one is green, the bottom one is not green, and the color of the middle block

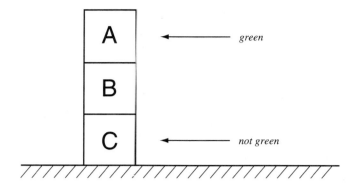

A Stack of Three Blocks

is not known. The question to consider is whether there is a green block directly on top of a nongreen one. The thing to observe about this question is that the answer (which happens to be *yes*) is not immediately obvious without some thinking.

We can formalize this problem in FOL, using $a$, $b$, and $c$ as the names of the blocks and predicate symbols $G$ and $O$ to stand for "green" and "on." The facts we have in $S$ are

$$\{O(a,b), O(b,c), G(a), \neg G(c)\}$$

and this is all we need. The claim we make here is that these four facts *entail* that there is indeed a green block on top of a nongreen one, that is, that $S \models \alpha$, where $\alpha$ is

$$\exists x \exists y.\, G(x) \wedge \neg G(y) \wedge O(x,y).$$

To see this, we need to show that any interpretation that satisfies $S$ also satisfies $\alpha$. So let $\Im$ be any interpretation, and assume that $\Im \models S$. There are two cases to consider:

1. Suppose $\Im \models G(b)$. Then because $\neg G(c)$ and $O(b,c)$ are in $S$,

$$\Im \models G(b) \wedge \neg G(c) \wedge O(b,c).$$

It follows from this that

$$\Im \models \exists x \exists y.\, G(x) \wedge \neg G(y) \wedge O(x,y).$$

2. Suppose on the other hand that it is not the case that $\Im \models G(b)$. Then it is the case that $\Im \models \neg G(b)$, and because $G(a)$ and $O(a,b)$ are in $S$,

$$\Im \models G(a) \wedge \neg G(b) \wedge O(a,b).$$

It follows from this that

$$\Im \models \exists x \exists y.\, G(x) \wedge \neg G(y) \wedge O(x,y).$$

Either way, it is the case that $\Im \models \alpha$. Thus, $\alpha$ is a logical consequence of $S$.

Even though this is a very simple example, we can see that calculating what is implicit in a given collection of facts will sometimes involve subtle forms of reasoning. Indeed, it is well known that for FOL the problem of determining whether one sentence is a logical consequence of others is in general *unsolvable:* No automated procedure can decide validity, and so no automated procedure can tell us in all cases whether or not a sentence is entailed.

## 2.5.2   Knowledge-Based Systems

To recap, we imagine that for knowledge representation we will start with a (large) KB representing what is explicitly known by a knowledge-based system. This KB could be the result of what the system is told, or perhaps what the system found out for itself through perception or learning. Our goal is to influence the behavior of the overall system based on what is *implicit* in this KB, or as close as possible.

In general, this will require reasoning. By *deductive inference*, we mean the process of calculating the entailments of a KB, that is, given the KB, and any sentence $\alpha$, determining whether or not $\text{KB} \models \alpha$.

We consider a reasoning process to be *logically sound* if whenever it produces $\alpha$, then $\alpha$ is guaranteed to be a logical consequence. This rules out the possibility of producing plausible assumptions that may very well be true in the intended interpretation but are not strictly entailed.

We consider a reasoning process to be *logically complete* if it is guaranteed to produce $\alpha$ whenever $\alpha$ is entailed. This rules out the possibility of missing some entailments, for example, when their status is too difficult to determine.

As noted, no automated reasoning process for FOL can be both sound and complete in general. However, the relative simplicity of FOL makes it a natural first step in the study of reasoning. The computational difficulty of FOL is one of the factors that will lead us to consider various other options in subsequent chapters.

## 2.6 BIBLIOGRAPHIC NOTES

For a history of the development of logic beginning in ancient Greece, refer to Kneale and Kneale [218]. Books on first-order logic tend to focus on three broad categories: philosophical logic [172, 187, 234], mathematical logic [26, 34, 119, 288], and computer science [194, 265]. The role of logic in Artificial Intelligence is treated by Genesereth and Nilsson [153]. The importance of first-order logic in knowledge representation is argued by Hayes [181], Israel [195] and Moore [294, 297]. John McCarthy, probably the first to advocate the use of formal logic as a basis for automated reasoning in Artificial Intelligence [275], also argues that first-order logic is sufficient for knowledge representation [281]. Interesting related works in the philosophy of language include those by Ayer [16] and Wittgenstein [429].

The distinction between explicit and implicit belief was first discussed in AI by Levesque [239] and further developed by Levesque and Lakemeyer [244]. Other approaches to the same issue were taken by Fagin and Halpern [123], Delgrande [100], and others. The topic is also discussed in the psychological literature (see [103], for example).

The semantics of first-order logic is largely due to Tarski [405]. For a proof of the undecidability of first-order logic, see Büchi [61] (the undecidability of FOL was first shown independently by Church and Turing in 1936). Completeness of first-order logic for a given set of axioms was first proven by Gödel [161]. Gödel's famous incompleteness theorem regarding number theory [163] is discussed in [301].

The *Handbook of Logic in Artificial Intelligence and Logic Programming* [139] and the *Handbook of Philosophical Logic* [138] are two series of volumes that are excellent sources of articles on a large variety of logics and their uses.

## 2.7 EXERCISES

1. For each of the following sentences, give a logical interpretation that makes that sentence false and the other two sentences true:

   (a) $\forall x \forall y \forall z[(P(x,y) \land P(y,z)) \supset P(x,z)]$;
   (b) $\forall x \forall y[(P(x,y) \land P(y,x)) \supset (x = y)]$;
   (c) $\forall x \forall y[P(a,y) \supset P(x,b)]$.

2. This question involves formalizing the properties of mathematical *groups* in FOL. Recall that a set is considered to be a group relative to a binary function $f$ and an object $e$ if and only if (1) $f$ is associative;

(2) $e$ is an identity element for $f$, that is, for any $x$, $f(e,x) = f(x,e) = x$; and (3) every element has an inverse, that is, for any $x$, there is an $i$ such that $f(x,i) = f(i,x) = e$. Formalize these as sentences of FOL with two nonlogical symbols, a function symbol f, and a constant symbol e, and show using interpretations that the sentences logically entail the following property of groups:

> For every $x$ and $y$, there is a $z$ such that $f(x,z) = y$.

Explain how your answer shows the value of $z$ as a function of $x$ and $y$.

3. This question involves formalizing some simple properties of *sets* in FOL. Consider the following three facts:

- *No set is an element of itself.*
- *A set $x$ is a subset of a set $y$ iff every element of $x$ is an element of $y$.*
- *Something is an element of the union of two sets $x$ and $y$ iff it is an element of $x$ or an element of $y$.*

(a) Represent the facts as sentences of FOL. As nonlogical symbols, use Sub$(x,y)$ to mean "$x$ is a subset of $y$," Elt$(e,x)$ to mean "$e$ is an element of $x$," and u$(x,y)$ to mean "the union of $x$ and $y$." Instead of using a special predicate to assert that something is a set, you may simply assume that in the domain of discourse (assumed to be nonempty) everything is a set. Call the resulting set of sentences $\mathcal{T}$.

(b) Show using logical interpretations that $\mathcal{T}$ entails that $x$ is a subset of the union of $x$ and $y$.

(c) Show using logical interpretations that $\mathcal{T}$ does not entail that the union of $x$ and $y$ is equal to the union of $y$ and $x$.

(d) Let $A$ be any set. Show using logical interpretations that $\mathcal{T}$ entails that there is a set $z$ such that the union of $A$ and $z$ is a subset of $A$.

(e) Does $\mathcal{T}$ entail that there is a set $z$ such that for any set $x$ the union of $x$ and $z$ is a subset of $x$? Explain.

(f) Write a sentence that asserts the existence of singleton sets, that is, for any $x$, the set whose only element is $x$. $\mathcal{T}_1$ is $\mathcal{T}$ with this sentence added.

(g) Prove that $\mathcal{T}_1$ is not finitely satisfiable (again, assuming the domain is nonempty). *Hint:* In a finite domain, consider $u$, the object interpreted as the union of all the elements in the domain.

(h) Prove or disprove that $\mathcal{T}$ entails the existence of an empty set.

**4.** In a certain town, there are the following regulations concerning the town barber:

- *Anyone who does not shave himself must be shaved by the barber.*
- *Whomever the barber shaves, must not shave himself.*

Show that no barber can fulfill these requirements. That is, formulate the requirements as sentences of FOL and show that in any interpretation where the first regulation is true, the second one must be false. (This is called the *barber's paradox* and was formulated by Bertrand Russell.)

# CHAPTER 3

# EXPRESSING KNOWLEDGE

▨
─────────────────────────────────────────────

▨

▨

The stage is now set for a somewhat more detailed exploration of the process of creating a knowledge base. Recall that knowledge involves taking the world to satisfy some property, as expressed by a declarative sentence. A KB will thus comprise a collection of such sentences, and we take the propositions expressed by these sentences to be beliefs of our putative agent.

Much of this book is an exploration of different languages that can be used to represent the knowledge of an agent in symbolic form with different consequences, especially regarding reasoning. As we suggested in Chapter 2, first-order logic, while by no means the only language for representing knowledge, is a convenient choice for getting started with the knowledge representation enterprise.

## 3.1 KNOWLEDGE ENGINEERING

Having outlined the basic principles of knowledge representation and decided on an initial representation language, we might be tempted to dive right in and begin the implementation of a set of programs that could reason over a specific KB of interest. But before doing so, there are key questions about the knowledge of the agent that need to be considered in the abstract. In the same way that a programmer who is thinking ahead would first outline an architecture for his or her planned system, it is essential that we consider the overall architecture of the system we are about to create. We must think ahead to what it is we ultimately want (or want our artificial agent) to compute. We need to make some commitments to the reasons and times that inference will be necessary in our system's behavior. Finally, we need to stake out what is sometimes called an *ontology*—the kinds of *objects* that will be important to the agent, the *properties* those objects will be thought to have, and the *relationships* among them—before we can start populating our agent's KB. This general process, which addresses the KB at the knowledge level, is often called *knowledge engineering*.

This chapter, then, will be an introductory exercise in knowledge engineering, intended to be specific enough to make vivid the import of the previous two chapters. There are any number of example domains that we might use to illustrate how to use a knowledge representation language to build a KB. Here we pick a common and commonsensical world to illustrate the process, with people and places and relationships that are representative of many of the types of domains that AI systems will address. Given the complexity of human relations and the kind of behaviors that regular people have, we can think of this example domain as a "soap opera" world. Think of a small town in the midst of a number of scandals and contorted relationships. This little world will include people, places, companies, marriages (and divorces), crimes, death, "hanky-panky," and, of course, money.

Our task is to create a KB that has appropriate entailments, and the first things we need to consider are what vocabulary to use and what facts to represent.

## 3.2   VOCABULARY

In creating a KB it is a good idea to start with the set of domain-dependent predicates and functions that provide the basis for the statement of facts about the KB's domain. What sorts of objects will there be in our soap-opera world?

The most obvious place to start is with the *named individuals* who are the actors in our human drama. In FOL, these would be represented by constant symbols, like maryJones, johnQSmith, and so on. We might need to allow multiple identifiers that could ultimately be found to refer to the same individual: At some point in the process our system might know about a "john" without knowing whether he is johnQSmith or johnPJones, or even the former joannaSmith. Beyond the human players on our stage, we could of course have animals, robots, ghosts, and other sentient entities.

Another class of named individuals would be the legal entities that have their own identities, such as corporations (faultyInsuranceCompany), governments (evilvilleTownCouncil), and restaurants (theRackAndRollRestaurant). Key places also need to be identified: tomsHouse, theAbandonedRailwayCar, norasJacuzzi, and so on. Finally, other important objects need to be scoped out, such as earring35, butcherknife1, and laurasMortgage (note that it is common to use the equivalent of numeric subscripts to distinguish among individuals that do not have uniquely referring names).

After capturing the set of individuals that will be central to the agent's world, it is next essential to circumscribe the basic *types* of objects that those individuals are. This is usually done with one-place predicates in FOL, such as Person($x$). Among the types of unary predicates we will want in our current domain we find Man, Woman, Place, Company, Jewelry, Knife, Contract, and so on. If we expect to be reasoning about certain places based on what types of entities they are, such as a restaurant as a place to eat that is importantly different than someone's living room, for example, then object types like Restaurant, Bar, House, and SwimmingPool will be useful.

Another set of one-place predicates that is crucial for our domain representation is the set of *attributes* that our objects can have. So we need a vocabulary of properties that can hold for individuals, such as Rich, Beautiful, Unscrupulous, Bankrupt, ClosedForRepairs, Bloody, and Foreclosed. The syntax of FOL is limited in that it does not allow us to distinguish between such properties and the object-types we suggested a moment ago, such as Man and Knife. This usually does not present a problem, although if it were important for the system to distinguish between such types, the language could be extended to do so.[1]

The next key predicates to consider are *n*-ary predicates that express *relationships* (obviously of crucial interest in any soap-opera world). We can start with obvious ones, like MarriedTo and DaughterOf, and related ones like LivesAt and HasCEO. We can then branch out to more esoteric relationships like HairDresserOf, Blackmails, and HadAnAffairWith. Also, we cannot forget relationships of higher arity than 2, as in LoveTriangle, ConspiresWith, and OccursInTimeInterval.

Finally, we need to capture the important *functions* of the domain. These can take more than one argument, but are most often unary, as in fatherOf, bestFriendOf, and ceoOf. One thing to note is that all functions are taken to be *total* in FOL. If we want to allow for the possibility of individuals without friends in our domain, we can use a binary BestFriend predicate instead of a unary bestFriendOf function.

## 3.3 BASIC FACTS

Now that we have our basic vocabulary in place, it is appropriate to start representing the simple core facts of our soap-opera world. Such facts are usually represented by atomic sentences and negations of

---

[1] FOL does not distinguish because in our semantic account, as presented in Chapter 2, both sorts of predicates will be interpreted as sets of individuals for which the descriptions hold.

atomic sentences. For example, we can use our type predicates, applied to individuals in the domain, to represent some basic truths: Man(john), Woman(jane), Company(faultyInsuranceCompany), Knife(butcherknife1). Such type predications would define the basic ontology of this world.[2]

Once we have set down the types of each of our objects, we can capture some of the properties of the objects. These properties will be the chief currency in talking about our domain, since we most often want to see what properties (and relationships) are implied by a set of facts or conjectures. In our sample domain, some useful property assertions might be Rich(john), ¬HappilyMarried(jim), WorksFor(jim,fic), Bloody(butcherknife1), and ClosedForRepairs(marTDiner).

Basic facts like these yield what amounts to a simple database. These facts could indeed be stored in relational tables. For example, each type predicate could be a table, with the table's entries being identifiers for all of the known satisfiers of that predicate. Of course, the details of such a storage strategy would be a symbol-level, not a knowledge-level issue.

Another set of simple facts that are useful in domain representation are those dealing with equality. To express the fact that John is the CEO of Faulty Insurance Company, we could use an equality and a one-place function: john = ceoOf(fic). Similarly, bestFriendOf(jim) = john would capture the fact that John is Jim's best friend. Another use of equalities would be for naming convenience, as when an individual has more than one name, for example, fic = faultyInsuranceCompany.

## 3.4  COMPLEX FACTS

Many of the facts we would like to express about a domain are more complex than can be captured using atomic sentences. Thus we need to use more complex formulas, with quantifiers and other connectives, to express various beliefs about the domain.

In the soap-opera domain, we might want to express the fact that all the rich men in our world love Jane. To do so, we would use universal quantification, ranging over all of the rich individuals in our world, and over all of the men:

$$\forall y[\text{Rich}(y) \land \text{Man}(y) \supset \text{Loves}(y, \text{jane})].$$

Note that "rich man" here is captured by a conjunction of predicates. Similarly, we might want to express the fact that in this world all the

---

[2]Note, by the way, that suggestive names are not a form of knowledge representation because they do not support logical inference. Just using "butcherknife1" as a symbol does not give the system any substantive information about the object. This is done using predicates, not orthography.

women, with the possible exception of Jane, love John. To do so, we would use a universal ranging over all of the women, and negate an equality to exclude Jane:

$$\forall y[\text{Woman}(y) \wedge y \neq \text{jane} \supset \text{Loves}(y, \text{john})].$$

Universals are also useful for expressing very general facts, not even involving any known individuals. For example,

$$\forall x \forall y[\text{Loves}(x, y) \supset \neg\text{Blackmails}(x, y)]$$

expresses the fact that no one who loves someone will blackmail the one he or she loves.

Note that these universal quantifications could each be expressed without quantifiers if all of the individuals in the soap-opera world were enumerated. It would be tedious if the world were at all large, so the universally quantified sentences are handy abbreviations. Further, as new individuals are born or otherwise introduced into our soap-opera world, the universals will cover them as well.

Another type of fact that needs a complex formula to express it is one that expresses *incomplete knowledge* about our world. For example, if we know that Jane loves one of John or Jim but not which, we would need to use a disjunction to capture that belief:

$$\text{Loves( jane, john)} \vee \text{Loves( jane, jim)}.$$

Similarly, if we knew that someone (an adult) was blackmailing John, but not who it was, we would use an existential quantifier to posit that unknown person:

$$\exists x[\text{Adult}(x) \wedge \text{Blackmails}(x, \text{john})].$$

This kind of fact would be quite prevalent in a soap-opera world story, although one would expect many such unknowns to be resolved over time.

In contrast to the prior use of universals, these cases of incomplete knowledge are not merely abbreviations. We cannot write a more complete version of the information in another form—it just isn't known.

Another useful type of complex statement about our soap-opera domain is what we might call a *closure* sentence, used to limit the domain of discourse. So, for example, we could enumerate if necessary all of the lawyers in our world:

$$\forall x[\text{Lawyer}(x) \supset x = \text{jane} \vee x = \text{jack} \vee x = \text{jim} \vee \ldots].$$

In a similar fashion, we could circumscribe the set of all married couples:

$$\forall x \forall y[\text{MarriedTo}(x, y) \supset (x = \text{ethel} \land y = \text{fred}) \lor \ldots].$$

It will then follow that any pair of individuals known to be different from those mentioned in the sentence are unmarried. In an even more general way, we can carve out the full set of individuals in the domain of discourse:

$$\forall x[x = \text{fic} \lor x = \text{jane} \lor x = \text{jim} \lor x = \text{marTDiner} \lor \ldots].$$

This ensures that a reasoner would not postulate a new, hitherto unknown object in the course of its reasoning.

Finally, it is useful to distinguish formally between all known individuals with a set of sentences like jane ≠ john. This would prevent the accidental postulation that two people were the same, for example, in trying to solve a crime.

## 3.5 TERMINOLOGICAL FACTS

The kinds of facts we have represented so far are sufficient to capture the basic circumstances in a domain, and give us grist for the reasoning mill. However, when thinking about domains like the soap-opera world, we would typically also think in terms of relationships among the predicate and function symbols we have exploited. For example, we would consider it quite "obvious" in this domain that if it were asserted that john were a Man, then we should answer "no" to the query Woman( john). Or we would easily accede to the fact that MarriedTo(jr,sueEllen) was true if it were already stated that MarriedTo(sueEllen,jr) was. But there is nothing in our current KB that would actually sanction such inferences. In order to support such common and useful inferences, we need to provide a set of facts about the *terminology* we are using.

Terminological facts come in many varieties. Here we look at a sample:

- *Disjointness:* Often two predicates are disjoint, and the assertion of one implies the negation of the other, as in

  $$\forall x[\text{Man}(x) \supset \neg\text{Woman}(x)]$$

- *Subtypes:* There are many predicates that imply a form of specialization, wherein one type is subsumed by another. For example, since a surgeon is a kind of doctor, we would want to capture the subtype relationship:

  $$\forall x[\text{Surgeon}(x) \supset \text{Doctor}(x)]$$

This way, we should be able to infer the reasonable consequence that anything true of doctors is also true of surgeons (but not vice versa).

■ *Exhaustiveness:* This is the converse of the subtype assertion, where two or more subtypes completely account for a supertype, as in

$$\forall x[\text{Adult}(x) \supset (\text{Man}(x) \vee \text{Woman}(x))]$$

■ *Symmetry:* As in the case of the MarriedTo predicate, some relationships are symmetric:

$$\forall x, y[\text{MarriedTo}(x, y) \supset \text{MarriedTo}(y, x)]$$

■ *Inverses:* Some relationships are the opposite of others:

$$\forall x, y[\text{ChildOf}(x, y) \supset \text{ParentOf}(y, x)]$$

■ *Type restrictions:* Part of the meaning of some predicates is the fact that their arguments must be of certain types. For example, we might want to capture the fact that the definition of marriage entails that the partners are persons:

$$\forall x, y[\text{MarriedTo}(x, y) \supset \text{Person}(x) \wedge \text{Person}(y)]$$

■ *Full definitions:* In some cases, we want to create compound predicates that are completely defined by a logical combination of other predicates. We can use a biconditional to capture such definitions:

$$\forall x[\text{RichMan}(x) \equiv \text{Rich}(x) \wedge \text{Man}(x)]$$

As can be seen from these examples, terminological facts are typically captured in a logical language as universally quantified conditionals or biconditionals.

## 3.6 ENTAILMENTS

Now that we have captured the basic structure of our soap-opera domain, it is time to turn to the reason that we have done this representation in the first place: deriving implicit conclusions from our explicitly represented KB. Here we briefly explore this notion in an intuitive fashion. This will give us a feel for the consequences of a particular characterization of a domain. In Chapter 4 we will consider how entailments can be computed in a more mechanical way.

Let us consider all of the basic and complex facts proposed so far in this chapter to be a knowledge base, called KB. Besides asking simple questions of KB like, "Is John married to Jane?" we will want to explore more complex and important ones, such as, "Is there a company whose CEO loves Jane?" Such a question would look like this in FOL:

$$\exists x[\text{Company}(x) \wedge \text{Loves}(\text{ceoOf}(x), \text{jane})]?$$

What we want to do is find out if the truth of this sentence is implicit in what we already know. In other words, we want to see if the sentence is entailed by KB.

To answer the question, we need to determine whether every logical interpretation that satisfies KB also satisfies the sentence. So let us imagine an interpretation $\Im$, and suppose that $\Im \models \text{KB}$. It follows then that $\Im$ satisfies Rich(john), Man(john), and $\forall y[\text{Rich}(y) \wedge \text{Man}(y) \supset \text{Loves}(y, \text{jane})]$, since these are all in KB. As a result, $\Im \models \text{Loves}(\text{john,jane})$. Now since (john = ceoOf(fic)) is also in KB, we can conclude that

$$\Im \models \text{Loves}(\text{ceoOf}(\text{fic}), \text{jane}).$$

Finally, since

$$\text{Company}(\text{faultyInsuranceCompany})$$

and

$$\text{fic} = \text{faultyInsuranceCompany}$$

are both in KB, it is the case that

$$\Im \models \text{Company}(\text{fic}) \wedge \text{Loves}(\text{ceoOf}(\text{fic}), \text{jane}),$$

from which it follows that

$$\Im \models \exists x[\text{Company}(x) \wedge \text{Loves}(\text{ceoOf}(x), \text{jane})].$$

Since this argument goes through for any interpretation $\Im$, we know that the sentence is indeed entailed by KB.

Observe that by looking at the argument we have made, we can determine not only that there is a company whose CEO loves Jane, but also what that company is. In many applications we will be interested in finding out not only whether something is true or not, but also which individuals satisfy a property of interest. In other words, we need answers not only to yes–no questions, but to *wh*-questions as well (who? what? where? when? how? why?).[3]

Let us consider a second example, which involves a hypothetical. Consider the question, "If no man is blackmailing John, then is he being blackmailed by someone he loves?" In logical terms, this question would be formulated this way:

$$\forall x[\text{Man}(x) \supset \neg\text{Blackmails}(x, \text{john})] \supset$$
$$\exists y[\text{Loves}(\text{john}, y) \wedge \text{Blackmails}(y, \text{john})]?$$

Again, we need to determine whether or not the sentence is entailed by KB. Here we use the easily verified fact that KB $\models (\alpha \supset \beta)$ if and only if KB $\cup \{\alpha\} \models \beta$. So let us imagine that we have an interpretation $\Im$ such that $\Im \models$ KB, and that

$$\Im \models \forall x[\text{Man}(x) \supset \neg\text{Blackmails}(x, \text{john})].$$

We must show that

$$\Im \models \exists y[\text{Loves}(\text{john}, y) \wedge \text{Blackmails}(y, \text{john})].$$

To get to this conclusion, there are a number of steps. First of all, we know that someone is blackmailing John,

$$\Im \models \exists x[\text{Adult}(x) \wedge \text{Blackmails}(x, \text{john})],$$

since this fact is in KB. Also, KB contains the fact that adults are either men or women,

$$\Im \models \forall x[\text{Adult}(x) \supset (\text{Man}(x) \vee \text{Woman}(x))],$$

and since by hypothesis no man is blackmailing John, we conclude that a woman is blackmailing him:

$$\Im \models \exists x[\text{Woman}(x) \wedge \text{Blackmails}(x, \text{john})].$$

Next, as seen in the previous example, we know that

$$\Im \models \text{Loves}(\text{john}, \text{jane}).$$

---

[3]In Chapter 4 we will propose a general mechanism for extracting answers from existential questions.

So, some woman is blackmailing John and John loves Jane. Could she be the blackmailer? Recall that all the women except possibly Jane love John,

$$\Im \models \forall y[\text{Woman}(y) \wedge y \neq \text{jane} \supset \text{Loves}(y, \text{john})],$$

and that no one who loves someone will blackmail them,

$$\Im \models \forall x \forall y[\text{Loves}(x, y) \supset \neg \text{Blackmails}(x, y)].$$

We can put these two conditionals together and conclude that no woman other than Jane is blackmailing John:

$$\Im \models \forall y[\text{Woman}(y) \wedge y \neq \text{jane} \supset \neg \text{Blackmails}(y, \text{john})].$$

Since we know that a woman is in fact blackmailing John, we are forced to conclude that it is Jane:

$$\Im \models \text{Blackmails}(\text{jane}, \text{john}).$$

Thus, in the end, we have concluded that John loves Jane and she is blackmailing him,

$$\Im \models [\text{Loves}(\text{john}, \text{jane}) \wedge \text{Blackmails}(\text{jane}, \text{john})],$$

and so

$$\Im \models \exists y[\text{Loves}(\text{john}, y) \wedge \text{Blackmails}(y, \text{john})],$$

as desired.

Here we have illustrated in intuitive form how a *proof* can be thought of as a sequence of FOL sentences, starting with those known to be true in the KB (or surmised as part of the assumptions dictated by the query), that proceeds logically using other facts in the KB and the rules of logic until a suitable conclusion is reached. In Chapter 4 we will examine a different style of proof based on negating the desired conclusion and showing that this leads to a contradiction.

To conclude this section, let us consider what is involved with an entailment question when the answer is *no*. In the previous example, we made the assumption that no man was blackmailing John. Now let us consider if this was necessary: Is it already implicit in what we have in the KB that someone John loves is blackmailing him? In other words, we wish to determine whether or not KB entails

$$\exists y[\text{Loves}(\text{john}, y) \wedge \text{Blackmails}(y, \text{john})].$$

To show that it does *not*, we must show an interpretation that satisfies KB but falsifies this sentence. That is, we must produce a specific interpretation $\Im = \langle \mathcal{D}, \mathcal{I} \rangle$ and argue that it satisfies every sentence in the KB as well as the negation of the sentence. For the number of sentences we have in KB this is a big job, since all of them must be verified, but the essence of the argument is that without contradicting anything already in KB, we can arrange $\Im$ in such a way that John only loves women, there is only one person in $\mathcal{D}$ who is blackmailing John, and it is a man. Thus it is not already implicit in KB that someone John loves is blackmailing him.

## 3.7   ABSTRACT INDIVIDUALS

The FOL language gives us the basic tools for representing facts in a domain, but in many cases there is a great deal of flexibility that can be exercised in mapping objects in that domain onto predicates and functions. There is also considerable flexibility in what we consider to be the individuals in the domain. In this section we will see that it is sometimes useful to introduce new *abstract individuals* that might not have been considered in a first analysis. This idea of making up new individuals is called *reification* and is typical, as we shall see in later chapters, of systems like description logics and frame languages.

To see why reification might be useful, consider how we might say that John purchased a bike:

Purchases(john,bike)   vs.

Purchases(john,sears,bike)   vs.

Purchases(john,sears,bike,feb14)   vs.

Purchases(john,sears,bike,feb14,$200)   vs. . . .

The problem here is that it seems that the arity of the Purchases predicate depends on how much detail we will want to express, which we may not be able to predict in advance.

A better approach is to take the purchase itself to be an abstract individual; call it p23. To describe this purchase at any level of detail we find appropriate, we need only use 1-place predicates and functions:

Purchase(p23) $\wedge$ agent(p23) = john $\wedge$ object(p23) = bike
$\wedge$ source(p23) = sears $\wedge$ amount(p23) = $200 $\wedge$ . . .

For less detail, we simply leave out some of the conjuncts; for more, we include others. The big advantage is that the arity of the predicate and function symbols involved can be determined in advance.

In a similar way we can capture in a reasonable fashion complex relationships of the sort that are common in our soap-opera world. For example, we might initially consider representing marriage relationships this way:

$$MarriedTo(x, y),$$

but we might also need to consider

$$PreviouslyMarriedTo(x, y)$$

and

$$ReMarriedTo(x, y).$$

Rather than create a potentially endless supply of marriage and remarriage (and divorce and annulment and so on) predicates, we can reify marriage and divorce events as abstract individuals and determine anyone's current marital status and complete marital history directly from them:

$$Marriage(m17) \land husband(m17) = x \land wife(m17) = y$$
$$\land\ date(m17) = \dots \land witness(m17) = \dots \land \dots$$

It is now possible to *define* these predicates (PreviouslyMarriedTo, etc.) in terms of the existence (and chronological order) of appropriate marriage and divorce events.

In representing commonsense information like this we also find that we need individuals for numbers, dates, times, addresses, and so on. Basically, any "object" about which we can ask a *wh*-question should have an individual standing for it in the KB so it can be returned as the result of a query.

The idea of reifying abstract individuals leads to some interesting choices concerning the representation of *quantities*. For example, an obvious representation for a person's age would be something like this:

$$ageInYears(suzy) = 14.$$

If a finer-grained notion of age is needed in an application, we might prefer to represent a person's age in months (this is particularly common when talking about young children):

$$ageInMonths(suzy) = 172.\,[4]$$

---

[4]For some purposes a more qualitative view of age might be in order, as in age(suzy) = teenager or age(suzy) = minor.

Of course, there is a relationship between ageInYears and ageInMonths. However, we have exactly the same relationship between quantities like durationInYears and durationInMonths, and between expectedLifeInYears and expectedLifeInMonths.

To capture all these regularities, it might be better to introduce an abstract individual to stand for a time duration, independent of any units. So we might take age(suzy) to denote an abstract quantity of time quite apart from Suzy and 14, and assert that

$$years(age(suzy)) = 14$$

as a way of saying what this quantity would be if measured in years. Now we can write very general facts about such quantities such as

$$months(x) = 12 * years(x)$$

to relate the two units of measurement. Similarly, we would have

$$centimeters(x) = 100 * meters(x).$$

We could continue in this vein with locations and times. For example, instead of

$$time(m17) = \text{"Jan 5 1992 4:47:03EST"}$$

where we are forced to decide on a fixed granularity, we could use

$$time(m17) = t41 \land year(t41) = 1992 \land month(t41) = Jan \land \ldots$$

where we have reified time points. This type of representation of abstract individuals for quantities, times, locations, and so on is a common technique similar to the reification of events illustrated earlier.

## 3.8  OTHER SORTS OF FACTS

With the apparatus described so far we have seen how to represent the basic facts and individuals of a commonsense domain like our soap-opera world. Before moving on to a look at the variations in different knowledge representation systems and their associated inference machinery, it is important to point out that there are a number of other types of facts about domains that we may want to capture. Each of these is problematical for a straightforward application of first-order logic, but as we shall see in the remainder of the book, they may be represented with extensions of FOL or with other knowledge representation languages. The choice of the language to use in a system or analysis will ultimately depend on what types of facts and conclusions are most important for the application.

Among the many types of facts in the soap-opera world that we have not captured are the following:

- *statistical and probabilistic facts:* These include those that involve portions of the sets of individuals satisfying a predicate, in some cases exact subsets and in other cases less exactly quantifiable:

  - Half of the companies are located on the East Side.
  - Most of the employees are restless.
  - Almost none of the employees are completely trustworthy.

- *default and prototypical facts:* These cite characteristics that are usually true, or reasonable to assume true unless told otherwise:

  - Company presidents typically have secretaries intercepting their phone calls.
  - Cars have four wheels.
  - Companies generally do not allow employees that work together to be married.
  - Birds fly.

- *intentional facts:* These express people's mental attitudes and intentions, that is, they can reflect the reality of people's beliefs but not necessarily the "real" world itself:

  - John believes that Henry is trying to blackmail him.
  - Jane does not want Jim to know that she loves him.
  - Tom wants Frank to believe that the shot came from the grassy knoll.

This is not the end of what we would like to be able to express in a KB, of course. In later chapters we will want to talk about the effects of actions and will end up reifying both actions and states of the world. Ultimately, a knowledge-based system should be able to express and reason with anything that can be expressed by a sentence of English, indeed, anything that we can imagine as being either true or false. Here we have only looked at simple forms that are easily expressible in FOL. In subsequent chapters we will examine other representation languages with different strengths and weaknesses. First, however, we turn to how we might compute entailments of a KB in FOL.

## 3.9  BIBLIOGRAPHIC NOTES

The catalogue of concepts (constants, relations, functions, etc.) used to represent knowledge about a problem domain has come to be called an *ontology* [1, 85, 171]. A very substantial, many-year attempt to develop a universal ontology for commonsense reasoning has been the CYC project [235]. Among some smaller projects with related ambitions is the KM project [71, 72].

A number of standards have been proposed for communicating knowledge between knowledge-based systems and for representing knowledge in a standard format. These include the *Knowledge Interchange Format* KIF [151, 152] (for a critique of KIF, see Ginsberg [159]), the *Knowledge Query Manipulation Language* KQML [229, 230], the *DARPA Agent Markup Language* DAML [185], the *Ontology Inference Layer* OIL [126], and the Web Ontology Language OWL [286]. Some of this work is making its way into the broader world of the World Wide Web via what is called the "Semantic Web" [27].

The domain closure assumption and unique names assumption were introduced by Reiter [341] and will be examined in detail in Chapter 11. As noted in Chapter 2, the formal truth-valued semantics for first-order logic is largely credited to Tarski [405], although it follows on from earlier work. For further discussion, see Etchemendy [121].

---

## 3.10  EXERCISES

**1.** (Adapted from [309], and see follow-up Exercise 2 of Chapter 4.)
   Consider the following piece of knowledge:

   *Tony, Mike, and John belong to the Alpine Club. Every member of the Alpine Club who is not a skier is a mountain climber. Mountain climbers do not like rain, and anyone who does not like snow is not a skier. Mike dislikes whatever Tony likes, and likes whatever Tony dislikes. Tony likes rain and snow.*

   (a) Prove that the given sentences logically entail that there is a member of the Alpine Club who is a mountain climber but not a skier.

   (b) Suppose we had been told that Mike likes whatever Tony dislikes, but we had not been told that Mike dislikes whatever Tony likes. Prove that the resulting set of sentences no longer logically entails that there is a member of the Alpine Club who is a mountain climber but not a skier.

**2.** Consider the following facts about the Elm Street Bridge Club:

   *Joe, Sally, Bill, and Ellen are the only members of the club. Joe is married to Sally. Bill is Ellen's brother. The spouse of every married person in the club is also in the club.*

From these facts, most people would be able to determine that Ellen is not married.

(a) Represent these facts as sentences in FOL, and show semantically that by themselves they do *not* entail that Ellen is not married.

(b) Write in FOL some additional facts that most people would be expected to know, and show that the augmented set of sentences now entails that Ellen is not married.

3. Donald and Daisy Duck took their nephews, age 4, 5, and 6, on an outing. Each boy wore a tee-shirt with a different design on it and of a different color. You are also given the following information:

   ■ *Huey is younger than the boy in the green tee-shirt.*
   ■ *The 5-year-old wore the tee-shirt with the camel design.*
   ■ *Dewey's tee-shirt was yellow.*
   ■ *Louie's tee-shirt bore the giraffe design.*
   ■ *The panda design was not featured on the white tee-shirt.*

(a) Represent these facts as sentences in FOL.

(b) Using your formalization, is it possible to conclude the age of each boy together with the color and design of the tee-shirt he is wearing? Show semantically how you determined your answer.

(c) If your answer was "no," indicate what further sentences you would need to add so that you could conclude the age of each boy together with the color and design of the tee-shirt he is wearing.

4. A Canadian variant of an old puzzle:

   *A traveler in remote Quebec comes to a fork in the road and does not know which way to go to get to Chicoutimi. Henri and Pierre are two local inhabitants nearby who do know the way. One of them always tells the truth, and the other one never does, but the traveler does not know which is which. Is there a single question the traveler can ask Henri (in French, of course) that will be sure to tell him which way to go?*

   We will formalize this problem in FOL. Assume there are only two sorts of objects in our domain: *inhabitants*, denoted by the constants henri and pierre; and *French questions*, which Henri and Pierre can answer. These questions are denoted by the following terms:

   ■ gauche, which asks if the traveler should take the left branch of the fork to get to Chicoutimi;
   ■ dit_oui($x, q$), which asks if inhabitant $x$ would answer yes to the French question $q$;

- dit_non($x, q$), which asks if inhabitant $x$ would answer no to the French question $q$.

Obviously this is a somewhat impoverished dialect of French, although a philosophically interesting one. For example, the term

$$\text{dit\_non(henri, dit\_oui(pierre, gauche))}$$

represents a French question that might be translated as, "Would Henri answer no if I asked him if Pierre would say yes I should go to the left to get to Chicoutimi?" The predicate symbols of our language are the following:

- Truth_teller($x$), which holds when inhabitant $x$ is a truth teller;
- Answer_yes($x, q$), which holds when inhabitant $x$ will answer yes to French question $q$;
- True($q$), which holds when the correct answer to the question $q$ is yes;
- Go_left, which holds if the direction to get to Chicoutimi is to go left.

For purposes of this puzzle, these are the only constant, function, and predicate symbols.

(a) Write FOL sentences for each of the following:

- *One of Henri or Pierre is a truth teller, and one is not.*
- *An inhabitant will answer yes to a question if and only if he is a truth teller and the correct answer is yes, or he is not a truth teller and the correct answer is not yes.*
- *The* gauche *question is correctly answered yes if and only if the proper direction to is to go is left.*
- *A* dit_oui($x, q$) *question is correctly answered yes if and only if x will answer yes to question q.*
- *A* dit_non($x, q$) *question is correctly answered yes if and only if x will not answer yes to q.*

Imagine that these facts make up the entire KB of the traveler.

(b) Show that there is a ground term $t$ such that

$$\text{KB} \models [\text{Answer\_yes(henri}, t) \equiv \text{Go\_left}].$$

In other words, there is a question $t$ that can be asked to Henri (and there is an analogous one for Pierre) that will be answered yes if and only if the proper direction to get to Chicoutimi is to go left.

(c) Show that this KB does not entail which direction to go, that is, show that there is an interpretation satisfying the KB where Go_left is true, and another one where it is false.

# CHAPTER 4

# RESOLUTION

■

■

■

In Chapter 3, we examined how FOL could be used to represent knowledge about a simple application domain. We also showed how logical reasoning could be used to discover facts that were only implicit in a given knowledge base. All of our deductive reasoning, however, was done by hand, and relatively informally. In this chapter, we will examine in detail how to automate a deductive reasoning procedure.

At the knowledge level, the specification for an idealized deductive procedure is clear: Given a knowledge base KB and a sentence $\alpha$, we would like a procedure that can determine whether or not KB $\models \alpha$; also, if $\beta[x_1, \ldots, x_n]$ is a formula with free variables among the $x_i$, we want a procedure that can find terms $t_i$, if they exist, such that KB $\models$ $\beta[t_1, \ldots, t_n]$. Of course, as discussed in Chapter 1, this is idealized; *no* computational procedure can fully satisfy this specification. What we are really after, in the end, is a procedure that does deductive reasoning in as sound and complete a manner as possible, and in a language as close as possible to that of full FOL.

One observation about this specification is that if we take the KB to be a finite set of sentences $\{\alpha_1, \ldots, \alpha_n\}$, there are several equivalent ways of formulating the deductive reasoning task:

$$\text{KB} \models \alpha$$
$$\text{iff} \quad \models [(\alpha_1 \wedge \cdots \wedge \alpha_n) \supset \alpha]$$
$$\text{iff} \quad \text{KB} \cup \{\neg\alpha\} \text{ is not satisfiable}$$
$$\text{iff} \quad \text{KB} \cup \{\neg\alpha\} \models \neg\text{TRUE}$$

where TRUE is any valid sentence, such as $\forall x(x = x)$. What this means is that if we have a procedure for testing the validity of sentences, or for testing the satisfiability of sentences, or for determining whether or not ¬TRUE is entailed, then that procedure can also be used to find the entailments of a finite KB. This is significant, because the Resolution procedure that we will consider in this chapter is in fact a procedure for determining whether certain sets of formulas are satisfiable.

In the next section, we begin by looking at a propositional version of Resolution, the clausal representation it depends on, and how it can be used to compute entailments. In Section 4.2, we generalize this account to deal with variables and quantifiers, and show how special answer predicates can be used to find bindings for variables in queries. Finally, in Section 4.3, we review the computational difficulties inherent in Resolution, and show some of the refinements to Resolution that are used in practice to deal with them.

## 4.1    THE PROPOSITIONAL CASE

The reasoning procedure we will consider in this chapter works on logical formulas in a special restricted form. It is not hard to see that every formula $\alpha$ of propositional logic can be converted into another formula $\alpha'$ such that $\models (\alpha \equiv \alpha')$, and where $\alpha'$ is a conjunction of disjunctions of *literals*, where a literal is either an atom or its negation. We say that $\alpha$ and $\alpha'$ are *logically equivalent*, and that $\alpha'$ is in *conjunctive normal form*, or CNF. In the propositional case, CNF formulas look like this:[1]

$$(p \vee \neg q) \wedge (q \vee r \vee \neg s \vee p) \wedge (\neg r \vee q).$$

The procedure to convert any propositional formula to CNF is as follows:

1. eliminate $\supset$ and $\equiv$, using the fact that these are abbreviations for formulas using only $\wedge$, $\vee$, and $\neg$;

2. move $\neg$ inward so that it appears only in front of an atom, using the following equivalences:

$$\models \neg\neg\alpha \equiv \alpha;$$

$$\models \neg(\alpha \wedge \beta) \equiv (\neg\alpha \vee \neg\beta);$$

$$\models \neg(\alpha \vee \beta) \equiv (\neg\alpha \wedge \neg\beta).$$

3. distribute $\wedge$ over $\vee$, using the following equivalences:

$$\models (\alpha \vee (\beta \wedge \gamma)) \equiv ((\beta \wedge \gamma) \vee \alpha) \equiv ((\alpha \vee \beta) \wedge (\alpha \vee \gamma)).$$

---

[1]In this chapter, to be consistent with common practice, we use lowercase letters for propositional symbols.

4. collect terms, using the following equivalences:

$$\models (\alpha \vee \alpha) \equiv \alpha;$$

$$\models (\alpha \wedge \alpha) \equiv \alpha.$$

The result of this procedure is a logically equivalent CNF formula (which can be exponentially larger than the original formula).[2] For example, for $((p \supset q) \supset r)$, by applying rule (1), we get $(\neg(\neg p \vee q) \vee r)$; applying rule (2), we then get $((p \wedge \neg q) \vee r)$; and with rule (3), we get $((p \vee r) \wedge (\neg q \vee r))$, which is in CNF. In this chapter, we will mainly deal with formulas in CNF.

It is convenient to use a shorthand representation for CNF. A *clausal formula* is a finite set of *clauses*, where a clause is a finite set of literals. The interpretation of clausal formulas is precisely as formulas in CNF: A clausal formula is understood as the conjunction of its clauses, where each clause is understood as the disjunction of its literals, and literals are understood normally. In representing clauses here, we will use the following notation:

- if $\rho$ is a literal then $\overline{\rho}$ is its *complement*, defined by $\overline{p} = \neg p$ and $\overline{\neg p} = p$, for any atom $p$;
- while we will always use the normal set notation involving "{" and "}" for clausal formulas (which are sets of clauses), we will sometimes use "[" and "]" as the delimiters for clauses (which are sets of literals) when we want to emphasize the difference between clauses and clausal formulas.

For example, $[p, \neg q, r]$ is the clause consisting of three literals, and understood as the disjunction $(p \vee \neg q \vee r)$, while $\{[p, \neg q, r], [q]\}$ is the clausal formula consisting of two clauses, and understood as $((p \vee \neg q \vee r) \wedge q)$. A clause like $[\neg p]$ with a single literal is called a *unit clause*.

Note that the empty clausal formula {} is not the same as {[]}, the formula containing just the empty clause. The empty clause [] is understood as a representation of ¬TRUE (the disjunction of no possibilities), and so {[]} also stands for ¬TRUE. However, the empty clausal formula {} (the conjunction of no constraints) is a representation of TRUE.

For convenience, we will move freely back and forth between ordinary formulas in CNF and their representations as sets of clauses.

Putting the comments made at the start of the chapter together with what we have seen about CNF, it is the case that as far as deductive

---

[2] An analogous procedure also exists to convert a formula into a disjunction of conjunctions of literals, which is called *disjunctive normal form*, or DNF.

reasoning is concerned, to determine whether or not KB $\models \alpha$ it will be sufficient to do the following:

1. put the sentences in KB and $\neg\alpha$ into CNF;

2. determine whether or not the resulting set of clauses is satisfiable.

In other words, any question about entailment can be reduced to a question about the satisfiability of a set of clauses.

### 4.1.1   Resolution Derivations

To discuss reasoning at the symbol level, it is common to posit what are called *rules of inference*, which are statements of what formulas can be inferred from other formulas. Here, we use a single rule of inference called (binary) *Resolution:*

> Given a clause of the form $c_1 \cup \{\rho\}$ containing some literal $\rho$, and a clause of the form $c_2 \cup \{\overline{\rho}\}$ containing the complement of $\rho$, infer the clause $c_1 \cup c_2$ consisting of those literals in the first clause other than $\rho$ and those in the second other than $\overline{\rho}$.[3]

We say in this case that $c_1 \cup c_2$ is a *resolvent* of the two input clauses with respect to $\rho$. For example, from clauses $[w,p,q]$ and $[s,w,\neg p]$, we have the clause $[w,s,q]$ as a resolvent with respect to $p$. The clauses $[p,q]$ and $[\neg p, \neg q]$ have two resolvents: $[q, \neg q]$ with respect to $p$, and $[p, \neg p]$ with respect to $q$. Note that $[]$ is not a resolvent of these two clauses. The only way to get the empty clause is to resolve two complementary unit clauses like $[\neg p]$ and $[p]$.

A *Resolution derivation* of a clause $c$ from a set of clauses $S$ is a sequence of clauses $c_1, \ldots, c_n$, where the last clause, $c_n$, is $c$, and where each $c_i$ is either an element of $S$ or a resolvent of two earlier clauses in the derivation. We write $S \vdash c$ if there is a derivation of $c$ from $S$.

Why do we care about Resolution derivations? The main point is that this purely symbol-level operation on finite sets of literals has a direct connection to knowledge-level logical interpretations.

Observe first of all that a resolvent is always entailed by the two input clauses. Suppose we have two clauses $c_1 \cup \{p\}$ and $c_2 \cup \{\neg p\}$. We claim that

$$\{c_1 \cup \{p\}, c_2 \cup \{\neg p\}\} \models c_1 \cup c_2.$$

To see why, let $\Im$ be any interpretation, and suppose that $\Im \models c_1 \cup \{p\}$ and $\Im \models c_2 \cup \{\neg p\}$. There are two cases: If $\Im \models p$, then $\Im \not\models \neg p$, but since

---

[3] Either $c_1$ or $c_2$ or both can be empty. In the case that $c_1$ is empty, $c_1 \cup \{\rho\}$ would be the unit clause $[\rho]$.

$\Im \models c_2 \cup \{\neg p\}$, it must be the case that $\Im \models c_2$, and so $\Im \models c_1 \cup c_2$; similarly, if $\Im \not\models p$, then since $\Im \models c_1 \cup \{p\}$, it must be the case that $\Im \models c_1$, and so again $\Im \models c_1 \cup c_2$. Either way, it is the case that $\Im \models c_1 \cup c_2$.

We can extend this argument to prove that any clause derivable by Resolution from $S$ is entailed by $S$, that is, if $S \vdash c$, then $S \models c$. We show by induction on the length of the derivation that for every $c_i$, $S \models c_i$: This is clearly true if $c_i \in S$, and otherwise, $c_i$ is a resolvent of two earlier clauses, and so is entailed by them, as argued, and hence by $S$.

The converse, however, does not hold: We can have $S \models c$ without having $S \vdash c$. For example, let $S$ consist of the single clause $[\neg p]$ and let $c$ be $[\neg q, q]$. Then, $S$ clearly entails $c$ even though it has no resolvents. In other words, as a form of reasoning, finding Resolution derivations is sound but not complete.

Despite this incompleteness, however, Resolution does have a property that allows it to be used without loss of generality to calculate entailments: Resolution is both sound and complete *when c is the empty clause*. In other words, there is a theorem that states that $S \vdash []$ if and only if $S \models []$.[4] This means that $S$ is unsatisfiable if and only if $S \vdash []$. This provides us with a way of determining the satisfiability of any set of clauses, because all we need to do is search for a derivation of the empty clause. Because this works for any set $S$ of clauses, we sometimes say that Resolution is *refutation-complete*.

## 4.1.2   An Entailment Procedure

We are now ready to consider a symbol-level procedure for determining if $KB \models \alpha$. The idea is to put both KB and $\neg\alpha$ into CNF, as discussed before, and then to check if the resulting set $S$ of clauses (for both) is unsatisfiable by searching for a derivation of the empty clause. As discussed, $S$ is unsatisfiable if and only if $KB \cup \{\neg\alpha\}$ is unsatisfiable, which holds if and only if $KB \models \alpha$. This can be done using the nondeterministic procedure in Figure 4.1. What the procedure does is to repeatedly add resolvents to the input clauses $S$ until either the empty clause is added (in which case there is a derivation of the empty clause) or no new clauses can be added (in which case there is no such derivation). Note that this is guaranteed to terminate: Each clause that gets added to the set is a resolvent of previous clauses, and so contains only literals mentioned in the original set $S$. There are only finitely many clauses with just these literals, and so eventually at step 2 we will not be able to find a pair of clauses that resolves to something new.

The procedure can be made deterministic quite simply: We need to settle on a strategy for choosing which pair of clauses to use when there

---

[4]This theorem will carry over to quantified clauses later.

**input:** a finite set $S$ of propositional clauses
**output:** satisfiable or unsatisfiable

1. check if [] ∈ $S$; if so, return unsatisfiable

2. otherwise, check if there are two clauses in $S$ such that they resolve to produce another clause not already in $S$; if not, return satisfiable

3. otherwise, add the new resolvent clause to $S$, and go back to step 1

▪ **FIGURE 4.1**

A Resolution Procedure

is more than one pair that would produce a new resolvent. One possibility is to use the first pair encountered; another is to use the pair that would produce the shortest resolvent. It might also be a good idea to keep track of which pairs have already been considered to avoid redundant checking. If we were interested in returning or printing out a derivation, we would of course also want to store with each resolvent pointers to its input clauses.

The procedure does not distinguish between clauses that come from the KB and those that come from the negation of $\alpha$, which we will call the *query*. Observe that if we have a number of queries we want to ask for the same KB, we need only convert the KB to CNF once and then add clauses for the negation of each query. Moreover, if we want to add a new fact $\alpha$ to the KB, we can do so by adding the clauses for $\alpha$ to those already calculated for KB. Thus, to use this type of entailment procedure, it makes good sense to keep KB in CNF, adding and removing clauses as necessary.

Let us now consider some simple examples of this procedure in action. We start with the following KB:

Toddler

Toddler ⊃ Child

Child ∧ Male ⊃ Boy

Infant ⊃ Child

Child ∧ Female ⊃ Girl

Female

We can read these sentences as if they were talking about a particular person: The person is a toddler; if the person is a toddler then the person is a child; if the person is a child and male, then the person is a boy; if the person is an infant, then the person is a child; if the person is a child and female, then the person is a girl; the person is female. In Figure 4.2, we graphically display a Resolution derivation showing that the person is a girl by showing that KB ⊨ Girl. Observe that in this diagram we use a dashed line to separate the clauses that come directly from the KB or the negation of the query from those that result from applying Resolution. There are six clauses from the KB, one from the negation of the query (i.e., ¬Girl) and four new ones generated by Resolution. Each resolvent in the diagram has two solid lines pointing up to its input clauses. The resulting graph will never have cycles, because input clauses must always appear earlier in the derivation. Note that there are two clauses in the KB that are not used in the derivation and could be left out of the diagram.

A second example uses the following KB:

Sun ⊃ Mail

(Rain ∨ Sleet) ⊃ Mail

Rain ∨ Sun

These formulas can be understood as talking about the weather and the mail service on a particular day. In Figure 4.3, we have a Resolution derivation showing that KB ⊨ Mail. Note that the formula ((Rain∨Sleet) ⊃ Mail) results in two clauses on conversion to CNF. If we wanted to show that KB ⊭ Rain for the same KB, we could do so by displaying a similar graph that contains the clause [¬Rain] and every possible resolvent, but does not contain the empty clause.

## 4.2   HANDLING VARIABLES AND QUANTIFIERS

Having seen how to do Resolution for the propositional case, we now consider reasoning with variables, terms, and quantifiers. Again, we will want to convert formulas into an equivalent clausal form. For simplicity, we begin by assuming that no existential quantifiers remain once negations have been moved inward.[5]

1. eliminate ⊃ and ≡, as before;

2. move ¬ inward so that it appears only in front of an atom, using the previous equivalences and the following two:

$$\models \neg\forall x. \alpha \equiv \exists x. \neg\alpha;$$

$$\models \neg\exists x. \alpha \equiv \forall x. \neg\alpha;$$

---

[5]We will see how to handle existentials in Section 4.2.3.

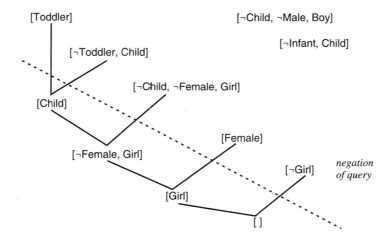

▪ **FIGURE 4.2**

A First Example Resolution Derivation

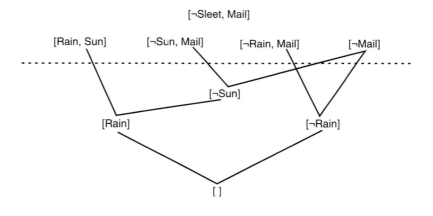

▪ **FIGURE 4.3**

A Second Example Resolution Derivation

3. standardize variables, that is, ensure that each quantifier is over a distinct variable by renaming them as necessary. This uses the following equivalences (provided that $x$ does not occur free in $\alpha$):

$$\models \forall y.\, \alpha \equiv \forall x.\, \alpha_x^y;$$

$$\models \exists y.\, \alpha \equiv \exists x.\, \alpha_x^y;$$

4. eliminate all remaining existentials (discussed later);

5. move universals outside the scope of $\land$ and $\lor$ using the following equivalences (provided that $x$ does not occur free in $\alpha$):

$$\models (\alpha \land \forall x. \beta) \equiv (\forall x. \beta \land \alpha) \equiv \forall x (\alpha \land \beta);$$

$$\models (\alpha \lor \forall x. \beta) \equiv (\forall x. \beta \lor \alpha) \equiv \forall x (\alpha \lor \beta);$$

6. distribute $\land$ over $\lor$, as before;

7. collect terms as before.

The result of this procedure is a quantified version of CNF, a universally quantified conjunction of disjunctions of literals that is once again logically equivalent to the original formula (ignoring existentials).

Again, it is convenient to use a *clausal form* of CNF. We simply drop the quantifiers (because they are all universal anyway), and we are left with a set of clauses, each of which is a set of literals, each of which is either an atom or its negation. An atom now is of the form $P(t_1, \ldots, t_n)$, where the terms $t_i$ may contain variables, constants, and function symbols.[6] Clauses are understood exactly as they were before, except that variables appearing in them are interpreted universally. So, for example, the clausal formula

$$\{[P(x), \neg R(a, f(b, x))], [Q(x, y)]\}$$

stands for the CNF formula

$$\forall x \forall y \, ([P(x) \lor \neg R(a, f(b, x))] \; \land \; Q(x, y)).$$

Before presenting the generalization of Resolution, it is useful to introduce special notation and terminology for substitutions. A *substitution* $\theta$ is a finite set of pairs $\{x_1/t_1, \ldots, x_n/t_n\}$ where the $x_i$ are distinct variables and the $t_i$ are arbitrary terms. If $\theta$ is a substitution and $\rho$ is a literal, then $\rho\theta$ is the literal that results from simultaneously replacing each $x_i$ in $\rho$ by $t_i$. For example, if $\theta = \{x/a, y/g(x, b, z)\}$, and $\rho = P(x, z, f(x, y))$, then $\rho\theta = P(a, z, f(a, g(x, b, z)))$. Similarly, if $c$ is a clause, $c\theta$ is the clause that results from performing the substitution on each literal. We say that a term, literal, or clause is *ground* if it contains no variables. We say that a literal $\rho$ is an *instance* of a literal $\rho'$ if for some $\theta$, $\rho = \rho'\theta$.

---

[6]For now, we ignore atoms involving equality.

### 4.2.1   First-Order Resolution

We now consider the Resolution rule as applied to clauses with variables. The main idea is that since clauses with variables are implicitly universally quantified, we want to allow Resolution inferences that can be made from any of their instances.

For example, suppose we have clauses

$$[P(x,a), \neg Q(x)] \quad \text{and} \quad [\neg P(b,y), \neg R(b,f(y))].$$

Then, implicitly at least, we also have clauses

$$[P(b,a), \neg Q(b)] \quad \text{and} \quad [\neg P(b,a), \neg R(b,f(a))],$$

which resolve to $[\neg Q(b), \neg R(b,f(a))]$. We will define the rule of Resolution so that this clause is a resolvent of the two original ones.

The general rule of (binary) Resolution is as follows:

> Suppose we are given a clause of the form $c_1 \cup \{\rho_1\}$ containing some literal $\rho_1$, and a clause of the form $c_2 \cup \{\overline{\rho_2}\}$ containing the complement of a literal $\rho_2$. Suppose we rename the variables in the two clauses so that each clause has distinct variables, and there is a substitution $\theta$ such that $\rho_1\theta = \rho_2\theta$. Then, we can infer the clause $(c_1 \cup c_2)\theta$ consisting of those literals in the first clause other than $\rho_1$ and those in the second other than $\overline{\rho_2}$, after applying $\theta$.

We say in this case that $\theta$ *unifies* $\rho_1$ and $\rho_2$, and that $\theta$ is a *unifier* of the two literals.

With this new general rule of Resolution, the definition of a derivation stays the same, and ignoring equality, it is the case that $S \vdash []$ if and only if $S \models []$ as before.[7]

We will use the same conventions as before to show Resolution derivations in diagrams, except that we will often show the unifying substitution as a label near one of the solid lines.[8]

Consider the following KB as an example:

$\forall x.\, \mathsf{GradStudent}(x) \supset \mathsf{Student}(x)$

$\forall x.\, \mathsf{Student}(x) \supset \mathsf{HardWorker}(x)$

$\mathsf{GradStudent}(\mathsf{sue})$

---

[7]For certain pathological cases, we actually require a slightly more general version of Resolution to get completeness. See Exercise 4.

[8]Because it is sometimes not obvious which literals in the input clauses are being resolved, for clarity we use the solid lines to point to them in the input clauses.

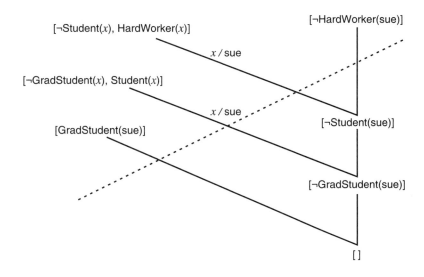

■ **FIGURE 4.4**

An Example Resolution Derivation with Variables

In Figure 4.4, we show that KB $\models$ HardWorker(sue). Note that the conversion of this KB to CNF did not require either existentials or equality.

A slightly more complex derivation is presented in Figure 4.5. This is a Resolution derivation corresponding to the three-block problem first presented in Figure 2.1 of Chapter 2: If there are three stacked blocks where the top one is green and the bottom one is not green, is there a green block directly on top of a nongreen block? The KB here is

$$On(a,b), \; On(b,c), \; Green(a), \; \neg Green(c)$$

where the three blocks are a, b, and c. Note that this KB is already in CNF. The query is

$$\exists x \exists y . On(x,y) \wedge Green(x) \wedge \neg Green(y)$$

whose negation contains no existentials or equalities.

Using a Resolution derivation it is possible to get answers to queries that we might think of as requiring computation. To do arithmetic, for example, we can use the constant zero to stand for 0, and succ to stand for the successor function. Every natural number can then be written as a ground term using these two symbols. For instance, the term

$$succ(succ(succ(succ(succ(zero)))))$$

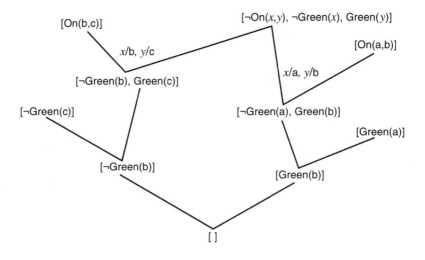

▪ **FIGURE 4.5**

The Three-Block Problem

stands for 5. We can use the predicate $\text{Plus}(x,y,z)$ to stand for the relation $x + y = z$, and start with a KB that formalizes the properties of addition as follows:

$\forall x. \text{Plus}(\text{zero}, x, x)$
$\forall x \forall y \forall z. \text{Plus}(x, y, z) \supset \text{Plus}(\text{succ}(x), y, \text{succ}(z)).$

All the expected relations among triples of numbers are entailed by this KB. For example, in Figure 4.6, we show that $2 + 3 = 5$ follows from this KB.[9] A derivation for an entailed existential formula like

$$\exists u. \text{Plus}(2, 3, u)$$

is similar, as shown in Figure 4.7. Here, we need to be careful to rename variables (using $v$ and $w$) to ensure that the variables in the input clauses are distinct. Observe that by examining the bindings for the variables we can locate the value of $u$: It is bound to $\text{succ}(v)$, where $v$ is bound to $\text{succ}(w)$, and $w$ to 3. In other words, the answer for the addition is correctly determined to be 5. As we will see in Chapter 5, this form of computation, including locating the answers in a derivation of an existential, is what underlies the PROLOG programming language.

---

[9]For readability, instead of using terms like succ(succ(zero)), we write the decimal equivalent, 2.

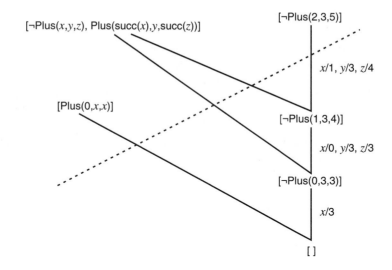

Arithmetic in FOL

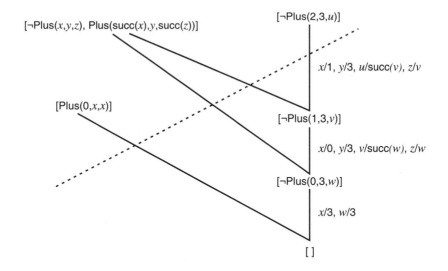

■ **FIGURE 4.7**

An Existential Arithmetic Query

## 4.2.2  Answer Extraction

While it is often possible to get answers to questions by looking at the
bindings of variables in a derivation of an existential, in full FOL the

situation is more complicated. Specifically, it can happen that a KB entails some $\exists x.\, P(x)$ without entailing $P(t)$ for any specific $t$. For example, in the three-block problem in Figure 4.5, the KB entails that *some* block must be green and on top of a nongreen block, but not which.

One general method that has been proposed for dealing with answers to queries even in cases like these is the *answer-extraction process*. Here is the idea: We replace a query such as $\exists x.\, P(x)$ (where $x$ is the variable we are interested in) by $\exists x.\, P(x) \wedge \neg A(x)$ where $A$ is a new predicate symbol occurring nowhere else, called the *answer predicate*. Since $A$ appears nowhere else, it will normally not be possible to derive the empty clause from the modified query. Instead, we terminate the derivation as soon as we produce a clause containing only the answer predicate.

To see this in action, we begin with an example having a definite answer. Suppose the KB is

Student(john)

Student(jane)

Happy(john)

and we wish to show that some student is happy. The query then is

$$\exists x.\, \text{Student}(x) \wedge \text{Happy}(x).$$

In Figure 4.8, we show a derivation augmented with an answer predicate to derive who that happy student is. The final clause can be interpreted as saying, "An answer is John." A normal derivation of the empty clause can be easily produced from this one by eliminating all occurrences of the answer predicate.

Observe that in this example we say that *an* answer is produced by the process. There can be many such answers, but each derivation only deals

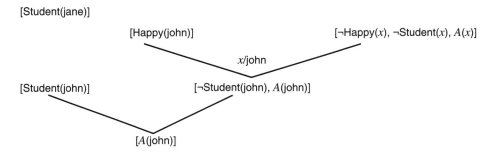

▪ **FIGURE 4.8**

Answer Predicate with a Definite Answer

with one. For example, if the KB had been

Student(john)

Student(jane)

Happy(john)

Happy(jane)

then in one derivation we might extract the answer jane, and in another, john.

Where the answer-extraction process especially pays off is in cases involving indefinite answers. Suppose, for example, our KB had been

Student(john)

Student(jane)

Happy(john) ∨ Happy(jane)

We can still see that there is a student who is happy, although we cannot say who. If we use the same query and answer extraction process, we get the derivation in Figure 4.9. In this case, the final clause can be interpreted as saying, "An answer is either Jane or John," which is as specific as the KB allows.

Finally, it is worth noting that the answer-extraction process can result in clauses containing variables. For example, if our KB is

$\forall w.\, \text{Student}(f(a, w))$

$\forall x \forall z.\, \text{Happy}(f(x, g(z)))$

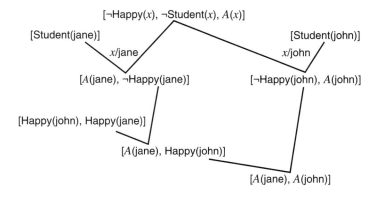

■ **FIGURE 4.9**

Answer Predicate with an Indefinite Answer

we get a derivation whose final clause is $[A(f(a,g(z)))]$, which can be interpreted as saying, "An answer is any instance of the term $f(a,g(z))$."

### 4.2.3  Skolemization

So far, in converting formulas to CNF, we have ignored existentials. For example, we could not handle facts in a KB like $\exists x \forall y \exists z. P(x,y,z)$, since we had no way to put them into CNF.

To handle existentials and represent such facts, we use the following idea: Because some individuals are claimed to exist, we introduce names for them (called *Skolem constants* and *Skolem functions*, for the logician who first introduced them) and represent facts using those names. If we are careful not to use the names anywhere else, what will be entailed will be precisely what was entailed by the original existential. For the formula just mentioned, for example, an $x$ is claimed to exist, so call it $a$; moreover, for each $y$, a $z$ is claimed to exist, call it $f(y)$. So instead of reasoning with $\exists x \forall y \exists z. P(x,y,z)$, we use $\forall y. P(a,y,f(y))$, where $a$ and $f$ are Skolem symbols appearing nowhere else. Informally, if we think of the conclusions we can draw from this formula, they will be the same as those we can draw from the original existential (as long as they do not mention $a$ or $f$).

In general, then, in our conversion to CNF we eliminate all existentials (at step 4) by what is called *Skolemization*: Replace each existential variable by a new function symbol with as many arguments as there are universal variables dominating the existential. In other words, if we start with

$$\forall x_1(\ldots \forall x_2(\ldots \forall x_3(\ldots \exists y[\ldots y \ldots] \ldots) \ldots) \ldots),$$

where existentially quantified $y$ appears in the scope of universally quantified $x_1, x_2, x_3$, and only these, we end up with

$$\forall x_1(\ldots \forall x_2(\ldots \forall x_3(\ldots [\ldots f(x_1,x_2,x_3) \ldots] \ldots) \ldots) \ldots),$$

where $f$ appears nowhere else.

If $\alpha$ is our original formula and $\alpha'$ is the result of converting it to CNF including Skolemization, then it is no longer the case that $\models (\alpha \equiv \alpha')$ as it was before. For example, $\exists x. P(x)$ is not logically equivalent to $P(a)$, its Skolemized version. What can be shown, however, is that $\alpha$ is satisfiable if and only if $\alpha'$ is satisfiable, and this is really all we need for Resolution.[10]

---

[10]We do need to be careful, however, with answer extraction, not to confuse real constants (which have meaning in the application domain) with Skolem constants, which are generated only to avoid existentials.

Note that Skolemization depends crucially on the universal variables that dominate the existential. A formula like $\exists x \forall y R(x,y)$ entails $\forall y \exists x R(x,y)$, but the converse does not hold. To show that the former holds using Resolution, we show that

$$\{\exists x \forall y R(x,y), \neg\forall y \exists x R(x,y)\}$$

is unsatisfiable. After conversion to CNF, we get the clauses

$$\{[R(a,y)], [\neg R(x,b)]\}$$

(where $a$ and $b$ are Skolem constants) that resolve to the empty clause in one step. If we were to try the same with the converse, we would need to show that

$$\{\neg\exists x \forall y R(x,y), \forall y \exists x R(x,y)\}$$

was unsatisfiable. After conversion to CNF, we get

$$\{[\neg R(x,g(x))], [R(f(y),y)]\}$$

where $f$ and $g$ are Skolem functions. In this case, there is no derivation of the empty clause (nor should there be) because the two literals $R(x,g(x))$ and $R(f(y),y)$ cannot be unified.[11] For logical correctness it is important to get the dependence of variables right. In one case, we had $R(a,y)$ where the value of the existential $x$ did not depend on universal $y$ (i.e., in $\exists x \forall y R(x,y)$); in the other case, we had the much weaker $R(f(y),y)$ where the value of the existential $x$ could depend on the universal (i.e., in $\forall y \exists x R(x,y)$).

## 4.2.4 Equality

So far, we have ignored formulas containing equality. If we were to simply treat equality as a normal predicate, we would miss many unsatisfiable sets of clauses, for example, $\{a = b, b = c, a \neq c\}$. To handle these, it is necessary to augment the set of clauses to ensure that all of the special properties of equality are taken into account. What we require are the clausal versions of the *axioms of equality:*

*reflexitivity:* $\forall x.\ x = x$;

*symmetry:* $\forall x \forall y.\ x = y \supset y = x$;

*transitivity:* $\forall x \forall y \forall z.\ x = y \land y = z \supset x = z$;

---

[11]To see this, note that if $x$ is replaced by $t_1$ and $y$ by $t_2$, then $t_1$ would have to be $f(t_2)$ and $t_2$ would have to be $g(t_1)$. So $t_1$ would have to be $f(g(t_1))$, which is impossible.

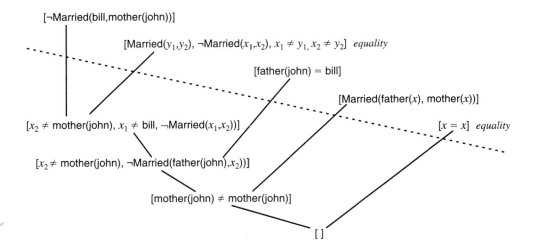

Using the Axioms of Equality

*substitution for functions:* for every function symbol $f$ of arity $n$, an axiom

$$\forall x_1 \forall y_1 \cdots \forall x_n \forall y_n. \; x_1 = y_1 \wedge \cdots \wedge x_n = y_n \supset$$
$$f(x_1,\ldots,x_n) = f(y_1,\ldots,y_n);$$

*substitution for predicates:* for every predicate symbol $P$ of arity $n$, an axiom

$$\forall x_1 \forall y_1 \cdots \forall x_n \forall y_n. \; x_1 = y_1 \wedge \cdots \wedge x_n = y_n \supset$$
$$P(x_1,\ldots,x_n) \equiv P(y_1,\ldots,y_n).$$

It can be shown that with the addition of these axioms, equality can be treated as a binary predicate, and soundness and completeness of Resolution for the empty clause will be preserved.

A simple example of the use of the axioms of equality can be found in Figure 4.10. In this example, the KB is

$\forall x. \, \text{Married}(\text{father}(x),\text{mother}(x))$

$\text{father}(\text{john}) = \text{bill}$

and the query to derive is

$\text{Married}(\text{bill},\text{mother}(\text{john})).$

Note that the derivation uses two of the axioms: reflexitivity and substitution for predicates.

Although the axioms of equality are sufficient for Resolution, they do result in a very large number of resolvents, and their use can easily come to dominate Resolution derivations. A more efficient treatment of equality is discussed in Section 4.3.7.

## 4.3  DEALING WITH COMPUTATIONAL INTRACTABILITY

The success we have had using Resolution derivations should not mislead us into thinking that Resolution provides a general effective solution to the reasoning problem.

### 4.3.1  The First-Order Case

Consider, for example, the KB consisting of a single formula (again in the domain of arithmetic):

$$\forall x \forall y.\ \mathsf{LessThan}(\mathsf{succ}(x), y) \supset \mathsf{LessThan}(x, y).$$

Suppose our query is LessThan(zero,zero). Obviously, this should fail because the KB does not entail the query (nor its negation). The problem is that if we pose it to Resolution, we get derivations like the one shown in Figure 4.11. Although we never generate the empty clause, we might generate an *infinite* sequence looking for it. Among other things,

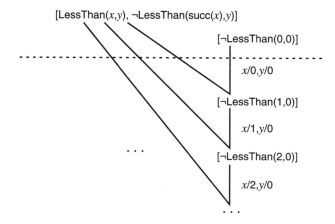

**■ FIGURE 4.11**

An Infinite Resolution Branch

this suggests that we cannot simply use a depth-first procedure to search for the empty clause, because we run the risk of getting stuck on such an infinite branch.

We might ask if there is any way to detect when we are on such a branch, so that we can give it up and look elsewhere. The answer unfortunately is no. The FOL language is very powerful and can be used as a full programming language. Just as there is no way to detect when a program is looping, there is no way to detect if a branch will continue indefinitely.

This is quite problematic from a knowledge representation point of view, because it means that there can be no procedure that, given a set of clauses, returns satisfiable when the clauses are satisfiable and unsatisfiable otherwise.[12] However, we do know that Resolution is refutation-complete: If the set of clauses is unsatisfiable, some branch will contain the empty clause (even if some branches may be infinite). So a breadth-first search is guaranteed to report unsatisfiable when the clauses are unsatisfiable. When the clauses are satisfiable, the search may or may not terminate.

## 4.3.2   The Herbrand Theorem

We saw in Section 4.1 that in the propositional case we can run Resolution to completion, so we never have the nontermination problem. An interesting fact about Resolution in FOL is that it sometimes reduces to this propositional case. Given a set $S$ of clauses, the *Herbrand universe* of $S$ (named after the logician who first introduced it) is the set of all ground terms formed using just the constants and function symbols in $S$.[13] For example, if $S$ mentions just constants $a$ and $b$ and unary function symbol $f$, then the Herbrand universe is the set

$$\{a, b, f(a), f(b), f(f(a)), f(f(b)), f(f(f(a))), \ldots\}$$

The *Herbrand base* of $S$ is the set of all ground clauses $c\theta$ where $c \in S$ and $\theta$ assigns the variables in $c$ to terms in the Herbrand universe.

Herbrand's Theorem states that a set of clauses is satisfiable if and only if its Herbrand base is.[14] The reason this is significant is that the Herbrand base is a set of clauses without variables, so it is essentially propositional. To reason with the Herbrand base it is not necessary to use unifiers and so on, and we have a sound and complete reasoning procedure that is guaranteed to terminate.

The catch in this approach (and there must be a catch, because no procedure can decide the satisfiability of arbitrary sets of clauses) is that

---

[12] We will see in Chapter 5 that this is also true for the much simpler case of Horn clauses.

[13] In case $S$ mentions no constant or function symbols, we use a single constant, say $a$.

[14] This applies to Horn clauses also, as discussed in Chapter 5.

the Herbrand base will typically be an *infinite* set of propositional clauses. It will, however, be finite when the Herbrand universe is finite (no function symbols and only finitely many constants appear in $S$). Moreover, sometimes we can keep the universe finite by considering the "type" of the arguments and values of functions, and include a term like $f(t)$ only if the type of $t$ is appropriate for the function $f$. For example, if our function is birthday (taking a person as argument and producing a date), we may be able to avoid meaningless terms like birthday(birthday(john)) in the Herbrand universe.

### 4.3.3 The Propositional Case

If we can get a finite set of propositional clauses, we know that the Resolution procedure in Figure 4.1 will terminate. But this does not make it practical. The procedure may terminate, but how long will it take? We might think that this depends on how good our procedure is at finding derivations. However, in 1985, Armin Haken proved that there are unsatisfiable propositional clauses $c_1, \ldots, c_n$ such that the *shortest* derivation of the empty clause has on the order of $2^n$ steps. This answers the question definitively: No matter how clever we are at finding derivations, and even if we avoid all needless searching, any Resolution procedure will still take *exponential* time on such clauses, because it takes that long to get to the end of the derivation.

We might then wonder if this is just a problem with Resolution: Might there not be a better way to determine whether a set of propositional clauses is satisfiable? As it turns out, this question is one of the deepest ones in all of computer science and still has no definite answer. In 1972, Stephen Cook proved that the satisfiability problem was *NP-complete:* Roughly, any search problem where we are searching for an item satisfying a certain property, and where we can test in polynomial time whether a candidate item satisfies the property, can be recast as a propositional satisfiability problem. The importance of this result is that many problems of practical interest (in areas such as scheduling, routing, and packing) can be formulated as search problems of this form.[15] Thus a polynomial time algorithm for satisfiability (which Haken proved Resolution is not) would imply a polynomial time algorithm for all of these tasks. Because so many people have been unable to find good algorithms for any of them, it is strongly believed that propositional

---

[15] An example is the so-called Traveling Salesman Problem: Given a graph with nodes standing for cities and edges with numbers on them standing for direct routes between cities that many kilometers apart, determine if there is a way to visit all the cities in the graph in less than some given number $k$ of kilometers.

satisfiability cannot be solved at all in polynomial time. Proofs, however, like Haken's for Resolution, have been very hard to obtain.

### 4.3.4 The Implications

So what are the implications of these negative results? At the very least, they tell us that Resolution is not a panacea. For knowledge representation purposes, we would like to be able to produce entailments of a KB for immediate action, but determining the satisfiability of clauses may simply be too difficult computationally for this purpose.

We may need to consider some other options. One is to give more control over the reasoning process to the user. This is a theme that will show up in the procedural representations in Chapters 5 and 6 and others. Another option is to consider the possibility of using representation languages that are less expressive than full FOL or even full propositional logic. This is a theme that will show up in Chapters 5 and 9, among others. Much of the research in knowledge representation and reasoning can be seen as attempts to deal with this issue, and we will return to it in detail in Chapter 16.

On the other hand, it is worth observing that in some applications of Resolution it is reasonable to wait for answers, even for a very long time. Using Resolution to do *mathematical theorem-proving*, for example, to determine whether or not Goldbach's Conjecture or its negation follows from the axioms of number theory, is quite different from using Resolution to determine whether or not an umbrella is needed when it looks like rain. In the former case, we might be willing to wait for months or even years for an answer. There is an area of AI called *automated theorem-proving* whose subject matter is precisely the development of procedures for such mathematical applications.

The best we can hope for in such applications of Resolution is not a guarantee of efficiency or even of termination, but a way to search for derivations that eliminates unnecessary steps as much as possible. In the rest of this section, we will consider strategies that can be used to improve the search in this sense.

### 4.3.5 SAT Solvers

In the propositional case, various procedures have been proposed for determining the satisfiability of a set of clauses more efficiently than the Resolution procedure of Figure 4.1. Examples are the DP, TAB, and LS procedures presented in Exercises 6, 7, and 8, respectively. Instead of searching for a derivation that would show a set of clauses to be unsatisfiable, these procedures search for an interpretation that would show the clauses to be satisfiable. For this reason, the procedures are called *SAT solvers*, and are often applied to clauses that are known to be satisfiable, but where the satisfying interpretation is not known.

However, the distance between the two sorts of procedures is not that great. For one thing, the Resolution procedure of Figure 4.1 can be adapted to finding a satisfying interpretation (see Exercise 9). Furthermore, as discussed in the exercises, the SAT solvers DP and TAB have the property that when they fail to find a satisfying interpretation, a Resolution derivation of the empty clause can be lifted directly from a trace of their execution. This implies that no matter how well DP or TAB work in practice, they must take exponential time on some inputs.

One interesting case is the procedure called GSAT in Exercise 10. This SAT solver is not known to be subject to any lower bounds related to the Haken result for Resolution. However, it does have drawbacks of its own: It is not even guaranteed to terminate with a correct answer in all cases.

### 4.3.6  Most General Unifiers

The most important way of avoiding needless search in a first-order derivation is to keep the search as general as possible. Consider, for example, two clauses $c_1$ and $c_2$, where $c_1$ contains the literal $P(g(x), f(x), z)$ and $c_2$ contains $\neg P(y, f(w), a)$. These two literals are unified by the substitution

$$\theta_1 = \{x/b, y/g(b), z/a, w/b\}$$

and also by

$$\theta_2 = \{x/f(z), y/g(f(z)), z/a, w/f(z)\}.$$

We may very well be able to derive the empty clause using $\theta_1$, but if we cannot, we will need to consider other substitutions like $\theta_2$ and so on.

The trouble is that both of these substitutions are overly specific. We can see that any unifier must give $w$ the same value as $x$, and $y$ the same as $g(x)$, but we do not need to commit yet to a value for $x$. The substitution

$$\theta_3 = \{y/g(x), z/a, w/x\}$$

unifies the two literals without making an arbitrary choice that might preclude a path to the empty clause. It is a *most general unifier* (MGU).

More precisely, a most general unifier $\theta$ of literals $\rho_1$ and $\rho_2$ is a unifier that has the property that for any other unifier $\theta'$, there is a further substitution $\theta^*$ such that $\theta' = \theta \cdot \theta^*$.[16] So starting with $\theta$ you can always

---

[16] By $\theta \cdot \theta^*$ we mean the substitution such that for any literal $\rho$, $\rho(\theta \cdot \theta^*) = (\rho\theta)\theta^*$, that is, we apply $\theta$ to $\rho$ and then apply $\theta^*$ to the result.

get to any other unifier by applying additional substitutions. For example, given $\theta_3$, we can get to $\theta_1$ by further applying $x/b$, and to $\theta_2$ by applying $x/f(z)$. Note that an MGU need not be unique, in that

$$\theta_4 = \{y/g(w), z/a, x/w\}$$

is also one for $c_1$ and $c_2$.

The key fact about MGUs is that (with certain restrictions that need not concern us here) we can limit the Resolution rule to MGUs without loss of completeness. This helps immensely in the search, because it dramatically reduces the number of resolvents that can be inferred from two input clauses. Moreover, an MGU of a pair of literals $\rho_1$ and $\rho_2$ can be calculated efficiently by the following procedure:

1. start with $\theta = \{\}$;

2. exit if $\rho_1\theta = \rho_2\theta$;

3. otherwise get the disagreement set, *DS*, which is the pair of terms at the first place where the two literals disagree;

   e.g., if $\rho_1\theta = P(a, f(a, g(z), \ldots))$ and $\rho_2\theta = P(a, f(a, u, \ldots))$, then $DS = \{u, g(z)\}$;

4. find a variable $v \in DS$, and a term $t \in DS$ not containing $v$; if none, fail;

5. otherwise, set $\theta$ to $\theta \cdot \{v/t\}$, and go to step 2.

This procedure works very well in practice, although it can take exponential time on certain pathological cases. Moreover, an even better but more complex *linear* time algorithm exists.

Because MGUs greatly reduce the search and can be calculated efficiently, all Resolution-based systems implemented to date use them.

### 4.3.7    Other Refinements

A number of other refinements to Resolution have been proposed to help improve the search.

**Clause Elimination**    The idea is to keep the number of clauses generated as small as possible, without giving up completeness, by using the fact that if there is a derivation to the empty clause at all, then there is one that does not use certain types of clause. Some examples are the following:

- *pure clauses:* these are clauses that contain some literal $\rho$ such that $\overline{\rho}$ does not appear anywhere;

- *tautologies:* these are clauses that contain both $\rho$ and $\overline{\rho}$, and can be bypassed in any derivation;

- *subsumed clauses:* these are clauses for which there already exists another clause with a subset of the literals (perhaps after a substitution).

**Ordering Strategies**   The idea here is to prefer to perform Resolution steps in a fixed order, trying to maximize the chance of deriving the empty clause. The best strategy found to date (but not the only one) is *unit preference*, that is, to use unit clauses first. This is because using a unit clause together with a clause of length $k$ always produces a clause of length $k - 1$. By going for shorter and shorter clauses, the hope is to arrive at the empty clause more quickly.

**Set of Support**   In a knowledge representation application, even if the KB and the negation of a query are unsatisfiable, we still expect the KB by itself to be satisfiable. It therefore makes sense not to perform Resolution steps involving only clauses from the KB. The *set of support* strategy says that we are only allowed to perform Resolution if at least one of the input clauses has an ancestor in the negation of the query. Under the right conditions, this can be done without loss of completeness.

**Special Treatment of Equality**   We examined earlier one way to handle equality using the axioms of equality explicitly. Because these can generate so many resolvents, a better way is to introduce a second rule of inference in addition to Resolution, called *Paramodulation:*

Suppose we are given a clause $c_1 \cup \{t = s\}$ where $t$ and $s$ are terms, and a clause $c_2 \cup \{\rho[t']\}$ containing some term $t'$. Suppose we rename the variables in the two clauses so that each clause has distinct variables, and that there is a substitution $\theta$ such that $t\theta = t'\theta$. Then, we can infer the clause $(\{c_1 \cup c_2 \cup \rho[s]\})\theta$, which eliminates the equality atom, replaces $t'$ by $s$, and then performs the $\theta$ substitution.

With this rule, it is no longer necessary to include the axioms of equality, and what would have required many steps of Resolution involving those axioms can be done in a single step. Using the earlier example, it is not hard to see that from

$$[\text{father(john)} = \text{bill}] \quad \text{and} \quad [\text{Married(father}(x), \text{mother}(x))],$$

we can derive the clause [Married(bill,mother(john))] in a single Paramodulation step.

**Sorted Logic**   The idea here is to associate sorts with all terms. For example, a variable $x$ might be of sort Male, and the function mother might be of sort [Person $\rightarrow$ Female]. We might also want to keep a taxonomy of sorts, for example, that Woman is a subsort of Person. With this information in place, we can refuse to unify $P(s)$ with $P(t)$ if the sorts of $s$ and $t$ are incompatible. The assumption here is that only meaningful (with respect to sorts) unifications can ever lead to the empty clause.

**Connection Graph**   In the connection graph method, given a set of clauses, we precompute a graph with edges between any two unifiable literals of opposite polarity and labeled with the MGU of the two literals. In other words, we start by precomputing all possible unifications. The Resolution procedure, then, involves selecting a link, computing a resolvent clause, and inheriting links for the new clause from its input clauses after substitution. No unification is done at "run time." With this, Resolution can be seen as a kind of state-space search problem—find a sequence of links that ultimately produces the empty clause—and any technique for improving a state-space search (such as using a heuristic function) can be applied to Resolution.

**Directional Connectives**   A clause like $[\neg p, q]$, representing "if $p$ then $q$," can be used in a derivation in two ways: In the forward direction, if we derive a clause containing $p$, we then derive the clause with $q$; in the backward direction, if we derive a clause containing $\neg q$, we then derive the clause with $\neg p$. The idea with directional connectives is to mark clauses to be used in one or the other direction only. For example, given a fact in a KB like

$$\forall x.\, \mathsf{Battleship}(x) \supset \mathsf{Gray}(x)$$

we may wish to use this only in the forward direction, because it is probably a bad idea to work on deriving that something is gray by trying to derive that it is a battleship. Similarly, a fact like

$$\forall x.\, \mathsf{Person}(x) \supset \mathsf{Has}(x, \mathsf{spleen})$$

might be used only in the backward direction, because it is probably a bad idea to derive having a spleen for every individual derived to be a person. This form of control over how facts are used is the basis for the procedural representation languages that will be discussed extensively in Chapter 6. From a logical point of view, however, great care is needed with directional connectives to ensure that completeness is not lost.

## 4.4   BIBLIOGRAPHIC NOTES

The Resolution principle was developed by Robinson [357]; Robinson also showed that Resolution is refutation-complete. An early, influential text on theorem proving was written by Chang and Lee [66]. Another text in the area is by Fitting [132], who contrasts the use of conjunctive normal form in Resolution (as presented here) and disjunctive normal form in another theorem-proving method known as *tableau*. Resolution and tableau are currently the predominant techniques in implementing automated theorem provers.

Wos [431] provides an interesting practical guide to the use of McCune's OTTER theorem prover as applied to the automated proof of theorems in algebra. Wos claims to have coined the term *automated reasoning* in 1980 [431, p. 2]. Leitsch [233] presents Resolution as a logical calculus. Wang [419] provides an early theorem prover based on another logical system known as Gentzen's "sequent calculus" [154]. Wang's theorem prover was capable of mechanically proving a number of the results in *Principia Mathematica* [422].

The idea of using answer predicates for answer extraction is due to Green [167]. Skolemization is named after Thoralf Skolem [387, 388]. Haken's result, showing the existence of unsatisfiable sets of clauses where the shortest derivation of the empty clause takes exponentially many steps in the number of clauses, can be found in [176]. Cook's landmark complexity result appeared in [78]. Garey and Johnson [145] present a comprehensive survey of the field of computational complexity, including discussion of the Traveling Salesman Problem and other related problems.

The study of SAT solvers has stimulated interesting interactions among researchers in AI (e.g., [293]), computational complexity (e.g., [5]), and statistical physics (e.g., [289]). SAT can be seen as a special type of *constraint satisfaction problem* (CSP) (see the textbook by Dechter [99]), and some of the research in the area concerns both notions. References to some of the existing algorithms for SAT are found in the exercises at the end of this chapter.

The set-of-support refinement is discussed by Wos et al. [433]. The paramodulation technique was developed by Wos and Robinson [432]. The collection by Meinke and Tucker [287] discusses aspects of sorted logic. The connection graph method of precomputing unifications was introduced by Stickel [400]. Boyer and Moore [39] introduce a theorem prover based on mathematical induction. Knuth and Bendix [219] introduce a procedure for equational reasoning that is commonly used in term-rewriting systems.

## 4.5    EXERCISES

**1.** Determine whether the following sentence is valid using Resolution:

$$\exists x \forall y \forall z ((P(y) \supset Q(z)) \supset (P(x) \supset Q(x))).$$

2. (Follow-up to Exercise 1 of Chapter 3)
   Use Resolution with answer extraction to find the member of the Alpine Club who is a mountain climber but not a skier.

3. (Adapted from [153])
   Victor has been murdered, and Arthur, Bertram, and Carleton are the only suspects (meaning exactly one of them is the murderer). Arthur says that Bertram was the victim's friend, but that Carleton hated the victim. Bertram says that he was out of town the day of the murder, and besides, he didn't even know the guy. Carleton says that he saw Arthur and Bertram with the victim just before the murder. You may assume that everyone—except possibly for the murderer—is telling the truth.

   (a) Use Resolution to find the murderer. In other words, formalize the facts as a set of clauses, prove that there is a murderer, and extract his identity from the derivation.

   (b) Suppose we discover that we were wrong—we cannot assume that there was only a single murderer (there may have been a conspiracy). Show that in this case the facts do not support anyone's guilt. In other words, for each suspect, present a logical interpretation that supports all the facts but where that suspect is innocent and the other two are guilty.

4. (See follow-up Exercise 3 of Chapter 5)
   The general form of Resolution with variables presented here is not complete as it stands, even for deriving the empty clause. In particular, note that the two clauses

   $$[P(x), P(y)] \quad \text{and} \quad [\neg P(u), \neg P(v)]$$

   are together unsatisfiable.

   (a) Argue that the empty clause cannot be derived from these two clauses.

   A slightly more general rule of Resolution handles cases such as these:

   > Suppose that $C_1$ and $C_2$ are clauses with disjoint atoms. Suppose that there are *sets* of literals $D_1 \subseteq C_1$ and $D_2 \subseteq C_2$ and a substitution $\theta$ such that $D_1\theta = \{\rho\}$ and $D_2\theta = \{\overline{\rho}\}$. Then, we conclude by Resolution the clause $(C_1 - D_1)\theta \cup (C_2 - D_2)\theta$.

   The form of Resolution considered in the text simply took $D_1$ and $D_2$ to be singleton sets.

(b) Show a refutation of the two clauses with this generalized form of Resolution.

(c) Another way to obtain completeness is to leave the Resolution rule unchanged (that is, dealing with pairs of literals rather than pairs of sets of literals), but to add a second rule of inference, sometimes called *factoring*, to make up the difference. Present such a rule of inference and show that it properly handles the earlier example.

In the remaining exercises of this chapter we consider a number of procedures for determining whether or not a set of propositional clauses is satisfiable. In most cases, we also would like to return a satisfying interpretation, if one exists.

5. In defining procedures for testing satisfiability, it is useful to have the following notation: When $C$ is a set of clauses and $m$ is a literal, define $C \bullet m$ to be the following set of clauses:

$$C \bullet m = \{c \mid c \in C, m \notin c, \overline{m} \notin c\} \cup \{(c - \overline{m}) \mid c \in C, m \notin c, \overline{m} \in c\}.$$

For example, if $C = \{[p,q], [\overline{p},a,b], [\overline{p},c], [d,e]\}$, it follows that $C \bullet p = \{[a,b], [c], [d,e]\}$ and $C \bullet \overline{p} = \{[q], [d,e]\}$.

Prove the following two properties of Resolution derivations:

(a) If $C \bullet m$ derives clause $c$ in $k$ steps, then $C$ derives $c^*$ in $k$ steps, where $c^*$ is either $c$ itself or the clause $c \cup [\overline{m}]$.

(b) If $C \bullet p$ derives $[]$ in $n_1$ steps and $C \bullet \overline{p}$ derives $[]$ in $n_2$ steps, then $C$ derives $[]$ in no more than $(n_1 + n_2 + 1)$ steps.

6. A very popular procedure for testing the satisfiability of a set of propositional clauses is the Davis-Putnam procedure (henceforth DP), shown in Figure 4.12, named after the two mathematicians who first presented it.[17]

(a) Sketch how DP could be modified to return a satisfying assignment (as a set of literals) instead of YES when the clauses are satisfiable.

(b) The main refinements to this procedure that have been proposed in the literature involve the choice of the atom $p$. As stated, the

---

[17]The version considered here is actually closer to the variant presented by Davis, Logemann, and Loveland *sans* Putnam [87].

**input:** a set of clauses $C$

**output:** are the clauses satisfiable, YES or NO?

**procedure** DP($C$)

> **if** $C$ is empty **then return** YES
> **if** $C$ contains [] **then return** NO
> let $p$ be some atom mentioned in $C$
> **if** DP($C \bullet p$) = YES **then return** YES
> **otherwise, return** DP($C \bullet \overline{p}$)

**end**

---

▪ **FIGURE 4.12**

The DP Procedure

---

choice is left to chance. Argue why it is useful to do at least the following: If $C$ contains a singleton clause $[p]$ or $[\overline{p}]$, then choose $p$ as the next atom.

(c) Another refinement is the following: Once it is established that $C$ is not empty and does not contain [], check to see if $C$ mentions some literal $m$ but not its complement $\overline{m}$. In this case, we return DP($C \bullet m$) directly and do not bother with $C \bullet \overline{m}$. Explain why this is correct.

(d) Among all known propositional satisfiability procedures, recent experimental results suggest that DP (including the refinements mentioned here) is the fastest one in practice. Somewhat surprisingly, it is possible to prove that DP can take an exponential number of steps on some inputs. Use the results from Exercise 5 and Haken's result mentioned in Section 4.3.3 to prove an exponential lower bound on the running time of DP. *Hint:* Prove by induction on $k$ that if DP($C$) returns NO after $k$ steps, then $C$ derives [] by Resolution in no more than $k$ steps.

(e) As stated, the choice of the next atom $p$ is left to chance. However, a number of selection strategies have been proposed in the literature, such as choosing an atom $p$ where

- $p$ appears in the most clauses in $C$, or
- $p$ appears in the fewest clauses in $C$, or
- $p$ is the most balanced atom in $C$ (the number of positive occurrences in $C$ is closest to the number of negative occurrences), or
- $p$ is the least balanced atom in $C$, or
- $p$ appears in the shortest clause(s) in $C$.

Choose any two of these selection strategies, implement two versions of DP, and compare how well they run (in terms of the number of recursive calls) on some hard test cases. To generate some sets of clauses that are known to be hard for DP (see [293] for details), randomly generate about $4.2n$ clauses of length 3, where $n$ is the number of atoms. (Each clause can be generated by choosing three atoms at random and flipping the polarity of each with a probability of .5.)

7. Until recently, a very popular way of testing the satisfiability of a set of propositional clauses was the *tableau* method. Rather than computing resolvents, the procedure TAB in Figure 4.13 tries to construct an interpretation $L$ that satisfies a set of clauses $C$ by picking literals from each clause.

   In this exercise, we begin by showing that the TAB procedure, like the DP procedure of Exercise 6, must have exponential running time on some inputs. First, we use the notation $C \vdash_N c$ to mean that clause $c$ (or a subset of it) can be derived by Resolution from the set of clauses $C$ in $N$ steps (or less). Observe that if $C \vdash_{N_1} c_1$ and $C \cup \{c_1\} \vdash_{N_2} c_2$, then $C \vdash_{(N_1+N_2)} c_2$, just by stacking the two derivations together.

   (a) Prove that if $C \cup \{c\} \vdash_N []$, then $C \cup \{(c \cup c')\} \vdash_N c'$.

**input:** a set of clauses $C$

**output:** are the clauses satisfiable, YES or NO?

**procedure** TAB($C$) = TAB1($C, \{\}$)

**procedure** TAB1($C, L$)

      **if** $L$ contains some $m$ and $\overline{m}$ **then return** NO

      **if** $C$ is empty **then return** YES

      **otherwise,** let $c$ be any clause in $C$

      **for** $m \in c$ **do**

          **if** TAB1($\{c \in C \mid m \notin c\}, L \cup \{m\}$) = YES

              **then return** YES

      **end for**

      **return** NO

**end**

■ **FIGURE 4.13**

The TAB Procedure

(b) Prove using part (a) and the earlier observation that if $m_1, \ldots, m_k$ are literals, and for each $i$, $C \cup \{[m_i]\} \vdash_{N_i} []$, then

$$C \cup \{[m_1, \ldots, m_k]\} \vdash_{(N_1 + \cdots + N_k)} [].$$

(c) Prove by induction on $N$ and using part (b) that if $\text{TAB1}(C, \{l_1, \ldots, l_r\})$ returns NO after a total of $N$ procedure calls, then there is a Resolution refutation of $(C \cup \{[l_1], \ldots, [l_r]\})$ that takes at most $N$ steps.

(d) As in Exercise 6, use Haken's result from Section 4.3.3 and part (c) to prove that there is a set of clauses $C$ for which $\text{TAB}(C)$ makes an exponential number of recursive procedure calls.

Finally, we consider an experimental question:

(e) As mentioned in Exercise 6, it was shown in [293] that the DP procedure often runs for a very long time with about $4.2n$ randomly generated clauses of length 3 (where $n$ is the number of atoms in the clauses). With fewer than $4.2n$ clauses, DP usually terminates quickly; with more, again DP usually terminates quickly.

Confirm (or refute) experimentally that the tableau method TAB also exhibits the same easy–hard–easy pattern around $4.2n$ on sets of clauses randomly generated as in Exercise 6.

8. Another method was proposed in [83] for testing the satisfiability of a set of propositional clauses. The procedure LS (for local search) tries to find an interpretation that satisfies a set of clauses by searching to within a certain distance from a given set of start points. In the simplest version, we consider two start points: the interpretation $\mathcal{I}_0$, which assigns all atoms false, and the interpretation $\mathcal{I}_1$, which assigns all atoms true. It is not hard to see that every interpretation lies within a distance of $n/2$ from one of these two start points, where $n$ is the number of atoms and where the distance between two interpretations is the number of atoms where they differ (the Hamming distance). The procedure is shown in Figure 4.14 using the $C \bullet m$ notation from Exercise 5.

*Note:* The correctness of the procedure depends on the following fact (discussed in [83]): In the final step, suppose $c \in C$ is a clause not satisfied by $\mathcal{I}$. Then there is an interpretation within distance $d$ of $\mathcal{I}$ that satisfies $C$ if and only if for some literal $m \in c$ there is an interpretation within distance $d - 1$ of $\mathcal{I}$ that satisfies $C \bullet m$.

**input:** a set of clauses $C$, over $n$ atoms

**output:** are the clauses satisfiable, YES or NO?

**procedure** $LS(C) = LS1(C, \mathcal{I}_0, n/2)$ **or** $LS1(C, \mathcal{I}_1, n/2)$

**procedure** $LS1(C, \mathcal{I}, d)$

    **if** $\mathcal{I} \models c$, for every $c \in C$, **then return** YES
    **if** $d \leq 0$ **then return** NO
    **if** $[] \in C$ **then return** NO
    **otherwise,** let $c$ be any clause in $C$ such that $\mathcal{I} \not\models c$
    **for** $m \in c$ **do**
        **if** $LS1(C \bullet m, \mathcal{I}, d - 1) = $ YES
            **then return** YES
    **end for**
    **return** NO

**end**

■ **FIGURE 4.14**

The LS Procedure

Confirm (or refute) experimentally that the LS method also exhibits the same easy–hard–easy pattern noted in Exercise 7.

9. In some applications we are given a set of clauses that is known to be satisfiable and our task is to find an interpretation that satisfies the clauses. We can use variants of the procedures presented in Exercises 6, 7, or 8 to do this, but we can also use Resolution itself. First we generate $R = RES(S)$, the set of all resolvents derivable from $S$. Then we run the procedure RES-SAT, shown in Figure 4.15.

Note that $\neg c$ refers to the set of literals that are the complements of those in $c$. Also, we are treating an interpretation as a set of literals $T$ containing exactly one of $p_i$ or $\neg p_i$, for each atom $p_i$.

(a) Show an example where this procedure would not correctly locate a satisfying interpretation if the original set $S$ were used instead of $R$ in the body.

(b) Given that the procedure works correctly for some set $R$, prove that it would also work correctly on just the minimal elements of $R$, that is, on those clauses in $R$ for which no proper subset is a clause in $R$.

**input:** a set of clauses $C$ over $n$ atoms

**output:** an interpretation satisfying $C$

**procedure** RES-SAT($C$)

$\quad T := \{\}$

$\quad$**for** $i := 1$ **to** $n$

$\quad\quad$**if** there is a clause $c \in R$ such that $\neg c \subseteq T \cup \{p_i\}$

$\quad\quad\quad$**then** $T := T \cup \{\neg p_i\}$

$\quad\quad\quad$**else** $T := T \cup \{p_i\}$

$\quad$**end for**

$\quad$**return** $T$

**end**

■ **FIGURE 4.15**

The RES-SAT Procedure

(c) Prove that the procedure correctly finds a satisfying interpretation when $R = RES(S)$. *Hint:* Begin by showing the following:

For any $T$, if for no clause $c \in R$ is it the case that $\neg c \subseteq T$, then there cannot be clauses $c_1$ and $c_2$ in $R$ such that $\neg c_1 \subseteq T \cup \{p\}$ and $\neg c_2 \subseteq T \cup \{\neg p\}$.

Then use induction to do the rest.

10. In [375], a procedure called GSAT is presented for finding interpretations for satisfiable sets of clauses. This procedure, shown in Figure 4.16, seems to have some serious drawbacks: It does not work at all on unsatisfiable sets of clauses, and even with satisfiable ones it is not guaranteed to eventually return an answer. Nonetheless, it appears to work quite well in practice.

The procedure uses two parameters: *flips* determines how many times the atoms in $\mathcal{I}$ should be flipped before starting over with a new random interpretation; *tries* determines how many times this process should be repeated before giving up and declaring failure. Both parameters need to be set by trial and error.

Implement GSAT and compare its performance to one of the other satisfiability procedures presented in these exercises on some satisfiable sets of clauses of your own choosing. Note that one of

**input:** a set of clauses $C$, and two parameters, *tries* and *flips*

**output:** an interpretation satisfying $C$, or failure

**procedure** GSAT($C$, *tries*, *flips*)

**for** $i := 1$ **to** *tries* **do**

    $\mathcal{I} :=$ a randomly generated truth assignment

    **for** $j := 1$ **to** *flips* **do**

        **if** $\mathcal{I} \models C$ **then return** $\mathcal{I}$

        $p :=$ an atomic symbol such that a change in its truth
            assignment gives the largest increase in the total
            number of clauses in $C$ that are satisfied by $\mathcal{I}$

        $\mathcal{I} := \mathcal{I}$ with the truth assignment of $p$ reversed

    **end for**

**end for**

**return** "no satisfying interpretation found"

**end**

■ **FIGURE 4.16**

The GSAT Procedure

the properties of GSAT is that because it counts the number of clauses not yet satisfied by an interpretation, it is very sensitive to how a problem is encoded as a set of clauses (that is, logically equivalent formulations could have very different computational consequences).

# CHAPTER 5

# REASONING WITH HORN CLAUSES

■

■

■

In Chapter 4, we saw how a Resolution procedure could in principle be used to calculate entailments of any first-order logic KB. But we also saw that in its most general form Resolution ran into serious computational difficulties. Although refinements to Resolution can help, the problem can never be completely eliminated. This is a consequence of the fundamental computational intractability of first-order entailment.

In this chapter, we will explore the idea of limiting ourselves to only a certain interesting subset of first-order logic, where the Resolution procedure becomes much more manageable. We will also see that from a representation standpoint, the subset in question is still sufficiently expressive for many purposes.

## 5.1 HORN CLAUSES

In a Resolution-based system, clauses end up being used for two different purposes. First, they are used to express ordinary disjunctions like

[Rain, Sleet, Snow].

This is the sort of clause we might use to express incomplete knowledge: There is rain or sleet or snow outside, but we don't know which. But consider a clause like

[¬Child, ¬Male, Boy].

Although this can certainly be read as a disjunction, namely, "either someone is not a child, or is not male, or is a boy," it is much more naturally understood as a *conditional:* "If someone is a child and is male then that someone is a boy." It is this second reading of clauses that will be our focus in this chapter.

We call a clause like this—containing at most one positive literal—a *Horn clause.* When there is exactly one positive literal in the clause, it is called a *positive* (or *definite*) Horn clause. When there are no positive literals, the clause is called a *negative* Horn clause. In either case, there can be zero negative literals, and so the empty clause is a negative Horn clause. Observe that a positive Horn clause $[\neg p_1, \ldots, \neg p_n, q]$ can be read as "if $p_1$ and ... and $p_n$, then $q$." We will sometimes write a clause like this as

$$p_1 \wedge \ldots \wedge p_n \Rightarrow q$$

to emphasize this conditional, "if–then" reading.

Our focus in this chapter will be on using Resolution to reason with if–then statements (which are sometimes called "rules"). Full first-order logic is concerned with disjunction and incomplete knowledge in a more general form, which we are putting aside for the purposes of this chapter.

### 5.1.1  Resolution Derivations with Horn Clauses

Given a Resolution derivation over Horn clauses, observe that two negative clauses can never be resolved together, because all of their literals are of the same polarity. If we are able to resolve a negative and a positive clause together, we are guaranteed to produce a negative clause: The two clauses must be resolved with respect to the one positive literal in the positive clause, and so it will not appear in the resolvent. Similarly, if we resolve two positive clauses together, we are guaranteed to produce a positive clause: The two clauses must be resolved with respect to one (and only one) of the positive literals, so the other positive literal will appear in the resolvent. In other words, Resolution over Horn clauses must always involve a positive clause, and if the second clause is negative, the resolvent is negative; if the second clause is positive, the resolvent is positive.

Less obvious, perhaps, is the following fact: Suppose $S$ is a set of Horn clauses and $S \vdash c$, where $c$ is a negative clause. Then there is guaranteed to be a derivation of $c$ where all the new clauses in the derivation (i.e., clauses not in $S$) are negative. The proof is detailed and laborious, but the main idea is this: Suppose we have a derivation with some new positive clauses. Take the last one of these, and call it $c'$. Since $c'$ is the last positive clause in the derivation, all of the Resolution steps after $c'$ produce negative clauses. We now change the derivation so that instead of generating negative clauses using $c'$, we generate these negative clauses using the positive parents of $c'$ (which is where all of the literals in $c'$ come from—$c'$

must have only positive parents, because it is a positive clause). We know we can do this because in order to get to the negative successor(s) of $c'$, we must have a clause somewhere that can resolve with it to eliminate the one positive literal in $c'$ (call that clause $d$ and the literal $p$). That $p$ must be present in one of the (positive) parents of $c'$, so we just use clause $d$ to resolve against the parent of $c'$, thereby eliminating $p$ earlier in the derivation and producing the negative clauses without producing $c'$. The derivation still generates $c$, but this time without needing $c'$. If we repeat this for every new positive clause introduced, we eliminate all of them.

We can go further: Suppose $S$ is a set of Horn clauses and $S \vdash c$, where $c$ is again a negative clause. Then there is guaranteed to be a derivation of $c$ where each new clause derived is not only negative, but is a resolvent of the previous one in the derivation and an original clause in $S$. The reason is this: By the earlier argument, we can assume that each new clause in the derivation is negative. This means that it has one positive and one negative parent. Clearly, the positive parent must be from the original set (because all the new ones are negative). Each new clause then has exactly one negative parent. So starting with $c$, we can work our way back through its negative ancestors and end up with a negative clause that is in $S$. Then, by discarding all the clauses that are not on this chain from $c$ to $S$, we end up with a derivation of the required form.

These observations lead us to the following conclusion:

> There is a derivation of a negative clause (including the empty clause) from a set of Horn clauses $S$ if and only if there is one where each new clause in the derivation is a negative resolvent of the previous clause in the derivation and some element of $S$.

We will look at derivations of this form in more detail in the next section.

## 5.2  SLD RESOLUTION

The observations of the previous section lead us to consider a very restricted form of Resolution that is sufficient for Horn clauses. This is a form of Resolution where each new clause introduced is a resolvent of the previous clause and a clause from the original set. This pattern showed up repeatedly in the examples of Chapter 4, and is illustrated schematically in Figure 5.1.[1]

Let us be a little more formal about this. For any set $S$ of clauses (Horn or not), an *SLD derivation* of a clause $c$ from $S$ is a sequence of clauses $c_1, c_2, \ldots, c_n$, such that $c_n = c$, $c_1 \in S$, and $c_{i+1}$ is a resolvent of $c_i$ and

---

[1] The pattern appears in Figure 4.4, but not Figure 4.5.

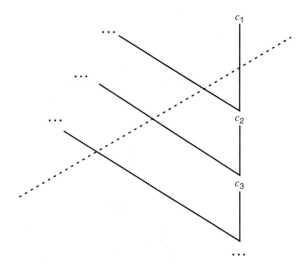

■ **FIGURE 5.1**

The SLD Resolution Pattern

some clause of $S$. We write $S \vdash_{\overline{SLD}} c$ if there is an SLD derivation of $c$ from $S$. Notationally, because of its structure, an SLD derivation is simply a type of Resolution derivation where we do not explicitly mention the elements of $S$ except for $c_1$.[2] We know that at each step of the way the obvious positive parent from $S$ can be identified, so we can leave it out of our description of the derivation and just show the chain of negative clauses from $c_1$ to $c$.

In the general case, it should be clear that if $S \vdash_{\overline{SLD}} []$ then $S \vdash []$. The converse, however, is not true in general. For example, let $S$ be the set of clauses $[p,q]$, $[\neg p,q]$, $[p, \neg q]$, and $[\neg p, \neg q]$. A quick glance at these clauses should convince us that $S$ is unsatisfiable (whatever values we pick for $p$ and $q$, we cannot make all four clauses true at the same time). Therefore, $S \vdash []$. However, to generate [] by Resolution, the last step must involve two complementary unit clauses $[\rho]$ and $[\overline{\rho}]$, for some atom $\rho$. Since $S$ contains no unit clauses, it will not be possible to use an element of $S$ for this last step. Consequently there is no SLD derivation of [] from $S$, even though $S \vdash []$.

In the previous section we argued that for Horn clauses we could get by with Resolution derivations of a certain shape, wherein each new clause in the derivation was a negative resolvent of the previous clause

---

[2] The name SLD stands for *Selected literals, Linear pattern, over Definite clauses.*

in the derivation and some element of $S$; we have now called such derivations SLD derivations. So although not the case for Resolution in general, it is the case that if $S$ is a set of Horn clauses, then $S \vdash []$ if and only if $S \vdash_{\text{SLD}} []$. So if $S$ is Horn, then it is unsatisfiable if and only if $S \vdash_{\text{SLD}} []$. Moreover, we know that each of the new clauses $c_2, \ldots, c_n$ can be assumed to be negative. So $c_2$ has a negative and a positive parent, and thus $c_1 \in S$ can be taken to be negative as well. Thus in the Horn case, SLD derivations of the empty clause must begin with a negative clause in the original set.

To see an example of an SLD derivation, consider the first example of Chapter 4. We start with a KB containing the following positive Horn clauses:

> Toddler
>
> Toddler $\supset$ Child
>
> Child $\wedge$ Male $\supset$ Boy
>
> Infant $\supset$ Child
>
> Child $\wedge$ Female $\supset$ Girl
>
> Female

and wish to show that $\text{KB} \models \text{Girl}$, that is, that there is an SLD derivation of $[]$ from KB together with the negative Horn clause $[\neg\text{Girl}]$. Because this is the only negative clause, it must be the $c_1$ in the derivation. By resolving it with the fifth clause in the KB, we get $[\neg\text{Child}, \neg\text{Female}]$ as $c_2$. Resolving this with the sixth clause, we get $[\neg\text{Child}]$ as $c_3$. Resolving this with the second clause, we get $[\neg\text{Toddler}]$ as $c_4$. And finally, resolving this with the first clause, we get $[]$ as the final clause. Observe that all the clauses in the derivation are negative. To display this derivation, we could continue to use Resolution diagrams from Chapter 4. However, for SLD derivations, it is convenient to use a special-purpose terminology and format.

### 5.2.1 Goal Trees

All the literals in all the clauses in a Horn SLD derivation of the empty clause are negative. We are looking for positive clauses in the KB to "eliminate" these negative literals to produce the empty clause. Sometimes, there is a unit clause in the KB that eliminates the literal directly. For example, if a clause like $[\neg\text{Toddler}]$ appears in a derivation using the earlier KB, then the derivation is finished, because there is a positive clause in the KB that resolves with it to produce the empty clause. We say in this case that the *goal* Toddler is *solved*. Sometimes there is a positive clause that eliminates the literal but introduces other negative literals.

For example, with a clause like [¬Child] in the derivation, we continue with the clause [¬Toddler], having resolved it against the second clause in our knowledge base ([¬Toddler, Child]). We say in this case that the goal Child *reduces to* the subgoal Toddler. Similarly, the goal Girl reduces to two subgoals, Child and Female, since two negative literals are introduced when it is resolved against the fifth clause in the KB.

A restatement of the SLD derivation is as follows: We start with the goal Girl. This reduces to two subgoals, Child and Female. The goal Female is solved, and Child reduces to Toddler. Finally, Toddler is solved.

We can display this derivation using what is called a *goal tree*. We draw the original goal (or goals) at the top, and point from there to the subgoals. For a complete SLD derivation, the leaves of the tree (at the bottom) will be the goals that are solved (see Figure 5.2). This allows us to easily see the form of the argument: We want to show that Girl is entailed by the KB. Reading from the bottom up, we know that Toddler is entailed because it appears in the KB. This means that Child is entailed. Furthermore, Female is also entailed (because it appears in the KB), so we conclude that Girl is entailed.

This way of looking at Horn clauses and SLD derivations, when generalized to deal with variables in the obvious way, forms the basis of the programming language PROLOG. We already saw an example of a PROLOG-style definition of addition in Chapter 4. Let us consider another example involving lists. For our purposes, list terms will either be variables, the constant nil, or a term of the form $cons(t_1, t_2)$, where $t_1$ is any term and $t_2$ is a list term. We will write clauses defining the Append$(x, y, z)$ relation, intended to hold when list $z$ is the result of appending list $y$ to list $x$:

Append$(nil, y, y)$

Append$(x, y, z) \Rightarrow$ Append$(cons(w, x), y, cons(w, z))$

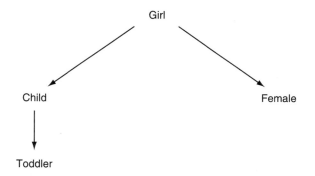

An Example Goal Tree

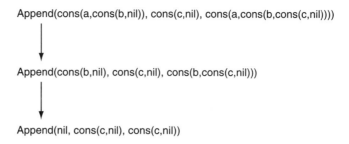

Append(cons(a,cons(b,nil)), cons(c,nil), cons(a,cons(b,cons(c,nil))))

Append(cons(b,nil), cons(c,nil), cons(b,cons(c,nil)))

Append(nil, cons(c,nil), cons(c,nil))

■ **FIGURE 5.3**

A Goal Tree for Append

If we wish to show that this entails

Append(cons(a,cons(b,nil)), cons(c,nil), cons(a,cons(b,cons(c,nil))))

we get the goal tree in Figure 5.3. We can also use a variable in the goal and show that the definition entails $\exists u.$ Append(cons(a,cons(b,nil)), cons(c,nil), $u$). The answer $u =$ cons(a,cons(b,cons(c,nil))) can be extracted from the derivation directly. Unlike ordinary Resolution, it is not necessary to use answer predicates with SLD derivations. This is because if $S$ is a set of Horn clauses, then $S \models \exists x. \alpha$ if and only if for some term $t$, $S \models \alpha_t^x$.

## 5.3    COMPUTING SLD DERIVATIONS

We now turn our attention to procedures for reasoning with Horn clauses. The idea is that we are given a KB containing a set of positive Horn clauses representing if–then sentences, and we wish to know whether or not some atom (or set of atoms) is entailed. Equivalently, we wish to know whether or not the KB together with a clause consisting of one or more negative literals is unsatisfiable. Thus the typical case, and the one we will consider here, involves determining the satisfiability of a set of Horn clauses containing exactly one negative clause.[3]

### 5.3.1    Backward Chaining

A procedure for determining the satisfiability of a set of Horn clauses with exactly one negative clause is presented in Figure 5.4. This procedure

---

[3]It is not hard to generalize the procedures presented here to deal with more than one negative clause (see Exercise 4). Similarly, the procedures can be generalized to answer entailment questions where the query is an arbitrary (non-Horn) formula in CNF.

**input:** a finite list of atomic sentences, $q_1, \ldots, q_n$

**output:** YES or NO according to whether a given KB entails all of the $q_i$

**procedure** SOLVE$[q_1, \ldots, q_n]$

    **if** $n = 0$ **then return** YES

    **for** each clause $c \in$ KB, **do**

        **if** $c = [q_1, \neg p_1, \ldots, \neg p_m]$

            and SOLVE$[p_1, \ldots, p_m, q_2, \ldots, q_n]$

        **then return** YES

    **end for**

    **return** NO

---

▪ **FIGURE 5.4**

A Recursive Backward-Chaining SLD Procedure

---

starts with a set of goals as input (corresponding to the atoms in the single negative clause) and attempts to solve them. If there are no goals, then it is done. Otherwise, it takes the first goal $q_1$ and looks for a clause in KB whose positive literal is $q_1$. Using the negative literals in that clause as subgoals, it then calls itself recursively with these subgoals together with the rest of the original goals. If this is successful, it is done; otherwise it must consider other clauses in the KB whose positive literal is $q_1$. If none can be found, the procedure returns NO, meaning the atoms are not entailed.

This procedure is called *backward chaining*, because it works backward from goals to facts in the KB. It is also called *depth-first*, because it attempts to solve the new goals $p_i$ before tackling the old goals $q_i$. Finally, it is called *left-to-right*, because it attempts the goals $q_i$ in order 1, 2, 3, and so on. This depth-first left-to-right backward-chaining procedure is the one normally used by PROLOG implementations to solve goals, although the first-order case obviously requires unification, substitution of variables, and so on.

This backward-chaining procedure also has a number of drawbacks. First, observe that even in the propositional case it can go into an infinite loop. Suppose we have the tautologous $[p, \neg p]$ in the KB.[4] In this case, a goal of $p$ can reduce to a subgoal of $p$, and so on, indefinitely.

Even if it does terminate, the backward-chaining algorithm can be quite inefficient and do a considerable amount of redundant searching. For example, imagine that we have $2n$ atoms $p_0, \ldots, p_{n-1}$ and $q_0, \ldots, q_{n-1}$,

---

[4]This corresponds to the PROLOG program "p :- p."

**input:** a finite list of atomic sentences, $q_1, \ldots, q_n$

**output:** YES or NO according to whether a given KB entails all of the $q_i$

1. if all of the goals $q_i$ are marked as solved, then return YES

2. check if there is a clause $[p, \neg p_1, \ldots, \neg p_n]$ in KB, such that all of its negative atoms $p_1$, ..., $p_n$ are marked as solved, and such that the positive atom $p$ is not marked as solved

3. if there is such a clause, mark $p$ as solved and go to step 1

4. otherwise, return NO

■ **FIGURE 5.5**

A Forward-Chaining SLD Procedure

and the following $4n - 4$ clauses: For $0 < i < n$,

$$p_{i-1} \Rightarrow p_i$$
$$p_{i-1} \Rightarrow q_i$$
$$q_{i-1} \Rightarrow p_i$$
$$q_{i-1} \Rightarrow q_i$$

For any $i$, both SOLVE[$p_i$] and SOLVE[$q_i$] will eventually fail, but only after at least $2^i$ steps. The proof is a simple induction argument.[5] This means that even for a reasonably sized KB (say 396 clauses when $n = 100$), an impossibly large amount of work may be required (over $2^{100}$ steps).

Given this exponential behavior, we might wonder if this is a problem with the backward-chaining procedure or another instance of what we saw in the last chapter where the entailment problem itself was simply too hard in its most general form. As it turns out, this time it is the procedure that is to blame.

## 5.3.2 Forward Chaining

In the propositional case, there is a much more efficient procedure to determine if a Horn KB entails a set of atoms, given in Figure 5.5. This is a *forward-chaining* procedure, because it works from the facts in the KB toward the goals. The idea is to mark atoms as "solved" as soon as we have determined that they are entailed by the KB.

---

[5] The claim is clearly true for $i = 0$. For the goal $p_k$, where $k > 0$, we need to try to solve both $p_{k-1}$ and $q_{k-1}$. By induction, each of these take at least $2^{k-1}$ steps, for a total of $2^k$ steps. The case for $q_k$ is identical.

Suppose, for example, we start with the earlier Girl example. At the outset Girl is not marked as solved, so we go to step 2. At this point, we look for a clause satisfying the given criteria. The clause [Toddler] is one such, because all of its negative literals (of which there are none) are marked as solved. So we mark Toddler as solved and try again. This time we might find the clause [Child, ¬Toddler], and so we can mark Child as solved and try again. Continuing in this way, we mark Female and finally Girl as solved and we are done.

Although this procedure appears to take about the same effort as the backward-chaining one, it has much better overall behavior. Note, in particular, that each time through the iteration we need to find a clause in the KB with an atom that has not been marked. Thus, we will iterate at most as many times as there are clauses in the KB. Each such iteration step may require us to scan the entire KB, but the overall result will never be exponential. In fact, with a bit of care in the use of data structures, a forward-chaining procedure like this can be made to run in time that is *linear* in the size of the KB, as will be demonstrated in Exercise 1.

### 5.3.3   The First-Order Case

Thus, in the propositional case at least, we can determine if a Horn KB entails an atom in a linear number of steps. But what about the first-order case? Unfortunately, even with Horn clauses, we still have the possibility of a procedure that runs forever. The example in Figure 4.11, where an infinite branch of resolvents was generated, only required Horn clauses. While it might seem that a forward-chaining procedure could deal with first-order examples like these, avoiding the infinite loops, this cannot be: The problem of determining whether a set of first-order Horn clauses entails an atom remains *undecidable*. So no procedure can be guaranteed to always work, despite the fact that the propositional case is so easy. This is not too surprising, because PROLOG is a full programming language, and being able to decide if an atom is entailed would imply being able to decide if a PROLOG program would halt.

As with non-Horn clauses, the best that can be expected in the first-order case is to give control of the reasoning to the user to help avoid redundancies and infinite branches. Unlike the non-Horn case, however, Horn clauses are much easier to structure and control in this way. In the next chapter, we will see some examples of how this can be done.

## 5.4   BIBLIOGRAPHIC NOTES

Horn formulas were first studied by Alfred Horn [190] and are named after him. The SLD Resolution procedure was introduced by Kowalski

[223] and referred to as SLD Resolution by Apt and van Emden [14]. The linear-time procedure for the satisfiability of Horn clauses is due to Dowling and Gallier [110].

What is called *backtracking* here is usually referred to as *chronological backtracking* [418]. Another common backtracking technique is dependency-directed backtracking, introduced by Stallman and Sussman [395].

Horn clauses and SLD Resolution form the basis of the logic programming language PROLOG [75]. Good introductions to reasoning with clauses are given by Kowalski [224] and Richards [353]. Further reference to material on PROLOG will be provided in the next chapter.

## 5.5 EXERCISES

1. Write, test, and document a program that determines the satisfiability of a set of propositional Horn clauses by forward chaining and that runs in linear time, relative to the size of the input. Use the following data structures:

   (a) a global variable STACK containing a list of atoms known to be true, but waiting to be propagated forward;

   (b) for each clause, an atom CONCLUSION, which is the positive literal appearing in the clause (or NIL if the clause contains only negative literals), and a number REMAINING, which is the number of atoms appearing negatively in the clause that are not yet known to be true;

   (c) for each atom, a flag VISITED indicating whether or not the atom has been propagated forward, and a list ON-CLAUSES of all the clauses where the atom appears negatively.

   You may assume the input is in suitable form. Include in the documentation an argument as to why your program runs in linear time. (If you choose to use LISP property lists for your data structures, you may assume that it takes constant time to go from an atom to any of its properties.)

2. As noted in Chapter 4, Herbrand's Theorem allows us to convert a first-order satisfiability problem into a propositional (variable-free) one, although the size of the Herbrand base, in general, is infinite. One way to deal with an infinite set $S$ of clauses is to look at progressively larger subsets of it to see if any of them are unsatisfiable, in which case $S$ must be as well. In fact, the converse is true: If $S$ is

unsatisfiable, then some finite subset of $S$ is unsatisfiable too. This is called the *compactness* property of FOL.

One way to generate progressively larger subsets of $S$ is as follows:

> For any term $t$, let $|t|$ be defined as 0 for variables and constants, and $1 + max|t_i|$ for terms $f(t_1, \ldots, t_n)$.
>
> Now for any set $S$ of formulas, define $S_k$ to be those elements $\alpha$ of $S$ such that every term $t$ of $\alpha$ has $|t| \le k$.

(a) Write and test a program that given a finite set $S$ of first-order clauses and a positive number $k$ returns as value $H_k$, where $H$ is the Herbrand base of $S$.

(b) When the original set $S$ is Horn, then for any $k$, your program returns a finite set of propositional Horn clauses. These can be checked for satisfiability using a propositional program like the one in Exercise 1. Briefly compare this way of testing the satisfiability of $S$ to the more standard way using SLD Resolution, as in PROLOG.

3. Consider the more general version of Resolution discussed in Exercise 4 of Chapter 4. Is that generalization required for SLD-resolution? Explain.

4. In this question, we will explore the semantic properties of propositional Horn clauses. For any set of clauses $S$, define $\mathcal{I}_S$ to be the interpretation that satisfies an atom $p$ if and only if $S \models p$.

(a) Show that if $S$ is a set of positive Horn clauses, then $\mathcal{I}_S \models S$.

(b) Give an example of a set of clauses $S$ where $\mathcal{I}_S \not\models S$.

(c) Suppose that $S$ is a set of positive Horn clauses and that $c$ is a negative Horn clause. Show that if $\mathcal{I}_S \not\models c$ then $S \cup \{c\}$ is unsatisfiable.

(d) Suppose that $S$ is a set of positive Horn clauses and that $T$ is a set of negative ones. Using part (c), show that if $S \cup \{c\}$ is satisfiable for every $c \in T$, then $S \cup T$ is satisfiable also.

(e) In the propositional case, the normal PROLOG interpreter can be thought of as taking a set of positive Horn clauses $S$ (the program) and a single negative clause $c$ (the query) and determining whether or not $S \cup \{c\}$ is satisfiable. Use part (d) to conclude that PROLOG can be used to test the satisfiability of an arbitrary set of Horn clauses.

5. In this question, we will formalize a fragment of high school geometry. We will use a single binary predicate symbol, which we write here as $\cong$. The objects in this domain are points, lines, angles,

and triangles. We will use constants only to name the points we need, and for the other individuals we will use function symbols that take points as arguments: first, a function that given two points is used to name the line between them, which we write here as $\overline{AB}$, where $A$ and $B$ are points; next, a function that given three points names the angle between them, which we write here as $\angle ABC$; and finally, a function that given three points names the triangle between them, which we write here as $\triangle ABC$.

Here are the axioms of interest:

- $\cong$ *is an equivalence relation.*
- $\overline{XY} \cong \overline{YX}$.
- $\angle XYZ \cong \angle ZYX$.
- *If* $\triangle XYZ \cong \triangle UVW$, *then the corresponding lines and angles are congruent* $(\overline{XY} \cong \overline{UV}, \angle XYZ \cong \angle UVW, etc.)$.
- **SAS:** *If* $\overline{XY} \cong \overline{UV}$, $\angle XYZ \cong \angle UVW$, *and* $\overline{YZ} \cong \overline{VW}$, *then* $\triangle XYZ \cong \triangle UVW$.

(a) Show that these axioms imply that the base angles of an isosceles triangle must be equal, that is, that

$$\text{Axioms} \cup \overline{AB} \cong \overline{AC} \models \angle ABC \cong \angle ACB.$$

Because the axioms can be formulated as Horn clauses and the other two sentences are atomic, it is sufficient to present an SLD derivation.

(b) The theorem in part (a) can also be proven by constructing the midpoint of the side $\overline{BC}$ (call it $D$), and showing that $\triangle ABD \cong \triangle ACD$ (by using **SSS**, the fact that two triangles are congruent if the corresponding sides are all congruent). What difficulties do you foresee in automated reasoning with constructed points like this?

# CHAPTER 6

# PROCEDURAL CONTROL OF REASONING

◼

◼

◼

Theorem-proving methods, like Resolution, are general, domain-independent ways of reasoning. A user can express facts in full FOL without having to know how this knowledge will ultimately be used for inference by an automated theorem-proving (ATP) procedure. The ATP mechanism will try all logically permissible uses of everything in the knowledge base in looking for an answer to a query.

This is a double-edged sword, however. Sometimes, it is not computationally feasible to try all logically possible ways of using what is known. Furthermore, we often do have an idea about how knowledge should be used or how to go about searching for a derivation. When we understand the structure of a domain or a problem, we may want to avoid using facts in every possible way or in every possible order. In cases like these, we would like to communicate *guidance* to an automatic theorem-proving procedure based on properties of the domain. This may be in the form of specific methods to use, or perhaps merely suggesting what to avoid in trying to answer a query.

For example, consider a variant on a logical language where some of the connectives are to be used only in one direction, as suggested at the end of Chapter 4. Instead of a simple implication symbol, for example, we might have a special forward implication symbol that suggests only going from antecedent to consequent but not the reverse. If we used the symbol "$\rightarrow$" to represent this one-way implication, then the sentence, $(\text{Battleship}(x) \rightarrow \text{Gray}(x))$, would allow a system to conclude in the forward direction for any specific battleship that it was gray, but would prevent it from trying to show that something was gray by trying to show that it was a battleship (an unlikely prospect for most gray things).

More generally, there are many cases in knowledge representation where we as users will want to control the reasoning process in various domain-specific ways. As noted in Chapter 4, this is often the best we can do to deal with an otherwise computationally intractable reasoning task. In this chapter, we will examine how knowledge can be expressed to provide control for the simple case of the backward-chaining reasoning procedure we examined in Chapter 5.

## 6.1 FACTS AND RULES

In a clausal representation scheme like those we considered in the chapter on Horn logic, we can often separate the clauses in a KB into two components: a database of *facts*, and a collection of *rules*. The facts are used to cover the basic truths of the domain and are usually ground atoms; the rules are used to extend the vocabulary, expressing new relations in terms of basic facts, and are usually universally quantified conditionals. Both the basic facts and the (conclusions of) rules can be retrieved by the sort of unification matching we have studied.

For example, we might have the following simple knowledge base fragment:

Mother(jane, billy)

Father(john, billy)

Father(sam, john)

...

Parent$(x, y) \Leftarrow$ Mother$(x, y)$

Parent$(x, y) \Leftarrow$ Father$(x, y)$

Child$(x, y) \Leftarrow$ Parent$(y, x)$

...

We can read the latter sentence, for example, as "$x$ is a child of $y$ if $y$ is a parent of $x$." In this case, if we ask the knowledge base if John is the father of Billy, we would find the answer by matching the base fact, Father(john, billy), directly. If we ask if John is a parent of Billy, we would need to chain backward and ask the KB if John was either the mother of Billy or the father of Billy (the latter would of course succeed). If we were to ask whether Billy is a child of John, then we would have to check whether John was a parent of Billy, and then proceed to the mother and father checks.

Because rules involve chaining, and the possible invocation of other rules that can in turn cause more chaining, the key control issue we need to think about is how to make the most effective use of the rules in a knowledge base.

## 6.2   RULE FORMATION AND SEARCH STRATEGY

Let's consider defining the notion of Ancestor in terms of the predicate Parent. Here are three logically equivalent ways to express the relationship between the two predicates:

1. $\text{Ancestor}(x,y) \Leftarrow \text{Parent}(x,y)$
   $\text{Ancestor}(x,y) \Leftarrow \text{Parent}(x,z) \wedge \text{Ancestor}(z,y)$

2. $\text{Ancestor}(x,y) \Leftarrow \text{Parent}(x,y)$
   $\text{Ancestor}(x,y) \Leftarrow \text{Parent}(z,y) \wedge \text{Ancestor}(x,z)$

3. $\text{Ancestor}(x,y) \Leftarrow \text{Parent}(x,y)$
   $\text{Ancestor}(x,y) \Leftarrow \text{Ancestor}(x,z) \wedge \text{Ancestor}(z,y)$

In the first case, we see that someone $x$ is an ancestor of someone else $y$ if $x$ is a parent of $y$, or if there is a third person $z$ who is a child of $x$ and an ancestor of $y$. So, for example, if Sam is the father of Bill, and Bill is the great-grandfather (an ancestor) of Sue, then Sam is an ancestor of Sue. The second case looks at the situation where Sam might be the great-grandfather of Fred, who is a parent of Sue, and therefore Sam is an ancestor of Sue. In the third case, we observe that if Sam is the great-grandfather of George who is in turn a grandfather of Sue, then again Sam is an ancestor of Sue. Although their forms are different, a close look reveals that all three of these yield the same results on all questions.

If we are trying to determine whether or not someone is an ancestor of someone else, in all three cases we would use backward chaining from an initial Ancestor goal, such as Ancestor(sam,sue), which would ultimately reduce to a set of Parent goals. But depending on which version we use, the rules could lead to substantially different amounts of computation. Consider the three cases:

1. the first version of Ancestor suggests that we start from Sam and look "downward" in the family tree; in other words (assuming that Sam is not Sue's parent), to find out whether or not Ancestor(sam, sue) is true, we first look for a $z$ that is Sam's child: Parent(sam, $z$). We then check to see if that $z$ is an ancestor of Sue: Ancestor($z$, sue).

2. the second option (again, assuming that Sam is not Sue's parent) suggests that we start searching "upward" in the family tree from Sue, looking for some $z$ that is Sue's parent: Parent($z$, sue). Once we

find one, we then check to see if Sam is an ancestor of that parent: Ancestor(sam, $z$).

3. the third option suggests a search in both directions, looking at individual Parent relationships both up and down at the same time.

The three search strategies implied by these (logically equivalent) representations are not equivalent in terms of the computational resources needed to answer the query. For example, suppose that people have on average one child, but two parents. With the first option, as we fan out from Sam, we search a tree downward that has about $d$ nodes where $d$ is the depth of the search; with the second option, as we fan out from Sue, we search a tree upward that has $2^d$ nodes where $d$ is the depth. So as $d$ gets larger, we can see that the first option would require much less searching. If, on the other hand, people had more than two children on average, the second option would be better. Thus we can see how the structure of a particular domain, or even a particular problem, can make logically equivalent characterizations of the rules quite different in their computational impact for a backward-chaining derivation procedure.

## 6.3    ALGORITHM DESIGN

The same kind of thinking about the structure of rules plays a significant role in a wide variety of problems. For example, familiar numerical relations can be expressed in forms that are logically equivalent, but with substantially different computational properties.

Consider the Fibonacci integer series, wherein each Fibonacci number is the sum of the previous two numbers in the series. Assuming that the first two Fibonacci numbers are 1 and 1, the series looks like this:

$$1, 1, 2, 3, 5, 8, 13, 21, 34, \ldots$$

One direct and obvious way to characterize this series is with the following two base facts and a rule, using a two-place predicate, Fibo($n, v$), intended to hold when $v$ is the $n$th Fibonacci number:

Fibo(0, 1)

Fibo(1, 1)

Fibo(s(s($n$)), $v$) $\Leftarrow$ Fibo($n, y$) $\wedge$ Fibo(s($n$), $z$) $\wedge$ Plus($y, z, v$)

This says explicitly that the zeroth and first Fibonacci numbers are both 1, and by the rule, that the $(n + 2)^{nd}$ Fibonacci number is the sum of the $(n + 1)^{st}$ Fibonacci number $z$ and the $n$th Fibonacci number $y$. Note that we use a three-place relation for addition: Plus($y, z, v$) means $v = y + z$.

This simple and direct characterization has significant computational drawbacks if used by an unguided backward-chaining theorem prover. In particular, it generates an exponential number of Plus subgoals. This is because each application of the rule calls Fibo twice, once each on the previous two numbers in the series. Most of this effort is redundant, because the call on the previous number makes a further call on the number before that, which has already been pursued in a different part of the proof tree by the former step. That is, Fibo(12, −) invokes Fibo(11, −) and Fibo(10, −); the call to Fibo(11, −) then calls Fibo(10, −) again. The resulting exponential behavior makes it virtually impossible to calculate the 100th Fibonacci number using these clauses.

An alternative (but still recursive) view of the Fibonacci series uses a four-place intermediate predicate, F. The definition is this:

$$\text{Fibo}(n, v) \Leftarrow \text{F}(n, 1, 0, v)$$

$$\text{F}(0, y, z, y)$$

$$\text{F}(\text{s}(n), y, z, v) \Leftarrow \text{Plus}(y, z, s) \wedge \text{F}(n, s, y, v)$$

Here, $\text{F}(n, y, z, v)$ will count down from $n$ using $y$ to keep track of the current Fibonacci number and $z$ to keep track of the one before that. Each time we reduce $n$ by 1, we get a new current number (the sum of the current and previous Fibonacci numbers) and we get a new previous number (which was the current one). At the end, when $n$ is 0, the final result $v$ is the current Fibonacci number $y$.[1] The important point about this equivalent characterization is that it avoids the redundancy of the previous version and requires only a linear number of Plus subgoals. Calculating the 100th Fibonacci number in this case is quite straightforward.

In a sense, looking for computationally feasible ways of expressing definitions of predicates using rules is not so different from looking for efficient algorithms for computational tasks.

## 6.4  SPECIFYING GOAL ORDER

When using rules to do backward chaining, we can try to solve subgoals in any order; all orderings of subgoals are logically permissible. But as we saw in the previous sections, the computational consequences of logically equivalent representations can be significant.

---

[1] To prove that $\text{F}(n, 1, 0, v)$ holds when $v$ is the $n$th Fibonacci number, we show by induction on $n$ that $\text{F}(n, y, z, v)$ holds if and only if $v$ is the sum of $y$ times the $n$th Fibonacci number and $z$ times the $(n − 1)^{\text{st}}$ Fibonacci number.

Consider this simple example:

$$\mathsf{AmericanCousin}(x, y) \Leftarrow \mathsf{American}(x) \wedge \mathsf{Cousin}(x, y)$$

If we are trying to ascertain the truth of AmericanCousin(fred, sally), there is not much difference between choosing to solve the first subgoal (American(fred)) or the second subgoal (Cousin(fred, sally)) first. However, there is a big difference if we are looking for an American cousin of Sally: AmericanCousin($x$, sally). Our two options are then

1. find an American and then check to see if she is a cousin of Sally; or

2. find a cousin of Sally and then check to see if she is an American.

Unless Sally has a lot of cousins (more than several hundred million), the second method will be much better than the first.

This illustrates the potential importance of ordering goals. We might think of the two parts of the earlier definition as suggesting that when we want to generate Sally's American cousins, what we want to do is to *generate* Sally's cousins one at a time and *test* to see if each is an American. Languages like PROLOG, which are used for programming and not just general theorem proving, take ordering constraints seriously, both of clauses and of the literals within them. In PROLOG notation,

$$G \; :- \; G_1, G_2, \ldots, G_n.$$

stands for

$$G \Leftarrow G_1 \wedge G_2 \wedge \ldots \wedge G_n$$

but goals are attempted exactly in the presented order.

## 6.5 COMMITTING TO PROOF METHODS

An appropriate PROLOG rendition of our American cousin case would take care of the inefficiency problem we pointed out earlier:

```
americanCousin(X,Y) :- cousin(X,Y), american(X).
```

In a construct like this, we need to allow for goal backtracking, because for a goal of, say, AmericanCousin($x$, sally), we may need to try American($x$) for various values of $x$. In other words, we may need to generate many cousin candidates before we find one that is American.

Sometimes, given a clause of the form

```
G :- T, S.
```

goal $T$ is needed only as a test for the applicability of subgoal $S$, and not as a generator of possibilities for subgoal $S$ to test further. In other words, if $T$ succeeds, then we want to *commit* to $S$ as the appropriate way of achieving goal $G$. So, if $S$ were then to fail, we would consider goal $G$ as having failed. A consequence is that we would not look for other ways of solving $T$, nor would we look for other clauses with $G$ as the head.

In PROLOG, this type of test/fail control is specified with the *cut symbol*, "!". Notationally, we would have a PROLOG clause that looks like this:

```
G :- T₁, T₂, ..., Tₘ, !, G₁, G₂, ..., Gₙ.
```

which would tell the interpreter to try each of the goals in this order, but if all the $T_i$ succeed, to commit to the $G_i$ as the only way of solving $G$.

A clear application of this construct is in the if–then–else construct of traditional programming languages. Consider, for example, defining a predicate $\text{Expt}(a, n, v)$ intended to hold when $v = a^n$. The obvious way of calculating $a^n$ (or reasoning about Expt goals) requires $n - 1$ multiplications. However, there is a much more efficient recursive method that only requires about $\log_2(n)$ multiplications: If $n$ is even, we continue recursively with $a^2$ and $n/2$ replacing $a$ and $n$, respectively; otherwise, if $n$ is odd, we continue recursively with $a^2$ and $(n - 1)/2$ and then multiply the result by $a$. In other words, we are imagining a recursive procedure with an if–then–else of the form

> **if** $n$ is even
> > **then** do one thing
> > **else** do another.

The details need not concern us, except to note the form of the clauses we would use to define the predicate:

$\text{Expt}(a, 0, 1)$

$\text{Expt}(a, n, v) \Leftarrow n > 0 \land \text{Even}(n) \land \text{Expt}(a^2, n/2, v)$

$\text{Expt}(a, n, v) \Leftarrow n > 0 \land \neg\text{Even}(n) \land$
$$\text{Expt}(a^2, (n - 1)/2, v') \land v = av'$$

The point of this example is that we need to use slightly different methods based on whether $n$ is even or odd. However, we would much prefer to test whether $n$ is even only once: We should attempt the goal $\text{Even}(n)$ and if it succeeds do one thing, if it fails do another. The goal $\neg Even(n)$ should in reality never be considered. A related but less serious consideration is the test for $n = 0$: If $n = 0$ we should commit to the first clause; we should not have to confirm that $n > 0$ in the other two clauses.

In PROLOG both of these concerns can be handled with the cut operator. We would end up with a PROLOG definition like this:

```
expt(A,0,V)  :- !, V=1.
expt(A,N,V)  :- even(N), !, ...what to do when n is even.
expt(A,N,V)  :- ...what to do when n is odd.
```

Note that we *commit* to the first clause when $n = 0$ regardless of the value of $a$ or $v$, but we only *succeed* when $v = 1$. Thus, while

```
expt(A,N,V)  :- N=0, !, V=1.
```

is correct and equivalent to the first clause,

```
expt(A,0,1)  :- !.
```

would be incorrect. In general, we can see that something like

```
G :- P, !, R.
G :- S.
```

is logically equivalent to "if $P$ holds then $R$ implies $G$, and if $\neg P$ holds then $S$ implies $G$," but that it only considers the $P$ once.

A less algorithmic example of the use of the cut operator might be to define a NumberOfParents predicate: For Adam and Eve, the number of parents is 0, but for everyone else, it is 2:

```
numberOfParents(adam,V)  :- !, V=0.
numberOfParents(eve,V)   :- !, V=0.
numberOfParents(P,2).
```

In this case, we do not need to confirm in the third clause that the person in question is not Adam or Eve.

## 6.6 CONTROLLING BACKTRACKING

Another application of the PROLOG cut operator involves control of back-tracking on failure. At certain points in a proof we can have an idea of which steps might be fruitful and which steps will come to nothing and waste resources in the process.

Imagine, for example, that we are trying to show that Jane is an American cousin of Billy. Two individuals can be considered to be (first) cousins if they share a grandparent but are not siblings:

$$\text{Cousin}(x,y) \Leftarrow (x \neq y) \wedge \neg\text{Sibling}(x,y) \wedge \text{GParent}(z,x) \wedge \text{GParent}(z,y)$$

Suppose that in trying to show that Jane is an American cousin of Billy, we find that Henry is a grandparent of both of them, but that Jane is not American. The question is what happens now. If it turns out that Elizabeth is also a grandparent of both Jane and Billy, we will find this second $z$ on backtracking and end up testing whether Jane is American a second time. This will of course fail once more, because nothing has changed.

What this example shows is that on failure we need to avoid trying to redo a goal that was not part of the reason we are failing. It was not the choice of grandparent that caused the trouble here, so there is no point in reconsidering it. Yet this is precisely what PROLOG backtracking would do.[2] To get the effect we want in PROLOG, we would need to represent our goal as

```
cousin(jane,billy), !, american(jane)
```

In other words, once we have found a way to show that Jane is a cousin of Billy (no matter how), we should commit to whatever result comes out of checking that she is American.

As a second example of controlling backtracking, consider the following definition of membership in a list:

$$\text{Member}(x,l) \Leftarrow \text{FirstElement}(x,l)$$

$$\text{Member}(x,l) \Leftarrow \text{RemainingElements}(l,l') \wedge \text{Member}(x,l')$$

with the auxiliary predicates FirstElement and RemainingElements defined in the obvious way. Now imagine that we are trying to establish that some object $a$ is an element of some (large) list $c$ and has property $Q$. That is, we have the goal

$$\text{Member}(a,c) \wedge Q(a).$$

If the Member$(a,c)$ subgoal were to succeed but $Q(a)$ fail, it would be silly to reconsider Member$(a,c)$ to see if $a$ also occurs later in the list. In PROLOG, we can control this by using the goal

```
member(a,C), !, q(a).
```

---

[2]A more careful but time-consuming version of backtracking (called *dependency-directed* backtracking) avoids the redundant steps here automatically.

More generally, if we know that the Member predicate will only be used to test for membership in a list (and not to generate elements of a list), we can use a PROLOG definition like this:

```
member(X,L) :- firstElement(X,L), !.
member(X,L) :- remainingElements(L,L1), member(X,L1).
```

This guarantees that once a membership goal succeeds (in the first clause) by finding a sublist whose first element is the item in question, the second clause, which looks farther down the list, will never be reconsidered on failure of a later goal. For example, if we had a list of our friends and some goal needed to check that someone (e.g., George) was both a friend and rich, we could simply write

```
member(george,Friends), rich(george).
```

without having to worry about including a cut. The definition of Member assures us that once an element is found in the list, if a subsequent test like Rich fails, we won't go back to see if that element occurs somewhere later in the list and try the failed test again.

## 6.7 NEGATION AS FAILURE

Perhaps the most interesting idea to come out of the study of the procedural control of reasoning is the concept of *negation as failure*. Procedurally, we can distinguish between two types of "negative" situations with respect to a goal $G$:

- being able to solve the goal $\neg G$; or
- being unable to solve the goal $G$.

In the latter case, we may not be able to find a fact or rule in the KB asserting that $G$ is false, but we may have run out of options in trying to show that $G$ is true. In general, we would like to be able to tell a reasoner what it should do after failing to prove a goal.

We begin by introducing a new type of goal, **not**($G$), which is understood to succeed when the goal $G$ fails and to fail when the goal $G$ succeeds (quite apart from the status of $\neg G$). In PROLOG, **not** behaves as if it were defined like this:

| | |
|---|---|
| **not**($G$) :- $G$, !, fail. | % fail if $G$ succeeds |
| **not**($G$). | % otherwise succeed |

This type of negation as failure is only useful when failure is *finite*. If attempting to prove $G$ results in an infinite branch with an infinite set of resolvents to try, then we cannot expect a goal of **not**($G$) to terminate either. However, if there are no more resolvents to try in a proof, then **not**($G$) will succeed.

Negation as failure is especially useful in situations where the collection of facts and the rules express complete knowledge about some predicate. If, for example, we have an entire family represented in a KB, we could define in PROLOG

```
noChildren(X) :- not(parent(X,Y)).
```

We know that someone has no children if we cannot find any in the database. With incomplete knowledge, on the other hand, we could fail to find any children in the database simply because we have not yet been told of any.

Another situation where negation as failure is useful is when we have a complete method for computing the complement of a predicate we care about. For example, if we have a rule for determining if a number is prime, we would not need to construct another one to show that a number is not prime; instead, we can use negation as failure:

```
composite(N) :- N > 1, not(primeNumber(N)).
```

In this case, failure to prove that a number greater than 1 is prime is sufficient to conclude that the number is composite.

Declaratively, **not** has the same reading as conventional negation, except when new variables appear in the goal. For example, the PROLOG clause for Composite can be read as saying that

for every number $n$, if $n > 1$ and $n$ is not a prime number,
then $n$ is composite.

However, the clause for NoChildren before that should not be read as saying that

for every $x$ and $y$, if $x$ is not a parent of $y$, then $x$ has no children.

For example, suppose that the goal Parent(sue, jim) succeeds, but that the goal Parent(sue, george) fails. Although we do want to conclude that Sue is not a parent of George, we do not want to conclude that she has no children. Logically, the rule needs to be read as

for every $x$, if for every $y$, $x$ is not a parent of $y$, then $x$ has no children.

Note that the quantifier for the new variable $y$ in the goal has moved inside the scope of the "if."

## 6.8  DYNAMIC DATABASES

In this chapter we have considered a KB consisting of a collection of ground atomic facts about the world and universally quantified rules defining new predicates. Because our most basic knowledge is expressed by the elementary facts, we can think of them as a database representing a snapshot of the world. It is natural, then, as properties of the world change over time, to think of reflecting these changes with additions and deletions to the database. The removed facts are a reflection of things that are no longer true, and the added facts are a reflection of things that have newly become true.

With this more dynamic view of the database, it is useful to consider three different procedural interpretations for a basic rule like $Parent(x, y) \Leftarrow Mother(x, y)$:

1. *if-needed*: Whenever we have a goal matching $Parent(x, y)$, we can solve it by solving $Mother(x, y)$. This is ordinary backward chaining. Procedurally, we wait to make the connection between mothers and parents until we need to prove something about parents.

2. *if-added*: Whenever a fact matching $Mother(x, y)$ is added to the database, we also add $Parent(x, y)$ to the database. This is forward chaining. In this case, the connection between mothers and parents is made as soon as we learn about a new mother relationship. A proof of a parent relationship would then be more immediate, but at the cost of the space needed to store facts that may never be used.

3. *if-removed*: Whenever something matching $Parent(x, y)$ is removed from the database, we should also remove $Mother(x, y)$. This is the dual of the *if-added* case, but there is a more subtle issue here. If the *only* reason we have a parent relationship in the database is because of the mother relationship, then if we remove that mother relationship, we should remove the parent one as well. To do this properly, we would need to keep track of *dependencies* in the database.

Interpretation (1) is of course the mainstay of PROLOG; interpretations (2) and (3) suggest the use of *demons*, which are procedures that actively monitor the database and trigger—or *fire*—when certain conditions are met. There can be more than one such demon matching a given change to the database, and each demon may end up further changing the database, causing still more demons to fire, in a pattern of spreading activation. This type of processing underlies the production systems of Chapter 7.

### 6.8.1 The PLANNER Approach

The practical implications of giving the user more direct control over the reasoning process have led over the years to the development of a set of programming languages based on ideas like the ones we have covered here. The PROLOG language is of course well known, but only covers some of these possibilities. A LISP-based language called PLANNER was invented at about the same time as PROLOG, and was designed specifically to give the user fine-grained control of a theorem-proving process.

The main ideas in PLANNER relevant to our discussion here are as follows:[3]

- The knowledge base of a PLANNER application is a database of facts, expressed in a notation like (Mother susan john) and (Person john).

- The rules of the system are formulated as a collection of *if-needed*, *if-added*, and *if-removed* procedures, each consisting of a *pattern* for invocation (e.g., (Mother $x$ $y$)) and a *body*, which is a program statement to execute once the invocation pattern is matched.

- Each program statement can succeed or fail:
  - (**goal** $p$), (**assert** $p$), and (**erase** $p$) specify, respectively, that a goal should be established (proven or made true), that a new fact should be added to the database, and that an old fact should be removed from the database;
  - (**and** $s_1 \ldots s_n$), where the $s_i$ are program statements, is considered to succeed if all the $s_i$ succeed, allowing for backtracking among them;
  - (**not** $s$) is negation as failure;
  - (**for** $p$ $s$) says to perform program statement $s$ for every way goal $p$ succeeds;
  - (**finalize** $s$) is similar to the PROLOG cut operator;
  - a lot more, including all of LISP.

Here is a simple PLANNER example:

> (**proc if-needed** (clearTable)
>     (**for** (on $x$ table)
>         (**and** (**erase** (on $x$ table)) (**goal** (putaway $x$)))))

> (**proc if-removed** (on $x$ $y$) (**print** $x$ "is no longer on" $y$))

The first procedure is invoked whenever the goal clearTable needs to be true, that is, in the blocks world of this example, whenever the table needs

---

[3]We are simplifying the original syntax somewhat.

to be free of objects. To solve this goal, for each item found on the table we remove the statement in the database that reflects its being on the table and solve the goal of putting that item away somewhere. We do not show here how those goals are solved, but presumably each putaway goal could trigger an action by a robot arm to put the item somewhere not on the table and subsequently to assert the new location in the database. The second procedure just alerts the user to a change in the database, printing a statement that the item is no longer on the surface it was removed from.

The type of program considered in PLANNER suggests an interesting shift in perspective on knowledge representation and reasoning. Instead of thinking of solving a goal as proving that a condition is logically entailed by a collection of facts and rules, we think of it as *making conditions hold*, using some combination of forward and backward chaining. This is the first harbinger of the use of a representation scheme to support the execution of *plans*; hence the name of the language.[4] We also see a shift away from rules with a clear logical interpretation (as universally quantified conditionals) toward arbitrary procedures, and specifically, arbitrary operations over a database of facts. These operations can correspond to deductive reasoning, but they need not. Although PLANNER itself is no longer used, we will see that this dynamic view of rules persists in the representation for production systems of the next chapter.[5]

## 6.9   BIBLIOGRAPHIC NOTES

The idea that logic could be used as the basis for a programming language is generally attributed to Kowalski and Colmerauer [259, p. 1]. The history of the development of logic programming is detailed in Kowalski [225] (see also Cohen [74] in the same issue). A good reference on the foundations of logic programming and PROLOG is Lloyd [259]. Hogger [188] also provides a good introduction. There are a number of textbooks on the PROLOG programming language, including Clocksin and Mellish [73], Covington et al. [80], Nilsson and Maluszynski [312], and Sterling and Shapiro [399]. The use of PROLOG in Artificial Intelligence is covered by Bratko [54] and Shoham [385].

For *definite logic programs* (consisting of clauses with exactly one atom in the head and no negation), the cut operator does not affect soundness but may lead to incompleteness. In *normal logic programs*, which may

---

[4]We will reconsider the issue of planning from a logical perspective in Chapter 15.
[5]Users of the language eventually wanted even more control, and gravitated toward using its implementation language and some of its data structures.

have negation in the body of the clause, the cut operator may also affect soundness [259].

Negation as failure was first introduced by Clark [70]. It has been widely studied in the logic programming literature and several different types of semantics have been suggested for logic programs with negation as failure. These include stable model semantics [147], which forms the basis of *answer set programming* (see, for instance, Baral [24]), and the well-founded semantics [146].

There are many extensions to the PROLOG language and logic programming, including versions capable of dealing with concurrency and with parallelism. One interesting extension involves the solving of constraints, termed *constraint logic programming* [198, 199]. This has led to work on constraint databases [351] and more directly to constraint programming [269]. Volume 138 of the journal *Artificial Intelligence* [2] contains a special issue on knowledge representation and logic programming. Research on logic programming also influenced, and was influenced by, work on database management, leading to the development of *deductive databases*, which highlight the distinction between facts (the "extensional" part of the database) and rules (the "intensional" part). See [140] for an early survey of work in this area, and [291] for a more recent account.

The PLANNER language was proposed by Hewitt [186] and portions of the language were implemented by Sussman and Winograd [404]. Many variants were also implemented (mostly at MIT), including CONNIVER [403] and AMORD [96]. Winograd discusses procedural representations more generally in [426].

## 6.10 EXERCISES

The exercises here all concern generalizing Horn derivations to incorporate negation as failure. For these questions, assume that a KB consists of a list of rules of the form $(q \leftarrow a_1, \ldots, a_n)$ where $n \geq 0$, $q$ is an atom, and each $a_i$ is either of the form $p$ or **not**$(p)$, where $p$ is an atom. The $q$ in this case is called the conclusion of the rule, and the $a_i$ make up the antecedent of the rule.

1. The forward-chaining procedure presented in Chapter 5 for Horn clause satisfiability can be extended to handle negation as failure by marking atoms incrementally with either a Y (when they are known to be solved), or with an N (when they are known to be unsolvable), using the following procedure:

For any unmarked atom $q$,

- if there is a rule $(q \leftarrow a_1, \ldots, a_n) \in$ KB, where all the positive $a_i$ are marked Y and all the negative $a_i$ are marked N, then mark $q$ with Y;
- if for every rule $(q \leftarrow a_1, \ldots, a_n) \in$ KB, some positive $a_i$ is marked N or some negative $a_i$ is marked Y, then mark $q$ with N.

Note that the first case trivially applies for rules where $n = 0$, and that the second case trivially applies if there are no rules with $q$ as the conclusion.

(a) Show how the procedure would label the atoms in the following KB:

```
a ←
b ← a
c ← b
d ← not(c)
e ← c, g
f ← d, e
f ← not(b), g
g ← not(h), not(f)
```

(b) Give an example of a KB where this procedure fails to label an atom as either Y or N, but where the atom is intuitively Y, according to negation as failure.

(c) A KB is defined to be *strongly stratified* if and only if there is a function $f$ from atoms to numbers such that for every rule $(q \leftarrow a_1, \ldots, a_n) \in$ KB, and for every $1 \le i \le n$, it is the case that $f(q) > f(a_i)$, where $f(\mathbf{not}(p_i)) = f(p_i)$. (In other words, the conclusion of a rule is always assigned a higher number than any atom used positively or negatively in the antecedent of the rule.) Is the example KB of part (a) strongly stratified?

(d) Prove by induction that this procedure will label every atom of a strongly stratified KB.

(e) Alternately, a KB is defined to be *weakly stratified* if and only if there is a function $g$ from atoms to numbers such that for every rule $(q \leftarrow a_1, \ldots, a_n) \in$ KB, and for every $1 \le i \le n$, $g(q) \ge g(a_i)$, where in this case, $g(\mathbf{not}(p_i)) = 1 + g(p_i)$. (In other words, the conclusion of a rule is always assigned a number no lower than any atom used positively in the antecedent of the rule, and higher than any atom used negatively in the antecedent of the rule.) Is the example KB of part (a) weakly stratified?

(f) Give an example of a weakly stratified KB where the procedure fails to label an atom.

(g) Assume you are given a KB that is weakly stratified and you are also given the function $g$ in question. Sketch a forward-chaining procedure that uses the $g$ to label every atom in the KB either Y or N.

2. Write, test, and document a program that performs the forward chaining of the previous question and that runs in linear time, relative to the size of the input. You should use data structures inspired by those of Exercise 1 of Chapter 5. Include in the documentation an argument as to why your program runs in linear time. Show that your program works properly on at least the KB of the previous question.

3. There are many ways of making negation as failure precise, but one way is as follows: We try to find a set of "negative assumptions" we can make, $\{\mathbf{not}(q_1), \ldots, \mathbf{not}(q_n)\}$, such that if we were to add these to the KB and use ordinary logical reasoning (now treating a $\mathbf{not}(p)$ as if it were a new atom unrelated to $p$), the set of atoms we could *not* derive would be exactly $\{q_1, \ldots, q_n\}$.

   More precisely, we define a sequence of sets as follows:

   $$N_0 = \{\}$$
   $$N_{k+1} = \{\mathbf{not}(q) \mid KB \cup N_k \not\models q\}$$

   The reasoning procedure then is this: We calculate the $N_k$, and if the sequence converges, that is, if $N_{k+1} = N_k$ for some $k$, then we consider any atom $p$ such that $\mathbf{not}(p) \notin N_k$ to be derivable by negation as failure.

   (a) Show how this procedure works on the KB of Exercise 1, by giving the values of $N_k$.

   (b) Give an example of a KB where the procedure does not terminate.

   (c) Explain why the procedure does the right thing for KBs that are pure Horn, that is, do not contain the **not** operator.

   (d) Suppose a KB is weakly stratified with respect to $g$, as defined in Exercise 1. For any pair of natural numbers $k$ and $r$, define $N(k, r)$ by

   $$N(k, r) = \{\mathbf{not}(q) \in N_k \mid g(q) < r\}.$$

   It can be shown that for any $k$ and any atom $p$ where $g(p) = r$

   $$KB \cup N_k \models p \quad \text{iff} \quad KB \cup N(k, r) \models p.$$

In other words, for a weakly stratified KB, when trying to prove $p$, we need only consider negative assumptions whose $g$ value is lower than $p$. Use this fact to prove that for any $k$ and $r$ where $r < k$, $N(k + 1, r) = N(k + 2, r)$. *Hint*: Prove this by induction on $k$. In the induction step, this will require assuming the claim for $k$ (which is that for any $r < k$, $N(k + 1, r) = N(k + 2, r)$) and then proving the claim for $k + 1$ (which is that for any $r < k + 1$, $N(k + 2, r) = N(k + 3, r)$.)

(e) Use part (d) to conclude that this negation as failure reasoning procedure always terminates for a KB that is weakly stratified.

# CHAPTER 7

# RULES IN PRODUCTION SYSTEMS

■

■

■

We have seen from our work on Horn clauses and procedural systems in previous chapters that the concept of an if–then conditional or rule—if *P* is true then *Q* is true—is central to knowledge representation. Whereas the semantics of the logical formula $(P \supset Q)$ is simple and clear, it suggests that a rule of this sort is no more than a form of disjunction: Either *P* is false or *Q* is true. However, as we saw in Chapter 6, from a reasoning point of view we can look at these rules in different ways. In particular, a rule can be understood procedurally as either

- moving from assertions of *P* to assertions of *Q*, or
- moving from goals of *Q* to goals of *P*.

We can think of these two cases this way:

$$(\textbf{assert } P) \Rightarrow (\textbf{assert } Q)$$

$$(\textbf{goal } Q) \Rightarrow (\textbf{goal } P).$$

Although both of these arise from the same connection between *P* and *Q*, they emphasize the difference between focusing on asserting facts and seeking the satisfaction of goals. We usually call the two types of reasoning that they suggest

- *data-directed reasoning*, that is, reasoning from *P* to *Q*, and
- *goal-directed reasoning*, that is, reasoning from *Q* to *P*.

Data-directed reasoning might be most appropriate in a database-like setting, when assertions are made and it is important to follow the implications of those assertions. Goal-directed reasoning might be most appropriate in a problem-solving situation, where a desired result is clear and the means to achieve that result—the logical foundations for a conclusion—are sought.

Quite separately, we can also distinguish the mechanical direction of the computation. Forward-chaining computations follow the "⇒" in the forward direction, independent of the emphasis on assertion or goal. Backward-chaining reasoning goes in the other direction. While the latter is almost always oriented toward goal-directed reasoning and the former toward data-directed reasoning, these associations are not exclusive. For example, using the notation of Chapter 6, we might imagine procedures of the following sort:

- (**proc if-added** (myGoal $Q$) ... (**assert** (myGoal $P$)) ...)
- (**proc if-needed** (myAssert $P$) ... (**goal** (myAssert $Q$)) ...)

In the former case, we use forward chaining to do a form of goal-directed reasoning: (myGoal $Q$) is a formula to be read as saying that $Q$ is a goal; if this is ever asserted (that is, if we ever find out that $Q$ is indeed a goal), we might then assert that $P$ is also a goal. In a complementary way, the latter case illustrates a way to use backward chaining to do a form of data-directed reasoning: (myAssert $P$) is a formula to be read as saying that $P$ is an assertion in the database; if this is ever a goal (that is, if we ever want to assert $P$ in the database), we might then also have the goal of asserting $Q$ in the database. This latter example suggests how it is possible, for example, to do data-directed reasoning in PROLOG, a backward-chaining system.

In the rest of this chapter, we examine a new formalism, *production systems*, that is used extensively in practical applications and emphasizes forward chaining over rules as a way of reasoning. We will see examples where the reasoning is data-directed, and others where it is goal-directed. Applications built using production systems are often called *rule-based systems* as a way of highlighting the emphasis on rules in the underlying knowledge representation.

## 7.1  PRODUCTION SYSTEMS: BASIC OPERATION

A *production system* is a forward-chaining reasoning system that uses rules of a certain form called *production rules* (or simply, *productions*) as its representation of general knowledge.[1] A production system keeps

---

[1] Many variants have been proposed; the version we present here is representative.

an ongoing memory of assertions in what is called its *working memory* (WM). The WM is like a database, but more volatile; it is constantly changing during the operation of the system.

A *production rule* is a two-part structure comprising an *antecedent* set of *conditions* and a *consequent* set of *actions*. We usually write a rule in this form:

IF *conditions* THEN *actions*

The antecedent conditions are tests to be applied to the current state of the WM. The consequent actions are a set of actions that modify the WM.

The basic operation of a production system is a *cycle* of three steps that repeats until no more rules are applicable to the WM, at which point the system halts. The three parts of the cycle are as follows:

1. *recognize*: find which rules are applicable, that is, those rules whose antecedent conditions are satisfied by the current working memory;

2. *resolve conflict*: among the rules found in the first step (called a *conflict set*), choose which of the rules should "fire," that is, get a chance to execute;

3. *act*: change the working memory by performing the consequent actions of all the rules selected in the second step.

As stated, this cycle repeats until no more rules can fire.

## 7.2  WORKING MEMORY

Working memory is composed of a set of *working memory elements* (WMEs). Each WME is a tuple of the form,

(*type attribute$_1$: value$_1$ ... attribute$_n$: value$_n$*),

where *type*, *attribute$_i$*, and *value$_i$* are all atoms. Here are some examples of WMEs:

■  (person  age: 27  home: toronto)

■  (goal  task: putDown  importance: 5  urgency: 1)

■  (student  name: john  department: computerScience)

Declaratively, we understand each WME as an existential sentence:

$$\exists x\,[\,type(x) \wedge attribute_1(x) = value_1 \wedge attribute_2(x) = value_2 \wedge \ldots$$
$$\wedge\ attribute_n(x) = value_n\,].$$

Note that the individual about whom the assertion is made is not explicitly identified in a WME. If we choose to do so, we can identify individuals by using an attribute that is expected to be unique for the individual. For example, we might use a WME of the form (person identifier: 777-55-1234 name: janeDoe ...). Note also that the order of attributes in a WME is not significant.

These example WMEs represent objects in an obvious way. Relationships among objects can be handled by reification.[2] For example, something like

(basicFact relation: olderThan firstArg: john secondArg: mary)

might be used to say that John is older than Mary.

## 7.3  PRODUCTION RULES

As mentioned, the antecedent of a production rule is a set of conditions. If there is more than one condition, they are understood conjunctively, that is, they all have to be true for the rule to be applicable. Each condition can be positive or negative (negative conditions will be expressed as $-cond$), and the body of each is a tuple of this form:

$$(type \; attribute_1: specification_1 \; ... \; attribute_k: specification_k),$$

where each specification is one of the following:

- ▪ an atom,
- ▪ a variable,
- ▪ an evaluable expression, within "[ ],"
- ▪ a test, within "{ },"
- ▪ the conjunction ($\wedge$), disjunction ($\vee$), or negation ($\neg$) of a specification.

Here are two examples of rule conditions:

$$(person \; age: [n + 4] \; occupation: x)$$

This condition is satisfied if there is a WME whose type is person and whose age attribute is exactly $n + 4$, where $n$ is specified elsewhere.

---

[2]The technique of encoding $n$-ary relationships using reified objects and a collection of unary functions was discussed in Section 3.7.

The result binds the occupation value to $x$, if $x$ is not already bound; if $x$ is already bound, then the occupation value in the WME needs to be the same as the value of $x$.

$$-(\text{person} \ \ \text{age:} \{< 23 \land > 6\})$$

This condition is satisfied if there is *no* WME in the WM whose type is person and whose age value is between 6 and 23.

Now we can be more precise about the applicability of rules: A rule is considered applicable if there are values for all the variables in the rule such that all the antecedent conditions are satisfied by the current WM. A positive condition is satisfied if there is a matching WME in the WM; a negative condition is satisfied if there is no matching WME. A WME matches a condition if the types are identical and for each attribute/specification pair mentioned in the condition there is a corresponding attribute/value pair in the WME, where the value matches the specification (under the given assignment of variables) in the obvious way. The matching WME may have attributes that are not mentioned in the condition.

Note that for a negated condition there must be no element in the entire WM that matches it. This interpretation is negation as failure, as in PROLOG-type systems (see Chapter 5). We do not need to prove that such a WME could never exist in WM—it just has to be the case that no matching WME can be found at the time the rule is checked for applicability.

The consequent sides of production rules are treated a little differently. They have a strictly procedural interpretation, all of the actions in the consequent are to be executed in sequence, and each action is one of the following:

- ADD *pattern*: this means that a new WME specified by *pattern* is added directly to the WM.

- REMOVE $i$: $i$ is an integer, and this means to remove (completely) from WM the WME that matched the $i$-th condition in the antecedent of the rule. This construct is not applicable if that condition was negative.

- MODIFY $i$ (*attribute specification*): this means to modify the WME that matched the $i$-th condition in the antecedent by replacing its current value for *attribute* by *specification*. MODIFY is also not applicable to negative conditions.

Note that in the ADD and MODIFY actions, any variables that appear refer to the values obtained when matching the antecedent of the rule. For example, the following rule might be used in an ordinary logical reasoning situation:

```
IF (student name: x) THEN ADD (person name: x)
```

In other words, if there is a WME of type student, with any name (and bind that name to $x$), then add to WM an element of type person with the same name. This is a production rule version of the conditional $\forall x$ (Student($x$) $\supset$ Person($x$)), here used in a data-directed way. This conditional could also be handled in a very different way with a user-defined assertion type and a rule like this:

```
IF   (assertion predicate: student)
THEN  MODIFY 1 (predicate person)
```

In this case, we lose the original fact stated in terms of student and replace it with one using the predicate person.

The following example implements a simple database update. It assumes that some rule has added a WME of type birthday to the WM at the right time:

```
IF   (person age: x name: n) (birthday who: n)
THEN MODIFY 1 (age [x + 1])
     REMOVE 2
```

Note that when the WME with the person's age is changed, the birthday WME is removed, so that the rule will not fire a second time.

The REMOVE action is also used on occasion to deal with control information. We might use a WME of type control to indicate what phase of a computation we are in. This can be initialized in the following way:

```
IF   (starting)
THEN  REMOVE 1
      ADD   (control phase: 1)
```

We could subsequently change phases of control with something like this:

```
IF   (control phase: x) ... other appropriate conditions ...
THEN  MODIFY 1 (phase [x + 1])
```

## 7.4  A FIRST EXAMPLE

In order to illustrate a production system in action, we consider the following task. We have three bricks, each of different size, sitting in a heap. We have three identifiable positions in which we want to place the bricks with a robotic "hand"; call these positions 1, 2, and 3. Our goal is to place the bricks in those positions in order of their size, with the largest in position 1 and the smallest in position 3.

Assume that when we begin, working memory has the following elements:

(counter value: 1)

(brick name: A size: 10 position: heap)

(brick name: B size: 30 position: heap)

(brick name: C size: 20 position: heap)

In this case, the desired outcome is brick B in position 1, brick C in position 2, and brick A in position 3.

We can achieve our goal with two production rules that work with any number of bricks. The first one will place the largest currently available brick in the hand, and the other one will place the brick currently in the hand into the next position, going through the positions sequentially:

1. IF (brick position: heap name: $n$ size: $s$)

   $-$(brick position: heap size: $\{> s\}$)

   $-$(brick position: hand)

   THEN MODIFY 1 (position hand)

   In other words, if there is a brick in the heap, and there is no bigger brick in the heap, and there is nothing currently in the hand, put the brick in the hand.

2. IF (brick position: hand)

   (counter value: $i$)

   THEN  MODIFY 1 (position $i$)

   MODIFY 2 (value $[i + 1]$)

   When there is a brick in the hand, this rule places it in the next position in sequence given by the counter, and increments the counter.

In this example, no conflict resolution is necessary, because only one rule can fire at a time: The second rule requires there to be a brick in the hand, and the first rule requires there to be none.

It is fairly simple to trace the series of rule firings and actions in this example. Recall that when we start, all bricks are in the heap and none are in the hand. The counter is initially set to 1.

1. Rule 2 is not applicable, since no brick is in the hand. Rule 1 attempts to match each of the three WMEs of type brick in WM, but only succeeds for brick B, because it is the only one for which no larger brick exists in the heap. When Rule 1 matches, $n$ is bound to B and $s$ to 30. The result of this rule's firing, then, is the modification of the brick B WME to be the following:

   (brick  name: B  size: 30  position: hand)

2. Now that there is a brick in the hand, Rule 1 cannot fire. Rule 2 is applicable, with $i$ being bound to 1. Rule 2's firing results in two modifications, one to the brick B WME (position now becomes 1) and one to the counter WME:

   (brick  name: B  size: 30  position: 1)

   (counter  value: 2)

3. Brick B no longer has its position as the heap, so now Rule 1 matches on brick C, whose position is modified as a result:

   (brick  name: C  size: 20  position: hand)

4. In a step similar to step 2, Rule 2 causes brick C to now be in position 2 and the counter to be reset to 3:

   (brick  name: C  size: 20  position: 2)

   (counter  value: 3)

5. Now A is the only brick left in the heap, so Rule 1 matches its WME and moves it to the hand:

   (brick  name: A  size: 10  position: hand)

6. Rule 2 fires again, this time moving brick A to position 3:

   (brick  name: A  size: 10  position: 3)

   (counter  value: 4)

7. Now that there are no bricks in either the heap or the hand, neither Rule 1 nor Rule 2 is applicable. The system halts, with the final configuration of WM as follows:

   (counter  value: 4)

   (brick  name: A  size: 10  position: 3)

   (brick  name: B  size: 30  position: 1)

   (brick  name: C  size: 20  position: 2)

## 7.5 A SECOND EXAMPLE

Next we look at an example of a slightly more complex computation that is easy to do with production systems; we present a set of rules that computes how many days there are in any given year. In this example, working memory will have two simple control elements in it. (wantDays year: $n$) will be our starting point and express the fact that our goal is to calculate the number of days in the year $n$. The WME (hasDays days: $m$) will express the result when the computation is finished. Finally, we will use a WME of type year to break the year down into its value *mod* 4, *mod* 100, and *mod* 400. Here are the five rules that capture the problem:

1. IF (wantDays year: $n$)
   THEN REMOVE 1
       ADD (year mod4: [$n\%4$] mod100: [$n\%100$] mod400: [$n\%400$])

2. IF (year mod400: 0)
   THEN REMOVE 1
       ADD (hasDays days: 366)

3. IF (year mod100: 0 mod400: {$\neq$ 0})
   THEN REMOVE 1
       ADD (hasDays days: 365)

4. IF (year mod4: 0 mod100: {$\neq$ 0})
   THEN REMOVE 1
       ADD (hasDays days: 366)

5. IF (year mod4: {$\neq$ 0})
   THEN REMOVE 1
       ADD (hasDays days: 365)

This rule set is structured in a typical way for goal-directed reasoning. The first rule initializes WM with the key values for a year that will lead to the calculation of the length of the year in days. Once it fires, it removes the wantDays WME and is never applicable again. Each of the other four rules check for their applicable conditions, and once one of them fires, it removes the year WME, so the entire system halts. Each antecedent expresses a condition that only it can match, so again no conflict resolution is needed. The order of the rules is also irrelevant.

It is easy to see how this rule set works. If the input is 2000, then we start with (wantDays year: 2000) in WM. The first rule fires, which then adds to WM the WME, (year mod4: 0 mod100: 0 mod400: 0). This matches only Rule 2, yielding (hasDays days: 366) at the end. If the input is 1900, the first rule adds the WME, (year mod4: 0 mod100: 0 mod400: 300), which then matches only Rule 3, for a value of 365. If the input is 1996, we get (year mod4: 0 mod100: 96 mod400: 396), which matches only Rule 4, for a value of 366.

## 7.6 CONFLICT RESOLUTION

Depending on whether we are doing data-directed reasoning or goal-directed reasoning, we may want to fire different numbers of rules in the case that more than one rule is applicable. In a data-directed context, we may want to fire all rules that are applicable, to get all consequences of a sentence added to working memory; in a goal-directed context, we may prefer to pursue only a single method at a time, and thus wish to fire only one rule.

In cases where we do want to eliminate some applicable rules, there are many *conflict resolution strategies* for arriving at the most appropriate rule(s) to fire. The most obvious one is to choose an applicable rule at random. Here are some other common approaches:

- *order*: Pick the first applicable rule in order of presentation. This is the type of strategy that PROLOG uses and is one of the most common ones. Production system programmers would take this strategy into account when formulating rule sets.

- *specificity*: Select the applicable rule whose conditions are most specific. One set of conditions is said to be more specific than another if the set of WMs that satisfy it is a subset of those that satisfy the other. For example, consider the three rules

  ```
  IF (bird) THEN ADD (canFly)
  IF (bird weight: {>100}) THEN ADD (cannotFly)
  IF (bird) (penguin) THEN ADD (cannotFly)
  ```

  Here the second and third rules are both more specific than the first. If we have a bird that is heavy or that is a penguin, then the first rule applies, but the others should take precedence. (Note that if the bird is a penguin *and* heavy, another conflict resolution criterion might still have to come into play to help decide between the second and third rules.)

- *recency*: Select an applicable rule based on how recently it has been used. There are different versions of this strategy, ranging from firing the rule that matches on the most recently created (or modified) WME to firing the rule that has been least recently used. The former could be used to make sure a problem solver stays focused on what it was just doing (typical of depth-first search); the latter would ensure that every rule gets a fair chance to influence the outcome (typical of breadth-first search).

- *refractoriness*: Do not select a rule that has just been applied with the same values of its variables. This prevents the looping behavior that results from firing a rule repeatedly because of the same WME. A variant forbids reusing a given rule–WME pair. Either the refractoriness can disappear automatically after a few cycles, or an explicit "refresh" mechanism can be used.

As implied in our penguin example, nontrivial rule systems often need to use more than one conflict resolution criterion. For example, the OPS5 production rule system uses the following criteria for selecting the rule to fire among those that are found to be applicable:

1. discard any rule that has just been used for the same values of variables;

2. order the remaining instances in terms of recency of WME matching the first condition, and then the second condition, and so on;

3. order the remaining rules by number of conditions;

4. if there is still a conflict, select arbitrarily among the remaining candidates.

One interesting approach to conflict resolution is provided by the SOAR system. This system is a general problem solver that attempts to find a path from a start state to a goal state by applying productions. It treats selecting which rule to fire as deciding what the system should do next. Thus, if unable to decide on which rule to fire at some point, SOAR sets up a new *metagoal* to solve, namely, the goal of selecting which rule to use, and the process iterates. When this metagoal is solved (which could in principle involve metametagoals, etc.), the system has made a decision about which base goal to pursue, and therefore the conflict is resolved.

## 7.7  MAKING PRODUCTION SYSTEMS MORE EFFICIENT

Early production systems, implemented in a straightforward way, ended up spending inordinate amounts of time (as much as 90%) in rule matching. Surprisingly, this remained true even when the matching was implemented using sophisticated indexing and hashing.

However, two key observations led to an implementation breakthrough: first, that the WM was modified only very slightly on each rule-firing cycle, and second, that many rules shared conditions. The idea behind what came to be called the RETE algorithm was to create a network from the rule antecedents. Because the rules in a production system do not change during its operation, this network could be computed in advance. During operation of the production system, "tokens" representing new or changed WMEs are passed incrementally through the network of tests. Tokens that make it all the way through the network on any given cycle are considered to satisfy all of the conditions of a rule. At each cycle, a new conflict set can then be calculated from the previous one and any incremental changes made to WM. This way, only a very small part of WM is rematched against any rule conditions, drastically reducing the time needed to calculate the conflict set.

A simple example will serve to illustrate. Consider a rule like the following (call it RULE23):

```
IF (person name:x age:{< 14} father:y)
   (person name:y occupation:doctor)
THEN...
```

This rule would cause the RETE network of Figure 7.1 to be created. The network has two types of nodes: *alpha* nodes, which represent simple, self-contained tests, and *beta* nodes, which take into account the fact that variables create constraints between different parts of an antecedent. Tokens for all new WMEs whose type was person would enter the network

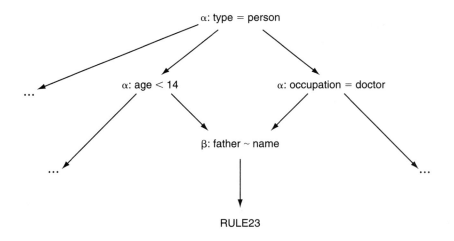

**▪ FIGURE 7.1**

A Sample RETE Network

at the topmost (alpha) node. If the age of the person was not known to be less than 14, or the person was not known to be a doctor, then the token would sit at the topmost node until one of the relevant attributes was modified by a rule. A person WME whose age was known to be less than 14 would pass down to the age alpha node; one whose occupation was doctor would pass to the other alpha node in the figure. In the case where a pair of WMEs residing at those alpha nodes also shared a common value between their respective father and name attributes, a token would pass through the lower beta node expressing the constraint, indicating that this rule was now applicable. For tokens left sitting in the network at the end of a cycle, any modifications to the corresponding WMEs would cause a reassessment, to see if they could pass further down the network, or combine with other WMEs at a beta node. Thus the work at each step is quite small and incremental.

## 7.8 APPLICATIONS AND ADVANTAGES

Production systems are a general computational framework, but one based originally on the observation that human experts appear to reason from "rules of thumb" in carrying out tasks. Systems based on the production system architecture were the first to attempt to model explicitly not only the knowledge that people have but also the *reasoning method* people use when performing mental tasks. Here, for example, is a production rule that suggests one step in the procedure a person might use in carrying out a subtraction:

```
IF (goal is: getUnitDigit)
    (minuend unit: d)
    (subtrahend unit: {> d})
THEN REMOVE 1
    ADD (goal is: borrowFromTens)
```

What was especially interesting to researchers in this area of psychology was the possibility of modeling the errors or misconceptions people might have in symbolic procedures of this sort.

Subsequently, what was originally a descriptive framework for psychological modeling was taken up in a more prescriptive fashion in what became known as *expert systems*. Expert systems, now a core technology in the field, use rules as a representation of knowledge for problems that ordinarily take human expertise to solve. But because human experts appear to reason from symptoms to causes in a heuristic fashion, production rules seem to be able to handle significant problems of great consequence, ranging from medical diagnosis to checking for credit-worthiness to configuration of complex products. We will look briefly at some of these rule-based systems in the next section.

There are many advantages claimed for production systems when applied to practical complex problems. Among the key advantages, the following are usually cited:

- *modularity*: In a production rule framework, each rule works independently of the others. This allows new rules to be added or old rules to be removed incrementally in a relatively easy fashion. This is especially useful for knowledge acquisition and for debugging.

- *fine-grained control*: Production systems have a very simple control structure. There are no complex goal or control stacks hidden in the implementation, among other things.

- *transparency*: Because rules are usually derived from expert knowledge or observation of expert behavior, they tend to use terminology that humans can resonate with. In contrast to formalisms like neural networks, the reasoning behavior of the system can be traced and explained in natural language, as discussed in Chapter 1.

In reality—especially when the systems get large and are used to solve complex problems—these advantages tend to wither. With hundreds or even thousands of rules, it is deceptive to think that rules can be added or removed with impunity. Often, more complex control structures than one might suppose are embedded in the elements of WM (remember attributes like phase and counter from earlier) and in very complex rule antecedents. But production rules have been used successfully on a very wide variety of practical problems, and are an essential element of every AI researcher's toolkit.

## 7.9  SOME SIGNIFICANT PRODUCTION RULE SYSTEMS

Given the many years that they have been used and the many problems to which they have been applied, there are many variants on the production system theme. While it is impossible to survey here even the most important developments in the area, one or two significant contributions are worth mentioning. Among other systems, work on MYCIN and XCON has influenced virtually all subsequent work in the area.

MYCIN was developed at Stanford University in the 1970s to aid physicians in the diagnosis of bacterial infections. After working with infectious disease specialists, the MYCIN team built a system with approximately 500 production rules for recognizing roughly 100 causes of infection. Although the system operated in the typical forward-chaining manner of production systems (using the recognize–resolve–act cycle we studied earlier), it performed its reasoning in a goal-directed fashion. Rules looked for symptoms in WM and used those symptoms to build evidence for certain hypotheses.

Here is a simplified version of a typical MYCIN rule:

IF
> the type of $x$ is primary bacteremia
> the suspected entry point of $x$ is the gastrointestinal tract
> the site of the culture of $x$ is one of the sterile sites

THEN
> there is evidence (0.8) that $x$ is bacteroides

MYCIN also introduced the use of other static data structures (not in WM) to augment the reasoning mechanism; these included things like lists of organisms and clinical parameters. But perhaps the most significant development was the introduction of a level of certainty in the accumulation of evidence and confidence in hypotheses. Because in medical diagnosis not all conclusions are obvious, and many diseases can produce the same symptoms, MYCIN worked by accumulating evidence and trying to ascertain what was the most likely hypothesis, given that evidence. The technical means for doing this was what were called *certainty factors*, which were numbers from $-1$ to 1 attached to the conclusions of rules; these allowed the rank ordering of alternative hypotheses. Because rules could introduce these numeric measures into working memory and newly considered evidence could change the confidence in various outcomes, MYCIN had to specify a set of combination rules for certainty factors. For example, the conjunction of two conclusions might take the minimum of the two certainty factors involved, and their disjunction might imply the maximum of the two.[3]

In a very different line of thinking, researchers at Carnegie-Mellon University produced an important rule-based system called XCON (originally called R1). The system was in use for many years at what was the Digital Equipment Corporation for configuring computers, starting with its VAX line of products. The most recent versions of the system had over 10,000 rules, covering hundreds of types of components. This system was the main stimulus for widespread commercial interest in rule-based expert systems. Substantial commercial development, including the formation of several new companies, has subsequently gone into the business of configuring complex systems, using the kind of technology pioneered by XCON.

---

[3]We address uncertainty and its relationship to other numerical means of combining evidence in Chapter 12.

Here is a simplified version of a typical XCON rule:

```
IF
        the context is doing layout and assigning a power supply
        an sbi module of any type has been put in a cabinet
        there is space available for the power supply
        there is no available power supply
        the voltage and frequency of the components are known
THEN
        add an appropriate power supply
```

XCON was the first rule-based system to segment a complex task into sections, or "contexts," to allow subsets of the very large rule base to work completely independently of one another. It broke the configuration task down into a number of major phases, each of which could proceed sequentially. Each rule would typically include a condition like (control phase: 6) to ensure that it was applicable to just one phase of the task. Then special *context-switching rules*, like the kind we saw at the end of Section 7.3, would be used to move from one phase of the computation to another. This type of framework allowed for more explicit emulation of standard control structures, although again, one should note that this type of architecture is not ideal for complex control scenarios.

While grouping rules into contexts is a useful way of managing the complexity of large knowledge bases, we now turn our attention to an even more powerful organizational principle, object orientation.

## 7.10 BIBLIOGRAPHIC NOTES

A good introduction to expert systems is provided by Jackson [196]; see also Waterman [421], and the collection by Hayes-Roth et al. [183]. Newell and Simon's *General Problem Solver* [306, 307] was an early, influential rule-based system. MYCIN is described by Shortliffe [386]. The R1 system (later renamed XCON) is described by McDermott [283, 284, 285]. Another early expert system is DENDRAL [60] (see also Lindsay et al. [257]). PROSPECTOR was introduced by Duda et al. [115].

General-purpose languages for building expert systems include OPS5 [59] and CLIPS [435]. OPS5 and its variants have had broad and extensive worldwide use. The RETE algorithm was designed by Forgy [134]. Apart from expert systems, it is used in the SOAR architecture [231].

As presented here, the rules of a production system are not allowed to change. The *ripple-down rules* [76] technique allows the rule base of an expert system to be incrementally modified and adapted (see also Kang et al. [209]).

## 7.11  EXERCISES

1. Consider the following strategy for playing tic-tac-toe:
   Put your mark in an available square that ranks the highest in the following list of descriptions:

   (i)   a square that gives you three in a row;
   (ii)  a square that would give your opponent three in a row;
   (iii) a square that is a double row for you;
   (iv)  a square that would be a double row for your opponent;
   (v)   a center square;
   (vi)  a corner square;
   (vii) any square.

   A double row square for a player is an available square that gives the player two in a row on two distinct lines (where the third square of each line is still available, obviously).

   (a) Encode this strategy as a set of production rules, and state what conflict resolution is assumed.

   Assumptions: To simplify matters, you may assume that there are elements in WM of the form (line sq1: $i$ sq2: $j$ sq3: $k$), for any three squares $i$, $j$, $k$, that form a straight line in any order. You may also assume that for each occupied square there is an element in WM of the form (occupied square: $i$ player: $p$) where $p$ is either X or 0. Finally, assume an element of the form (want-move player: $p$), that should be replaced once a move has been determined by something of the form (move player: $p$ square: $i$).

   (b) It is impossible to guarantee a win at tic-tac-toe, but it is possible to guarantee a draw. Describe a situation where your rule set fails to chose the right move to secure a draw.

   (c) Suggest a small addition to your rule set that is sufficient to guarantee a draw.

2. In the famous Towers of Hanoi problem, you are given three pegs, A, B, and C, and $n$ disks of different sizes with holes in them. Initially all the disks are located on peg A arranged in order, with the smallest one at the top. The problem is to get them all to peg C, but where only the top disk on a peg can be moved, a disk can only be moved from one peg to another, and at no time can a disk be placed on top of a smaller disk.

While this problem has an elegant recursive solution, it also has a less well known iterative solution, as follows: First, we arrange the pegs in a circle, so that clockwise we have A, B, C, and then A again. Following this, assuming we never move the same disk twice in a row, there will always only be one disk that can be legally moved, and we transfer it to the first peg it can occupy, moving in a clockwise direction, if $n$ is even, and counterclockwise, if $n$ is odd.

Write a collection of production rules that implement this procedure. Initially, the working memory will have elements (on peg: A disk: $i$), for each disk $i$, and an element (solve). When your rules stop firing, your working memory should contain (done) and (on peg: C disk: $i$), for each disk $i$.

3. This question concerns computing subtraction using a production system. Assume that WM initially contains information to deal with individual digits in the following form:

> (digitMinus top: $n$  bot: $m$  ans: $k$  borrow: $b$), where $n$ and $m$ are any digits, and if $n \geq m$, then $k$ is $n - m$ and $b$ is 0, else $k$ is $10 + n - m$ and $b$ is 1.

For example, (digitMinus top: 7 bot: 3 ans: 4 borrow: 0) would be in WM, as would (digitMinus top: 3 bot: 7 ans: 6 borrow: 1). The working memory also specifies the first and second arguments of a subtraction problem (the subtrahend and minuend):

> (topNum pos: $i$ digit: $d$ left: $j$) and (botNum pos: $i$ digit: $d$ left: $j$), where $d$ is a digit, and $i$ and $j$ are indices indicating the current position of the digit and its neighbor to the left, respectively.

For example, if the subtrahend were 465, the WM would contain

(topNum  pos: 0  digit: 5  left: 1)

(topNum  pos: 1  digit: 6  left: 2)

(topNum  pos: 2  digit: 4  left: 3)

Finally, the WM contains the goal (start). Your job is to write a collection of production rules that removes (start) and eventually stops with additional elements in WM of the form (ansNum pos: $i$ digit: $d$ left: $j$), indicating digit by digit what the answer to the subtraction is. Be sure to specify which conflict resolution strategy you are using; you may use any strategy described in the text. You may not use any arithmetic operators in your rules.

# CHAPTER 8

# OBJECT-ORIENTED REPRESENTATION

■

■

■

One property shared by all of the representation methods we have considered so far is that they are *flat*: Each piece of representation is self-contained and can be understood independently of any other. Recall that when we discussed logical representations in Chapter 3, we observed that information about a given object we might care about could be scattered among any number of seemingly unrelated sentences. With production system rules and the procedures in procedural systems, we have the corresponding problem: Knowledge about a given object or type of object could be scattered around the knowledge base.

As the number of sentences or procedures in a KB grows, it becomes critical to organize them in some way. As we have seen, in a production system, rule sets can be organized by their context of application, but this is primarily a control structure convenience for grouping items by when they might execute. A more representationally motivated approach would be to group facts or rules in terms of the kinds of *objects* they pertain to. Indeed, it is very natural to think of knowledge itself not as a mere collection of sentences, but rather as structured and organized in terms of what the knowledge is *about*, the objects of knowledge. In this chapter, we will examine a procedural knowledge representation formalism that is object-oriented in this way.

## 8.1 OBJECTS AND FRAMES

The objects that we care about range far and wide, from physical objects like houses and people, to more conceptual objects like courses and trips, and even to reified abstractions like events and relations. Each of these types of object has its own *parts*, some physical (roof, doors, rooms, fixtures, etc.; arms, torso, head, etc.), and some more abstract (course title, teacher, students, meeting time, etc.; destination, conveyance, departure date, etc.). The parts are constrained in various ways: The roof has to be connected to the walls in a certain way, the departure date and the first leg of a trip have to be related, and so on. The constraints between the parts might be expressed procedurally, such as by the registration procedure that connects a student to a course, or the procedure for reserving an airline seat that connects the second leg of a trip to the first. Also, some types of objects might have procedures of other sorts that are crucial to our understanding of them: procedures for recognizing bathrooms in houses, for reserving hotel rooms on trips, and so on. In general, in a procedural object-oriented representation system, we consider the kinds of reasoning operations that are relevant for the various types of objects in our application, and we design procedures to deal with them.

In one of the more seminal papers in the history of knowledge representation, Marvin Minsky in 1975 suggested the idea of using object-oriented groups of procedures to recognize and deal with new situations. Minsky used the term *frame* for the data structure used to represent these situations. Although the original intended application of frames as a knowledge representation was for recognition, the idea of grouping related procedures in this way for reasoning has much wider applicability. Among its more natural applications we might find the kind of relationship recognition common in story understanding, data monitoring in which we look for key situations to arise, and propagation and enforcement of constraints in planning tasks.

## 8.2    A BASIC FRAME FORMALISM

To examine the way frames can be used for reasoning, it will help us to have a formal representation language to express their structure. For the sake of discussion, we will keep the language simple, although extremely elaborate frame languages have been developed.

### 8.2.1    Generic and Individual Frames

For our purposes, there are two types of frames: *individual frames*, used to represent single objects, and *generic frames*, used to represent categories or classes of objects. An individual frame is a named list of "buckets" into which values can be dropped. The buckets are called *slots*, and the items that go into them are called *fillers*. Individual frames are similar to the working memory elements of production systems seen in Chapter 7. Schematically, an individual frame looks like this:

(*Frame-name*
    <*slot-name1 filler1*>
    <*slot-name2 filler2*>
    ...)

The frame and slot names are atomic symbols; the fillers are either atomic values (like numbers or strings) or the names of other individual frames.

Notationally, the names of generic frames appear here capitalized, while individual frames will be in uncapitalized mixed case. Slot names will be capitalized and prefixed with a ":". For example, we might have the following frames:

(tripLeg123
    <**:INSTANCE-OF** TripLeg>
    <:Destination toronto> ...)

(toronto
    <**:INSTANCE-OF** CanadianCity>
    <:Province ontario>
    <:Population 4.5M> ...)

Individual frames also have a special distinguished slot called **:INSTANCE-OF**, whose filler is the name of a generic frame indicating the category of the object being represented. We say that the individual frame is an *instance* of the generic one, so, in the example, toronto is an instance of CanadianCity.

Generic frames, in their simplest form, have a syntax that is similar to individual frames:

(CanadianCity
    <**:IS-A** City>
    <:Province CanadianProvince>
    <:Country canada>)

In this case, slot fillers are the names of either generic frames (like CanadianProvince) or individual ones (like canada). Instead of an **:INSTANCE-OF** slot, generic frames can have a distinguished slot called **:IS-A**, whose filler is the name of a more general generic frame. We say that the generic frame is a *specialization* of the more general one, for example, CanadianCity is a specialization of City.

Slots of generic frames can also have *attached procedures*. In the simple case we consider here, there are two types, **IF-ADDED** and **IF-NEEDED**, which are object-oriented versions of the if-added and if-needed procedures from Chapter 6. The syntax is illustrated in these examples:

```
(Table
    <:Clearance [IF-NEEDED ComputeClearanceFromLegs]> ...)

(Lecture
    <:DayOfWeek WeekDay>
    <:Date [IF-ADDED ComputeDayOfWeek]> ...)
```

Note that a slot can have both a filler and an attached procedure in the same frame.

## 8.2.2    Inheritance

As we will see, much of the reasoning that is done with a frame system involves creating individual instances of generic frames, filling some of the slots with values, and inferring some other values. The **:INSTANCE-OF** and **:IS-A** slots have a special role to play in this process. In particular, the generic frames can be used to fill in values that are not mentioned explicitly in the creation of the instance, and they can also trigger additional actions when slot fillers are provided.

For example, if we ask for the :Country of the toronto frame, we can determine that it is canada by using the **:INSTANCE-OF** slot, which points to CanadianCity, where that value is given. The process of passing information from generic frames down through their specializations and eventually to their instances is called *inheritance of properties* (the "child" frames inherit properties from their "parents"), and we say that toronto inherits the :Country property from CanadianCity. If we had not provided a filler for the :Province of toronto, we would still know by inheritance that we were looking for an instance of CanadianProvince (which could be useful in a recognition task). Similarly, if we had not provided a filler for :Population, but we also had the following frame,

```
(City
    <:Population NonNegativeNumber> ...)
```

then by using both the **:INSTANCE-OF** slot of toronto and the **:IS-A** slot of CanadianCity, we would know by inheritance that we were looking for an instance of NonNegativeNumber.

The inheritance of attached procedures works analogously. If we create an instance of Table, and we need to find the filler of the :Clearance slot for that instance, we can use the attached **IF-NEEDED** procedure to compute the clearance of that table from the height of its legs. This procedure would also be used through inheritance if we created an instance of the frame MahoganyCoffeeTable, where we had the following:

```
(CoffeeTable
    <:IS-A Table> ...)

(MahoganyCoffeeTable
    <:IS-A CoffeeTable> ...)
```

Similarly, if we create an instance of the Lecture frame with a lecture date specified explicitly, the attached **IF-ADDED** procedure would fire immediately to calculate the day of the week for the lecture, filling the slot :DayOfWeek. If we later changed the :Date slot, the :DayOfWeek slot would again be changed by the same procedure.

One of the distinguishing features of the inheritance of properties in frame systems is that it is *defeasible*. By this we mean that we use an inherited value only if we cannot find a filler otherwise. So a slot filler in a generic frame can be overridden explicitly in its instances and in its specializations. For example, if we have a generic frame like

```
(Elephant
    <:IS-A Mammal>
    <:EarSize large>
    <:Color gray> ...)
```

we are saying that instances of Elephant have a certain :EarSize and :Color property by *default*. We might have the following other frames:

```
(raja
    <:INSTANCE-OF Elephant>
    <:EarSize small> ...)

(RoyalElephant
    <:IS-A Elephant>
    <:Color white> ...)

(clyde
    <:INSTANCE-OF RoyalElephant> ...)
```

In this case, raja inherits the gray color of elephants, but has small ears; clyde inherits the large ears from Elephant via RoyalElephant, but inherits the white color from RoyalElephant, overriding the default from Elephant.

Normally in frame systems, all values are understood as default values, and nothing is done automatically to check the validity of an explicitly provided filler. So, for example, nothing stops us from creating an individual frame like

```
(city135
    <:INSTANCE-OF CanadianCity>
    <:Country holland>)
```

It is also worth mentioning that in many frame systems, individual frames are allowed to be instances of (and generic frames are allowed to be specializations of) more than one generic frame. For example, we might want to say that

```
(AfricanElephant
    <:IS-A Elephant>
    <:IS-A AfricanAnimal> ...)
```

with properties inherited from both generic frames. This, of course, complicates inheritance considerably, because the values from Elephant may conflict with those from AfricanAnimal. We will further examine this more general form of inheritance in Chapter 10.

## 8.2.3  Reasoning with Frames

The procedures attached to frames give us a flexible, organized framework for computation. Reasoning within a frame system usually starts with the system's "recognizing" an object as an instance of a generic frame, and then applying procedures triggered by that recognition. Such procedure invocations can then produce more data or changes in the knowledge base that can cascade to other procedure calls. When no more procedures are applicable, the system halts.

More specifically, the basic reasoning loop in a frame system has these three steps:

1. a user or external system using the frame system as its knowledge representation declares that an object or situation exists, thereby instantiating some generic frame;

2. any slot fillers that are not provided explicitly but can be inherited by the new frame instance are inherited;

3. for each slot with a filler, any **IF-ADDED** procedure that can be inherited is run, possibly causing new slots to be filled, or new frames to be instantiated, and the cycle repeats.

If the user, the external system, or an attached procedure requires the filler of a slot, then we get the following behavior:

1. if there is a filler stored in the slot, then that value is returned;

2. otherwise, any **IF-NEEDED** procedure that can be inherited is run, calculating the filler for the slot, but potentially also causing other slots to be filled, or new frames to be instantiated.

If neither of these produce a result, then the value of the slot is considered to be unknown. Note that in this account, the inheritance of property values is done at the time the individual frame is created, but **IF-NEEDED** procedures, which calculate property values, are only invoked as required. Other schemes are possible.

This comprises the local reasoning involving a single frame. When constructing a frame knowledge base, one would also think about the global structure of the KB and how computation should produce the desired overall reasoning. Typically, generic frames are created for any major object-type or situation-type required in the problem-solving. Any constraints between slots are expressed by the attached **IF-ADDED** and **IF-NEEDED** procedures. As in the procedural systems of Chapter 6, it is up to the designer to decide whether reasoning should be done in a data-directed or goal-directed fashion.

In this account, default values are filled in whenever they are available on slots. It is worth noting that in the original, psychological view that first gave rise to frames, defaults were considered to play a major role in scene, situation, and object recognition; it was felt that people were prone to generalize from situations they had seen before, and that they would assume that objects and situations were "typical"—had key aspects taking on their normal default values—unless specific features in the individual case were noticed to be exceptional.

Overall, given the constraints between slots that are enforced by attached procedures, we can think of a frame knowledge base as a symbolic "spreadsheet," with constraints between the objects we care about being propagated by attached procedures. But the procedures in a frame KB can do a lot more, including invoking complex actions by the system.

---

## 8.3 AN EXAMPLE: USING FRAMES TO PLAN A TRIP

We now turn our attention to developing an example frame system to see how these representations work in practice. This is a form of knowledge engineering that is quite different from the logical approach considered in Chapter 3. The example will be part of a scheme for planning trips.

We will see how the "symbolic spreadsheet" style of reasoning in frame systems is used. This might be particularly useful in supporting the documentation one often uses in a company for reporting expenses.

The basic structure of our representation involves two main types of frames: Trip and TravelStep. A Trip will have a sequence of TravelSteps, linked together by appropriate slots. A TravelStep will usually terminate in a LodgingStay, except when there are two travel legs in a single day, or when it is the last leg of a trip.

In order to make the correspondences work out correctly (and to be able to keep track of what is related to what), a LodgingStay will use slots to point to its arriving TravelStep and its departing TravelStep. Similarly, TravelSteps will indicate the LodgingStays at their origin and destination. Graphically, for a trip with three legs (instances of TravelStep), we might sketch the relationships as in Figure 8.1.

Using the obvious slot names, a Trip in general will look like this:

```
(Trip
       <:FirstStep   TravelStep>
       <:Traveler    Person>
       <:BeginDate   Date>
       <:EndDate     Date>
       <:TotalCost   Price>
       …)
```

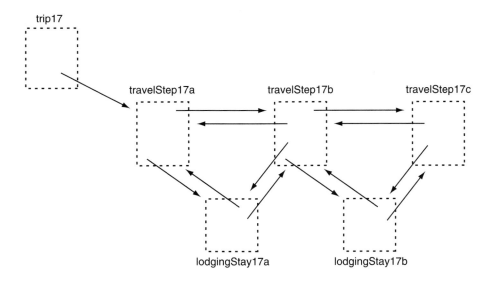

■ **FIGURE 8.1**

Sketch of Structure of a Trip

A specific Trip, say trip17, might look like this:

```
(trip17
    <:INSTANCE-OF  Trip>
    <:FirstStep  travelStep17a>
    <:Traveler  ronB>
    <:BeginDate  11/13/98>
    <:EndDate  11/18/98>
    <:TotalCost  $1752.45>
    ...)
```

In general, instances of TravelStep and LodgingStay will share some properties (e.g., each has a beginning date, an end date, a cost, and a payment method), so for representational conciseness, we might posit a more general category, TripPart, of which the two other frames would be specializations:

```
(TripPart
    <:BeginDate  Date>
    <:EndDate  Date>
    <:Cost  Price>
    <:PaymentMethod  FormOfPayment>
    ...)
```

```
(LodgingStay
    <:IS-A  TripPart>
    <:Place  City>
    <:LodgingPlace  LodgingPlace>
    <:ArrivingTravelStep  TravelStep>
    <:DepartingTravelStep  TravelStep>
    ...)
```

```
(TravelStep
    <:IS-A  TripPart>
    <:Origin  City>
    <:Destination  City>
    <:OriginLodgingStay  LodgingStay>
    <:DestinationLodgingStay  LodgingStay>
    <:Means  FormOfTransportation>
    <:DepartureTime  Time>
    <:ArrivalTime  Time>
    <:NextStep  TravelStep>
    <:PreviousStep  TravelStep>
    ...)
```

This gives us our basic overall structure for a trip. Next we embellish the frame structure with various defaults as well as procedures that will help us enforce constraints. For example, our trips might most often be made by air, in which case the default filler for the :Means slot of a TravelStep should be airplane:

```
(TravelStep
    <:Means   airplane> ...)
```

We might also make a habit of paying for parts of trips with a Visa card:

```
(TripPart
    <:PaymentMethod   visaCard> ...)
```

However, perhaps because it provides insurance, we may prefer American Express for travel steps, overriding this default:

```
(TravelStep
    <:PaymentMethod   americanExpressCard> ...)
```

As indicated earlier, not all inherited fillers of slots will necessarily be specified as fixed values; it may be more appropriate to compute them from the current circumstances. For example, it would be appropriate to automatically set up the origin of a travel step as our home airport, say Newark, as long as there was no previous travel step—in other words, Newark is the default airport for the beginning of a trip. To do this we introduce two pieces of notation:

- if $x$ refers to an individual frame and $y$ to a slot, then $xy$ refers to the filler of the slot for the frame;[1]
- SELF will be a way to refer to the frame currently being processed.

Our travel step description would then be augmented to look like this:

```
(TravelStep
    <:Origin
        [IF-NEEDED
            {if no SELF:PreviousStep
                then  newark
                else  SELF:PreviousStep:Destination}]> ...)
```

---

[1] Note that we do not write $x : y$, because we are assuming that the slot $y$ already begins with a ":".

This attached procedure says that for any TravelStep, if we want its origin city, use the destination of the previous TravelStep, or newark if there is none.

Another useful thing to do with a travel planning symbolic spreadsheet would be to compute the total cost of a trip from the costs of each of its parts:

```
(Trip
    <:TotalCost
      [IF-NEEDED
        {let result ← 0;
         let x ← SELF:FirstStep;
         repeat
           {if exists x:NextStep
              then
                {result ← result + x:Cost
                 if exists x:DestinationLodgingStay then
                     result ← result + x:DestinationLodgingStay:Cost;
                 x ← x:NextStep}
              else return result + x:Cost}]]> ...)
```

This **IF-NEEDED** procedure (written in a suggestive pseudocode) iterates through the travel steps, starting at the trip's :FirstStep. At each step, it adds the cost of the step itself (x:Cost) to the previous result, and if there is a subsequent step, the cost of the lodging stay between those two steps, if any (x:DestinationLodgingStay:Cost).

Another useful thing to expect an automatic travel documentation system to do would be to create a skeletal lodging stay instance each time a new travel leg was added. The following **IF-ADDED** procedure does a basic form of this:

```
(TravelStep
    <:NextStep
      [IF-ADDED
        {if SELF:EndDate ≠ SELF:NextStep:BeginDate
           then
             SELF:DestinationLodgingStay ←
             SELF:NextStep:OriginLodgingStay ←
             create new LodgingStay
                 with :BeginDate = SELF:EndDate
                 and with :EndDate = SELF:NextStep:BeginDate
                 and with :ArrivingTravelStep = SELF
                 and with :DepartingTravelStep = SELF:NextStep
         ...}]]> ...)
```

Note that the first thing done is to confirm that the next travel leg begins on a different day than the one we are starting with ends; presumably no lodging stay is needed if the two travel legs join on the same day.

Note also that the default :Place of a LodgingStay (and other fillers) could also be calculated as another piece of automatic processing:

```
(LodgingStay
     <:Place [IF-NEEDED
                 {SELF:ArrivingTravelStep:Destination}]> ...)
```

This might be a fairly weak default, however, and its utility would depend on the particular application. It is quite possible that a traveller's preferred default city for lodging is different than the destination city for the arriving leg of the trip (e.g., flights may arrive in San Francisco, but I may prefer as a default to stay in Palo Alto).

## 8.3.1   Using the Example Frames

We now consider how the various frame fragments we have created might work together in specifying a trip. Imagine that we propose a trip to Toronto on December 21, 2006, returning home the following day. First, we create an individual frame for the overall trip (call it trip18), and one for the first leg of the trip:

```
(trip18
     <:INSTANCE-OF Trip>
     <:FirstStep travelStep18a>)

(travelStep18a
     <:INSTANCE-OF TravelStep>
     <:Destination toronto>
     <:BeginDate 12/21/06>
     <:EndDate 12/21/06>)
```

Because we know we are to return home the next day, we create the second leg of the trip:

```
(travelStep18b
     <:INSTANCE-OF TravelStep>
     <:Destination newark>
     <:BeginDate 12/22/06>
     <:EndDate 12/22/06>
     <:PreviousStep travelStep18a>)
```

The state of affairs after creating travelStep18b is pictured in Figure 8.2.

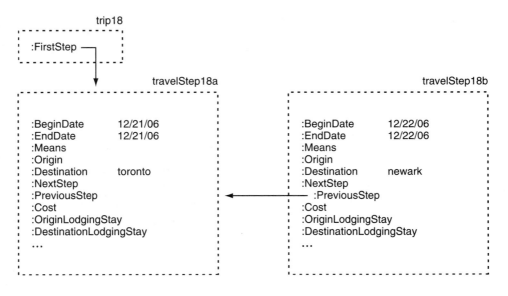

■ **FIGURE 8.2**

Travel Example with Two Legs

To complete the initial setup, travelStep18a will need its :NextStep slot filled with travelStep18b. (Note that this could be done automatically with an **IF-ADDED** procedure on travelStep:PreviousStep triggered from travelStep18b.) As a consequence of the assignment of travelStep18b as the :NextStep of travelStep18a, a default LodgingStay is automatically created to represent the overnight stay between those two legs of the trip (using the **IF-ADDED** procedure on the :NextStep slot):

```
(lodgingStay18a
      <:INSTANCE-OF LodgingStay>
      <:BeginDate  12/21/06>
      <:EndDate  12/22/06>
      <:ArrivingTravelStep  travelStep18a>
      <:DepartingTravelStep  travelStep18b>)
```

Note that the **IF-NEEDED** procedure for the :Place slot of LodgingStay would infer a default filler of toronto for lodgingStay18a, if required. Once we have established the initial structure, we can see how the :Means slot of either step would be filled by default, and a query about the :Origin slot of either step would produce an appropriate default value, as in Figure 8.3 (note that we have included in the figure the values derived by the **IF-NEEDED** procedures).

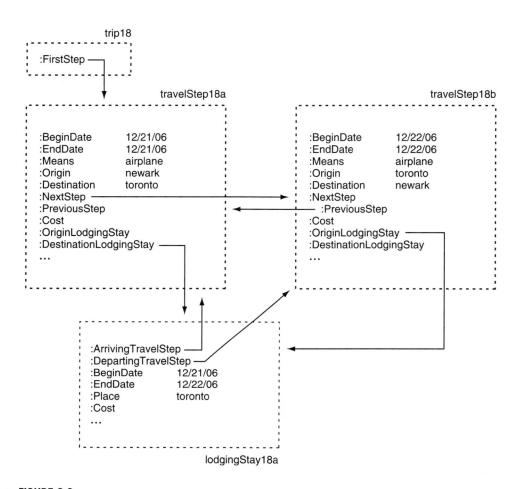

■ **FIGURE 8.3**

The Travel Example with Lodging Stay

For a final illustration, imagine that we have over the course of our trip filled in the :Cost slots for each of the instances of TripPart as follows: travelStep18a:Cost is $321.00; travelStep18b:Cost is $321.00; and lodgingStay18b:Cost is $124.75. If we ask for the :TotalCost of the entire trip, the **IF-NEEDED** procedure defined earlier will come into play (assuming the :TotalCost slot has not already been filled manually). Given the final state of the trip as completed by the cost assertions, the calculation proceeds as follows:

■  *result* is initialized to 0, and *x* is initialized to travelStep18a, which makes *x*:NextStep be travelStep18b;

- the first time through the `repeat` loop, *result* is set to the sum of *result* (0), the cost of *x* ($321.00), and the cost of the :DestinationLodgingStay of the current step (lodgingStay18a) ($124.75); *x* is then set to travelStep18b;

- the next time through, because *x* (travelStep18b) has no following step, the loop is broken and the sum of *result* ($445.75) and the cost of *x* ($321.00) is returned.

As a result, a grand total of $766.75 is taken to be the :TotalCost of trip18.

## 8.4  BEYOND THE BASICS

The trip planning example considered here is typical of how frame systems have been used: Start with a sketchy description of some circumstance and embellish it with defaults and implied values. The **IF-ADDED** procedures can make updates easier and help to maintain consistency; the **IF-NEEDED** procedures allow values to be computed only when they are needed. There is a tradeoff here, of course, and which type of procedure to use in an application will depend on the potential value to the user of seeing implied values computed up front versus the value of waiting to do computation only as required.

### 8.4.1  Other Uses of Frames

There are other types of applications for frame systems. One would be to use a frame system to provide a structured, knowledge-based monitoring function over a database. By hooking the frames to items in a database, changes in values and newly added values could be detected by the frame system, and new frame instances or implied slot values could be computed and added to the database, without having to modify the DBMS itself to handle rules. In some ways, this combination would act like an expert system. But database monitors are probably more naturally thought of as object-centered (generic frames could line up with relations in the schema, for example), in which case a frame representation is a better fit than a flat production system.

Other uses of frame systems come closer to the original thinking about psychologically oriented recognition processes espoused by Minsky in 1975. These include, for example, structuring views of typical activities of characters in stories. The frame structures for such activities have been called *scripts*, and have been used to recognize the motivations of characters in the stories and set up expectations for their later behavior. More general commonsense reasoning of the sort that Minsky envisioned would use local cues from a situation to suggest potentially relevant frames, which in turn would set up further expectations that could drive investigation procedures.

Consider, for example, a situation where many people in a room were holding what appeared to be wrapped packages, and balloons and cake were in evidence. This would suggest a birthday party, and prompt us to look for the focal person at the party (a key slot of the birthday party frame) and to interpret the meaning of lit candles in a certain way. Expectations set up by the suggested frames could be used to confirm the current hypothesis (that this is a birthday party). If they were subsequently violated, then an appropriately represented "differential diagnosis" attached to the frame could lead the system to suggest other candidate frames, taking the reasoning in a different direction. For example, no candles on the cake and an adult focal person or persons could suggest a retirement or anniversary party.

## 8.4.2   Extensions to the Frame Formalism

As with other knowledge representation formalisms, frame systems have been subject to many extensions to handle ever more complex applications. Here we briefly review some of these extensions.

**Other Procedures**   An obvious way to increase the expressiveness and utility of the frame mechanism is to include other types of procedures. The whole point of object-oriented reasoning is to determine the sort of questions appropriate for a type of object and to design procedures to answer them. For trips, for example, we have only considered two forms of questions, exemplified by "What is the total cost of a trip?" (handled by an **IF-NEEDED** procedure) and "What should I do if I find out about a new leg of a trip?" (handled by an **IF-ADDED** procedure). Other questions that do not fit these two patterns are certainly possible, such as "What should I do if I cancel a leg of a trip?" (requiring some sort of "if-removed" procedure), "How do I recognize an overly expensive trip?" (along the lines of the birthday party recognition example), or "What do I need to look out for in an overseas trip?" and so on.

**Multiple Slot Fillers**   In addition to extending the repertoire of procedures attached to a frame knowledge base, we can also expand the types of slots used to express parts and features of objects. One obvious extension is to allow *sets* of frames to fill slots. Procedures attached to the slot could then operate on the entire set of fillers, and constraints on the cardinality of these sets could be used in reasoning, as we will see in the description logics of Chapter 9. One complication this raises concerns inheritance: With multiple slot fillers, we need to know whether the fillers of a slot given explicitly should or should not be augmented by other fillers through inheritance.

**Other Slot Facets**  So far, we have seen that both default fillers and procedures can be associated with a slot. We can imagine dealing with other aspects of the relationship between a slot and a frame. For example, we might want to be able to *insist* that instances of a generic frame provide a filler of a certain type (or perhaps check the validity of the provided filler with a procedure), rather than being merely a default. Another possibility is to state *preferences* we might have regarding the filler of a slot. Preferences could be used to help select a filler among a number of competing inherited values.

**Metaframes**  Generic frames can sometimes usefully be considered to be instances of higher-level metaframes. For example, generic frames like CanadianCity and NewJerseyCity represent a type of city defined by a geographic region. So we might think of them as being instances (not specializations) of a metaframe like GeographicalCityType, and have something like this:

```
(GeographicalCityType
    <:IS-A CityType>
    <:DefiningRegion GeographicalRegion>
    <:AveragePopulation NonNegativeNumber> ...)
```

An instance of this frame, like CanadianCity, would have a particular value for the :DefiningRegion slot, namely canada. The filler for the :AveragePopulation slot for CanadianCity could be calculated by an **IF-NEEDED** procedure, by iterating through all the Canadian cities. Observe that individual cities themselves do not have a defining region or an average population, so we need to ensure that frames like toronto do not inherit these slots from CanadianCity. The usual way this is done is to distinguish the "member" slots of a generic frame, which apply to instances (members) of the frame (like the :Country of a CanadianCity), from the "own" slots of the frame, which apply to the frame itself (like the :AveragePopulation of CanadianCity).

### 8.4.3  Object-Driven Programming with Frames

Frame-structured knowledge bases are the first instance we have seen of an object-oriented representation. Careful attention to the mapping of generic frames to categories of objects in a domain of interest can yield a simple declarative knowledge base, emphasizing taxonomies of objects and their structural relationships. However, as we have seen, attached procedures can be a useful adjunct to a pure object-oriented representation structure, and in practice, we are encouraged to take advantage of their power to build a complex, highly procedural knowledge base. In this case, what is known about the connections among the various symbols used is expressed through the attached procedures, just as it was in the procedural and production systems of previous chapters. Although there is nothing intrinsically wrong with this, it does mean moving away from the original declarative view of knowledge—taking the world to be one way and not another—presented in the first chapter.

The shift to a more procedural view of frames moves us close to conventional object-oriented programming (OOP). Indeed, frame-based representation languages and OOP systems were developed concurrently, and share many of the same intuitions and techniques. A procedural frame system shares the advantages of a conventional OOP system: Definition is done primarily by specialization of more general classes, control is localized, methods can be inherited, encapsulation of abstract procedures is possible, and so on. The main difference is that frame systems tend to have a centralized, conventional control regime, whereas OOP systems have objects acting as small, independent agents sending each other messages. Frame systems tend to work in a cycle: Instantiate a frame and declare some slot fillers, inherit values from more general frames, trigger appropriate forward-chaining procedures, and then, when quiescent, stop and wait for the next input. OOP systems tend to be more decentralized and less patterned. As a result, there can be some applications for which a frame-based system can provide some advantages over a more generic OOP system, for example, in the style of applications that we touched on earlier. But if the primary use of a frame system is as an organizing method for procedures, this contrast should be examined carefully to be sure that the system is best suited to the task.

In Chapter 9 we will continue our investigation of object-oriented knowledge representation, but now without procedures, in a more logical and declarative form.

## 8.5 BIBLIOGRAPHIC NOTES

A collection of papers about frames and other structured representations was edited by Bobrow and Collins [31]. The key concepts of frame representations are generally credited to a seminal paper by Minsky [292], although many of the ideas were in the air and pursued by others in the early 1970s. FRL [356] was one of the first implemented reasoning systems to be based on the frames idea and procedural attachment. In some respects, the apotheosis of frame systems was KRL [32], a very ambitious effort based, among other things, on insight into the use of descriptions in natural language. Scripts [366] were an attempt to apply the idea of frames to natural language story understanding.

Frame-style representations eventually found their way into the commercial arena in systems like KEE [3, 127].

For a critique of frames and the difficulty of providing a logical semantics for framelike languages, see Hayes [182].

## 8.6 EXERCISES

1. Imagine a frame-based travel-planning assistant, as discussed in the text. Let us focus on two of the generic frames used there, LodgingStay (which represents a hotel stay in a city while on a trip) and TravelStep (which represents any travel from one city to another). A LodgingStay has a :Place, in which the lodging is located, an :ArrivingTravelStep, and a :DepartingTravelStep, both of which are TravelSteps. A TravelStep has an :Origin and a :Destination, each of which is a city, a possible :OriginLodgingStay, and a possible :DestinationLodgingStay, each of which is a LodgingStay. For simplicity, assume that there is always a LodgingStay between any two TravelSteps.

   Write in English some combination of **IF-NEEDED** and/or **IF-ADDED** procedures that could be attached to the city slots of the various LodgingStay and TravelStep frames to keep them consistent. Statements like "set the :Place of my :OriginLodgingStay to be the same as this one" in a procedure are fine. Make sure that a change to one of these city slots does not cause an infinite loop.

   In the remaining exercises, we consider two possible frame-based applications:

   **Classroom Scheduler**   Imagine we want to build a program that helps schedule rooms for classes of various size at a university, using the sort of frame technology (frames, slots, and attached procedures) discussed in the text. Slots of frames might be used to record when and where a class is to be held, the capacity of a room, and so on, and **IF-ADDED** and other procedures might be used to encode constraints as well as to fill in implied values when the KB is updated.

   In this problem, we want to consider updating the KB in several ways: (1) asserting that a class of a given size is to be held in a given room at a given time; the system would either go ahead and add this to its schedule or alert the user that it was not possible to do so; (2) asserting that a class of a given size is to be held at a given time, with the system providing a suitable room (if one is available) when queried; (3) asserting that a class of a given size is desired, with the system providing a time and place when queried.

**Olympic Assistant**   Imagine we want to help the International Olympic Committee in the smooth running of the next Olympic games. In particular, we want to select an event and write a program to deal with that event including facilities for handling the preliminary rounds/heats and finals. Slots of frames might be used to record athletes in a heat/final, the location and time of that heat/final, and so on, and **IF-ADDED/IF-NEEDED** and other procedures might be used to encode constraints as well as to fill in implied values when the knowledge base is updated.

We particularly wish to consider several ways of updating the knowledge base: (1) asserting that a heat will take place with certain athletes; the system should add this and determine what time and the location of the venue the athletes need to be at for their heat, and so on; (2) asserting that a particular semifinal/final should take place, the system should determine the participating athletes; and (3) asserting that the medal ceremony should take place at a particular time and location, the system should add this and provide the medalists plus appropriate national anthem when queried. To simplify matters, we assume that an athlete takes part in only the event we have chosen.

**2.** For either application, the questions are the same:

  (a) Design a set of frames and slots to represent the schedule and any ancillary information needed by the assistant.

  (b) For all slots of all frames, write in English pseudocode the **IF-ADDED** or **IF-NEEDED** procedures that would appear there. Annotate these procedures with comments explaining why they are there (e.g., what constraints they are enforcing).

  (c) Briefly explain how your system would work (what procedures would fire and what they would do) on concrete examples of your choosing, illustrating each of the three situations (1, 2, and 3) mentioned in the description of the application.

# CHAPTER 9

# STRUCTURED DESCRIPTIONS

■

■

■

In Chapter 8, we looked at knowledge organization inspired by our natural tendency to think in terms of categories of *objects*. However, the frame representation seen there focused more on the organization and invocation of *procedures* than on inferences about the objects and categories themselves. Reasoning about objects in everyday thinking goes well beyond the simple cascaded computations seen in that chapter, and is based on considerations like the following:

- objects naturally fall into categories (e.g., my pet is a dog, my wife is a physician), but are very often thought of as being members of multiple categories (e.g., I am an author, an employee, and a father);

- categories can be more general or more specific than others (e.g., Westie and Schnauzer are types of dogs, a rheumatologist is a type of physician, a father is a type of parent);

- in addition to generalization being common for categories with simple names, it is also natural for those with more complex descriptions (e.g., a part-time employee is an employee, a Canadian family with at least one child is a family, a family with three children is a family that is not childless);

- objects have parts, sometimes in multiples (e.g., books have titles, tables have legs, automobiles have wheels);

- the relationships among an object's parts is essential to its being considered a member of a category (e.g., a stack of bricks is not the same as a pile of the very same bricks).

In this chapter we will delve into representation techniques that look more directly at these aspects of objects and categories than frames did. In focusing on the more declarative aspects of an object-oriented representation, our analysis will take us back to concepts like predicates and entailment from FOL. But as we shall see, what matters about these predicates and the kind of entailments we will consider here will be quite different.

## 9.1 DESCRIPTIONS

Before we look at the details of a formal knowledge representation language in the next section, one useful way to get our bearings is to think in terms of the expressions of a natural language like English. In our discussion of knowledge in Chapter 1, and in our presentation of FOL, we focused mainly on *sentences*, because it is sentences, after all, that express what is known. Here, we want to talk about *noun phrases*. Like sentences, noun phrases can be simple or complex, and they give us a nice window onto our thinking about objects.

### 9.1.1 Noun Phrases

Recall that in our introduction to expressing knowledge in FOL-like languages (Chapter 3), we represented categories of objects with one-place predicates using common nouns like Company($x$), Knife($x$), and Contract($x$). But there is more to noun phrases than just nouns. To capture more interesting types of nominal constructions, such as "a hunter-gatherer" or "a man whose children are all female," we would need predicates with internal structure.

For example, if we had a truly compound predicate like

Hunter&Gatherer($x$),

then we would expect that for any $x$ for which Hunter&Gatherer($x$) was true, both Hunter($x$) and Gatherer($x$) would also be true.[1] Most important, this connection among the three predicates would hold not by virtue of some fact believed about the world, but by *definition* of what we meant by the compound predicate.

Similarly, we would expect that if Child($x,y$) and FatherOfOnlyGirls($x$) were both true, $y$ would have to be a girl, again (somehow), by definition. Note that this would be so even if we had a simple name that served as an abbreviation for a concept like this, which is very often the case

---

[1] We are using the "&" and complex predicate names suggestively here; we will introduce formal machinery shortly.

in natural language (e.g., Teenager is synonymous with PersonWithAge-Between13and19).

Traditional first-order logic does not provide any tools for dealing with compound predicates of this sort. In a sense, the only noun phrases in FOL are the nouns. But given the prominence and naturalness of such constructs in natural language, it is worthwhile to consider knowledge representation machinery that does provide such tools. Because a logic that would allow us to manipulate complex predicates would be working mainly with *descriptions*, we call a logical system based on these ideas a *description logic* (DL).[2]

## 9.1.2   Concepts, Roles, and Constants

Looking at our earlier examples, we can already see that two sorts of nouns are involved: There are category nouns like Hunter, Teenager, and Girl describing basic classes of objects, and there are relational nouns like Child and Age that describe objects that are parts or attributes or properties of other objects.[3] We saw a similar distinction in Chapter 8 between a frame and a slot. In a description logic, we refer to the first type of description as a *concept* and to the second type as a *role*.

As with frames, we will think of concepts as being organized into a generalization hierarchy where, for example, Hunter&Gatherer is a specialization of Hunter. However, we will see that much of the generalization hierarchy in a description logic follows logically from the meaning of the compound concepts involved, quite unlike the case with frames where hierarchies were stipulated by the user. As we will see, much of the reasoning performed by a description logic system centers around automatically computing this generalization relation.

For simplicity, we will not consider roles to be organized hierarchically in this way except briefly in Section 9.6. In contrast to the slots in frame systems, however, roles will be allowed to have multiple fillers. This way we can naturally describe a person with several children, a function with multiple arguments, a desk with many drawers, or a wine made from more than one type of grape.

Finally, although much of the reasoning we perform in a description logic concerns generic categories, we will want to know how these descriptions apply to individuals as well. Consequently, we will also include *constants* like johnSmith in our description logic language.

---

[2]Other names used in the literature include "terminological logics," "term subsumption systems," "taxonomic logics," or even "KL-One-like systems," because of their origin in early work on a representation system called KL-One.

[3]Many nouns can be used both ways. For example, "child" can refer to a relation (the inverse of parent) or a category (a person of a young age).

## 9.2  A DESCRIPTION LANGUAGE

We begin here with the syntax of a very simple but illustrative description logic language that we call $\mathcal{DL}$. Like FOL, $\mathcal{DL}$ has two types of symbols: logical symbols, which have a fixed meaning or use, and nonlogical symbols, which are application-dependent. There are four sorts of logical symbols in $\mathcal{DL}$:

1. *punctuation*: "[," "]," "(," ")";

2. *positive integers*: 1, 2, 3, etc.;

3. *concept-forming operators*: "**ALL**," "**EXISTS**," "**FILLS**," "**AND**";

4. *connectives*: "⊑," "≐," "→."

We distinguish three sorts of nonlogical symbols in $\mathcal{DL}$:

1. *atomic concepts*, written in capitalized mixed case, e.g., Person, WhiteWine, FatherOfOnlyGirls; $\mathcal{DL}$ also has a special atomic concept, Thing;

2. *roles*, written like atomic concepts, but preceded by ":," e.g., :Child, :Height, :Employer, :Arm;

3. *constants*, written in uncapitalized mixed case, e.g., desk13, maryAnnJones.

There are four types of legal syntactic expressions in $\mathcal{DL}$: *constants*, *roles* (both seen earlier), *concepts*, and *sentences*. We use $c$ and $r$ to range over constants and roles, respectively, $d$ and $e$ to range over concepts, and $a$ to range over atomic concepts. The set of concepts of $\mathcal{DL}$ is the least set satisfying the following:

■  every atomic concept is a concept;

■  if $r$ is a role and $d$ is a concept, then [**ALL** $r$ $d$] is a concept;

■  if $r$ is a role and $n$ is a positive integer, then [**EXISTS** $n$ $r$] is a concept;

■  if $r$ is a role and $c$ is a constant, then [**FILLS** $r$ $c$] is a concept;

■  if $d_1 \ldots d_n$ are concepts, then [**AND** $d_1 \ldots d_n$] is a concept.

Finally, there are three types of sentences in $\mathcal{DL}$:

■  if $d_1$ and $d_2$ are concepts, then $(d_1 \sqsubseteq d_2)$ is a sentence;

■  if $d_1$ and $d_2$ are concepts, then $(d_1 \doteq d_2)$ is a sentence;

■  if $c$ is a constant and $d$ is a concept, then $(c \rightarrow d)$ is a sentence.

A KB in a description logic like $\mathcal{DL}$ is considered to be any collection of sentences of this form.

What are these syntactic expressions supposed to mean? Constants are intended to stand for individuals in some application domain as they did in FOL, atomic concepts (and indeed all concepts in general) are intended to stand for categories or classes of individuals, and roles are intended to stand for binary relations over those individuals.

As for the complex concepts, their meanings are derived from the meanings of their parts the way the meanings of noun phrases are. Imagine that we have a role $r$ standing for some binary relation. Then the concept [**EXISTS** $n$ $r$] stands for the class of individuals in the domain that are related by relation $r$ to at least $n$ other individuals. So the concept [**EXISTS** 1 :Child] could represent someone who was not childless. Next, imagine that constant $c$ stands for some individual; then the concept [**FILLS** $r$ $c$] stands for those individuals that are $r$-related to that individual. So [**FILLS** :Cousin vinny] would then represent someone, one of whose cousins was Vinny. Next, imagine that concept $d$ stands for some class of individuals; then the concept [**ALL** $r$ $d$] stands for those individuals who are $r$-related only to elements of that class. For example, [**ALL** :Employee UnionMember] describes something whose employees, if any, are all union members. Finally, the concept [**AND** $d_1 \ldots d_n$] stands for anything that is described by $d_1$ and $\ldots d_n$.

Turning now to sentences, these expressions are intended to be true or false in the domain, as they would be in FOL. Imagine that we have two concepts $d_1$ and $d_2$, standing for two classes of individuals, and a constant $c$, standing for some individual. Then $(d_1 \sqsubseteq d_2)$ says that concept $d_1$ is *subsumed* by concept $d_2$, that is, all individuals that satisfy $d_1$ also satisfy $d_2$. For example, (Surgeon $\sqsubseteq$ Doctor) says that any surgeon is also a doctor (among other things). Similarly, $(d_1 \doteq d_2)$ will mean that the two concepts are *equivalent*, that is, the individuals that satisfy $d_1$ are precisely those that satisfy $d_2$. This is just a convenient way of saying that both $(d_1 \sqsubseteq d_2)$ and $(d_2 \sqsubseteq d_1)$ are true. Finally, $(c \rightarrow d)$ says that the individual denoted by $c$ satisfies the description expressed by concept $d$.

While the sentences of $\mathcal{DL}$ are all atomic, it is easy to create complex concepts. For example,

> [**AND** Wine
>     [**FILLS** :Color red]
>     [**EXISTS** 2 :GrapeType]]

would represent the category of a blended red wine (literally, a wine, one of whose colors is red, and which has at least two types of grape in it).

A typical sentence in a description logic KB is one that assigns a name to a complex concept:

(ProgressiveCompany ≐ [**AND** Company
                            [**EXISTS** 7 :Director]
                            [**ALL** :Manager [**AND** Woman
                                                      [**FILLS** :Degree phD]]]
                            [**FILLS** :MinSalary $24.00/hour]])

The concept on the right-hand side represents the notion of a company with at least seven directors, and all of whose managers are women with Ph.D.s and whose minimum salary is $24.00/hour. The sentence as a whole says that ProgressiveCompany, as a concept, is equivalent to the one on the right. If this sentence is in a KB, we consider ProgressiveCompany to be fully *defined* in the KB, that is, we have a set of necessary and sufficient conditions for being a ProgressiveCompany, exactly expressed by the right-hand side. If we used the ⊑ connective instead, the sentence would say only that ProgressiveCompany as a concept was subsumed by the one on the right. Without a ≐ sentence in the KB defining it, we consider ProgressiveCompany to be a *primitive concept* in that we only have necessary conditions it must satisfy. As a result, although we could draw conclusions about an individual ProgressiveCompany once we were told it was one, we would not have a way to recognize an individual definitively as a ProgressiveCompany.

## 9.3 MEANING AND ENTAILMENT

As we saw in the previous section, there are four different sorts of syntactic expressions in a description logic—constants, roles, concepts, and sentences—with different intended uses. In this section, we will explain precisely what these expressions are supposed to mean, and under what circumstances a collection of sentences in this logic entails another. As in ordinary FOL, it is this entailment relation that a description logic reasoner will be required to calculate.

### 9.3.1 Interpretations

The starting point for the semantics of description logics is the *interpretation*, just as it was for FOL. An interpretation $\Im$ for $\mathcal{DL}$ is a pair $\langle \mathcal{D}, \mathcal{I} \rangle$ as before, where $\mathcal{D}$ is any set of objects called the *domain* of the interpretation, and $\mathcal{I}$ is a mapping called the *interpretation mapping* from the nonlogical symbols of $\mathcal{DL}$ to elements and relations over $\mathcal{D}$, where

1. for every constant $c$, $\mathcal{I}[c] \in \mathcal{D}$;[4]

2. for every atomic concept $a$, $\mathcal{I}[a] \subseteq \mathcal{D}$;

3. for every role $r$, $\mathcal{I}[r] \subseteq \mathcal{D} \times \mathcal{D}$.

Comparing this to FOL, we can see that constants have the same meaning as they would as terms in FOL, that atomic concepts are understood as unary predicates, and that roles are understood as binary predicates. The set $\mathcal{I}[d]$ associated with a concept $d$ in an interpretation is called its *extension*, and $\mathcal{I}$ is sometimes called an extension function.

As we have emphasized, a distinguishing feature of description logics is the existence of nonatomic concepts whose meanings are completely determined by the meanings of their parts. For example, the extension of [**AND** Doctor Female] is required to be the intersection of the extension of Doctor and that of Female. More generally, we can extend the definition of $\mathcal{I}$ to all concepts as follows:

- for the distinguished concept Thing, $\mathcal{I}[\text{Thing}] = \mathcal{D}$;
- $\mathcal{I}[[\textbf{ALL } r \ d]] = \{x \in \mathcal{D} \mid \text{ for any } y, \text{ if } \langle x, y \rangle \in \mathcal{I}[r], \text{ then } y \in \mathcal{I}[d]\}$;
- $\mathcal{I}[[\textbf{EXISTS } n \ r]] =$
  $\{x \in \mathcal{D} \mid \text{ there are at least } n \text{ distinct } y \text{ such that } \langle x, y \rangle \in \mathcal{I}[r]\}$;
- $\mathcal{I}[[\textbf{FILLS } r \ c]] = \{x \in \mathcal{D} \mid \langle x, \mathcal{I}[c] \rangle \in \mathcal{I}[r]\}$;
- $\mathcal{I}[[\textbf{AND } d_1 \ldots d_n]] = \mathcal{I}[d_1] \cap \ldots \cap \mathcal{I}[d_n]$.

So if we are given an interpretation $\mathfrak{I}$, with an interpretation mapping for constants, atomic concepts, and roles, these rules tell us how to find the extension of any concept.

## 9.3.2 Truth in an Interpretation

Given an interpretation, we can now specify which sentences of $\mathcal{DL}$ are true and which are false according to that interpretation. A sentence $(c \rightarrow d)$ will be true when the object denoted by $c$ is in the extension of $d$; a sentence $(d \sqsubseteq d')$ will be true when the extension of $d$ is a subset of the extension of $d'$; a sentence $(d \doteq d')$ will be true when the extension of $d$ is the same as that of $d'$. More formally, given an interpretation $\mathfrak{I} = \langle \mathcal{D}, \mathcal{I} \rangle$, we say that $\alpha$ is *true* in $\mathfrak{I}$, written $\mathfrak{I} \models \alpha$, according to these rules:

---

[4]Note that, as in FOL, different constants can map to the same individual in the domain.

Assume that $d$ and $d'$ are concepts, and that $c$ is a constant.

1. $\Im \models (c \rightarrow d)$ iff $\mathcal{I}[c] \in \mathcal{I}[d]$;
2. $\Im \models (d \sqsubseteq d')$ iff $\mathcal{I}[d] \subseteq \mathcal{I}[d']$;
3. $\Im \models (d \doteq d')$ iff $\mathcal{I}[d] = \mathcal{I}[d']$.

As in FOL, we will also use the notation $\Im \models S$, where $S$ is a set of sentences, to mean that all the sentences in $S$ are true in $\Im$.

### 9.3.3 Entailment

The definition of entailment in $\mathcal{DL}$ is exactly like it is in FOL. Let $S$ be a set of sentences, and $\alpha$ any individual sentence. We say that $S$ logically *entails* $\alpha$, which we write $S \models \alpha$, if and only if for every interpretation $\Im$, if $\Im \models S$ then $\Im \models \alpha$. As a special case of this definition, we say that a sentence $\alpha$ is logically *valid*, which we write $\models \alpha$, when it is logically entailed by the empty set.

There are two basic sorts of reasoning we will be concerned with in description logics: determining whether or not some constant $c$ satisfies a certain concept $d$, and determining whether or not a concept $d$ is subsumed by another concept $d'$. Both of these involve calculating entailments of a KB: In the first case, we need to determine if the KB entails $(c \rightarrow d)$, and in the second case, if the KB entails $(d \sqsubseteq d')$. So, as in FOL, reasoning in a description logic means calculating entailments.

Note that in some cases the entailment relationship will hold because the sentences themselves are valid. For example, consider the sentence

([**AND** Doctor Female] $\sqsubseteq$ Doctor).

This sentence is valid according to the definition just mentioned: The sentence must be true in every interpretation $\Im$ because no matter what extension it assigns to Doctor and Female, the extension of the **AND** concept (which is the intersection of the two sets) will always be a subset of the extension of Doctor. Consequently, for any KB, the first concept is subsumed by the second—in other words, a female doctor is always a doctor. Similarly, the sentence

(john $\rightarrow$ Thing)

is valid: The sentence must be true in every interpretation $\Im$ because no matter what extension it assigns to john, it must be an element of $\mathcal{D}$, which is the extension of Thing. Consequently, for any KB, the constant satisfies that concept—in other words, the individual John is always something.

In more typical cases, the entailment relationship will depend on the sentences in the KB. For example, if a knowledge base, KB, contains the sentence

(Surgeon ⊑ Doctor),

then we get the following entailment:

KB ⊨ ([**AND** Surgeon Female] ⊑ Doctor).

To see why, consider any interpretation $\Im$, and suppose that $\Im \models$ KB. Then, for this interpretation, the extension of Surgeon is a subset of that of Doctor, and so the extension of the **AND** concept (that is, the intersection of the extensions of Surgeon and Female) must also be a subset of that of Doctor. So for this KB, the **AND** concept is subsumed by Doctor: If a surgeon is a doctor (among other things), then a female surgeon is also a doctor. This conclusion would also follow if instead of (Surgeon ⊑ Doctor), the KB were to contain

(Surgeon ≐ [**AND** Doctor [**FILLS** :Specialty surgery]]).

In this case we are defining a surgeon to be a certain kind of doctor, which again requires the extension of Surgeon to be a subset of that of Doctor. With the empty KB, on the other hand, there would be no subsumption relation, because we can find an $\Im$ where the extension of the **AND** concept is not a subset of the extension of Doctor: Let $\mathcal{D}$ be the set of all integers, and let $\mathcal{I}$ assign Doctor to the empty set, and both Surgeon and Female to the set of all integers.

## 9.4 COMPUTING ENTAILMENTS

As stated, there are two major types of reasoning that we care about with a description logic: Given a knowledge base, KB, we want to be able to determine if KB ⊨ $\alpha$ for sentences $\alpha$ of the form

- $(c \rightarrow d)$, where $c$ is a constant and $d$ is a concept; and
- $(d \sqsubseteq e)$, where $d$ and $e$ are both concepts.[5]

In fact, the first of these depends on being able to handle the second, and so we begin by considering how to compute subsumption. As with

---

[5]As noted, KB ⊨ $(d \doteq e)$ if and only if KB ⊨ $(d \sqsubseteq e)$ and KB ⊨ $(e \sqsubseteq d)$.

Resolution for FOL, the key fact about the symbol-level computation that we are about to present is that it is correct (sound and complete) relative to the knowledge-level definition of entailment given earlier.

## 9.4.1  Simplifying the Knowledge Base

First, it can be shown that subsumption entailments are unaffected by the presence of sentences of the form $(c \rightarrow d)$ in the KB. In other words, if KB$'$ is just like KB except that all the $(c \rightarrow d)$ sentences have been removed, then it can be shown that KB $\models (d \sqsubseteq e)$ if and only if KB$'$ $\models (d \sqsubseteq e)$.[6] So we can assume that for subsumption questions, the KB in question contains no $(c \rightarrow d)$ sentences.

Furthermore, we can eliminate sentences of the form $(d \sqsubseteq e)$ from the KB, replacing them by sentences of the form $(d \doteq [\textbf{AND } e\ a])$, where $a$ is a new atomic concept used nowhere else. In other words, to think of $d$ as a primitive sort of $e$ is the same as thinking of it as being defined to be exactly those $e$ things that also satisfy some new unaccounted-for concept $a$.

For pragmatic purposes, it is useful to make the following restriction: We insist that the left-hand sides of the $\doteq$ sentences in the KB be atomic concepts other than Thing and that each atom appears on the left-hand side of a sentence exactly once in the KB. We can think of such sentences as providing definitions of the atomic concepts. We will, however, still be able to compute KB $\models \alpha$ for sentences $\alpha$ of the more general form (e.g., subsumption between two complex concepts). Finally, we assume that the $\doteq$ sentences in the KB are *acyclic*. Informally we want to rule out a KB like

$$\{ (d_1 \doteq [\textbf{AND } d_2 \ \ldots]),\ (d_2 \doteq [\textbf{ALL } r\ d_3]),\ (d_3 \doteq [\textbf{AND } d_1 \ldots]) \},$$

which has a cycle $(d_1, d_2, d_3, d_1)$. While this type of cycle is meaningful in our semantics, it complicates the calculation of subsumption.

With these restrictions in place, to determine whether KB $\models (d \sqsubseteq e)$ it will be sufficient to do the following:

1. using the definitional declarations ($\doteq$) in KB, put $d$ and $e$ into a special normalized form;

2. determine whether each part of the normalized $e$ is accounted for by some part of the normalized $d$.

---

[6]This would not hold if the sentences involving constants could be inconsistent.

So subsumption in a description logic KB reduces to a question about a structural relationship between two normalized concepts.[7]

### 9.4.2 Normalization

Normalization in description logics is similar in spirit to the derivation of normal forms like CNF in FOL. During this phase, we draw some inferences, but only small, obvious ones. This preprocessing makes the subsequent structure-matching step straightforward.

Normalization applies to one concept at a time and involves a small number of steps. Here we outline the steps and then review the whole process on a larger expression.

1. **expand definitions:** Any atomic concept that appears as the left-hand side of a $\doteq$ sentence in the KB is replaced by its definition. For example, if we have the following sentence in KB,

   (Surgeon $\doteq$ [**AND** Doctor [**FILLS** :Specialty surgery]]),

   then the concept [**AND** ... Surgeon ...] expands to

   [**AND** ... [**AND** Doctor [**FILLS** :Specialty surgery]] ...].

2. **flatten the AND operators:** Any subconcept of the form

   [**AND** ... [**AND** $d_1$ ... $d_n$] ...]

   can be simplified to [**AND** ... $d_1$ ... $d_n$ ...].

3. **combine the ALL operators:** Any subconcept of the form

   [**AND** ... [**ALL** $r$ $d_1$] ... [**ALL** $r$ $d_2$] ...]

   can be simplified to [**AND** ... [**ALL** $r$ [**AND** $d_1$ $d_2$]] ...].

4. **combine EXISTS operators:** Any subconcept of the form

   [**AND** ... [**EXISTS** $n_1$ $r$] ... [**EXISTS** $n_2$ $r$] ...]

   can be simplified to the concept [**AND** ... [**EXISTS** $n$ $r$] ...], where $n$ is the maximum of $n_1$ and $n_2$.

---

[7]There are other ways of computing subsumption; this is probably the most common and direct way that takes concept structure into account.

5. **deal with** Thing: Certain concepts are vacuous and should be removed as an argument to **AND**: Thing, [**ALL** *r* Thing], and **AND** with no arguments. In the end, the concept Thing should only appear if this is what the entire expression simplifies to.

6. **remove redundant expressions:** Eliminate any expression that is an exact duplicate of another within the same **AND** expression.

To normalize a concept, these operations can be applied repeatedly in any order and at any level of embedding within **ALL** and **AND** operators. The process only terminates when no further steps are applicable.

In the end, the result of a normalization is either Thing, an atomic concept, or a concept of the following form:

$$[\textbf{AND } a_1 \ldots a_m$$
$$[\textbf{FILLS } r_1\ c_1] \ldots [\textbf{FILLS } r_{m'}\ c_{m'}]$$
$$[\textbf{EXISTS } n_1\ s_1] \ldots [\textbf{EXISTS } n_{m''}\ s_{m''}]$$
$$[\textbf{ALL } t_1\ e_1] \ldots [\textbf{ALL } t_{m'''}\ e_{m'''}]\,]$$

where the $a_i$ are primitive atomic concepts other than Thing, the $r_i$, $s_i$, and $t_i$ are roles, the $c_i$ are constants, the $n_i$ are positive integers, and the $e_i$ are themselves normalized concepts. We call the arguments to **AND** in a normalized concept the *components* of the normalized concept. In fact, we can think of Thing itself as an **AND** that has no components, and an atomic concept as an **AND** with one component.

To illustrate the normalization process, we consider an example. Assume that KB has the following definitions:

WellRoundedCo $\doteq$
    [**AND** Company [**ALL** :Manager [**AND** B-SchoolGrad
                                        [**EXISTS** 1 :TechnicalDegree]]]]

HighTechCo $\doteq$
    [**AND** Company [**FILLS** :Exchange nasdaq] [**ALL** :Manager Techie]]

Techie $\doteq$ [**EXISTS** 2 :TechnicalDegree]

These definitions amount to a WellRoundedCo being a company whose managers are business school graduates who each have at least one technical degree, a HighTechCo being a company listed on the NASDAQ whose managers are all Techies, and a Techie being someone with at least two technical degrees.

Given these definitions, let us examine how we would normalize the concept

[**AND** WellRoundedCo HighTechCo].

First, we would expand the definitions of WellRoundedCo and HighTechCo, and then Techie, yielding this:

[**AND** [**AND** Company
          [**ALL** :Manager [**AND** B-SchoolGrad
                              [**EXISTS** 1 :TechnicalDegree]]]]
      [**AND** Company
          [**FILLS** :Exchange nasdaq]
          [**ALL** :Manager [**EXISTS** 2 :TechnicalDegree]]]]

Next, we flatten the **AND** operators at the top level and then combine the **ALL** operators over :Manager:

[**AND** Company
      [**ALL** :Manager [**AND** B-SchoolGrad
                          [**EXISTS** 1 :TechnicalDegree]
                          [**EXISTS** 2 :TechnicalDegree]]]
      Company
      [**FILLS** :Exchange nasdaq]]

Finally, we remove the redundant Company concept and combine the **EXISTS** operators over :TechnicalDegree, yielding the following:

[**AND** Company
      [**ALL** :Manager [**AND** B-SchoolGrad [**EXISTS** 2 :TechnicalDegree]]]
      [**FILLS** :Exchange nasdaq]]

This is the concept of a company listed on the NASDAQ exchange whose managers are business school graduates with at least two technical degrees.

### 9.4.3 Structure Matching

In order to compute whether KB $\models$ $(d \sqsubseteq e)$, we need to compare the normalized versions of $d$ and $e$. The idea behind structure-matching is that for $d$ to be subsumed by $e$, the normalized $d$ must account for each component of the normalized $e$ in some way. For example, if $e$ contains the component [**ALL** $r$ $e'$], then $d$ must contain some [**ALL** $r$ $d'$], where $d'$ is subsumed by $e'$. The full procedure for structure matching is shown in Figure 9.1.

To illustrate briefly the structure-matching algorithm, consider the following normalized concept:

[**AND** Company
      [**ALL** :Manager B-SchoolGrad]
      [**EXISTS** 1 :Exchange]]

**input:** Two normalized concepts $d$ and $e$ where

$$d \text{ is } [\mathbf{AND}\ d_1 \ldots d_m] \quad \text{and} \quad e \text{ is } [\mathbf{AND}\ e_1 \ldots e_{m'}]$$

**output:** YES or NO, according to whether KB $\models (d \sqsubseteq e)$

Return YES iff for each component $e_j$, for $1 \le j \le m'$, there exists a component $d_i$ where $1 \le i \le m$, such that $d_i$ *matches* $e_j$, as follows:

1. if $e_j$ is an atomic concept, then $d_i$ must be identical to $e_j$;

2. if $e_j$ is of the form [**FILLS** $r\ c$], then $d_i$ must be identical to it;

3. if $e_j$ is of the form [**EXISTS** $n\ r$], then the corresponding $d_i$ must be of the form [**EXISTS** $n'\ r$], for some $n' \ge n$; in the case where $n = 1$, the matching $d_i$ can be of the form [**FILLS** $r\ c$], for any constant $c$;

4. if $e_j$ is of the form [**ALL** $r\ e'$], then the corresponding $d_i$ must be of the form [**ALL** $r\ d'$], where recursively $d'$ is subsumed by $e'$.

---

▪ **FIGURE 9.1**

A Procedure for Structure Matching

This is the concept of a company listed on some stock exchange whose managers are business school graduates. This concept (call it $d$) can be seen to subsume the concept that resulted from the normalization example in the previous section (call it $d'$) by looking at each of the three components of $d$ and seeing that there exists in $d'$ a matching component:

- ▪ Company is an atomic concept that appears as a component of $d'$;

- ▪ for the **ALL** component of $d$, whose restriction is B-SchoolGrad, there is an **ALL** component of $d'$ such that the restriction on that **ALL** component is subsumed by B-SchoolGrad (namely, the conjunction [**AND** B-SchoolGrad [**EXISTS** 2 :TechnicalDegree]]).

- ▪ for the [**EXISTS** 1 :Exchange] component of $d$, there is a corresponding **FILLS** component of $d'$.

## 9.4.4   The Correctness of the Subsumption Computation

We conclude our discussion of subsumption by claiming correctness for the procedure presented here: KB $\models (d \sqsubseteq e)$ (according to the definition in terms of interpretations) if and only if $d$ normalizes to some $d'$, $e$ normalizes to some $e'$, and for every component of $e'$ there is a corresponding matching component of $d'$ as in the procedure of Figure 9.1. We will not present a full proof, because it is quite involved, but merely sketch the argument.

The first observation is that given a KB in the simplified form discussed in Section 9.4.1, every concept can be put into normal form, and moreover, each step of the normalization preserves concept equivalence. Once the concepts have been put into normal form, the KB itself is no longer needed. It follows that KB $\models (d \sqsubseteq e)$ if and only if $(d' \sqsubseteq e')$ is valid.

The next part of the proof is to show that if the procedure returns YES given $d'$ and $e'$, then $(d' \sqsubseteq e')$ is valid. So suppose that each component of $e'$ has a corresponding component in $d'$. To show subsumption, imagine that we have some interpretation $\Im = \langle \mathcal{D}, \mathcal{I} \rangle$ and some $x \in \mathcal{D}$ such that $x \in \mathcal{I}[d']$, and therefore in all of its components, $d_i$. To prove that $x \in \mathcal{I}[e']$ (and consequently that $d'$ is subsumed by $e'$), we look at each of the components $e_j$ of $e'$ and note that $x \in \mathcal{I}[e_j]$ for each $e_j$ because it has a matching component $d_i$ in $d'$ and $x \in \mathcal{I}[d_i]$.

The final part of the proof is the trickiest. We must show that if the procedure returns NO, then $(d' \sqsubseteq e')$ is not valid. To do so, we need to construct an interpretation where for some $x \in \mathcal{D}$, $x \in \mathcal{I}[d']$ but $x \notin \mathcal{I}[e']$.

Here is how to do so in the simplest case where there are no **EXISTS** concepts involved. Let the domain $\mathcal{D}$ be the set of all constants together with the set of *role chains*, defined to be all sequences of roles (including the empty sequence). Then, for every constant $c$, let $\mathcal{I}[c]$ be $c$; for every atomic concept $a$, let $\mathcal{I}[a]$ be all constants and all role chains $\sigma$ where $\sigma = r_1 \cdots r_k$ for some $k \geq 0$ and such that $d'$ is of the form

$$[\textbf{AND} \ldots [\textbf{ALL } r_1 \ldots [\textbf{AND} \ldots [\textbf{ALL } r_k\, a] \ldots ] \ldots ] \ldots ];$$

finally, for every role $r$, let $\mathcal{I}[r]$ be every pair of constants, together with every pair $(\sigma, \sigma \cdot r)$ where $\sigma$ is a role chain, together with every pair $(\sigma, c)$ where $c$ is a constant, $\sigma = r_1 \cdots r_k$ where $k \geq 0$, and such that $d'$ is of the form

$$[\textbf{AND} \ldots [\textbf{ALL } r_1 \ldots [\textbf{AND} \ldots [\textbf{ALL } r_k\, [\textbf{FILLS } r\, c]] \ldots ] \ldots ] \ldots ].$$

Assuming the procedure returns NO, it can be shown for this interpretation that the empty role chain is in the extension of $d'$, but not in the extension of $e'$, and consequently that $d'$ does not subsume $e'$. We omit all further details.

## 9.4.5  Computing Satisfaction

Computing whether an individual denoted by a constant satisfies a concept is very similar to computing subsumption between two concepts. The main difference is that we need to take the $\rightarrow$ sentences in the KB into account. In general, we wish to determine whether or not KB $\models (b \rightarrow e)$, where $b$ is a constant and $e$ is a concept. For example, if we have a KB that contains $(b \rightarrow d)$ and where KB $\models (d \sqsubseteq e)$, then we clearly have a case where KB $\models$ ($b \rightarrow e$). This suggests that we should collect together all sentences of the form ($b \rightarrow d_i$) in the KB, and answer YES when the concept [**AND** $d_1 \ldots d_n$] is subsumed by $e$. However, this would miss some necessary inferences. For example, suppose we have a KB that contains

```
joe  →  Person
canCorp  →  [AND Company
                 [ALL :Manager Canadian]
                 [FILLS :Manager joe]]
```

It is not hard to see that KB $\models$ (joe $\rightarrow$ Canadian), even though the $\rightarrow$ sentence in the KB about joe does not lead us to this conclusion. In general, to find out if an individual satisfies a description, we will need to *propagate* the information implied by what we know about other individuals (either named by constants or unnamed fillers of roles) before checking for subsumption.

This can be done with a form of forward chaining, similar to how we dealt with entailment for Horn clauses. Assuming for the moment that there are no **EXISTS** terms in any concept, we can use the following procedure:

1. Construct a list $S$ of pairs ($b, d$), where $b$ is any constant mentioned in the KB and $d$ is the normalized version of the **AND** of all concepts $d'$ such that ($b \rightarrow d'$) is in the KB.

2. Try to find two constants, $b_1$ and $b_2$, such that ($b_1, d_1$) and ($b_2, d_2$) are in $S$ and where for some role $r$, [**FILLS** $r$ $b_2$] and [**ALL** $r$ $e$] are both components of $d_1$, but it is not the case that KB $\models$ ($d_2 \sqsubseteq e$).

3. If no such pair of constants can be found, exit. Otherwise, replace the pair ($b_2, d_2$) in $S$ by ($b_2, d_2'$), where $d_2'$ is the normalized version of [**AND** $d_2$ $e$], and then go to step 2.

This procedure has the effect of computing for each constant $b$ the most specific concept $d$ such that KB $\models$ ($b \rightarrow d$). Once it has been run, to test whether or not KB $\models$ ($b \rightarrow e$), we need only test whether or not KB $\models$ ($d \sqsubseteq e$). Observe that the forward chaining will terminate in time that is polynomial in the size of the KB, because, at the very worst, for each constant $b$ we will end up with a pair ($b, d$) where $d$ is the **AND** of every component mentioned in the KB, after which no further propagation will be possible.

To handle terms of the form [**EXISTS** 1 $r$], a similar idea can be used. Instead of having pairs ($b, d$) in $S$, we allow pairs ($b \cdot \sigma, d$), where $\sigma$ is a role chain (as in the previous subsection). Intuitively, $b \cdot r_1 \cdot r_2$ can be understood as an individual that is an $r_2$ of an $r_1$ of $b$ (perhaps unnamed). When $\sigma$ is empty, this corresponds to $b$ itself. We then extend the forward chaining procedure to these new terms by inserting some additional steps in the procedure just before the end, as follows:

- Try to find a constant $b$, a role chain $\sigma$ (possibly empty), and a role $r$, such that $(b \cdot \sigma, d_1)$ is in $S$ and some $(b \cdot \sigma \cdot r, d_2)$ is in $S$ (or if no such pair exists, take $d_2$ to be Thing), and where [**EXISTS** 1 $r$] and [**ALL** $r$ $e$] are both components of $d_1$, but it is not the case that KB $\models (d_2 \sqsubseteq e)$.

- If these can be found, remove the pair $(b \cdot \sigma \cdot r, d_2)$ from $S$ (if applicable), and add the pair $(b \cdot \sigma \cdot r, d_2')$ where $d_2'$ is the normalized version of [**AND** $d_2$ $e$]. Repeat.

This extends the propagation procedure to anonymous individuals: We start with some property of the individual $b \cdot \sigma$ and conclude something new about the individual $b \cdot \sigma \cdot r$. Eventually, this can lead us to conclude something new about a named individual. For example, it would allow us to conclude correctly that (marianne $\rightarrow$ Scandinavian), assuming we have the following in the KB:

ellen $\rightarrow$ [**AND** [**EXISTS** 1 :Child]
                [**ALL** :Child [**AND** [**FILLS** :Pediatrician marianne]
                                    [**ALL** :Pediatrician Scandinavian]]]]

If we did not allow this propagation, the original procedure would not draw the conclusion about Marianne, because there is no constant in the KB corresponding to a child of Ellen.

Finally, to handle terms of the form [**EXISTS** $n$ $r$] where $n > 1$, we observe that it is not necessary to create $n$ different anonymous individuals, because they would all get exactly the same properties in the forward chaining. So the more general case is handled the same as when $n = 1$.

## 9.5 TAXONOMIES AND CLASSIFICATION

In practice, there are a small number of key questions that would typically be asked of a description logic KB. Because these KBs resemble databases, where the concepts correspond roughly to elements of a schema and constants correspond to records, it is common to ask for all of the instances of a concept:

given some query concept, $q$, find all $c$ in KB such that KB $\models (c \rightarrow q)$.

On the other hand, because these KBs resemble frame systems in some ways, it is common to ask for all of the known categories that an individual satisfies, in order, for example, to trigger procedures associated with those classes:

given a constant $c$, find all atomic concepts $a$ such that $\text{KB} \models (c \to a)$.

While the logic and computational methods we have presented so far are adequate for finding the answers to these questions, a naïve approach might consider doing a full scan of the KB, requiring time that grows linearly with the number of sentences in the KB. However, one of the key reasons for using a description logic in the first place is to exploit the fact that concepts are naturally thought of as organized hierarchically, with the most general ones at the top and the more specialized ones further down. In this section, we will consider a special treelike data structure that we call a *taxonomy* for representing sentences in a description logic KB. This taxonomy will allow us to answer queries like the above much more efficiently, requiring time that in many cases grows linearly with the *depth* of the taxonomy, rather than its *size*. The net result: It becomes practical to consider extremely large knowledge bases, with thousands or even millions of concepts and constants.

## 9.5.1  A Taxonomy of Atomic Concepts and Constants

The key observation is that subsumption is a partial order, and a taxonomy naturally falls out of any given set of concepts. Assume that $a_1, \ldots, a_n$ are all the atomic concepts that occur on the left-hand sides of $\doteq$ or $\sqsubseteq$ sentences in KB. The resultant taxonomy will have nodes for each of the $a_i$ and edges from $a_i$ up to $a_j$, whenever $a_i \sqsubseteq a_j$ and there is no distinct $a_k$ such that $a_i \sqsubseteq a_k \sqsubseteq a_j$. This will produce a directed acyclic graph. The graph will have no redundant links in it, and the transitivity of the links will capture all of the subsumption relationships implied by the declarations defining $a_i$. If we add to this the requirement that each constant $c$ in KB be linked only to the most specific atomic concepts $a_i$ such that $\text{KB} \models (c \to a_i)$, we have a hierarchical representation of KB that makes our key questions easier to answer.[8]

Once we have a taxonomy of concepts corresponding to some KB, we can consider adding a sentence to the KB for some new atomic concept or constant. This will involve creating some links from the new concept or constant to existing ones in the taxonomy, and perhaps redirecting some existing links. This process is called *classification*. Because classification itself exploits the structure of the taxonomy, the process can be done efficiently. Furthermore, we can think of building the entire taxonomy by

---

[8]We assume that with each node in the taxonomy we also store the concept making up the right-hand side of the sentence it appeared in.

classification: We start with a single concept Thing in the taxonomy, and then add new atomic concepts and constants to it incrementally.

## 9.5.2 Computing Classification

We begin by considering how to add a sentence $(a_{new} \doteq d)$ to a taxonomy where $a_{new}$ is an atomic concept not appearing anywhere in the KB and $d$ is any concept:

1. We first calculate $S$, the *most specific subsumers* of $d$, that is, the set of atomic concepts $a$ in the taxonomy such that $\text{KB} \models (d \sqsubseteq a)$, but such that there is no $a'$ other than $a$ such that $\text{KB} \models (d \sqsubseteq a')$ and $\text{KB} \models (a' \sqsubseteq a)$. We will see how to do this efficiently in a moment.

2. We next calculate $G$, the *most general subsumees* of $d$, that is, the set of atomic concepts $a$ in the taxonomy such that $\text{KB} \models (a \sqsubseteq d)$, but such that there is no $a'$ other than $a$ such that $\text{KB} \models (a' \sqsubseteq d)$ and $\text{KB} \models (a \sqsubseteq a')$. We will also see how to do this efficiently.

3. If there is a concept $a$ in $S \cap G$, then the new concept $a_{new}$ is already present in the taxonomy under a different name (namely, $a$), and no action is necessary.

4. Otherwise, if there are any links from concepts in $G$ up to concepts in $S$, we remove them, because we will be putting $a_{new}$ between the two groups.

5. We add links from $a_{new}$ up to each concept in $S$, and links from each concept in $G$ up to $a_{new}$.

6. Finally, we handle constants: We calculate $C$, the set of constants $c$ in the taxonomy such that for every $a \in S$, $\text{KB} \models (c \rightarrow a)$, but such that there is no $a' \in G$ such that $\text{KB} \models (c \rightarrow a')$. (This is done by doing intersections and set differences on the sets of constants below concepts in the obvious way.) Then, for each $c \in C$, we test if $\text{KB} \models (c \rightarrow d)$, and if so, we remove the links from $c$ to the concepts in $S$ and add a single link from $c$ to $a_{new}$.

To add a sentence $(a_{new} \sqsubseteq d)$ to a taxonomy, the procedure is similar, but simpler. Because $a_{new}$ is a new primitive, there will be no concepts or constants below it in the taxonomy. So we need only link $a_{new}$ to the most specific subsumers of $d$. Similarly, to add a sentence $(c_{new} \rightarrow d)$, we again link $c_{new}$ to the most specific subsumers of $d$.

Now, to calculate the most specific subsumers of a concept $d$, we begin at the very top of the taxonomy with the set {Thing} as our first $S$. Assume we have a list $S$ of subsumers of $d$. Suppose that some $a \in S$

has at least one child $a'$ immediately below it in the taxonomy such that KB $\models (d \sqsubseteq a')$. Then we remove $a$ from $S$ and replace it with all those children $a'$. We keep doing this until no element of $S$ has a child that subsumes $d$.

Observe that if we have an atomic concept $a'$ below $a \in S$ that does *not* subsume $d$, then we will not use any other concept below this $a'$ during the classification. If $a'$ is high enough in the taxonomy, such as just below Thing, an entire subtree can be safely ignored. This is the sense in which the structure of the taxonomy allows us to do classification efficiently even for very large knowledge bases.

Finally, to calculate the most general subsumees $G$ of a concept $d$, we start with the most specific subsumers $S$ as our first $G$. Because $d$ is subsumed by the elements of $S$, we know that any concept that is below $d$ will be below the elements of $S$ as well. Again, other distant parts of the taxonomy will not be used. Suppose that for some $a \in G$ it is not the case that KB $\models (a \sqsubseteq d)$. Then we remove $a$ from $G$ and replace it with all the children of $a$ (or simply delete $a$, if it has no children). We keep doing this, working our way down the taxonomy, until every element of $G$ is subsumed by $d$. Finally, we repeatedly delete any $a \in G$ that has a parent that is also subsumed by $d$.

Following this procedure, Figure 9.2 shows how a new concept, Surgeon, defined by the sentence (Surgeon $\doteq$ [**AND** Doctor [**FILLS** :Specialty surgery]]), can be classified, given a taxonomy that already includes appropriate

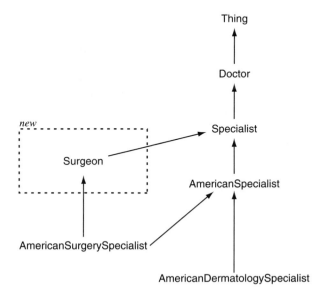

▪ **FIGURE 9.2**

Classifying a New Concept in a Taxonomy

definitions for concepts like Doctor, AmericanSpecialist, and so on. First, we calculate the most specific subsumers of Surgeon, $S$. We start with $S = \{Thing\}$. Assume that none of the direct subsumees of Thing except for Doctor subsume Surgeon. Given that, and the fact that (Surgeon $\sqsubseteq$ Doctor), we replace Thing in the set $S$ by Doctor. The concept Specialist is immediately below Doctor, and (Surgeon $\sqsubseteq$ Specialist), so we then replace Doctor in $S$ with Specialist. Finally, we see that no child of Specialist subsumes Surgeon (i.e., not all surgeons are American specialists), so we have computed the set of most specific subsumers, $S = \{Specialist\}$.

Now we turn our attention to the most general subsumees. We start with $G = S = \{Specialist\}$. It is not the case that (Specialist $\sqsubseteq$ Surgeon), so we replace Specialist in $G$ with its one child in the taxonomy; now $G = \{AmericanSpecialist\}$. Similarly, it is not the case that (AmericanSpecialist $\sqsubseteq$ Surgeon), so we replace that concept in $G$ with its children, resulting in $G = \{AmericanDermatologySpecialist, AmericanSurgerySpecialist\}$. Then, since AmericanDermatologySpecialist is not subsumed by Surgeon, and that concept has no children, it is deleted from $G$. Finally, we see that it is the case that (AmericanSurgerySpecialist $\sqsubseteq$ Surgeon), and we are done, with $G = \{AmericanSurgerySpecialist\}$. As a result of this classification process, the new concept, Surgeon, is placed between the two concepts Specialist and AmericanSurgerySpecialist.

### 9.5.3 Answering the Questions

If we construct in this manner a taxonomy corresponding to a knowledge base, we are in a position to answer the key description logic questions quite easily. To find all of the constants that satisfy a query concept, $q$, we simply classify $q$ and then collect all constants at the fringe of the tree below $q$. This would involve a simple tree walk in only the part of the taxonomy subtended by $q$. Similarly, to find all atomic concepts that are satisfied by a constant $c$, we start at $c$ and walk up the tree, collecting all concept nodes that can be reached by following the links representing subsumption.

### 9.5.4 Taxonomies versus Frame Hierarchies

The taxonomies we derive by classification in a description logic KB look a lot like the hierarchies of frames we encountered in the preceding chapter. In the case of frames, the KB designer could create the hierarchy in any arbitrary way desired, simply by adding whatever **:IS-A** and **:INSTANCE-OF** slot-fillers seemed appropriate. However, with DLs the logic of concepts dictates what each concept means, as well as what must be above or below it in the resulting taxonomy. As a result, we cannot just throw labeled nodes together in a hierarchy or arbitrarily change a taxonomy—we must honor the relationships implicit in the structures of the concepts. A concept of the form [**AND** Fish [**FILLS** :Size large]...] *must* appear in a taxonomy below Fish, even if we originally (perhaps mistakenly) constructed it to be the referent of Whale. If we at some point realized that that was an inaccurate rendition of Whale, what would have to be changed is the association of the symbol Whale with the expression, changing it to perhaps [**AND** Mammal [**FILLS** :Size large]...]. But the compound concept with Fish in it could not possibly go anywhere in the taxonomy but under Fish.

### 9.5.5   Inheritance and Propagation

Recall that in our frames chapter (Chapter 8) we introduced the notion of *inheritance*, whereby individual frames were taken to have values (and attached procedures) represented in parent frames somewhere up the generalization hierarchy. The same phenomenon can be seen here with description logic taxonomies: A constant in the taxonomy should be taken as having all properties (as expressed by **ALL**, **FILLS**, and **EXISTS**) that appear both on it locally (as part of the right-hand side of the sentence where it was first introduced) and on any parent concept further up the taxonomy.

Inheritance here tends to be much simpler than inheritance found in most frame systems, because it is *strict*: There are no exceptions permitted by the logic of the concept-forming operators. It is important to note, though, that these inferences are sanctioned by the logic, and issues of how to compute them using the taxonomy are purely implementation considerations. We will return to a much richer notion of inheritance in the next chapter.

Another important inference in practical description logic systems involves the *propagation* of properties to an individual caused by an assertion. We are imagining, in other words, that we can add a sentence $(c \rightarrow d)$ to the KB even if we had already previously classified $c$. This can then cause other constants to be reclassified. For example, suppose we introduce Lauren with the sentence (lauren → [**FILLS** :Child rebecca]), and we define ParentOfDocs by

(ParentOfDocs $\doteq$ [**ALL** :Child Doctor]).

Then, as soon as it is asserted that (lauren → ParentOfDocs), we are forced to conclude that Rebecca is a doctor. (This is what would happen with the forward-chaining procedure of Section 9.4.5.) If it were also the case that (rebecca → Woman), and we had the atomic concept FemaleDoc defined as [**AND** Woman Doctor], then the assertion about Lauren should result in Rebecca being reclassified as a FemaleDoc.

This kind of cascaded inference is interesting in applications where membership in classes is monitored and changes in class membership are considered significant (e.g., imagine we are monitoring the stock market and have concepts representing stocks whose values are changing in significant ways). It is also reminiscent of the kind of cascaded computation we saw with frame systems, except that here again the computations are dictated by the logic.

## 9.6  BEYOND THE BASICS

In this final section, we examine briefly how we can move beyond the simple picture of description logics presented so far.

### 9.6.1  Extensions to the Language

First, we consider some extensions to $\mathcal{DL}$ that would make it more useful. Each of the extensions ends up having serious consequences for computing subsumption or satisfaction. In many cases, it is no longer possible to use normalization and structure matching to do the job; in some cases, subsumption can even be shown to be undecidable.[9]

**Bounds on the Number of Role Fillers**   The $\mathcal{DL}$ construct **EXISTS** is used to say that a role has a minimum number of fillers. We can think of the dual operator **AT-MOST** where [**AT-MOST** $n\ r$] describes individuals related by role $r$ to *at most* $n$ individuals. This seemingly small addition to $\mathcal{DL}$ in fact allows a wide range of new inferences. First of all, we can have descriptions like

[**AND** [**EXISTS** 4 $r$] [**AT-MOST** 3 $r$]],

which are *inconsistent* in that their extension is guaranteed to be the empty set. Moreover, a simple concept like [**ALL** $r\ d$] now subsumes one like

[**AND** [**FILLS** $r\ c$] [**AT-MOST** 1 $r$] [**ALL** $s\ d$] [**FILLS** $s\ c$]]

even though there is no obvious structure to match.

We should also note that as soon as inconsistency is allowed into the language, computation gets complex. Besides the difficulties with structure matching just noted, normalization also suffers. For example, if we have found $d$ to be inconsistent, then although [**ALL** $r\ d$] is not inconsistent by itself, the result of conjoining it with [**EXISTS** 1 $r$] is inconsistent, and this would need to be detected during normalization.

---

[9]We will revisit this important issue in detail in Chapter 16.

**Sets of Individuals**  Another important construct would package up a set of individuals into a set concept, which could then be used, for example, in restricting the values of roles. [**ONE-OF** $c_1$ $c_2$ ... $c_n$] would be a concept that could only be satisfied by the $c_i$. In an **ALL** restriction, we might find such a set:

[**ALL** :BandMember [**ONE-OF** john paul george ringo]]

would represent the concept of something whose band members could only be taken from the specified set. Note that such a combination would have consequences for the cardinality of the :BandMember role, implying [**AT-MOST** 4 :BandMember], although it would imply nothing about the minimum number of band members.

**Relating the Roles**  While we have discussed classes of objects with internal structure (via their roles), we have ignored a key ingredient of complex terms—how the role fillers actually interrelate. A simple case of this is when fillers for two roles are required to be identical. Consider a construct [**SAME-AS** $r_1$ $r_2$], which equates the fillers of roles $r_1$ and $r_2$. [**AND** Company [**SAME-AS** :CEO :President]] would thus mean a company whose CEO was identical to its president. Despite its apparent simplicity, without some restrictions, **SAME-AS** makes subsumption difficult to compute (even undecidable, with the right other constructs). This is especially true if we allow a very natural extension to the **SAME-AS** construct— allowing it to take as arguments chains of roles, rather than single roles. In that case, [**SAME-AS** (:Mother :Sister)(:Father :Partner :Lawyer)] would represent something whose mother's sister is its father's partner's lawyer. Computation can be simplified by restricting **SAME-AS** to chains of "features" or "attributes"—roles that have exactly one filler.

**Qualified Number Restrictions**  Another natural extension to $\mathcal{DL}$ is what has been called a "qualified number restriction." [**EXISTS** $n$ $r$ $d$] would allow us to represent something that is $r$-related to $n$ individuals who are also instances of $d$. For example, [**EXISTS** 2 :Child Female] would represent someone with at least two daughters. This is a very natural and useful construct, but as we will explore in detail in Chapter 16, it causes surprising computational difficulties, even if the rest of the language is kept very simple.

**Complex Roles**  So far we have taken roles to be primitive atomic constructs. It is plausible to consider a logic of roles reminiscent of the logic of concepts. For example, some description logics have role-forming operators that construct *conjunctive roles* (much like **AND** over concepts). This would imply a role taxonomy akin to the concept taxonomy. Another extension that has been explored is that of *role inverses*.

If we have introduced a role like :Parent, it is quite natural to think of introducing :Child to be defined as its inverse.

**Rules**   In $\mathcal{DL}$, there is no way to *assert* that all instances of one concept are also instances of another. Consider, for example, the concept of a red Bordeaux wine, which we might define as follows:

(RedBordeauxWine $\doteq$ [**AND** Wine
                      [**FILLS** :Color red]
                      [**FILLS** :Region bordeaux]])

We might also have the following concept:

(DryRedBordeauxWine $\doteq$ [**AND** Wine
                         [**FILLS** :Color red]
                         [**FILLS** :Region bordeaux]
                         [**FILLS** :SugarContent dry]])

These two concepts are clearly not equivalent. But suppose that we want to assert that all red Bordeaux wines are in fact dry. If we were to try to do this by using the second concept as the definition of RedBordeauxWine, we would be saying in effect that red Bordeaux wines are dry *by definition*. In this case, the status of the first concept would be unclear: Should the subsumption relation be changed somehow so that the two concepts end up being equivalent? To avoid this difficulty, we can keep the original definition of RedBordeauxWine, but extend $\mathcal{DL}$ with a simple form of *rules*, which capture universal assertions. A rule will have an atomic concept as its antecedent and an arbitrary concept as its consequent:

(**if** RedBordeauxWine **then** [**FILLS** :SugarContent dry])

Rules of this sort give us a new and quite useful form of propagation: A constant gets classified, then inherits rules from concepts that it satisfies, which then are applied and yield new properties for the constant (and possibly other constants), which can then cause a new round of classification. This is reminiscent of the triggering of **IF-ADDED** procedures in frame systems, except that the classification is done automatically.

## 9.6.2   Applications of Description Logics

We now turn our attention to how description logic systems can be utilized in practical applications.

**Assertion and Query**   One mode of use is the exploration of the consequences of axiomatizing a domain by describing it in a concept hierarchy.

In this scenario, we generate a taxonomy of useful general categories and then describe individuals in terms of those categories. The system then classifies the individuals according to the general scheme and propagates to related individuals any new properties that they should accrue. We might then ask if a given individual satisfies a certain concept, or we might ask for the entire set of individuals satisfying a concept.

This would be appealing in a situation where a catalogue of products was described in terms of a complex domain model. The system may be able to determine that a product falls into some categories unanticipated by the user.

Another situation in which this style of interaction is important involves configuration of complex structured items. Asserting that a certain board goes in a certain slot of a computer hardware assembly could cause the propagation of constraints to other boards, power supplies, software, and so on. The domain theory then acts as a kind of object-oriented constraint propagator. One could also ask questions about properties of an incrementally evolving configuration, or even "what if" questions.

**Contradiction Detection in Configuration** Configuration-style applications can also make good use of contradiction-detection facilities for those DLs that have enough power to express them. In particular, as an incremental picture of the configured assembly evolves, it is useful to detect when a proposed part or subassembly violates some constraint expressed in the knowledge base. This keeps us from making invalid configurations. It is also possible to design explanation mechanisms so that the reasons for the violation can be outlined to the user.

**Classification and Contradiction Detection in Knowledge Acquisition** In a similar way, some of the inferential properties of a description logic system can be used as partial validation during knowledge acquisition. As we add more concepts or constants to a DL knowledge base, a DL system will notice if any inconsistencies are introduced. This can alert us to mistakes. Because of its classification property, a DL can make us aware of certain failures of domain modeling in a way that frame systems cannot, for example, the unintended merger of two concepts that look different on the surface but mutually subsume one another, or the unintended classification of a new item below one that the user had not expected.

**Assertion and Classification in Monitoring Scenarios** In some applications, it is normal to build the description of an individual incrementally over time. This might be the case in a diagnosis scenario, where information about a suspected fault is gathered in pieces, or in a situation with a hardware device sending a stream of status and error reports. Such an incremental setting leads one to expect the refinement of classifications of individuals over time. If we are on the lookout for members of certain classes (e.g., Class1CriticalError), we can alert a user when new members for those classes are generated by new data. We can also imagine actions (external procedures) being triggered automatically when such class members are found. Although this begins to sound like the sort of operation done with a procedural system, in the case of a DL the detection of interesting situations is handled automatically once the situations are described as concepts.

**Working Memory for a Production System**    This scenario is somewhat reminiscent of a common use of production systems; in situations where the description logic language is expressive enough, a DL could in fact be used entirely to take the place of a production system. In other cases, it may be useful to preserve the power and style of a production system, but a DL might provide some very useful added value. In particular, if the domain of interest has a natural object-oriented, hierarchical structure, as so many do, a true picture of the domain can only be achieved in a pure production system if there are explicit rules capturing the inheritance relationships, part–whole relationships, and so on. An alternative would be to use a DL as the working memory. The DL would encode the hierarchical domain theory and take care of classification and inheritance automatically. The production system could then restrict its attention to complex pattern detection and action—where it belongs—with its rules represented at just the right, natural level (the antecedents could refer to classes at any level of a DL generalization hierarchy), avoiding any *ad hoc* attempts to encode inheritance or classification procedurally.

**Using Concepts as Queries and Access to Databases**    It is possible to think of a concept as a query asking for all of its instances. Imagine we have "raw" data stored in a relational database system. We can then develop an object-oriented model of the world in our DL and specify a mapping from that model to the schema used in the conventional database management system (DBMS). This would then allow us to ask questions of a relational database mediated by an object-oriented domain model. One could implement such a hybrid system either by preclassifying in the KB all objects from the DB and using classification of a DL query to find answers, or leaving the data in the DB and dynamically translating a DL query into a DB query language like SQL.

## 9.7    BIBLIOGRAPHIC NOTES

Description logics grew out of research in the 1970s and 1980s driven by interest in overcoming representational and semantic difficulties in "semantic network" and frame languages (see the notes for Chapter 10 and Chapter 8). The original work was done in the context of a knowledge representation system called KL-ONE [41, 49]. An important development in this line of work was the differentiation between "terminological" information, which captured definitions and relations among concepts, and "assertional" information, which captured information about individuals in the domain [45]. The first system to make this distinction explicit was KRYPTON [51, 52]. KANDOR [316] was a related, but more compact version (see also [317]). Besides being useful in certain types of information retrieval tasks [318], KANDOR helped start thinking in the emerging description logic community about the value of expressively limited representation systems, as we will discuss in detail in Chapter 16.

The recent *Description Logic Handbook* [18] is an excellent comprehensive resource for information on all aspects of this kind of representation system, including interesting extensions to the basic framework.

While subsumption was originally most often computed structurally in the way presented here, most modern systems use a tableau-style computation regime [18]. A good account of the original notion of classification is provided by Schmolze and Lipkis [368].

For examples of possible applications of description logics, see Baader et al. [17] and Wright et al. [434]. [44] looks at the potential of database access mediated by a DL-based object-oriented view mechanism. Brachman et al. [53] discuss how the implementation and deployment of the CLASSIC system [36] influenced the theory underlying it (and vice versa). Recent work on OWL [191], which provides knowledge-structuring primitives that can be used to build ontologies for the Semantic Web [27], is based on description logics.

## 9.8  EXERCISES

1. In this chapter, we considered the semantics of a description logic language that includes concept-forming operators such as **FILLS** and **EXISTS** but no role-forming operators. In this question, we extend the language with new concept-forming operators and role-forming operators.

   (a) Present a formal semantics in the style of Section 9.3.1 for the following concept-forming operators:

      ▪ [**SOME** $r$]   Role existence.
        Something with at least 1 $r$.
      ▪ [**AT-MOST** $n$ $r$]   Maximum role cardinality.
        Something with at most $n$ $r$'s.

(b) Do the same for the following role-forming operators:

- [**INVERSE** $r$]    Role inverse.
  So the :Child role could be defined as [**INVERSE** :Parent].
- [**COMPOSE** $r_1 \dots r_{n-1}\ r_n$]    Role composition.
  The $r_n$'s of the $r_{n-1}$'s ... of the $r_1$'s.
  So [**ALL** [**COMPOSE** :Parent :BrotherInLaw] Rich] would mean
  something all of whose uncles are rich (where an uncle is
  a brother-in-law of a parent).

(c) Use this semantic specification to show that for any roles $r$, $s$,
and $t$, the concept

[**ALL** [**COMPOSE** $r$ $s$] [**SOME** $t$]]

subsumes the concept

[**ALL** $r$ [**AND** [**ALL** $s$ [**EXISTS** 2 $t$]] [**ALL** $s$ [**AT-MOST** 2 $t$]]]]

by showing that the extension of the latter concept is always
a subset of the extension of the former.

2. Consider a new concept-forming operator, **AMONG**, which takes two
   arguments, each of which can be a role chain (a sequence of one or
   more roles). The description [**AMONG** $(r_1 \dots r_n)\ (s_1 \dots s_m)$] is intended
   to apply to an individual whose $r_n$'s of its $r_{n-1}$'s of its ... of its
   $r_1$'s are a subset of its $s_m$'s of its $s_{m-1}$'s of its ... of its $s_1$'s. For
   example,

   [**AMONG** (:Brother :Friend) (:Sister :Enemy)]

   would mean "something whose friends of its brothers are among the
   enemies of its sisters."

   (a) Give a formal semantics for **AMONG** in the style of Section 9.3.1.
   (b) Use this semantics to show that for any roles $r_i$, the concept

   [**AMONG** $(r_1)\ (r_2\ r_3\ r_4)$]

   subsumes the concept

   [**AND** [**AMONG** $(r_1)\ (r_2\ r_5)$] [**ALL** $r_2$ [**AMONG** $(r_5)\ (r_3\ r_4)$]]].

   (c) Does the subsumption also work in the opposite direction (that is,
   are the two concepts equivalent)? Show why or why not.

(d) Construct an interpretation that shows that neither of the following two concepts subsumes the other:

[**AMONG** $(r_1)$ $(r_2\ r_3\ r_4)$]

and

[**AMONG** $(r_1\ r_2)$ $(r_3\ r_4)$].

3. The procedure given in Section 9.5.2 for finding the most general subsumees $G$ of a concept $d$ says at the very end that we should remove any $a \in G$ that has a parent that is also subsumed by $d$. Explain why this is necessary by presenting an example where the procedure would produce an incorrect answer without it.

4. When building a classification hierarchy, once we have determined that one concept $d_1$ subsumes another $d_2$, it is often useful to calculate the *difference* between the two—the concept that needs to be conjoined to $d_1$ to produce $d_2$. As a trivial example, if we have

$d_1 = $ [**AND** $p$ [**AND** $q\ r$]]

$d_2 = $ [**AND** [**AND** $q\ t$] [**AND** $p\ s$] $r$]

then the difference in question is [**AND** $t\ s$] since $d_2$ is equivalent to

[**AND** $d_1$ [**AND** $t\ s$]].

(a) Implement and test a procedure that takes as arguments two concepts in the following simple language, and when the first subsumes the second, returns a difference as above. You may assume that your input is well-formed. The concept language to use is

*<concept>* ::= [**AND** *<concept>* ... *<concept>*]
*<concept>* ::= [**ALL** *<role> <concept>*]
*<concept>* ::= *<atom>*
*<role>* ::= *<atom>*

with the semantics as presented in the text.

(b) The earlier definition of "difference" is not precise. If all we are after is a concept $d$ such that $d_2$ is equivalent to [**AND** $d_1$ $d$], then $d_2$ itself would qualify as the difference, because $d_2$ is equivalent to [**AND** $d_1$ $d_2$], whenever $d_1$ subsumes $d_2$. Make the definition of what your program calculates precise.

**5.** For this question, you will need to write, test, and document a program that performs normalization and subsumption for a description logic language. The input will be a pair of syntactically correct expressions encoded in a list-structured form. Your system should output a normalized form of each, and a statement of which subsumes the other, or that neither subsumes the other.

The description language your program needs to handle should contain the concept-forming operators **AND**, **ALL**, and **EXISTS** (as described in the text), **AT-MOST** (as used in Exercise 1), but no role-forming operators, so that roles are all atomic. You may assume that all named concepts and roles other than Thing are primitive, so that you do not have to maintain a symbol table or classification hierarchy. Submit output from your program working on at least the following pairs of descriptions:

(a) (1) [**AND** [**ALL** :Employee Canadian]]
    (2) [**ALL** :Employee [**AND** American Canadian]]

(b) (1) [**EXISTS** 0 :Employee]
    (2) [**AT-MOST** 2 :Employee]

(c) (1) [**AND** [**ALL** :Friend [**EXISTS** 3 Teacher]]
          [**ALL** :Friend [**AND** [**ALL** Teacher Person]
                                     [**AT-MOST** 2 Teacher]]]]
    (2) [**ALL** :Friend [**ALL** Teacher Female]]

(d) (1) [**EXISTS** 1 Teacher]
    (2) [**AND** [**EXISTS** 2 Teacher] [**ALL** Teacher Male]]

(e) (1) [**EXISTS** 1 Teacher]
    (2) [**AND** [**AT-MOST** 2 Teacher] [**ALL** Teacher Male]]

(f) (1) [**AND** [**ALL** :Cousin [**EXISTS** 0 :Friend]]
          [**ALL** :Employee Female]]
    (2) [**AND** [**AT-MOST** 0 :Employee]
          [**ALL** :Friend [**AT-MOST** 3 :Cousin]]]

**6.** This question involves writing and running a program to do a simple form of normalization and classification, building a concept hierarchy incrementally. We will use the very simple description language specified by the grammar in Exercise 4a. The atomic concepts here are either primitives or the names of previously classified descriptions.

There are two main programs to write: NORMALIZE and CLASSIFY.

NORMALIZE takes a concept description as its single argument, and returns a normal form description, an **AND** expression where every argument is either a primitive atom or an **ALL** expression whose concept argument is itself in normal form. Within this **AND**, primitives should occur at most once, and **ALL** expressions with the same role should be combined. Nonprimitive atomic concepts need to be replaced by their definitions. (It may simplify the code to leave out the atoms **AND** and **ALL** within normalized descriptions, and just deal with the lists.)

CLASSIFY should take as its two arguments an atom and a description. The idea is that a new concept of that name (the atom) is being defined, and CLASSIFY should first link the name to a normalized version of the description as its definition. CLASSIFY should then position the newly defined concept in a hierarchy of previously defined concepts. Initially, the hierarchy should contain a single concept named Thing. Subsequently, all new concepts can work their way down the hierarchy to their correct position starting at Thing, as explained in the text. (Something will need to be done if there is already a defined concept at that position.)

Show your program working on some examples of your own choosing.

# CHAPTER 10

# INHERITANCE

■

■

■

As we saw in earlier chapters on frames and description logics, when we think about the world in an object-centered way we inevitably end up thinking in terms of hierarchies or taxonomies. This reflects the importance of abstraction, classification, and generalization in the enterprise of knowledge representation. Groups of things in the world naturally share properties, and we talk about them most concisely using words for abstractions like "furniture" or "situation comedy" or "seafood." Further, hierarchies allow us to avoid repeating representations—it is sufficient to say that "elephants are mammals" to immediately know a great deal about them. Taxonomies of kinds of objects are so fundamental to our thinking about the world that they are found everywhere, especially when it comes to organizing knowledge in a comprehensible form for human consumption, in encyclopedias, dictionaries, scientific classifications, and so on.

What does reasoning with a taxonomy amount to? When we are told that elephants are mammals what we expect to conclude is that elephants (by and large) inherit the properties of mammals. In the kind of classification networks we built using description logics, inheritance was just a way of doing a certain type of logical reasoning in a graphically oriented way: If we have a network where the concept PianoConcerto is directly below Concerto, which is directly below MusicalWork, then instances of PianoConcerto inherit properties from MusicalWork because logically all instances of PianoConcerto are also instances of Concerto and thus also instances of MusicalWork. Similar considerations apply in the case of frames, although the reasoning there is not strict: If the **:IS-A** slot of frame AdultHighSchoolStudent points to HighSchoolStudent and HighSchool

Student points to Teenager, then instances of AdultHighSchoolStudent may inherit properties from HighSchoolStudent and in turn from Teenager, but we are no longer justified in concluding that an instance of AdultHigh-SchoolStudent must be an instance of Teenager. In both cases, however, "can (instances of) *a* inherit properties from *b*?" involves asking if we can get from *a* to *b* along some sort of path of generalization relationships.

In order to highlight the richness of this type of reasoning, in this chapter we are going to concentrate just on inheritance and generalization relationships among nodes in a network, suppressing a great deal of representational detail. This will also allow us to introduce a simple but fundamental form of default reasoning, which will be the topic of the next chapter.

## 10.1  INHERITANCE NETWORKS

In this chapter, we reduce the frames and descriptions of previous chapters to simple *nodes* that appear in *inheritance networks*, like the one expressed in Figure 10.1. For our discussion, we treat objectlike concepts, like Elephant, and properties, like Gray, equivalently as nodes. If we wanted to be more precise, we could use terms like GrayThing (for a Thing whose Color role was filled with the individual gray), but for our purposes here that is not really necessary. Also, we normally will not distinguish which nodes at the bottom of the hierarchy stand for individuals like Clyde and which stand for kinds like Elephant. We will capitalize the names of both. We will use the following concepts in our discussion:

- *edges* in the network, connecting one node directly to another. In Figure 10.1, Clyde · Elephant and Elephant · Gray are the two edges.

■ **FIGURE 10.1**

A Simple Inheritance Network

These represent instance or generalization relationships (Clyde is an elephant, an elephant is a gray thing).

- *paths* included in the network; a path is a sequence of one or more edges. So edges are paths, and in Figure 10.1, Clyde · Elephant · Gray is the only other path.

- *conclusions* supported by the paths. In Figure 10.1, three conclusions are supported: Clyde → Elephant; Elephant → Gray; and Clyde → Gray. The last conclusion is supported because the edges represent relationships that are transitive (and so Clyde is a gray thing).

Before getting into some of the interesting complications with inheritance networks, we begin with some simple cases.

## 10.1.1   Strict Inheritance

The simplest form of inheritance is the kind used in description logics and other systems based on classical logic: *strict inheritance*. In a strict inheritance network, conclusions are produced by the complete transitive closures of all paths in the network. Any traversal procedure for computing the transitive closure will do for determining the supported conclusions.

In a tree-structured strict inheritance network, inheritance is very simple. As in Figure 10.2, all nodes reachable from a given node are implied. In this figure, supported conclusions include the fact that Ben is gray and that Clyde is gray.

In a strict inheritance network that is a *directed acyclic graph* (DAG), the results are the same as for trees: All conclusions you can reach by

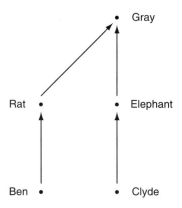

**■ FIGURE 10.2**

Strict Inheritance in a Tree

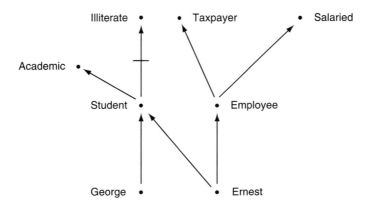

■ **FIGURE 10.3**

Strict Inheritance in a DAG

any path are supported. This includes conclusions found by traversing different branches upward from a node in question. Figure 10.3 illustrates a strict DAG. It says that Ernest is both a student and an employee. The network supports the conclusions that Ernest is an academic, as well as a taxpayer, and salaried.

Note that in this figure we introduce a negative edge with a bar through it, between Student and Illiterate, meaning that a student is *not* an illiterate thing. So edges in these networks have *polarity*—positive or negative. Thus the conclusion that Ernest is not illiterate is supported by the network in the figure.[1]

Inheritance in directed acyclic networks is often called *multiple inheritance* when a node has more than one parent node; in such cases, because of the meaning of the edges, the node must inherit from all of its parents.

## 10.1.2  Defeasible Inheritance

In our study of frame systems, we saw numerous illustrations of a nonstrict inheritance policy. In these representations, inherited properties do not always hold; they can be *defeated*, or overridden. This is most obviously true in the case of default values for slots, such as the default origin of a trip. But a closer examination of the logic of

---

[1]As we will see more precisely in Section 10.3, when a network contains negative edges, a path is considered to be zero or more *positive* edges followed by a single positive or negative edge.

frame systems such as those that we covered in Chapter 8 would suggest that in fact virtually *all* properties (and procedures) can be overridden. We call the kind of inheritance in which properties can be defeated *defeasible inheritance*.

In a defeasible inheritance scheme, one way to determine conclusions is by searching upward from a *focus node*—the one about which we are trying to draw a conclusion—and selecting the first version of the property being considered. An example will make this clear. In Figure 10.4 there is an edge from Clyde to Elephant and one from Elephant to Gray. There is also, however, a negative edge from Clyde directly to Gray. This network is intended to capture the knowledge that while elephants in general are gray, Clyde is not. Intuitively, if we were trying to find what conclusion this network supported about Clyde's color, we would first find the negative conclusion about Gray, because that is directly asserted of Clyde.

In general, what will complicate defeasible reasoning, and what will occupy us for much of this chapter, is the fact that different paths in a network can support conflicting conclusions and a reasoning procedure needs to decide which conclusion should prevail, if any. In the example, there is an argument for Clyde being gray: He is an elephant and elephants are gray; however, there is a "better" argument for concluding that he is not gray, because this has been asserted of him specifically.

In some cases, we will not be able to say which conclusion is better or worse. In Figure 10.5 there is nothing obvious that tells us how to choose between the positive or negative conclusions about Nixon's pacifism. The network tells us that by virtue of his being a Quaker he is a pacifist; it also tells us that by virtue of his being a Republican, he is not. This type of network is said to be *ambiguous*.

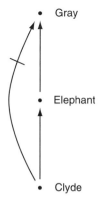

Gray

Elephant

Clyde

■ **FIGURE 10.4**

Defeasible Inheritance

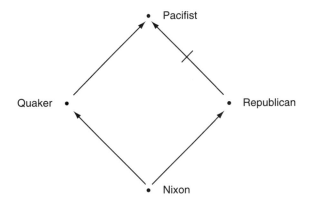

Is Nixon a Pacifist or Not?

When exploring different accounts for reasoning under this kind of circumstance, we typically see two types of approaches: *credulous* (or brave or choice) accounts allow us to choose arbitrarily between conclusions that appear equally well supported; *skeptical* (or cautious) accounts are more conservative, often accepting only conclusions that are not contradicted by other paths. In the Nixon case, a credulous account would in essence flip a coin and choose one of Nixon → Pacifist or Nixon → ¬Pacifist, because either conclusion is as good as the other. A skeptical account would draw no conclusion about Nixon's pacifism.

## 10.2   STRATEGIES FOR DEFEASIBLE INHERITANCE

For DAGs with defeasible inheritance, we need a method for deciding which conclusion to choose (if any) when there are contradictory conclusions supported by different paths through the network. In this section, we examine two possible ways of doing this informally, before moving to a precise characterization of inheritance reasoning in the next section.

### 10.2.1   The Shortest Path Heuristic

Figure 10.6 shows two examples of defeasible inheritance networks that produce intuitively plausible conclusions. In the one on the left, we see that while Royal Elephants are elephants, and elephants are (typically) gray, Royal Elephants are not. Since Clyde is a Royal Elephant, it would be reasonable to assume he is not gray.

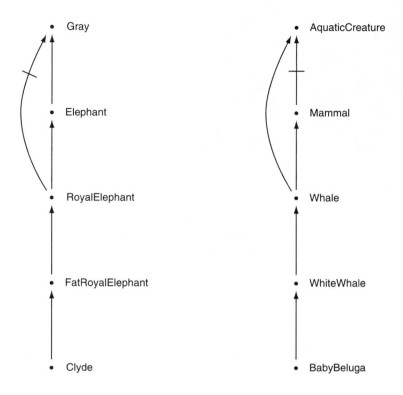

■ **FIGURE 10.6**

Shortest Path Heuristic

To decide this in an automated way, the *shortest path heuristic* says that we should prefer conclusions resulting from shorter paths in the network. Because there are fewer edges in the path from Clyde to Gray that includes the negative edge than in the path that includes the positive edge, the negative conclusion prevails.

In the network on the right, we see the opposite polarity conclusion being supported. Whales are mammals, but mammals are typically not aquatic creatures. Whales are exceptional in that respect, and are directly asserted to be aquatic creatures. We infer using the shortest path heuristic that BabyBeluga is an AquaticCreature.

The intuition behind the shortest path heuristic is that it makes sense to inherit from the most specific subsuming class. If two superclasses up the chain disagree on a property (e.g., Gray vs. ¬Gray), we take the value from the more specific one, because that is likely to be more directly relevant.[2]

_____

[2] A similar consideration arises in probabilistic reasoning in Chapter 12 regarding choosing what is called a "reference class": Our degree of belief in an individual having a certain property depends on the most specific class he or she belongs to for which we have statistics.

Notice then that in defeasible inheritance networks not all paths count in generating conclusions. It makes sense to think of the paths in the network as *arguments* in support of conclusions. Some arguments are *preempted* by others. Those that are not we might call "admissible." The inheritance problem, then, is "What are the admissible conclusions supported by the network?"

### 10.2.2    Problems with Shortest Path

While intuitively plausible, and capable of producing correct conclusions in many cases, the shortest path heuristic has serious flaws. Unfortunately, it can produce intuitively incorrect answers in the presence of redundant edges—those that are already implied by the basic network. Look at the network in Figure 10.7. The edge labeled $q$ is simply redundant, in that it is clear from the rest of the network that Clyde is unambiguously an elephant. But by creating an edge directly from Clyde

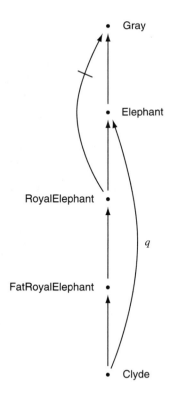

■ **FIGURE 10.7**

Shortest Path in the Face of Redundant Links

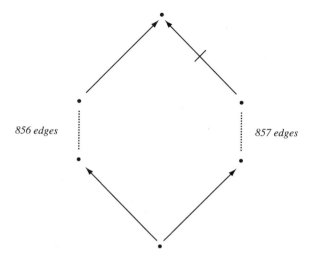

*856 edges*                                        *857 edges*

■ **FIGURE 10.8**

Very Long Paths

to Elephant we have inadvertently changed the polarity of the conclusion about Clyde's color. The path from Clyde to Gray that goes through
edge $q$ is now shorter (length = 2) than the one with the negative edge
from RoyalElephant to Gray (length = 3). So the inclusion of an edge that
is already implicitly part of the network undermines the shortest path
heuristic.

Another problem with the shortest path heuristic is the fact that
the length of a path through the network does not necessarily reflect
anything salient about the domain. Depending on the problem or application, some paths may describe object hierarchies in excruciating detail,
whereas others may be very sketchy. Just because an inheritance chain
makes many fine-grained distinctions, there should not be a bias against
it in drawing conclusions. Figure 10.8 illustrates in a somewhat extreme
way how this causes problems. The left-hand path has a very large number of nodes in it and ends with a positive edge. The right-hand path has
just one more edge and ends with a negative edge. So for this network the
shortest path heuristic supports the positive conclusion. But if we were to
add another two edges—anywhere in the path—to the left-hand side, the
conclusion would be reversed. This seems rather silly; the network should
be considered ambiguous in the same manner as the one in Figure 10.5.

## 10.2.3  Inferential Distance

Shortest path is what is considered to be a *preemption strategy*, which
allows us to make admissibility choices among competing paths. It tries

to provide what is called a *specificity criterion*, matching our intuition that more specific information about an item is more relevant than information more generally true about a broader class of items of which it is a member.

As we have seen, shortest path has its problems. Fortunately, it is not the only possible specificity criterion. A more plausible strategy is *inferential distance*, which rather than being linear distance based, is topologically based.

Consider Figure 10.7 once again. Starting at the node for Clyde, we would like to say that RoyalElephant is more specific than Elephant despite the redundant edge *q* because there is a path to Elephant that passes through RoyalElephant. Because it is more specific, we then prefer the negative edge from RoyalElephant to Gray over the positive one from Elephant to Gray. More generally, a node *a* is considered closer to node *b* than to node *c* according to inferential distance if and only if there is a path from *a* to *c* through *b*, regardless of the actual length of any paths from *a* to *b* and to *c*.

This criterion handles the earlier simple cases of inheritance from Figure 10.6. Furthermore, in the case of the ambiguous network of Figure 10.8, inferential distance prefers neither conclusion, as desired.

Unfortunately, inferential distance has its own problems. What should happen, for example, when the path from *a* through *b* to *c* is itself contradicted by another path? Rather than attempt to patch the definition to deal with such problematic cases, we will consider a different formalization of inheritance that incorporates a version of inferential distance as well as other reasonable accounts of defeasible inheritance networks.

## 10.3  A FORMAL ACCOUNT OF INHERITANCE NETWORKS

The discussion so far has been intended to convey some of the intent and issues behind defeasible inheritance networks, but has been somewhat informal. The ideas in these networks can be captured and studied in a much more formal way. We here briefly present one of the clearer formal accounts of inheritance networks (there are many that are impenetrable), owing to Lynn Stein.

An *inheritance hierarchy* $\Gamma = \langle V, E \rangle$ is a directed, acyclic graph with positive and negative edges, intended to denote "(normally) is-a" and "(normally) is-not-a," respectively (*V* are the nodes, or vertices, in the graph; *E* are the edges). Positive edges will be written as $(a \cdot x)$ and negative edges will be written as $(a \cdot \neg x)$.

A *positive path* is a sequence of one or more positive edges $a \cdot \ldots \cdot x$. A *negative path* is a sequence of zero or more positive edges followed by a single negative edge: $a \cdot \ldots \cdot v \cdot \neg x$. A *path* is either a positive or negative path.

Note that there are no paths with more than one negative edge, although a negative path could have no positive edges (i.e., be just a negative edge).

A path (or *argument*) supports a *conclusion* in the following ways:

- $a \cdot \ldots \cdot x$ supports the conclusion $a \rightarrow x$ ($a$ is an $x$);
- $a \cdot \ldots \cdot v \cdot \neg x$ supports the conclusion $a \not\rightarrow x$ ($a$ is not an $x$).

A single conclusion can be supported by many arguments. However, not all arguments are equally believable. We now look at what makes an argument prevail, given other arguments in the network. This stems from a formal definition of admissibility:

> $\Gamma$ *supports a path* if the corresponding set of edges are in $E$, and the path is admissible according to the definition that follows. The hierarchy *supports a conclusion* $a \rightarrow x$ (or $a \not\rightarrow x$) if it supports some corresponding path between $a$ and $x$.
>
> A path $a \cdot s_1 \cdot \ldots \cdot s_n \cdot (\neg)x$ is *admissible* if every edge in it is admissible with respect to $a$.
>
> An edge $v \cdot (\neg)x$ is *admissible in* $\Gamma$ *with respect to* $a$ if there is a positive path $a \cdot s_1 \cdot \ldots s_n \cdot v$ ($n \geq 0$) in $E$ and

1. each edge in $a \cdot s_1 \cdot \ldots s_n \cdot v$ is admissible in $\Gamma$ with respect to $a$ (recursively);

2. no edge in $a \cdot s_1 \cdot \ldots s_n \cdot v$ is redundant in $\Gamma$ with respect to $a$ (discussed later);

3. no intermediate node $a, s_1, \ldots, s_n$ is a preemptor of $v \cdot (\neg)x$ with respect to $a$ (discussed later).

So, an edge is admissible with respect to $a$ if there is a nonredundant, admissible path leading to it from $a$ that contains no preempting intermediaries. This situation is sketched in Figure 10.9.

*the edge under consideration*

$a \qquad s_i \qquad v \qquad x$

■ **FIGURE 10.9**

Basic Path Situation for Formalization

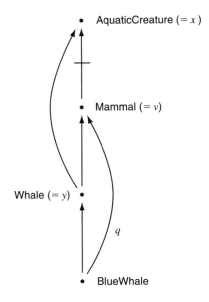

■ **FIGURE 10.10**

A Preempting Node

The definitions of preemption along a path and of redundancy will complete the basic formalization:

A node $y$ along path $a \cdot \ldots \cdot y \cdot \ldots \cdot v$ is a *preemptor* of $v \cdot x$ $(v \cdot \neg x)$ *with respect to* $a$ if $y \cdot \neg x \in E$ $(y \cdot x \in E)$. For example, in Figure 10.10, the node Whale preempts the negative edge from Mammal to AquaticCreature with respect to both Whale and BlueWhale.

A positive edge $b \cdot w$ is a *redundant* in $\Gamma$ with respect to node $a$ if there is some positive path $b \cdot t_1 \cdot \ldots \cdot t_m \cdot w \in E$ $(m \geq 1)$ for which

1. each edge in $b \cdot t_1 \cdot \ldots \cdot t_m$ is admissible in $\Gamma$ with respect to $a$ (i.e., none of the edges are themselves preempted);

2. there are no $c$ and $i$ such that $c \cdot \neg t_i$ is admissible in $\Gamma$ with respect to $a$;

3. there is no $c$ such that $c \cdot \neg w$ is admissible in $\Gamma$ with respect to $a$.

By this definition, the edge labeled $q$ in Figure 10.10 is redundant with respect to BlueWhale. The definition of redundancy for a negative edge is analogous.

### 10.3.1 Extensions

Now that we have covered the basics of admissibility and preemption, we can finally look at how to calculate what conclusions should be believed given an inheritance network. As noted in Section 10.1.2, we do not expect an ambiguous network to specify a unique set of conclusions. We use the term *extension* to mean a possible set of beliefs supported by the network. Ambiguous networks will have multiple extensions. More formally, we have the following:

> $\Gamma$ is *a-connected* iff for every node $x$ in $\Gamma$, there is a path from $a$ to $x$, and for every edge $v \cdot (\neg)x$ in $\Gamma$, there is a positive path from $a$ to $v$. In other words, every node and edge is reachable from $a$.

> $\Gamma$ is (potentially) *ambiguous* with respect to node $a$ at $x$ if there is some node $x \in V$ such that both $a \cdot s_1 \cdot \ldots \cdot s_n \cdot x$ and $a \cdot t_1 \cdot \ldots \cdot t_m \cdot \neg x$ are paths.

> A *credulous extension* of an inheritance hierarchy $\Gamma$ with respect to a node $a$ is a maximal unambiguous $a$-connected subhierarchy of $\Gamma$ with respect to $a$.

So if $X$ is a credulous extension of $\Gamma$, then adding an edge of $\Gamma$ to $X$ makes $X$ either ambiguous or not $a$-connected.

Figure 10.11 illustrates an ambiguous network and Figure 10.12 shows its two credulous extensions. Note that adding the edge from Mammal

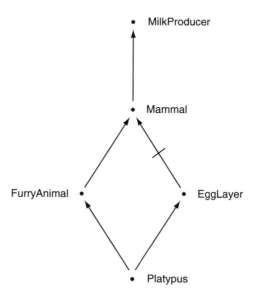

■ **FIGURE 10.11**

An Ambiguous Network

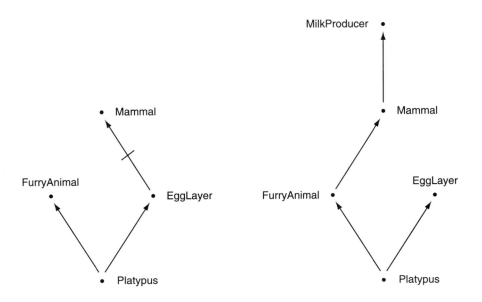

Two Credulous Extensions

to MilkProducer in the extension on the left would cause that extension to no longer be *a*-connected (where *a* is Platypus), because there is no positive path from Platypus to Mammal. Adding the edge from FurryAnimal to Mammal in the extension on the left, or the edge from EggLayer to Mammal in the extension on the right, would make the extensions ambiguous. Thus, both extensions in the figure are credulous extensions.

Credulous extensions do not incorporate any notion of admissibility or preemption. For example, the network of Figure 10.4 has two credulous extensions with respect to node Clyde. However, given our earlier discussion and our intuition about reasoning about the natural world, we would like our formalism to rule out one of these extensions. This leads us to a definition of *preferred extensions*:

Let $X$ and $Y$ be credulous extensions of $\Gamma$ with respect to a node $a$. $X$ is *preferred* to $Y$ iff there are nodes $v$ and $x$ such that

- $X$ and $Y$ agree on all edges whose endpoints precede $v$ topologically;
- there is an edge $v \cdot x$ (or $v \cdot \neg x$) that is *inadmissible* in $\Gamma$; and
- this edge is in $Y$ but not in $X$.

A credulous extension is a *preferred extension* if there is no other credulous extension that is preferred to it.

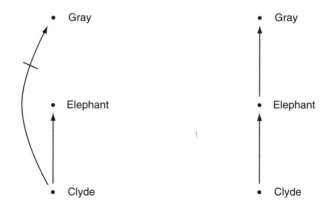

■ **FIGURE 10.13**

A Preferred Credulous Extension

The key part of this definition is that it appeals to the notion of admissibility defined earlier. So, for example, for the Γ shown in Figure 10.4, the extension on the left in Figure 10.13 is a preferred extension, whereas the one on the right is not. If we use the assignment $a$ = Clyde, $v$ = Elephant, and $x$ = Gray, we can see that the two extensions agree up to Elephant, but the edge Elephant·Gray is not admissible because it has a preemptor, Clyde, and that edge is in the extension on the right but not on the left.

### 10.3.2  Some Subtleties of Inheritance Reasoning

Although we have detailed some reasonable formal definitions that allow us to distinguish between different types of extensions, an agent still needs to make a choice based on such a representation of what actually to believe. The extensions offer sets of consistent conclusions, but one's attitude toward such extensions can vary. Different forms of reasoning have been proposed based on the type of formalization we have presented here:

- *credulous reasoning*: Choose a preferred extension, perhaps arbitrarily, and believe all of the conclusions supported by it.

- *skeptical reasoning*: Believe the conclusions supported by any path that is present in all preferred extensions.

- *ideally skeptical reasoning*: Believe the conclusions that are supported by all preferred extensions. This is subtly different from skeptical reasoning, in that these conclusions may be supported by different paths in each extension. One significant consequence of this is that ideally skeptical reasoning cannot be computed in a path-based way.

One final point to note is that our emphasis in this chapter has been on "upward" reasoning: In each case, we start at a node and see what can be inherited from its ancestor nodes further "up" the tree. There are actually many variations on this definition, and none has emerged as the agreed upon, or "correct" one. One alternative, for example, looks from the top and sees what propagates downward through the network.

In Chapter 11, we will reconsider in more general logical terms the kind of defeasible reasoning seen here in inheritance networks. We will study some very expressive representation languages for this that go well beyond what can be represented in a network. Although these languages have a clear logical foundation, we will see that it is quite difficult to get them to emulate in a convincing way the subtle path-based account of reasoning we have investigated here.

## 10.4    BIBLIOGRAPHIC NOTES

Inheritance networks, as described in the text, grew out of a more general-purpose representation formalism that used inheritance, known as *semantic networks*. Early and influential work in this area, inspired by the semantics of verbs and nouns in natural language, was done by Quillian [335, 336] and, for the application of computer vision, Winston [427]. Other important semantic network systems include Fahlman's NETL [124] and Shapiro's SNePS [381], which is still in use today (see, for example, [382]) and has also been used to develop a system for belief revision [270, 383]. For a more recent collection of articles on semantic networks, see Sowa [393].

The ideas in semantic networks were refined by a number of researchers trying to give such networks a clear semantics, most notably Woods [430] and Brachman [40, 42, 43] (see also the collections by Findler [130], Lehmann and Rodin [232], and Lenzerini et al. [236]). The work by Brachman eventually led to the development of description logics, described in Chapter 9.

The formal characterization of inheritance networks presented here is due to Stein [398] (see also [396, 397]). Variants of the definition, and the problems they raise, are discussed by Touretzky et al. [413]. Etherington and Reiter [122] studied exceptions in inheritance networks using default logic (see Chapter 11) and pointed out inadequacies with the shortest path heuristic. The notion of inferential distance is examined in Touretzky [412]. The *conceptual graph* [392] combines ideas from inheritance networks and Peirce's *existential graphs* [323, 325, 355], a graphical form of logic (allowing for propositional, first-order, and even some forms of modal logic).

---

## 10.5  EXERCISES

In these exercises, we consider three collections of assertions:

**George:** *George is a Marine.*

*George is a chaplain.*

*A Marine is typically a beer drinker.*

*A chaplain is typically not a beer drinker.*

*A beer drinker is typically overweight.*

*A Marine is typically not overweight.*

**Polly:** *Polly is a platypus.*

*Polly is an Australian animal.*

*A platypus is typically a mammal.*

*An Australian animal is typically not a mammal.*

*A mammal is typically not an egg layer.*

*A platypus is typically an egg layer.*

**Dick:** *Dick is a Quaker.*

*Dick is a Republican.*

*Quakers are typically pacifists.*

*Republicans are typically not pacifists.*

*Republicans are typically promilitary.*

*Pacifists are typically not promilitary.*

*Promilitary (people) are typically politically active.*

*Pacifists are typically politically active.*

For each collection, the questions are the same (and see the follow-up Exercise 1 in Chapter 11):

1.  Represent the assertions in an inheritance network.

2.  What are the credulous extensions of the network?

**3.** Which of them are preferred extensions?

**4.** Give a conclusion that a credulous reasoner might make but that a skeptical reasoner would not.

**5.** Are there conclusions where a skeptical reasoner and an ideally skeptical reasoner would disagree given this network?

# CHAPTER 11

# DEFAULTS

■

---

■

■

In Chapter 8 on frames, the kind of reasoning we saw exemplified by the inheritance of properties was actually a simple form of *default reasoning*, where a slot was assumed to have a certain value unless a different one was provided explicitly. In Chapter 10 on inheritance, we also considered a form of default reasoning in hierarchies. We might know, for example, that elephants are gray, but understand that there could be special kinds of elephants that are not. In this chapter, we look at this form of default reasoning in detail and in logical terms, without tying our analysis either to procedural considerations or to the topology of a network as we did earlier.

## 11.1 INTRODUCTION

Despite the fact that FOL is an extremely expressive representation language, it is nonetheless restricted in the patterns of reasoning it admits. To see this, imagine that we have a KB in FOL that contains facts about animals of various sorts, and that we would like to find out whether a particular individual, Fido, is a carnivore. Assuming that the KB contains the sentence Dog(fido), there are only two possibilities for getting to the conclusion Carnivore(fido):

1. the KB contains other facts that mention the constant fido explicitly;

2. the KB entails a universal of the form $\forall x. \text{Dog}(x) \supset \text{Carnivore}(x)$.

It is not too hard to see that if neither of these two conditions are satisfied, the desired conclusion simply cannot be derived: There is a logical interpretation that satisfies the KB but not Carnivore(fido).[1] So it is clear that if we want to deduce something about a particular dog that we know nothing else about, the only option available to us in FOL is to use what we know about *each and every* dog. In general, to reason from $P(a)$ to $Q(a)$ in FOL where we know nothing else about $a$ itself, we need to use what is known to hold for all instances of $P$.

## 11.1.1   Generics and Universals

So what is the problem? All along, we have been imagining that we will build a KB that contains facts about a wide variety of topics, somewhat like an encyclopedia. There would be "entries" on turtles, violins, wildflowers, and ferris wheels as in normal encyclopedias, as well as entries on more mundane subjects, like grocery stores, birthday parties, rubber balls, and haircuts. Clearly, what we would like to say about these topics goes beyond facts about particular cases of turtles or violins. The troublesome fact of the matter is that although we may have a great deal to write down about violins, say, almost none of it applies to *all* violins. The problem is how to express what we know about the topics *in general* using FOL, and in particular using universal quantification.

We might want to state, for example,

*Violins have four strings*

to distinguish them from guitars, which have six. But we most assuredly do *not* want to state,

*All violins have four strings*

because, obviously, this would rule out a violin with a string added or removed. One possible solution is to attempt to enumerate the conditions under which violins would not have four strings:

*All violins that are not $P_1$ or $P_2$ or ... or $P_n$ have four strings*

where the $P_i$ state the various exceptional cases. The challenge is to characterize these cases. We would need to cover at least the following: natural manufacturing (or genetic) varieties, like electric violins; cases in exceptional circumstances, like violins that have been modified or damaged; borderline cases, like miniature toy violins; imagined cases, like

---

[1]The construction is as follows: Take any model $\Im = \langle \mathcal{D}, \mathcal{I} \rangle$ of the KB that satisfies the first, but not the second, of the two conditions. So there is a dog $d$ in $\mathcal{D}$ that is not a carnivore. Let $\Im' = \langle \mathcal{D}, \mathcal{I}' \rangle$ be just like $\Im$ except that $\mathcal{I}'[\text{fido}] = d$. Because KB contains no facts other than Dog(fido) that mention fido, $\Im'$ still satisfies KB, but $\Im'$ satisfies ¬Carnivore(fido).

multiplayer violins (whatever they might be); and so on. Because of the range of possibilities, we are almost reduced to saying,

*All violins have four strings except those that do not*

a true but vacuous universal.

This is obviously not just a problem with the topic of violins. When we say that lemons are yellow and tart, that polar bears are white and live in Arctic regions, that birds have wings and fly, that children sing "Happy Birthday" at birthday parties, that banks are closed on Sundays, and on and on, we do not mean to say that such sentences hold of each and every instance of the corresponding class. Yet the facts are true; it would be wrong to say that at birthday parties children sing "Oh! Susanna," for example.

So we need to distinguish between *universals*, properties that do hold for all instances, easily expressible in FOL, and *generics*, properties that hold "in general." Much of our commonsense knowledge of the world appears to be concerned with generics, so it is quite important to consider formalisms that go beyond FOL in allowing us to handle general, but not truly universal, knowledge.

## 11.1.2  Default Reasoning

Assuming we know that dogs are, generally speaking, carnivores, and that Fido is a dog, under what circumstances is it appropriate to infer that Fido is a carnivore? The answer we will consider in very general terms is this:

Given that a *P* is generally a *Q*, and given that *P*(*a*) is true, it is reasonable to conclude that *Q*(*a*) is true unless there is a good reason not to.

This answer is unfortunately somewhat vague: Exactly what constitutes a good reason not to conclude something? Different ways of making this precise will be the subject of the rest of the chapter.[2]

One thing to notice, however, is that if absolutely nothing is known about the individual *a* except that it is an instance of *P*, then we ought to be able to conclude that it is an instance of *Q*, because there can be nothing that would urge us not to. When we happen to know that a polar bear has been rolling in the mud, or swimming in an algae-ridden pool, or playing with paint cans, then we may not be willing to conclude anything about its color; but if *all* we know is that the individual is a polar bear, it seems perfectly reasonable to conclude that it is white.

---

[2]In Chapter 12 we consider ways of dealing with this issue numerically. Here our approach is qualitative.

Note, however, that just because we don't know that the bear has been blackened by soot, for example, doesn't mean that it hasn't been. The conclusion does not have the guarantee of logical soundness; everything else we believe about polar bears could be true without this particular bear being white. It is only a reasonable *default*. That is to say, if we are pressed for some reason to come to some decision about its color, white is a reasonable choice. We would be prepared to retract that belief if appropriate evidence were encountered later. In general, this form of reasoning, which involves applying some general though not universal fact to a particular individual, is called *default reasoning*.

We do not want to suggest, however, that the only source of default reasoning has to do with general properties of kinds like violins, polar bears, or birthday parties. There are a wide variety of reasons for wanting to conclude $Q(a)$ given $P(a)$ even in the absence of true universal quantification. Here are some examples:

## General Statements

■ *normal*: Under typical circumstances, $P$s are $Q$s.
(People work close to where they live. Children enjoy singing.)

■ *prototypical*: The prototypical $P$ is a $Q$.
(Apples are red. Owls hunt at night.)

■ *statistical*: Most $P$s are $Q$s.
(The people in the waiting room are growing impatient.)

## Lack of Information to the Contrary

■ *familiarity*: If a $P$ was not a $Q$, you would know it.
(No nation has a political leader more than 7 feet tall.)

■ *group confidence*: All the known $P$s are known (or assumed) to be $Q$s.
(Natural languages are easy for children to learn.)

## Conventional Uses

■ *conversational*: A $P$ is a $Q$, unless I tell you otherwise.
(Being told "The closest gas station is two blocks east," the assumed default is that the gas station is open.)

■ *representational*: A $P$ is a $Q$, unless otherwise indicated.
(The speed limit in a city. An open door to an office, meaning that the occupant can be disturbed.)

## Persistence

■ *inertia*: A $P$ is a $Q$ unless something changes it.
(Marital status. The position of objects [within limits].)

- *time*: A *P* is a *Q* if it used to be a *Q*.
  (The color of objects. Their sizes.)

This list is not intended to be exhaustive. But it does suggest the very wide variety of sources of default information. In all cases, our concern in this chapter will be the same: how to characterize precisely when, in the absence of universals, it is appropriate to draw a default conclusion. In so doing, we will only use the simplest of examples, like the default that birds fly, which in FOL would have to be approximated by $\forall x(\mathsf{Bird}(x) \supset \mathsf{Flies}(x))$. But the techniques considered here apply to all the various forms of defaults, which, as we have argued, cover much of what we know.

### 11.1.3 Nonmonotonicity

In the rest of this chapter, we will consider four approaches to default reasoning: closed-world reasoning, circumscription, default logic, and autoepistemic logic. In all cases, we start with a KB from which we wish to derive a set of implicit beliefs. In the simple case with no default reasoning, implicit beliefs are just the entailments of the KB; with defaults, we go beyond these by making various assumptions.

Ordinary deductive reasoning is *monotonic*, which is to say that new facts can only produce additional beliefs. In other words, if $\mathsf{KB}_1 \models \alpha$, then $\mathsf{KB}_2 \models \alpha$, for any $\mathsf{KB}_2$ such that $\mathsf{KB}_1 \subseteq \mathsf{KB}_2$. However, default reasoning is *nonmonotonic*: New facts will sometimes invalidate previous beliefs. For example, if we are only told that Tweety is a bird, we may believe that Tweety flies. However, if we are now told that Tweety is an emu, we may no longer believe that she flies. This is because the belief that Tweety flies was a default based on an *absence* of information to the contrary. When we find out that Tweety is an exceptional bird, we reconsider.

For this reason, default reasoning of the kind we will discuss in this chapter is often called *nonmonotonic reasoning*, where the emphasis is not so much on how assumptions are made or where they come from, but on inference relations that are similar to entailment, but which are nonmonotonic.

## 11.2 CLOSED-WORLD REASONING

The simplest formalization of default reasoning we will consider was also the first to be developed, and is based on the following observation:

Imagine representing facts about the world in FOL with some natural vocabulary of predicate, function, and constant symbols. Of the large (but finite) number of atomic sentences that can be formed, only a very small fraction are expected to be *true*. A reasonable representational convention, then, is to explicitly represent the true atomic sentences, and to assume that any unmentioned atomic sentence is false.

Consider, for example, information sources like an airline flight guide. The kind of information we find in a such a guide might be roughly represented in FOL by sentences like

DirectConnect(cleveland,toronto),
DirectConnect(toronto,northBay),
DirectConnect(cleveland,phoenix),

telling us which cities have flights between them. What we do not expect to find in such a guide are statements about which cities do *not* have flights between them:

¬DirectConnect(northBay,phoenix).

The convention is that if an airline guide does not list a flight between two cities, then there is none. Similar conventions are used, of course, in encyclopedias, dictionaries, maps, and many other information sources. It is also the assumption used in computerized databases, modeled exactly on such information sources.[3]

## 11.2.1   The Closed-World Assumption

In general terms, the assumption here, called the *closed-world assumption* (CWA), is the following:

*Unless an atomic sentence is known to be true,
it can be assumed to be false.*

Note that expressed this way, the CWA can be seen to involve a form of default reasoning. A sentence assumed to be false could later be determined in fact to be true.

Perhaps the easiest way to formalize the reasoning inherent in the CWA is to consider a new form of entailment, $\models_c$, where we say that KB $\models_c \alpha$ if and only if $\text{KB}^+ \models \alpha$, where

$$\text{KB}^+ = \text{KB} \cup \{\neg p \mid p \text{ is atomic and KB} \not\models p\}.$$

So $\models_c$ is just like ordinary entailment, except with respect to an augmented KB, namely one that includes all negative atomic facts not

---

[3]Note that it is clearly possible to represent knowledge in a dual vocabulary where most of the atomic sentences would be true and where the opposite convention would be more appropriate. In everyday information sources, we tend not to do this.

explicitly ruled out by the KB.[4] In the airline guide example, $KB^+$ would include all the appropriate $\neg DirectConnect(c_1, c_2)$ sentences.

## 11.2.2 Consistency and Completeness of Knowledge

It is useful to introduce two terms at this point: We say that a KB exhibits *consistent* knowledge if and only if there is no sentence $\alpha$ such that both $\alpha$ and $\neg\alpha$ are known. This is the same as requiring the KB to be satisfiable. We also say that a KB exhibits *complete* knowledge if and only if for every sentence $\alpha$ (within its vocabulary), either $\alpha$ or $\neg\alpha$ is known.

In general, of course, knowledge can be incomplete. For example, suppose KB consists of a single sentence, $(p \vee q)$. Then, KB does not entail either $p$ or $\neg p$, and so exhibits incomplete knowledge. If we consider the CWA as we have formalized it, however, for any sentence $\alpha$, it holds that either $KB \models_c \alpha$ or $KB \models_c \neg\alpha$. (The argument is by induction on the length of $\alpha$.) So with the CWA we have completely filled out the entailment relation for the KB. Every sentence is *decided* by $KB^+$, that is, either it or its negation is entailed by $KB^+$.

It is not hard to see that if a KB is complete in this sense (the way $KB^+$ is), it also has the property that if it tells us that one of two sentences is true, then it must also tell us which. In other words, if KB exhibits complete knowledge and $KB \models (\alpha \vee \beta)$, then $KB \models \alpha$ or $KB \models \beta$. Again, note that this is not the case in general, for example, for the KB comprising only $(p \vee q)$, as described a moment ago.

The idea behind the CWA then, is to act *as if* the KB represented complete knowledge. Whenever $KB \not\models p$, then either $KB \models \neg p$ directly, or the assumption is that $\neg p$ is what was intended and it is conceptually added to the KB.

## 11.2.3 Query Evaluation

The fact that every sentence is decided by the CWA allows queries to be handled in a very direct way. The question as to whether $KB \models_c \alpha$ ends up reducing to a collection of questions about the literals in $\alpha$. We begin with the following general properties of entailment:

1. $KB \models (\alpha \wedge \beta)$ iff $KB \models \alpha$ and $KB \models \beta$.

2. $KB \models \neg\neg\alpha$ iff $KB \models \alpha$.

3. $KB \models \neg(\alpha \vee \beta)$ iff $KB \models \neg\alpha$ and $KB \models \neg\beta$.

---

[4]This definition applies to the propositional subset of FOL. We will deal with quantifiers later.

Next, because KB$^+$ is complete, we also have the following properties:

    4.  KB $\models_{\overline{c}} (\alpha \vee \beta)$ iff KB $\models_{\overline{c}} \alpha$ or KB $\models_{\overline{c}} \beta$.

    5.  KB $\models_{\overline{c}} \neg(\alpha \wedge \beta)$ iff KB $\models_{\overline{c}} \neg\alpha$ or KB $\models_{\overline{c}} \neg\beta$.

Putting all of these together, we can recursively reduce any question about whether KB $\models_{\overline{c}} \alpha$ to a set of questions about the literals in $\alpha$. For example, it is the case that

$$\text{KB} \models_{\overline{c}} ((p \wedge q) \vee \neg(r \wedge \neg s)) \quad \text{iff}$$
$$\text{either both KB} \models_{\overline{c}} p \text{ and KB} \models_{\overline{c}} q, \text{ or KB} \models_{\overline{c}} \neg r, \text{ or KB} \models_{\overline{c}} s.$$

If we further assume that KB$^+$ is consistent (which we discuss later), we get the following:

    6.  If KB$^+$ is consistent, KB $\models_{\overline{c}} \neg\alpha$ iff KB $\not\models_{\overline{c}} \alpha$.

With this extra condition, we can reduce a query to a set of questions about the *atoms* in $\alpha$. For example, assuming consistency, the sentence $((p \wedge q) \vee \neg(r \wedge \neg s))$ will be entailed under the CWA if and only if either both $p$ and $q$ are entailed or $r$ is not entailed or $s$ is entailed. What this suggests is that for a KB that is consistent and complete, entailment conditions are just like truth conditions: A conjunction is entailed if and only if both conjuncts are, a disjunction is entailed if and only if either disjunct is, and a negation is entailed if and only if the negated sentence is not entailed. As long as we have a way of handling atomic queries, all other queries can be handled recursively.[5]

## 11.2.4  Consistency and a Generalized Assumption

Just because a KB is consistent does not mean that KB$^+$ will also be consistent. Consider, for example, the consistent KB composed of the single sentence $(p \vee q)$, mentioned earlier. Because KB $\not\models p$, it is the case that $\neg p \in$ KB$^+$. Similarly, $\neg q \in$ KB$^+$. So KB$^+$ contains $\{(p \vee q), \neg p, \neg q\}$, and thus is inconsistent. In this case, KB $\models_{\overline{c}} \alpha$, for *every* sentence $\alpha$.

On the other hand, it is clear that if a KB consists of just atomic sentences (like the DirectConnect KB, which was discussed earlier) and is itself consistent, then KB$^+$ will be consistent. The same is true if the KB contains conjunctions of atomic sentences (or of other conjunctions). It is also true if the KB contains disjunctions of negative literals.

---

[5]We will explore the implications of this for reasoning procedures in Chapter 16.

But it is not clear what a reasonable closure assumption should be for disjunctions like $(p \lor q)$.

One possibility is to apply the CWA only to atoms that are completely "uncontroversial." For example, in the earlier case, although we might not apply the CWA to either $p$ or $q$, because they are both controversial (because we know that one of them is true, but not which), we might be willing to apply it to any other atom. This suggests a version of the CWA, which we call the *generalized closed-world assumption* (GCWA), where $\text{KB} \models_{\overline{\text{GC}}} \alpha$ if and only if $\text{KB}^\star \models \alpha$, where $\text{KB}^\star$ is defined as follows:

$$\text{KB}^\star = \text{KB} \cup \{\neg p \mid \text{for all collections of atoms } q_1, \ldots, q_n,$$
$$\text{if } \text{KB} \models (p \lor q_1 \lor \ldots \lor q_n), \text{ then } \text{KB} \models (q_1 \lor \ldots \lor q_n)\}.$$

So an atom $p$ can be assumed to be false only if it is the case that whenever a disjunction of atoms including that atom is entailed by the KB the smaller disjunction without the atom is also entailed. In other words, we will not assume that $p$ is false if an entailed disjunction of atoms including $p$ exists that cannot be reduced to a smaller entailed disjunction not involving $p$.

For example, suppose that KB is $(p \lor q)$, and consider the atom $p$. Then it is the case that $\text{KB} \models (p \lor q)$, but $\text{KB} \not\models q$. So $\neg p \notin \text{KB}^\star$. Similarly, $\neg q \notin \text{KB}^\star$. However, consider an atom $r$. Here it is the case that $\neg r \in \text{KB}^\star$, because although $\text{KB} \models (r \lor p \lor q)$, we also have the reduced disjunction $\text{KB} \models (p \lor q)$.[6]

It is not hard to see that entailments under the GCWA are a subset of those under the CWA, and in particular, that if $\neg p \in \text{KB}^\star$, then $\neg p \in \text{KB}^+$. Moreover, the GCWA agrees completely with the CWA in those cases where the KB has no disjunctive knowledge, that is, in those cases where $\text{KB} \models (q_1 \lor \ldots \lor q_n)$ implies that $\text{KB} \models q_i$ for some $i$. Finally, unlike the CWA, the GCWA preserves consistency: If KB is consistent then $\text{KB}^\star$ is also consistent. To summarize, then, the GCWA is a weaker version of the CWA that agrees with the CWA in the absence of disjunctions, but that remains consistent in the presence of disjunctions.

## 11.2.5  Quantifiers and Domain Closure

So far we have only considered the properties of the CWA in terms of sentences without quantifiers. Unfortunately, its most desirable

---

[6]The intuition behind this is as follows: Say that we know that there is a flight from Cleveland either to Dallas or to Houston (but not which one). As a result, we also know that there is a flight from Cleveland to one of Dallas, Houston, or Austin. But because we know that there is definitely a flight to one of the first two, it makes sense, under normal closed-world reasoning, to assume that there is no flight to Austin.

properties do not immediately generalize to sentences with quantifiers. To see why, consider a simple representation language containing a single predicate DirectConnect as before and constants $c_1, \ldots, c_n$. If we start with a KB containing only atomic sentences of the form DirectConnect($c_i, c_j$), the CWA will add to this a collection of literals of the form ¬DirectConnect($c_i, c_j$). In the resulting KB$^+$, for any pair of constants $c_i$ and $c_j$, either DirectConnect($c_i, c_j$) is in KB$^+$ or ¬DirectConnect($c_i, c_j$) is in KB$^+$.

Let us suppose that there is a city smallTown that has no airport and does not appear in the imagined guide, so that for every $c_j$, ¬DirectConnect($c_j$, smallTown) is in KB$^+$. Now consider the query, ¬∃xDirectConnect($x$, smallTown). Ideally, by closed-world reasoning, this sentence should be entailed: There is no city that has a direct connection to smallTown. However, even under the CWA, neither this sentence nor its negation is entailed: The CWA precludes any of the *named* cities, $c_1, \ldots, c_n$, flying to smallTown, but it does not preclude some other *unnamed* city doing so. That is, there is a model of KB$^+$ where the domain includes a city not named by any $c_i$ such that it and the denotation of smallTown are in the extension of DirectConnect. The problem is that the CWA has not gone far enough: Not only do we want to assume that none of the $c_i$ have a direct connection to smallTown, we want to assume that no city does so.

Perhaps the easiest way to achieve this effect is to assume that the named constants are the only individuals of interest, in other words, that every individual is named by one of the $c_i$. This leads to a stronger form of closed-world reasoning, which is the *closed world assumption with domain closure*, and a new form of entailment: KB $\models_{\text{CD}} \alpha$ if and only if KB$^\circ \models \alpha$, where

$$\text{KB}^\circ = \text{KB}^+ \cup \{\forall x[x = c_1 \vee \ldots \vee x = c_n]\},$$

where $c_1, \ldots, c_n$, are all the constant symbols appearing in KB.

This is exactly like the CWA, but with the additional assumption that no objects exist apart from the named constants. Returning to the smallTown example, because ¬DirectConnect($c_i$, smallTown) is entailed under the CWA for every $c_i$, it will follow that ¬∃xDirectConnect($x$, smallTown) is entailed under the CWA with domain closure.

The main properties of this extension to the CWA are the following:

$$\text{KB} \models_{\text{CD}} \forall x\alpha \quad \text{iff} \quad \text{KB} \models_{\text{CD}} \alpha^x_c, \text{ for every } c \text{ appearing in KB};$$

$$\text{KB} \models_{\text{CD}} \exists x\alpha \quad \text{iff} \quad \text{KB} \models_{\text{CD}} \alpha^x_c, \text{ for some } c \text{ appearing in KB}.$$

This means that the correspondence between entailment conditions and truth conditions now generalizes to quantified sentences. With this additional completeness assumption, it is the case that KB $\models_{\text{CD}} \alpha$ or KB $\models_{\text{CD}} \neg\alpha$ for any $\alpha$, even with quantifiers. Similarly, the recursive query operation, which reduces queries to the atomic case, now works for quantified sentences as well. This property can also be extended to deal with formulas with equality (and hence all of FOL) by including a *unique name assumption*, which adds to KB$^{\diamond}$ all sentences of the form $(c \neq c')$, for distinct constants $c$ and $c'$.

Finally, there is the issue of consistency. First note that domain closure does not rule out the use of function symbols. If we use sentences like $\forall x P(x) \supset P(f(x))$, then under the CWA with domain closure, we end up assuming that each term $f(t)$ is equal to one of the constants. In other words, even though individuals have unique constant names, they can have other nonconstant names.

However, it is possible to construct a KB that is inconsistent with domain closure in more subtle ways. Consider, for instance, the following:

$$P(c), \ \forall x \neg R(x,x), \forall x[P(x) \supset \exists y(R(x,y) \wedge P(y))]$$

This KB is consistent and does not even use equality. However, KB$^{\diamond}$ is inconsistent. The individual denoted by $c$ cannot be the only instance of $P$, because the other two sentences in effect assert that there must be another one. It is also possible to have a consistent KB that asserts the existence of infinitely many instances of $P$, guaranteeing that domain closure cannot be used for any finite set of constants. But these examples are somewhat far-fetched; they look more like formulas that might appear in axiomatizations of set theory than in databases. For "normal" applications, domain closure is much less of a problem.

## 11.3 CIRCUMSCRIPTION

In general terms, the CWA is the convention that arbitrary atomic sentences are taken to be false by default. Formally, $\models_{\text{C}}$ is defined as the entailments of KB$^{+}$, which is KB augmented by a set of negative literals. For a sentence $\alpha$ to be believed (under the CWA), it is not necessary for $\alpha$ to be true in all models of the KB, but only those that are also models of KB$^{+}$. In the first-order case, because of the presence of the negated literals in KB$^{+}$, we end up looking at models of the KB where the extension of the predicates is made as small as possible. This suggests a natural generalization: Consider forms of entailment where the extension of certain predicates (perhaps not all) is as small as possible.

One way to handle default knowledge is to assume that we have a predicate Ab to talk about the exceptional or abnormal cases where a default should not apply. Instead of saying that all birds fly, we might say:

$$\forall x[\mathsf{Bird}(x) \wedge \neg\mathsf{Ab}(x) \supset \mathsf{Flies}(x)].$$

This can be read as saying that all birds that are not in some way abnormal fly, or more succinctly, that all normal birds fly.[7] Now imagine we have this fact in a KB along with these facts:

$$\mathsf{Bird(chilly), Bird(tweety), (tweety \neq chilly), \neg Flies(chilly)}.$$

The intent here is clear: We would like to conclude by default that Tweety flies, whereas Chilly (the black and white Antarctic bird), of course, does not.

Note, however, that KB $\not\models$ Flies(tweety): There are interpretations satisfying the KB where Flies(tweety) is false. However, note that in these interpretations, the denotation of Tweety is contained in the extension of Ab. This then suggests a strategy for making default conclusions: As with the CWA, we will only consider certain interpretations of the KB, but in this case, only those where the Ab predicate is as small as possible. In other words, the strategy is to *minimize abnormality*. Intuitively, the default conclusions are taken to be those that are true in models of the KB where as few of the individuals as possible are abnormal.

In this example, we already know that Chilly is an abnormal bird, but we do not know one way or another about Tweety. The default assumption we wish to make is that the extension of Ab is only as large as it has to be given what we know; hence it includes Chilly, because it must, but excludes Tweety, because nothing we know dictates that Ab must include her. This is called *circumscribing* the predicate Ab, and as a whole, the technique is called *circumscription*.

Note that while Chilly is abnormal in her flying ability, she may be quite normal in having two legs, laying eggs, and so on. This suggests that we do not really want to use a single predicate Ab and not be able to assume any defaults at all about Chilly, but rather have a family of predicates $\mathsf{Ab}_i$ for talking about the various aspects of individuals. Chilly might be in the extension of $\mathsf{Ab}_1$, but not in that of $\mathsf{Ab}_2$, and so on.

## 11.3.1   Minimal Entailment

Circumscription is intended to be a much more fine-grained tool than the CWA, and because of this and the fact that we wish to apply it in much broader settings, the formalization we use does not involve

---

[7]We are not suggesting that this is exactly what is meant by the sentence, "Birds fly."

adding negative literals to the KB. Instead, we characterize a new form of entailment directly in terms of properties of interpretations themselves.

Let $P$ be a fixed set of unary predicates, which we will intuitively understand to be the Ab predicates. Let $\Im_1$ and $\Im_2$ be logical interpretations over the same domain such that every constant and function is interpreted the same. So $\Im_1 = \langle \mathcal{D}, \mathcal{I}_1 \rangle$ and $\Im_2 = \langle \mathcal{D}, \mathcal{I}_2 \rangle$. Then we define the relationship, $\leq$:

$$\Im_1 \leq \Im_2 \text{ iff for every } P \in P, \text{ it is the case that } \mathcal{I}_1[P] \subseteq \mathcal{I}_2[P].$$

Also, $\Im_1 < \Im_2$ if and only if $\Im_1 \leq \Im_2$ but $\Im_2 \nleq \Im_1$. Intuitively, given two interpretations over the same domain, we are saying that one is less than another in this ordering if it makes the extension of all the abnormality predicates smaller. Informally, then, we can think of an interpretation that is less than another as *more normal*.

With this idea, we can define a new form of entailment $\models_{\leq}$ (which we call *minimal entailment*) as follows:

> $KB \models_{\leq} \alpha$ iff for every interpretation $\Im$ such that $\Im \models KB$,
> either $\Im \models \alpha$ or there is an $\Im'$ such that $\Im' < \Im$ and $\Im' \models KB$.

This is very similar to the definition of entailment itself: We require each interpretation that satisfies KB to satisfy $\alpha$ except that it may be excused when there is another more normal interpretation that also satisfies the KB. Roughly speaking, we do not require $\alpha$ to be true in *all* interpretations satisfying the KB, but only in the minimal or *most normal* ones satisfying the KB.[8]

Consider, for example, the KB with Tweety and Chilly we defined earlier. As noted, $KB \nmodels \text{Flies(tweety)}$. However, $KB \models_{\leq} \text{Flies(tweety)}$. The reason is this: If $\Im \models KB$ but $\Im \nmodels \text{Flies(tweety)}$, then $\Im \models \text{Ab(tweety)}$. So let $\Im'$ be exactly $\Im$ except that we remove the denotation of tweety from the extension of Ab. Then $\Im' < \Im$ (assuming $P = \{Ab\}$, of course), and $\Im' \models KB$. Thus, in the minimal models of the KB, Tweety is a normal bird: $KB \models_{\leq} \neg\text{Ab(tweety)}$, from which we can infer that Tweety flies. We cannot do the same for Chilly, because in all models of the KB, normal or not, Chilly is an abnormal bird. Note that the only default step in this reasoning was to conclude that Tweety was normal; the rest was ordinary deductive reasoning given what we know about normal birds. This then is the circumscription proposal for formalizing default reasoning.

---

[8]This is a convenient but slightly inaccurate way of putting it. In fact, there may be no "most normal" models; in pathological cases, we could have an infinite descending chain of ever more normal models. In such cases, the definition would have every sentence minimally entailed, but a more complex account of minimal entailment can be made to do something more reasonable.

Note that, in general, we do not expect the "most normal" models of the KB all to satisfy exactly the same sentences. Suppose, for example, a KB contains Bird($c$), Bird($d$), and (¬Flies($c$) ∨ ¬Flies($d$)). Then in any model of the KB the extension of Ab must contain either the denotation of $c$ or the denotation of $d$. Any model that contains other abnormal individuals (including ones where the denotations of both $c$ and $d$ are abnormal) would not be minimal. Because we need to consider what is true in *all* minimal models, we see that KB $\not\models_\leq$ Flies($c$) and KB $\not\models_\leq$ Flies($d$). In other words, we cannot conclude by default that $c$ is a normal bird, nor that $d$ is. However, what we can conclude by default is that *one of them* is normal: KB $\models_\leq$ Flies($c$) ∨ Flies($d$).

This is very different from the behavior of the CWA. Under similar circumstances, because it is consistent with what is known that $c$ is normal, using the CWA we would add the literal ¬Ab($c$), and by similar reasoning, ¬Ab($d$), leading to inconsistency. Thus circumscription is more cautious than the CWA in the assumptions it makes about "controversial" individuals, like those denoted by $c$ and $d$. However, circumscription is less cautious than the GCWA: The GCWA would not conclude anything about either the denotation of $c$ or $d$, whereas circumscription is willing to conclude by default that one of them flies.

Another difference between circumscription and the CWA involves quantified sentences. By using interpretations directly rather than adding literals to the KB, circumscription works equally well with unnamed individuals. For example, if the KB contains

$$\exists x[\text{Bird}(x) \wedge (x \neq \text{chilly}) \wedge (x \neq \text{tweety}) \wedge \text{InTree}(x)],$$

then with circumscription we would conclude by default that this unnamed individual flies:

$$\exists x[\text{Bird}(x) \wedge (x \neq \text{chilly}) \wedge (x \neq \text{tweety}) \wedge \text{InTree}(x) \wedge \text{Flies}(x)].$$

The reason here is the same as before: In the minimal models there will be a single abnormal individual, Chilly. This also carries over to unnamed abnormal individuals. If our KB contains the assertion that

$$\exists x[\text{Bird}(x) \wedge (x \neq \text{chilly}) \wedge (x \neq \text{tweety}) \wedge \neg\text{Flies}(x)],$$

then a model of the KB will be minimal if and only if there are exactly two abnormal individuals: Chilly and the unnamed one. Thus, we conclude by default that

$$\exists x \forall y[(\text{Bird}(y) \wedge \neg\text{Flies}(y)) \equiv (y = \text{chilly} \vee y = x)].$$

Unlike the CWA and the GCWA, we do not need to name exceptions explicitly to avoid inconsistency. Indeed, the issue of consistency for circumscription is considerably more subtle than it was for the CWA, and characterizing it precisely remains an open question.

## 11.3.2 The Circumscription Axiom

One of the conceptual advantages of the CWA is that, although it is a form of non-monotonic reasoning, we can understand its effect in terms of ordinary deductive reasoning over a KB that has been augmented by certain assumptions. As we saw earlier, we cannot duplicate the effect of circumscription by simply adding a set of negative literals to a KB.

We can, however, view the effect of circumscription in terms of ordinary deductive reasoning from an augmented KB if we are willing to use so-called second-order logic, that is, logic where we can quantify not only over objects in the domain, but also over relations over the domain. Without going into detail, it is worth observing that for any KB there is a second-order sentence $\tau$ such that $KB \models_\leq \alpha$ if and only if $KB \cup \{\tau\} \models \alpha$ in second-order logic. What is required here of the sentence $\tau$ is that it should restrict interpretations to be minimal in the ordering. That is, if an interpretation $\Im$ is such that $\Im \models KB$, what we need (to get the correspondence with $\models_\leq$) is that $\Im \models \tau$ if and only if there does not exist $\Im' < \Im$ such that $\Im' \models KB$. The idea here (due to John McCarthy) is that instead of talking about another interpretation $\Im'$, we could just as well have said that a smaller extension for the Ab predicates that would also satisfy the KB must not exist. This requires quantification over the extensions of Ab predicates, and is what makes $\tau$ second-order.

## 11.3.3 Fixed and Variable Predicates

Although the default assumptions made by circumscription are usually weaker than those of the CWA, there are cases where they appear too strong. Suppose, for example, that we have the following KB:

$\forall x[\text{Bird}(x) \wedge \neg\text{Ab}(x) \supset \text{Flies}(x)]$,
$\text{Bird}(tweety)$,
$\forall x[\text{Penguin}(x) \supset (\text{Bird}(x) \wedge \neg\text{Flies}(x))]$.

It then follows that $\forall x[\text{Penguin}(x) \supset \text{Ab}(x)]$, that is, with respect to flying anyway, penguins are abnormal birds.

The problem is this: To make default assumptions using circumscription, we end up minimizing the set of abnormal individuals. For this KB, we conclude that there are no abnormal individuals at all:

$$KB \models_\leq \neg\exists x \text{Ab}(x).$$

But this has the effect of also minimizing penguins. In the process of wanting to derive the conclusion that Tweety flies, we end up concluding not only that Tweety is not a penguin, which is perhaps reasonable, but also that there are no penguins, which seems unreasonable:

$$\text{KB} \models_\le \neg\exists x \text{Penguin}(x).$$

In our zeal to make things as normal as possible, we have ruled out penguins. What would be much better in this case, it seems, is to be able to conclude by default merely that penguins are the only abnormal birds.

One solution that has been proposed is to redefine $\models_\le$ so that in looking at more normal worlds we do not in the process exclude the possibility of exceptional classes like penguins. What we should say is something like this: We can ignore a model of the KB if there is a similar model with fewer abnormal individuals, *but with exactly the same penguins*. That is, in the process of minimizing abnormality, we should not be allowed to also minimize the set of penguins. We say that the extension of Penguin remains *fixed* in the minimization. But it is not as if all predicates other than Ab will remain fixed. In moving from a model $\Im$ to a lesser model $\Im'$ where Ab has a smaller extension, we are willing to change the extension of Flies and indeed to conclude that Tweety flies. We say that the extension of Flies is *variable* in the minimization.

More formally, we redefine $\le$ with respect to a set of unary predicates $\boldsymbol{P}$ (understood as the ones to be minimized) and a set of arbitrary predicates $\boldsymbol{Q}$ (understood as the predicates that are fixed in the minimization). Let $\Im_1$ and $\Im_2$ be as before. Then $\Im_1 \le \Im_2$ if and only if for every $P \in \boldsymbol{P}$ it is the case that $\mathcal{I}_1[P] \subseteq \mathcal{I}_2[P]$, and for every $Q \in \boldsymbol{Q}$ it is the case that $\mathcal{I}_1[Q] = \mathcal{I}_2[Q]$. The rest of the definition of $\models_\le$ is as before. Taking $\boldsymbol{P} = \{\text{Ab}\}$ and $\boldsymbol{Q} = \{\text{Penguin}\}$ amounts to saying that we want to minimize the instances of Ab holding constant the instances of Penguin. The earlier version of $\models_\le$ was simply one where $\boldsymbol{Q}$ was empty.

Returning to the example bird KB, there will now be minimal models where there are penguins: $\text{KB} \not\models_\le \neg\exists x \text{Penguin}(x)$. In fact, a model of the KB will be minimal if and only if its abnormal individuals are precisely the penguins. Obviously the penguins must be abnormal. Conversely, assume to the contrary that in interpretation $\Im$ we have an abnormal individual $o$ who is not one of the penguins. Then construct $\Im'$ by moving $o$ out of the extension of Ab and, if it is in the extension of Bird, into the extension of Flies. Clearly, $\Im'$ satisfies KB and $\Im' < \Im$. So it follows that

$$\text{KB} \models_\le \forall x[(\text{Bird}(x) \wedge \neg\text{Flies}(x)) \equiv \text{Penguin}(x)].$$

Unfortunately, this version of circumscription still has some serious problems. For one thing, our method of using circumscription requires us to specify not only which predicates to minimize, but also which additional predicates to keep fixed: We need to be able to figure out somehow beforehand that flying should be a variable predicate, for example, and it is far from clear how.

More seriously, perhaps, KB $\not\models_{\leq}$ Flies(tweety). The reason is this: Consider a model of the KB where Tweety happens to be a penguin; we can no longer find a lesser model where Tweety flies, because that would mean changing the set of penguins, which must remain fixed. What we do get is that

$$\text{KB} \models_{\leq} \neg\text{Penguin(tweety)} \supset \text{Flies(tweety)}.$$

So if we know that Tweety is not a penguin, as in

$$\text{Canary(tweety)}, \quad \forall x[\text{Canary}(x) \supset \neg\text{Penguin}(x)],$$

we then get the desired conclusion. But this is not derivable by default. Even if we add something saying that birds are normally not penguins, as in

$$\forall x[\text{Bird}(x) \wedge \neg\text{Ab}_2(x) \supset \neg\text{Penguin}(x)],$$

Tweety still does not fly, because we cannot change the set of penguins. Various solutions to this problem have been proposed in the literature, but none are completely satisfactory.

In fact, this sort of problem was already there in the background with the earlier version of circumscription. For example, consider the KB we had before with Tweety and Chilly, but this time without (tweety $\neq$ chilly). Then, as with the penguins, we lose the assumption that Tweety flies and only get

$$\text{KB} \models_{\leq} (\text{tweety} \neq \text{chilly}) \supset \text{Flies(tweety)}.$$

The reason is that there is a model of the KB with a minimal number of abnormal birds where Tweety does not fly, namely, one where Chilly and Tweety are the same bird.[9] Putting Chilly aside, all it really takes is the existence of a single abnormal bird: If the KB contains $\exists x[\text{Bird}(x) \wedge \neg\text{Flies}(x)]$, then although we can assume by default that this flightless bird is unique, we have not ruled out the possibility that Tweety is that bird and we can no longer assume by default that Tweety flies.

---

[9]It would be nice here to be able to somehow conclude *by default* that any two named constants denote distinct individuals. Unfortunately, it can be shown that this cannot be done using a mechanism like circumscription (see Exercise 2).

This means that there is a serious limitation in using circumscription for default reasoning: We must ensure that any abnormal individual is known to be distinct from the other individuals.

## 11.4    DEFAULT LOGIC

In the previous section, we introduced the idea of circumscription as a generalization of the CWA: Instead of minimizing all predicates, we minimize abnormality predicates. Of course, in the CWA section, we looked at it differently: We thought of it as deductive reasoning from a KB that had been enlarged by certain default assumptions, the negative literals that are added to form KB$^+$.

A generalization in a different direction then suggests itself: Instead of adding to a KB all negative literals that are consistent with the KB, we provide a mechanism for specifying explicitly which sentences should be added to the KB when it is consistent to do so. For example, if Bird($t$) is entailed by the KB, we might want to add the default assumption Flies($t$), if it is consistent to do so. Or perhaps this should only be done in certain contexts.

This is the intuition underlying *default logic*. A KB is now thought of as a *default theory* consisting of two parts, a set $\mathcal{F}$ of first-order sentences as usual, and a set $\mathcal{D}$ of *default rules*, which are specifications of what assumptions can be made and when. The job of a default logic is then to specify what the appropriate set of implicit beliefs should be, somehow incorporating the facts in $\mathcal{F}$; as many default assumptions as we can, given the default rules in $\mathcal{D}$; and the logical entailments of both. As we will see, defining these implicit beliefs is nontrivial: In some cases, there will be more than one candidate set of sentences that could be regarded as a reasonable set of beliefs (just as there could be multiple preferred extensions in Chapter 10); in other cases, no set of sentences seems to work properly.

### 11.4.1    Default Rules

Perhaps the most general form of default rule that has been examined in the literature is due to Ray Reiter: It consists of three sentences: a *prerequisite* $\alpha$, a *justification* $\beta$, and a *conclusion* $\delta$. The informal interpretation of this triple is that $\delta$ should be believed if $\alpha$ is believed and it is consistent to believe $\beta$. That is, if we have $\alpha$ and we do not have $\neg\beta$, then we can assume $\delta$. We will write such a rule as $\langle\, \alpha : \beta\, /\, \delta\, \rangle$.

A typical rule is $\langle\, \text{Bird(tweety)} : \text{Flies(tweety)}\, /\, \text{Flies(tweety)}\, \rangle$. This says that if we know that Tweety is a bird, then we should assume that Tweety flies if it is consistent to assume that Tweety flies. This type of rule, where the justification and conclusion are the same, is called a *normal default rule* and is by far the most common case. We will sometimes write such rules as Bird(tweety) $\Rightarrow$ Flies(tweety). We call a default theory all of whose rules are normal a *normal default theory*. As we will see, there are cases where nonnormal defaults are useful.

Note that these rules are particular to Tweety. In general, we would like rules that could apply to any bird. To do so, we allow a default rule to use formulas with free variables. A rule like this should be understood as an abbreviation for the set of all its instances (formed by replacing its variables by ground terms). So, for example, $\langle$ Bird$(x)$ : Flies$(x)$ **/** Flies$(x)$ $\rangle$ stands for all rules of the form $\langle$ Bird$(t)$ : Flies$(t)$ **/** Flies$(t)$ $\rangle$, where $t$ is any ground term. This will allow us to conclude by default of any bird that it flies without also forcing us to believe by default that *all* birds fly, a useful distinction.

## 11.4.2 Default Extensions

Given a default theory KB $= (\mathcal{F}, \mathcal{D})$, what sentences ought to be believed? We will call a set of sentences that constitute a reasonable set of beliefs given a default theory an *extension* of the theory. In this subsection, we present a simple and workable definition of extension; in the next, we will argue that sometimes a more complex definition is called for.

For our purposes, a set of sentences $\mathcal{E}$ is an extension of a default theory $(\mathcal{F}, \mathcal{D})$ if and only if for every sentence $\pi$,

$$\pi \in \mathcal{E} \quad \text{iff} \quad \mathcal{F} \cup \{\delta \mid \langle\, \alpha : \beta\, \textbf{/}\, \delta\, \rangle \in \mathcal{D}, \alpha \in \mathcal{E}, \neg\beta \notin \mathcal{E}\} \models \pi.$$

Thus, a set of sentences is an extension if it is the set of all entailments of $\mathcal{F} \cup \Delta$, where $\Delta$ is a suitable set of assumptions. In this respect, the definition of extension is similar to the definition of the CWA: We add default assumptions to a set of basic facts. Here, the assumptions to be added are those that are applicable to the extension $\mathcal{E}$: An assumption is *applicable* to an extension if and only if it is the conclusion of a default rule whose prerequisite is in the extension and the negation of whose justification is not. Note that we require $\alpha$ to be in $\mathcal{E}$, not in $\mathcal{F}$. This has the effect of allowing the prerequisite to be believed as the result of other default assumptions, and therefore of allowing default rules to chain. Note also that this definition is not constructive: It does not tell us how to find an $\mathcal{E}$ given $\mathcal{F}$ and $\mathcal{D}$, or even if there is one or more than one to be found. However, given $\mathcal{F}$ and $\mathcal{D}$, the $\mathcal{E}$ is completely characterized by its set of applicable assumptions, $\Delta$.

For example, suppose we have the following normal default theory:

$\mathcal{F} = \{\text{Bird(tweety)}, \text{Bird(chilly)}, \neg\text{Flies(chilly)}\}$
$\mathcal{D} = \{\text{Bird}(x) \Rightarrow \text{Flies}(x)\}$.

We wish to show that there is a unique extension to this default theory characterized by the assumption Flies(tweety). To show this, we must first establish that the entailments of $\mathcal{F} \cup \{\text{Flies(tweety)}\}$—call this set $\mathcal{E}$—are indeed an extension according to the definition. This means showing that Flies(tweety) is the only assumption applicable to $\mathcal{E}$: It is applicable because $\mathcal{E}$ contains Bird(tweety) and does not contain ¬Flies(tweety). Moreover, for no other $t$ is Flies($t$) applicable, because $\mathcal{E}$ contains Bird($t$) additionally only for $t = $ chilly, for which $\mathcal{E}$ also contains ¬Flies(chilly). So this $\mathcal{E}$ is indeed an extension. Observe that unlike circumscription, we do not require Tweety and Chilly to be distinct to draw the default conclusion.

But are there other extensions? Assume that some $\mathcal{E}'$ is also an extension for some applicable set of assumptions Flies($t_1$), ... , Flies($t_n$). First observe that no matter what Flies assumptions we make, we will never be able to conclude that ¬Flies(tweety). Thus Flies(tweety) must be applicable to $\mathcal{E}'$. However, we will not be able to conclude Bird($t$) for any $t$ other than tweety or chilly. So Flies(tweety) is the only applicable assumption, and therefore $\mathcal{E}'$ must again be the entailments of $\mathcal{F} \cup \{\text{Flies(tweety)}\}$.

In arguing that there was a unique extension, we made statements like, "No matter what assumptions we make, we will never be able to conclude $\alpha$." Of course, if $\mathcal{E}$ is *inconsistent* we can conclude anything we want. For example, if we could somehow add the assumption Flies(chilly), then we could conclude Bird(george). It turns out that such contradictory assumptions are never possible: An extension $\mathcal{E}$ of a default theory $(\mathcal{F}, \mathcal{D})$ is inconsistent if and only if $\mathcal{F}$ is inconsistent.

### 11.4.3  Multiple Extensions

Now consider the following default theory:

$$\mathcal{F} = \{\text{Republican(dick), Quaker(dick)}\}$$
$$\mathcal{D} = \{\text{Republican}(x) \Rightarrow \neg\text{Pacifist}(x), \text{Quaker}(x) \Rightarrow \text{Pacifist}(x)\}.$$

Here, there are two defaults that are in conflict for Dick. There are, correspondingly, two extensions:

1. $\mathcal{E}_1$ is characterized by the assumption Pacifist(dick).

2. $\mathcal{E}_2$ is characterized by the assumption ¬Pacifist(dick).

Both of these are extensions, because their assumption is applicable and no other assumption (for any $t$ other than dick) is. Moreover, there are no other extensions: The empty set of assumptions does not give an extension, because both Pacifist(dick) and ¬Pacifist(dick) would be applicable; for any other potential extension, assumptions would be of the form Pacifist($t$) or ¬Pacifist($t$), none of which are applicable for any $t$ other than dick, because we will never have the corresponding prerequisite Quaker($t$) or Republican($t$) in $\mathcal{E}$. Thus, $\mathcal{E}_1$ and $\mathcal{E}_2$ are the only extensions.

Thus, what default logic tells us here is that we may choose to assume that Dick is a pacifist or that he is not a pacifist. On the basis of what we have been told, either set of beliefs is reasonable. As in the case of inheritance hierarchies in Chapter 10, there are two immediate possibilities:

1. a *skeptical* reasoner will only believe those sentences that are common to all extensions of the default theory;

2. a *credulous* reasoner will simply choose arbitrarily one of the extensions of the default theory as the set of sentences to believe.

Arguments for and against each type of reasoning have been made. Note that minimal entailment, in giving us what is true in *all* minimal models, is much more like skeptical reasoning.

In some cases, the existence of multiple extensions is merely an indication that we have not said enough to make a reasonable decision. In the example, we may want to say that the default regarding Quakers should only apply to individuals not known to be politically active. Assuming we have the fact

$$\forall x[\text{Republican}(x) \supset \text{Political}(x)],$$

we can replace the original rule with Quaker($x$) as the prerequisite by a nonnormal one like

$$\frac{\text{Quaker}(x) \; : \; [\text{Pacifist}(x) \wedge \neg\text{Political}(x)]}{\text{Pacifist}(x).}$$

Then, for ordinary Republicans and ordinary Quakers, the assumption would be as before; for Quaker Republicans like Dick, we would assume (unequivocally) that they were not pacifists. Note that if we merely say that Republicans are politically active *by default*, we would again be left with two extensions.

This idea of arbitrating among conflicting default rules is crucial when it comes to dealing with concept hierarchies. For example, suppose we have a KB that contains $\forall x[\text{Penguin}(x) \supset \text{Birds}(x)]$, together with two default rules:

$$\text{Bird}(x) \Rightarrow \text{Flies}(x)$$
$$\text{Penguin}(x) \Rightarrow \neg\text{Flies}(x).$$

If the KB also contains Penguin(chilly), we get two extensions: one where Chilly is assumed to fly and one where Chilly is assumed not to fly. Unlike the Quaker Republican example, however, what ought to have happened here is clear: The default that penguins do not fly should *preempt* the more general default that birds fly. In other words, we only want one extension, where Chilly is assumed not to fly. To get this in default logic, it is necessary to encode the penguin case as part of the justification in a nonnormal default for birds:

$$\frac{\text{Bird(tweety)} : [\text{Flies(tweety)} \wedge \neg\text{Penguin(tweety)}]}{\text{Flies(tweety)}}.$$

This is not a very satisfactory solution, because there may be a very large number of interacting defaults to consider:

$$\frac{\text{Bird(tweety)} : \begin{array}{l}[\text{Flies(tweety)} \wedge \neg\text{Penguin(tweety)} \wedge \neg\text{Emu(tweety)} \\ \wedge \neg\text{Ostrich(tweety)} \wedge \neg\text{Dead(tweety)} \wedge \ldots]\end{array}}{\text{Flies(tweety)}}.$$

It is a severe limitation of default logic and indeed of all the default formalisms considered in this chapter that, unlike the inheritance formalism of Chapter 10, they do not automatically prefer the most specific defaults in cases like this.

Now consider the following example. Suppose we have a default theory $(\mathcal{F}, \mathcal{D})$, where $\mathcal{F}$ is empty and $\mathcal{D}$ contains a single nonnormal default $\langle \text{TRUE}:p \, / \, \neg p \, \rangle$, where $p$ is any atomic sentence. This default theory has *no* extensions: If $\mathcal{E}$ were an extension, then $\neg p \in \mathcal{E}$ if and only if $\neg p$ is an applicable assumption if and only if $\neg p \notin \mathcal{E}$. This means that with this default rule, there is no reasonable set of beliefs to hold. Having no extension is very different from having a single but inconsistent one, such as when $\mathcal{F}$ is inconsistent. A skeptical believer might go ahead and believe all sentences (because every sentence is trivially common to all the extensions), but a credulous believer is stuck (because there are none). Fortunately, this situation does not arise with normal defaults, as it can be proven that every normal default theory has at least one extension.

An even more serious problem is shown in the following example. Suppose we have a default theory $(\mathcal{F}, \mathcal{D})$, where $\mathcal{F}$ is empty and $\mathcal{D}$ contains a normal default $p \Rightarrow p$, where again $p$ is atomic. This theory has two extensions, one of which is the set of all valid sentences and the other of which is the set $\mathcal{E}$ consisting of the entailments of $p$. (The assumption $p$ is applicable here, because $p \in \mathcal{E}$ and $\neg p \notin \mathcal{E}$.) However, on intuitive grounds, this second extension is quite inappropriate. The default rule says that $p$ can be assumed if $p$ is believed. This really should not allow us to conclude by default that $p$ is true any more than a fact saying that $p$ is true if $p$ is true would. It would be much better to end up with a single extension consisting of just the valid sentences, because there is no good reason to believe $p$ by default.

One way to resolve this problem is to rule out any extension for which a proper subset is also an extension. This works for this example, but fails on other examples. A more complex definition of extension, due to Ray Reiter, appears to handle all such anomalies: Let $(\mathcal{F}, \mathcal{D})$ be any default theory. For any set $S$, let $\Delta(S)$ be the least set containing $\mathcal{F}$, closed under entailment, and satisfying the following:

$$\text{If } \langle\, \alpha : \beta\, /\, \delta\, \rangle \in \mathcal{D},\ \alpha \in \Delta(S),\ \neg\beta \notin S,\ \text{then } \delta \in \Delta(S).$$

Then a set $\mathcal{E}$ is a *grounded extension* of $(\mathcal{F}, \mathcal{D})$ if and only if $\mathcal{E} = \Delta(\mathcal{E})$. This definition is considerably more complex to work with than the one we have considered, but does have some desirable properties, including handling the example correctly and agreeing with the simpler definition on all of the earlier examples.

We will not pursue this version in any more detail except to observe one simple feature: In the definition of $\Delta(S)$, we test if $\neg\beta \notin S$, rather than $\neg\beta \notin \Delta(S)$. Had we gone with the latter, the definition of $\Delta(S)$ would have been this: the least set containing $\mathcal{F}$, closed under entailment, and containing all of its applicable assumptions. Except for the part about "least set," this is precisely our earlier definition of extension. So this very small change to how justifications are used in the definition of extension ends up making all the difference.

## 11.5 AUTOEPISTEMIC LOGIC

One advantage circumscription has over default logic is that defaults end up as ordinary *sentences* in the language (using abnormality predicates). In default logic, although we can reason *with* defaults, we cannot reason *about* them. For instance, suppose we have the default $\langle\, \alpha : \beta\, /\, \delta\, \rangle$. It would be nice to say that we also implicitly have the defaults $\langle\, (\alpha \wedge \alpha') : \beta\, /\, \delta\, \rangle$ and $\langle\, \alpha : \beta\, /\, (\delta \vee \delta')\, \rangle$. Similarly, we might want to say that we also have the "contrapositive" default $\langle\, \neg\delta : \beta\, /\, \neg\alpha\, \rangle$. But these questions cannot even be posed in default logic because, despite its name, it is not a logic of defaults at all, as there is no notion of entailment among defaults. On the other hand, default logic deals more directly with what it is consistent to assume, whereas circumscription forces us to handle defaults in terms of abnormalities. The consistency in default logic is, of course, relative to what is currently believed. This suggests another approach to default reasoning where, like circumscription, defaults are represented as sentences, but like default logic, these sentences talk about what it is consistent to assume.

Roughly speaking, we will represent the default about birds, for example, by

*Any bird that can be consistently believed to fly does fly.*

Given that beliefs (as far as we are concerned) are closed under entailment, then a sentence can be consistently believed if and only if its negation is not believed. So we can restate the default as

*Any bird not believed to be flightless flies.*

To encode defaults like these as sentences in a logic, we extend the FOL language to talk about belief directly. In particular, we will assume that for every formula $\alpha$, there is another formula $\mathbf{B}\alpha$ to be understood informally as saying "$\alpha$ is believed to be true." The $\mathbf{B}$ should be thought of as a new unary connective (like negation). Defaults, then, are represented by sentences like

$$\forall x[\mathsf{Bird}(x) \wedge \neg\mathbf{B}\neg\mathsf{Flies}(x) \supset \mathsf{Flies}(x)].$$

For this to work, it must be the case that saying that a bird is *believed* to be flightless is not the same as saying that the bird is flightless. Suppose, for example, that we know that either bird $a$ or bird $b$ is flightless, but we do not know which.[10] In this case, we know that one of them is flightless, but neither of them is believed to be flightless. Because we imagine reasoning using sentences like these, we will be reasoning about birds, of course, but also about *what we believe about birds*. The fact that this is a logic about our own beliefs is why it is called *autoepistemic logic*.

## 11.5.1   Stable Sets and Expansions

As usual, our primary concern is to determine a reasonable set of beliefs in the presence of defaults. With autoepistemic logic, the question is the following: Given a KB that contains sentences using the $\mathbf{B}$ operator, what is a reasonable set of beliefs to hold? To answer this question, we begin by examining some minimal properties we expect any set of beliefs $\mathcal{E}$ to satisfy. We call a set $\mathcal{E}$ *stable* if and only if it satisfies these three properties:

1. Closure under entailment: if $\mathcal{E} \models \alpha$, then $\alpha \in \mathcal{E}$.

2. Positive introspection: if $\alpha \in \mathcal{E}$, then $\mathbf{B}\alpha \in \mathcal{E}$.

3. Negative introspection: if $\alpha \notin \mathcal{E}$, then $\neg\mathbf{B}\alpha \in \mathcal{E}$.

---

[10]As we have been doing throughout the book, we use "know" and "believe" interchangeably. Unless otherwise indicated, "believe" is what is intended, and "know" is used for stylistic variety.

So first, we want $\mathcal{E}$ to be closed under entailment. Because we have not yet defined entailment for a language with **B** operators, we take this simply to mean ordinary logical entailment, where we treat

$$\forall x[\mathsf{Bird}(x) \wedge \neg\mathbf{B}\neg\mathsf{Flies}(x) \supset \mathsf{Flies}(x)]$$

as if it were something like

$$\forall x[\mathsf{Bird}(x) \wedge \neg Q(x) \supset \mathsf{Flies}(x)]$$

where $Q$ is a new predicate symbol.

The other two properties of a stable set deal with the **B** operator. They ensure that if $\alpha$ is believed then so is $\mathbf{B}\alpha$, and if $\alpha$ is not believed then $\neg\mathbf{B}\alpha$ is believed. These are called introspection constraints, because they deal with beliefs about beliefs.

Given a KB, there will be many stable sets $\mathcal{E}$ that contain it. In deciding what sentences to believe, we want a stable set that contains the entailments of the KB and the appropriate introspective beliefs, but nothing else. This is called a *stable expansion* of the KB and its formal definition, due to Robert Moore, is this: A set $\mathcal{E}$ is a stable expansion of KB if and only if for every sentence $\pi$ it is the case that

$$\pi \in \mathcal{E} \quad \text{iff} \quad \mathrm{KB} \cup \{\mathbf{B}\alpha \mid \alpha \in \mathcal{E}\} \cup \{\neg\mathbf{B}\alpha \mid \alpha \notin \mathcal{E}\} \models \pi.$$

This is a familiar pattern: The implicit beliefs $\mathcal{E}$ are those sentences that are entailed by $\mathrm{KB} \cup \Delta$, where $\Delta$ is a suitable set of assumptions. In this case, the assumptions are those arising from the introspection constraints.

To see how this leads to default reasoning, suppose we a have a KB that consists of the following:

> $\mathsf{Bird}(\mathsf{chilly}), \mathsf{Bird}(\mathsf{tweety}), (\mathsf{tweety} \neq \mathsf{chilly}), \neg\mathsf{Flies}(\mathsf{chilly}),$
> $\forall x[\mathsf{Bird}(x) \wedge \neg\mathbf{B}\neg\mathsf{Flies}(x) \supset \mathsf{Flies}(x)].$

Let's consider the consequences of this KB informally. First, we see that there is no way to conclude $\neg\mathsf{Flies}(\mathsf{tweety})$: $\neg\mathsf{Flies}(\mathsf{tweety})$ is not explicitly in the knowledge base, and there is no rule that would allow us to conclude it, even by default (the conclusion of our one rule is of the form $\mathsf{Flies}(x)$). This means that if $\mathcal{E}$ is a stable expansion of the KB, it will not include this fact. But because of our negative introspection property, a stable expansion that did not include the fact $\neg\mathsf{Flies}(\mathsf{tweety})$ would include the assumption, $\neg\mathbf{B}\neg\mathsf{Flies}(\mathsf{tweety})$.[11] Now, given this assumption, and the

---

[11] This really is an assumption, because $\neg\mathbf{B}\neg\mathsf{Flies}(\mathsf{tweety})$ does not follow from what is in the KB; the KB does not specify one way or another.

fact that $\forall x[\text{Bird}(x) \wedge \neg\mathbf{B}\neg\text{Flies}(x) \supset \text{Flies}(x)]$ is in the KB, we conclude Flies(tweety) using ordinary logical entailment. In autoepistemic logic, default assumptions are typically of the form $\neg\mathbf{B}\alpha$, and new default beliefs about the world, like Flies(tweety), are deduced from these assumptions.

## 11.5.2  Enumerating Stable Expansions

The previous section illustrated informally how the notion of a stable expansion of a knowledge base can account for default reasoning of a certain sort. To be more precise, and show that the KB does in fact have a stable expansion containing Flies(tweety) and that it is unique, we will consider the simpler propositional version of the definition and show how to enumerate stable expansions. In the propositional case, we replace the sentence,

$$\forall x[\text{Bird}(x) \wedge \neg\mathbf{B}\neg\text{Flies}(x) \supset \text{Flies}(x)]$$

by all of its instances, as we did with default rules in the previous section.

Let us call a sentence *objective* if it does not contain any $\mathbf{B}$ operators. The first thing to observe is that in the propositional case a stable expansion is completely determined by its objective subset; the nonobjective part can be reconstructed using the two introspection constraints and logical entailment.

So imagine that we have a KB that contains objective and nonobjective sentences, where $\mathbf{B}\alpha_1, \mathbf{B}\alpha_2, \dots, \mathbf{B}\alpha_n$ are all the $\mathbf{B}$ formulas mentioned. Assume for simplicity that all the $\alpha_i$ are objective. If we knew which of the $\mathbf{B}\alpha_i$ formulas were true in a stable expansion, we could calculate the objective part of that stable expansion using ordinary logical reasoning. The procedure we will use is to *guess* nondeterministically which of the $\mathbf{B}\alpha_i$ formulas are true, and then check whether the result makes sense as the objective part of a stable expansion: If we guessed that $\mathbf{B}\alpha_i$ was true, we need to confirm that $\alpha_i$ is entailed; if we guessed that $\mathbf{B}\alpha_i$ was false, we need to confirm that $\alpha_i$ is not entailed. A more precise version of this procedure is shown in Figure 11.1. Observe that using this procedure we can generate at most $2^n$ stable expansions.

To see this procedure in action, consider a propositional version of the flying bird example. In this case, our KB is

> Bird(chilly), Bird(tweety), ¬Flies(chilly),
> [Bird(tweety) $\wedge$ $\neg\mathbf{B}\neg$Flies(tweety) $\supset$ Flies(tweety)],
> [Bird(chilly) $\wedge$ $\neg\mathbf{B}\neg$Flies(chilly) $\supset$ Flies(chilly)].

There are two subformulas with $\mathbf{B}$ operators, $\mathbf{B}\neg$Flies(tweety) and $\mathbf{B}\neg$Flies(chilly), and so at most $2^2 = 4$ stable expansions. For each constant $c$, if $\mathbf{B}\neg$Flies($c$) is true, then [Bird($c$) $\wedge$ $\neg\mathbf{B}\neg$Flies($c$) $\supset$ Flies($c$)]

**input:** a propositional KB, containing subformulas $\mathbf{B}\alpha_1, \mathbf{B}\alpha_2, \ldots, \mathbf{B}\alpha_n$

**output:** the objective part of a stable expansion of the KB

1. Replace each $\mathbf{B}\alpha_i$ in KB by either TRUE or ¬TRUE.

2. Simplify, and call the resulting objective knowledge base KB°.

3. If $\mathbf{B}\alpha_i$ was replaced by TRUE, confirm that KB° $\models \alpha_i$; if $\mathbf{B}\alpha_i$ was replaced by ¬TRUE, confirm that KB° $\not\models \alpha_i$.

4. If the condition is confirmed for every $\mathbf{B}\alpha_i$, then return KB°, whose entailments form the objective part of a stable expansion.

■ **FIGURE 11.1**

A Procedure to Generate Stable Expansions

simplifies to TRUE; if $\mathbf{B}$¬Flies($c$) is false, then the sentence simplifies to [Bird($c$) $\supset$ Flies($c$)], which will reduce to Flies($c$), because the KB contains Bird($c$). So, our four cases are these:

1. $\mathbf{B}$¬Flies(tweety) true and $\mathbf{B}$¬Flies(chilly) true, for which KB° is

    Bird(tweety), Bird(chilly), ¬Flies(chilly).

    This is the case because the two implications each simplify to TRUE. Then, following Step 3, for each of the two $\mathbf{B}\alpha_i$ formulas, which were replaced by TRUE, we need to confirm that the $\alpha_i$ are entailed by KB°. KB° does not entail ¬Flies(tweety). As a result, this is not a stable expansion.

2. $\mathbf{B}$¬Flies(tweety) true and $\mathbf{B}$¬Flies(chilly) false, for which KB° is

    Bird(tweety), Bird(chilly), ¬Flies(chilly), Flies(chilly).

    Following Step 3, we need to confirm that KB° entails ¬Flies(tweety) and that it does not entail ¬Flies(chilly). Because KB° entails ¬Flies(chilly), this is not a stable expansion (actually, this KB fails on both counts).

3. $\mathbf{B}$¬Flies(tweety) false and $\mathbf{B}$¬Flies(chilly) true, for which KB° is

    Bird(tweety), Bird(chilly), ¬Flies(chilly), Flies(tweety).

    Step 3 tells us to confirm that KB° entails ¬Flies(chilly) and does not entail ¬Flies(tweety). In this case, we succeed on both counts, and this characterizes a stable expansion.

4. Finally, **B**¬Flies(tweety) false and **B**¬Flies(chilly) false, for which KB° is

Bird(tweety), Bird(chilly), ¬Flies(chilly), Flies(tweety), Flies(chilly).

Because KB° entails ¬Flies(chilly), this is not a stable expansion.

Thus, this KB has a unique stable expansion, and in this expansion, Tweety flies.

As another example, we can use the procedure to show that the KB consisting of the sentence ($\neg$**B**$p \supset p$) has no stable expansion: If **B**$p$ is false, then the KB° is $p$, which entails $p$; conversely, if **B**$p$ is true, then KB° is TRUE, which does not entail $p$. So there is no stable expansion.

Similarly, we can use the procedure to show that the KB consisting of the sentences ($\neg$**B**$p \supset q$) and ($\neg$**B**$q \supset p$) has exactly two stable expansions: If **B**$p$ is true and **B**$q$ false, the KB° is $p$, which entails $p$ and does not entail $q$, and so this is the first stable expansion; symmetrically, the other stable expansion is when **B**$p$ is false and **B**$q$ true; if both are true, the KB° is TRUE, which neither entails $p$ nor $q$, and if both are false, the KB° is ($p \wedge q$), which entails both.

It is worth noting that as with default logic, in some cases this definition of stable expansion may not be strong enough. Consider, for example, a KB consisting of a single sentence, (**B**$p \supset p$). Using the procedure, we can see that there are two stable expansions: one that contains $p$ and one that does not. Intuitively it seems like the first expansion is inappropriate: The only possible justification for believing $p$ is **B**$p$ itself. As in the default logic case, it seems that the assumption is not properly grounded.

A new definition of stable expansion (due to Kurt Konolige) has been proposed to deal with this problem: A set of sentences is a *minimal stable expansion* if and only if it is a stable expansion that is minimal in its objective sentences. In the earlier example, only the stable expansion not containing $p$ would be a minimal stable expansion. However, further examples suggest that an even stronger definition may be required, resulting in an exact correspondence between stable expansions and the grounded extensions of default logic.

## 11.6  CONCLUSION

In this chapter, we have examined four different logical formalisms for default reasoning. Although each of them does the job in many cases, they each have drawbacks of one sort or another. Getting a logical account of default reasoning that is simple, broadly applicable, and intuitively correct remains an open problem, unfortunately. In fact, because so much of what we know involves default reasoning, it is perhaps *the* open problem in the whole area of knowledge representation. Not surprisingly, much of the theoretical research over the last twenty years has been on this topic.

## 11.7  BIBLIOGRAPHIC NOTES

Default reasoning and, in general, nonmonotonic reasoning are covered in most textbooks on AI. Books devoted to nonmonotonic reasoning include those by Antoniou [13], Łukaszewicz [261], Marek and Truszczyński [267], and Brewka et al. [57]. Besnard [28] concentrates on default logic. Ginsberg edited an early collection of readings in nonmonotonic reasoning [157]. For an early overview, see Reiter [344].

The closed-world assumption is due to Reiter [345], as were the domain closure assumption and unique names assumption [341]. The generalized closed-world assumption was suggested by Minker [290]. Circumscription and minimal entailment were introduced by McCarthy [278, 279] (see also the work of Lifschitz [249, 250, 253] and McCarthy [280]). Default logic was developed by Reiter [342, 343]. An alternative formulation is given by Poole [330]. This idea was extended by Brewka [55] (see also [56]). Autoepistemic logic was introduced by Moore [295, 296, 298]. Konolige [222] and Marek and Truszczyński [266] relate autoepistemic logic to default logic.

A semantics for negation as failure was proposed by Clark [70]. The work by Kraus, Lehmann, and Magidor investigates the notion of nonmonotonic consequence relations [227]. This type of work is also considered by Schlecta [367]. Makinson [262] relates nonmonotonic logics to classical logics.

## 11.8  EXERCISES

**1.** Although the inheritance networks of Chapter 10 are in a sense much weaker than the other formalisms considered in this chapter for default reasoning, they use default assertions more fully. Consider the following assertions:

> *Canadians are typically not francophones.*

> *All Québecois are Canadians.*

> *Québecois are typically francophones.*

> *Robert is a Québecois.*

Here is a case where it seems plausible to conclude by default that Robert is a francophone.

(a) Represent these assertions in an inheritance network (treating the second one as defeasible), and argue that it unambiguously supports the conclusion that Robert is a francophone.

(b) Represent them in first-order logic using two abnormality predicates, one for Canadians and one for Québecois, and argue that, as it stands, minimizing abnormality would *not* be sufficient to conclude that Robert is a francophone.

(c) Show that minimizing abnormality will work if we add the assertion

*All Québecois are abnormal Canadians,*

but will not work if we only add

*Québecois are typically abnormal Canadians.*

(d) Repeat the exercise in default logic: Represent the assertions as two facts and two normal default rules, and argue that the result has two extensions. Eliminate the ambiguity using a nonnormal default rule. You may use a variable-free version of the problem where the letters $q$, $c$, and $f$ stand for the propositions that Robert is a Québecois, Canadian, and francophone, respectively, and where defaults are considered only with respect to Robert.

(e) Write a variable-free version of the assertions in autoepistemic logic, and show that the procedure described in the text generates two stable expansions. How can the unwanted expansion be eliminated?

2. Consider the Chilly and Tweety KB presented in the text.

(a) We showed that for this KB, if we write the default that birds fly using an abnormality predicate, the resulting KB minimally entails that Tweety flies. Prove that without (chilly $\neq$ tweety), the conclusion no longer follows.

(b) Suppose that for any two constants $c$ and $c'$, we hoped to conclude by default that they were unequal. Imagine that we have a binary predicate $\text{Ab}_e$ and an FOL sentence

$$\forall x \forall y \, (\neg \text{Ab}_e(x, y) \supset (x \neq y)).$$

Would using minimal entailment work? Explain.

3. Consider the following proposal for default reasoning. As with minimal entailment, we begin with a KB that uses one or more Ab predicates. Then, instead of asking what is entailed by the KB, we ask what is entailed by KB′, where

$$\text{KB}' = \text{KB} \cup \{\neg \text{Ab}(t) \mid \text{KB} \not\models \text{Ab}(t)\}.$$

Compare this form of default reasoning to minimal entailment. Show an example where the two methods disagree on some default conclusions. State a sufficient condition for them to agree.

4. This question concerns the interaction between defaults and knowledge that is *disjunctive*. Starting with autoepistemic logic, there are different ways one might represent a default like "Birds fly." The first way, as in the text, is what we might call a *strong* default:

$$\forall x(\text{Bird}(x) \land \neg\mathbf{B}\neg\text{Flies}(x) \supset \text{Flies}(x)).$$

Another way is what we might call a *weak* default:

$$\forall x(\mathbf{B}\text{Bird}(x) \land \neg\mathbf{B}\neg\text{Flies}(x) \supset \text{Flies}(x)).$$

In this question, we will work with the following KB:

$$\text{Bird}(a), \text{Bird}(b), (\text{Bird}(c) \lor \text{Bird}(d)), \neg\text{Flies}(b),$$

where we assume that all names denote distinct individuals.

(a) Propositionalize and show that the strong and weak defaults lead to different conclusions about flying ability.

(b) Consider the following version of the default:

$$\forall x(\mathbf{B}\text{Bird}(x) \land \neg\mathbf{B}\neg\text{Flies}(x) \supset \mathbf{B}\text{Flies}(x)).$$

Show that this version does not lead to reasonable conclusions.

(c) Now consider using default logic and circumscription to represent the default. Show that one of them behaves more like the strong default, while the other is more like the weak one.

(d) Consider the following representation of the default in default logic:

$$\langle \text{TRUE} \Rightarrow [\text{Bird}(x) \supset \text{Flies}(x)] \rangle.$$

Discuss how this representation handles disjunctive knowledge.

# CHAPTER 12

# VAGUENESS, UNCERTAINTY, AND DEGREES OF BELIEF

■

■

■

In earlier chapters, we learned how precise logical statements about the world, in many different forms, can be useful for capturing knowledge and applying it. However, when we try to emulate the more common-sensical kinds of reasoning that people do, we find that the crisp precision of classical logics may fall short of what we want. As we saw in Chapter 11, trying to represent what is known about a typical bird stretches our logical forms in one direction—not every bird has all of what we usually think of as the characteristics of birds in general. But there are additional needs in Artificial Intelligence that ask us to extend our representations in other ways.

Sometimes it is not appropriate to express a general statement with the totality of a logical universal. In other words, not every generality has the force of "*P*s are always, purely, exactly, and unarguably *Q*s." As we have seen, there are circumstances where *P*s might *usually* (or perhaps only *rarely*) be *Q*s; for example, birds usually fly, but not always. In other cases, *P*s might be fair, but not excellent examples of *Q*s; we might, for example, prefer to say that someone is barely competent, or somewhat tall. In situations where we use physical sensors, we might also have some unavoidable imprecision, as with, for example, a thermometer that is only accurate to a certain precision.

These cases show that in many situations it may be hard to gauge something precisely or categorically. In addition to the intrinsic imperfection of statements like those just mentioned, the way that we generate conclusions from data may also be imprecise. For example, if we learn a fact or a rule from some other person, we may need to discount for that person's untrustworthiness, fallibility, or past inaccuracies. Similarly, we may only understand a physical system to a modest level of depth, and not be able to confidently apply rules in 100% of the cases; such is the case with many types of medical knowledge.

In cases like these, the use of equivocal information and imperfect rules can yield conclusions that "follow" from premises, but not in the standard logical sense we have been investigating so far. The "conclusions" that we come to may not be categorical: We may not be confident in an answer, or only be able to come within some error range of the true answer, or only really be able to say that something is "pretty good." As a result of this fairly common need to equivocate on specific data and general rules, we need to find ways to stretch the types of knowledge representation techniques we have investigated so far in this book. In this chapter, we look at some of the more common ways to expand our core representations to include frequencies, impurity of examples, doubt, and other modes of noncategorical description.

## 12.1   NONCATEGORICAL REASONING

A natural first reaction to the need to expand our interpretation of what follows from some premises would be to suggest using *probabilities*. A probability is a number expressing the chance that a proposition will be true or that an event will occur. The introduction of numbers—especially real numbers—would seem to be the key to avoiding the categorical nature of binary logical values. Given the introduction of the notion of "less than 100%" into the knowledge representation mix, we can easily see a way to go from "all birds fly" to "95% of birds fly."

But as appealing as probabilities are, they won't fit the bill in all ways. Certainly there will be repeatable sequences of events for which we will want to represent the likelihood of the next outcome—probabilities work well for sequences like coin tosses—but we also need to capture other senses of "less than 100%." For example, when we talk about the chances that the Blue Jays will win the World Series, or that Tweety will fly, we are not talking really about the laws of chance (as we would in assessing the probability of "heads" in tossing a fair coin), but rather about the development of opinions based on evidence and an inference about the possibility of the occurrence of an individual event or the property of a specific bird. Finally, in a somewhat different vein, to speak of someone being "fairly tall" doesn't feel like the use of a probability at all.

So let us take a moment to sort out some different ways to loosen the categorical grip of standard logics. We start by looking at a typical logical sentence of the form $\forall x P(x)$, as in "Everyone in this room is married," or "Everyone in my class is tall." We can distinguish at least three different types of modification we might try in order to make this logical structure more flexible:

1. We can relax the strength of the *quantifier*. Instead of "for *all x*," we might want to say "for *most x*" or "for 95% of *x*," as in "95% of the people in this room are married." This yields an assertion about frequency—a *statistical* interpretation. We say that our use of probability in such sentences is *objective*, because it is about the world, pure and simple, and not subject to interpretation or degrees of confidence.

2. We could relax the applicability of the *predicate*. Instead of only strict assertions like "Everyone in my class is (absolutely) tall," we could have statements like "Everyone in my class is moderately tall." This yields the notion of a predicate like "tall" that applies to an individual to a greater or lesser extent. We call these *vague predicates*. Note that with the relaxation of the predicate, a person might be considered simultaneously to be both tall (strongly) and short (weakly).

3. We could relax our degree of belief in the *sentence* as a whole. Instead of saying, "Everyone in the room is married," we might say, "I believe that everyone in the room is married, but I am not very sure." This lack of confidence can come from many sources, but it does not reflect a probabilistic concern (either everyone is married or they're not) or a less-than-categorical predicate (a person is either fully married or not married at all). Here we are dealing with *uncertain knowledge*; when we can quantify our lack of certainty, we are using a notion of *subjective* probability, because it reflects some individual's personal degree of belief, and not the objective frequency of an event.

We now look at objective probabilities, subjective probabilities, and vague predicates, in turn. This separation of concerns allows us to better determine appropriate representational mechanisms for less-than-categorical statements. However, nothing says that these three representational approaches cannot work together: We may need to represent statements like "I am pretty sure that most of the people in the room are fairly short." Also, many of the concepts we introduce (like the basic postulates of probability) will connect all three approaches.

## 12.2  OBJECTIVE PROBABILITY

Objective probabilities are about *frequency*. Even though we like to talk in terms of the probability or chance of a single event happening, for example, whether the next card I am dealt will be the ace of spades, or whether tomorrow will be rainy, the "chance of rain" we speak of actually refers to the percentage of time that a rain event will happen *in the long run*, when the conditions are exactly the same as they are now. In frequentist terms, the "chance of *x*" is really the percentage of times *x* is expected to happen out of a sequence of many events, when the basic process is repeated over and over, each event is independent of those that have gone before, and the conditions each time are exactly the same. As a result, the notion of objective probability, or chance of something, is best applied to processes like coin flipping and card drawing. Weather forecasting draws on the fact that the conditions today are similar enough to the conditions on prior days to help us decide how to place our bets—whether or not to carry an umbrella or go ahead with a planned picnic.

The kind of probability that deals with factual frequencies is called *objective* because it does not depend on who is assessing the probability. (In Section 12.3, we will talk about *subjective* probabilities, which deal with degrees of belief.) Because this is a statistical view, it does not directly support the assignment of a belief about a random event that is not part of any obvious repeatable sequence.

### 12.2.1  The Basic Postulates

Technically, a probability is a number between 0 and 1 (inclusive) representing the frequency of an event (e.g., a coin's landing on "heads" two times in a row) in a large enough space of random samples (e.g., a long sequence of coin flips). An event with probability 1 is considered to always happen, and one with probability 0 to never happen. More formally, we begin with a universal set $U$ of all possible occurrences, for example, the result of a large set of coin flips. An event $a$ is understood to be any subset of $U$. A *probability measure* **Pr** is a function from events to numbers in the interval $[0, 1]$ satisfying the following two basic postulates:

1. $\mathbf{Pr}(U) = 1$.

2. If $a_1, \ldots, a_n$ are disjoint events, then
   $\mathbf{Pr}(a_1 \cup \cdots \cup a_n) = \mathbf{Pr}(a_1) + \cdots + \mathbf{Pr}(a_n)$.

It follows immediately from these two postulates that

$$\mathbf{Pr}(\overline{a}) = 1 - \mathbf{Pr}(a),$$

and hence that

$$\mathbf{Pr}(\{\}) = 0.$$

It also follows (less obviously) from these that for any two events $a$ and $b$,

$$\mathbf{Pr}(a \cup b) = \mathbf{Pr}(a) + \mathbf{Pr}(b) - \mathbf{Pr}(a \cap b).$$

Another useful consequence is the following:

If $b_1, b_2, \ldots, b_n$ are disjoint events and exhaust all the possibilities, that is, if $(b_i \cap b_j) = \{\}$ for $i \neq j$, and $(b_1 \cup \cdots \cup b_n) = U$, then

$$\mathbf{Pr}(a) = \mathbf{Pr}(a \cap b_1) + \cdots + \mathbf{Pr}(a \cap b_n).$$

When thinking about probability, it is sometimes helpful to think in terms of a very simple interpretation of $\mathbf{Pr}$: We imagine that $U$ is a finite set of some sort and that $\mathbf{Pr}(a)$ is the number of elements in $a$ divided by the size of $U$, in other words, the proportion of elements of $U$ that are also in $a$. It is easy to confirm that this particular set-theoretic interpretation of $\mathbf{Pr}$ satisfies the two basic postulates stated earlier, and hence all the other properties as well.

## 12.2.2  Conditional Probability and Independence

A key idea in probability theory is *conditioning*. The probability of one event may depend on its interaction with others. We write a conditional probability with a vertical bar ("|") between the event in question and the conditioning event; for example, $\mathbf{Pr}(a|b)$ means the probability of $a$, given that $b$ has occurred. In terms of our simple finite set interpretation, whereas $\mathbf{Pr}(a)$ means the proportion of elements that are in $a$ among all the elements of $U$, $\mathbf{Pr}(a|b)$ means the proportion of elements that are in $a$ among the elements of $b$. This is defined more formally by the following:[1]

$$\mathbf{Pr}(a|b) \stackrel{def}{=} \frac{\mathbf{Pr}(a \cap b)}{\mathbf{Pr}(b)}.$$

Note that we cannot predict in general the value of $\mathbf{Pr}(a \cap b)$ given the values of $\mathbf{Pr}(a)$ and $\mathbf{Pr}(b)$. In other words, in terms of our simple set-theoretic interpretation, we cannot predict the size of $(a \cap b)$ given only the sizes of $a$ and $b$.

It does follow immediately from the definition of conditioning that

$$\mathbf{Pr}(a \cap b) = \mathbf{Pr}(a|b) \times \mathbf{Pr}(b),$$

---

[1]This conditional probability is considered to be undefined if $b$ has zero probability.

and more generally, we have the following *chain rule*:

$$\mathbf{Pr}(a_1 \cap \cdots \cap a_n) = \mathbf{Pr}(a_1 \,|\, a_2 \cap \cdots \cap a_n) \times$$
$$\mathbf{Pr}(a_2 \,|\, a_3 \cap \cdots \cap a_n) \times \cdots \times \mathbf{Pr}(a_{n-1} \,|\, a_n) \times \mathbf{Pr}(a_n).$$

We also get conditional versions of the properties noted earlier, such as

$$\mathbf{Pr}(\overline{a}|b) = 1 - \mathbf{Pr}(a|b),$$

and the following:

If $b_1, b_2, \ldots, b_n$ are disjoint events and exhaust all the possibilities, then

$$\mathbf{Pr}(a|c) = \mathbf{Pr}(a \cap b_1|c) + \cdots + \mathbf{Pr}(a \cap b_n|c).$$

A very useful rule, called *Bayes' rule*, uses the definition of conditional probability to relate the probability of $a$ given $b$ to the probability of $b$ given $a$:

$$\mathbf{Pr}(a|b) = \frac{\mathbf{Pr}(a) \times \mathbf{Pr}(b|a)}{\mathbf{Pr}(b)}.$$

Imagine, for example, that $a$ is a disease and $b$ is a symptom, and we wish to know the probability of someone having the disease given that they exhibit the symptom. Although it may be hard to estimate directly the frequency with which the symptom indicates the disease, it may be much easier to provide the numbers on the right-hand side of the equation, that is, the unconditional (or a priori) probabilities of the disease and of the symptom in the general population, and the probability that the symptom will appear given that the disease is present. We will find Bayes' rule especially helpful when we consider subjective probabilities.

Finally, we say that an event $a$ is *conditionally independent* of event $b$ if $b$ does not affect the probability of $a$, that is, if

$$\mathbf{Pr}(a|b) = \mathbf{Pr}(a).$$

This says that the chance of getting event $a$ is unaffected by whether or not event $b$ has occurred. In terms of our simple set-theoretic interpretation, $a$ is conditionally independent of $b$ if the proportion of $a$ elements within set $b$ is the same as the proportion of $a$ elements in the general population $U$. It follows from the definition that event $a$ is independent of $b$ if and only if

$$\mathbf{Pr}(a \cap b) = \mathbf{Pr}(a) \times \mathbf{Pr}(b),$$

if and only if *b* is independent of *a*. So the relation of conditional independence is symmetric. We also say that *a and b are conditionally independent given c* if

$$\mathbf{Pr}(a|b \cap c) = \mathbf{Pr}(a|c).$$

Observe that when we are trying to assess the likelihood of some event *a* given everything we know, it will not be sufficient to know only some of the conditional probabilities regarding *a*. For example, it does not help to know the value of $\mathbf{Pr}(a|c)$ when we want to calculate $\mathbf{Pr}(a|b \cap c)$, because the probability of *a* given both *b* and *c* is unrelated to the probability of *a* given just *c*, unless *a* is known to be independent from *b* given *c*.

## 12.3 SUBJECTIVE PROBABILITY

As proposed in Section 12.1, an agent's *subjective* degree of confidence or certainty in a sentence is separable from and indeed orthogonal to the propositional content of the sentence itself. Regardless of how vague or categorical a sentence may be, the degree of belief in it can vary. We might be absolutely certain, for example, that Bill is quite tall; similarly, we might only suspect that Bill is married.

Degrees of beliefs of this sort are often derived from observations about groups of things in the world. We may be confident that it will rain today because of the statistical observation about similar-looking days in the past. Moving from statistics to graded beliefs about individuals thus seems similar to the move we make from general facts about the world to defaults. We may conclude that Tweety the bird flies based on a belief that birds generally fly, but default conclusions tend to be all or nothing: We conclude that Tweety flies or we do not. With subjective beliefs, we are expressing levels of confidence rather than all-or-nothing conclusions.

Because degrees of belief often derive from statistical considerations, they are usually referred to as *subjective probabilities*. Subjective probabilities and their computations work mechanically like objective ones, but are used in a different way. We work with them typically in seeing how evidence combines to change our confidence in a belief about the world, rather than to simply derive new conclusions.

In the world of subjective probability, we define two types of probability relative to drawing a conclusion. The *prior* probability of a sentence $\alpha$ involves the prior state of information or background knowledge (which we indicate by $\beta$): $\mathbf{Pr}(\alpha|\beta)$. For example, suppose we know that .2% of the general population has hepatitis. Given just this, our degree of belief that some randomly chosen individual, John, has hepatitis is .002. This would be the subjective probability prior to any specific evidence to consider about John. A *posterior* probability is derived when new evidence is taken into account: $\mathbf{Pr}(\alpha|\beta \wedge \gamma)$, where $\gamma$ is the new evidence. If we take into account evidence that John is jaundiced, for example, we may conclude that the posterior probability of John's having hepatitis, given his symptoms and the prior probability, is .65. A key issue then, is how we *combine evidence* from various sources to reevaluate our beliefs.

## 12.3.1   From Statistics to Belief

As we have pointed out, there is a basic difference between statistical information like "the probability that an adult male is married is .43" and a graded belief about whether a particular individual is married. Intuitively, it ought to be reasonable to try to derive beliefs from statistical information. The traditional approach to doing this is to find a *reference class* for which we have statistical information, and use the statistics about the class to compute an appropriate degree of belief for the individual. A reference class would be a general class into which the individual in question would fit and information about which would comfortably seem to apply.

For example, imagine trying to assign a degree of belief to the proposition "Eric is tall," where Eric is an American male. If all we knew was this,

**A** 20% of American males are tall,

we might be inclined to assign a value of .2 to our belief about Eric's height. This move from statistics to belief is usually referred to as *direct inference*.

But there is a problem with such a simpleminded technique. Individuals will in general belong to many classes. For example, we might know that Eric is from California, and that

**B** 32% of Californian males are tall.

In general, more specific reference classes would seem to be more informative. So we should now be inclined to assign a higher degree of belief to "Eric is tall," because (B) gives us more specific information. But suppose we also know that

**C** 1% of jockeys are tall.

If we do not know Eric's occupation, should we leave our degree of belief unchanged? Or do we have to estimate the probability of his also being a jockey before we can decide? Imagine we also know that

**D** 8% of American males ride horses,

and

**E** Eric collects unusual hats.

Does this change anything, or is it irrelevant? Simple direct inference computations are full of problems because of multiple reference classes. This is reminiscent of our description of specificity in inheritance networks and the problems with simple algorithms like shortest path.

## 12.3.2   A Basic Bayesian Approach

Given problems like these, it would be nice to have a more principled way of calculating subjective probabilities and how these are affected by new evidence.

As a starting point, we might assume that we have a number of propositional variables (or atomic sentences) of interest, $p_1, \ldots, p_n$. For example, $p_1$ might be the proposition that Eric is a lawyer, $p_2$ might be the proposition that Sue is married, $p_3$ might be the proposition that Linda is rich, and so on. In different states of the world, different combinations of these sentences will be true. We can think of each state of the world as characterized by an interpretation $\mathcal{I}$ that specifies which atomic sentences are true and which are false. By a *joint probability distribution* $J$ we mean a specification of the degree of belief for each of the $2^n$ truth assignments to the propositional variables. In other words, for each interpretation $\mathcal{I}$, $J(\mathcal{I})$ is a number between 0 and 1 such that $\sum J(\mathcal{I}) = 1$, where the sum is over all $2^n$ possibilities. Intuitively, we are imagining a scenario where an agent does not know the true state of the world and $J(\mathcal{I})$ is the degree of belief the agent assigns to the world state specified by $\mathcal{I}$.

Using a joint probability like this, we can calculate the degree of belief in any sentence involving any subset of the variables. The idea is that the degree of belief in $\alpha$ is the sum of $J$ over all interpretations where $\alpha$ is true. In other words, we believe $\alpha$ to the extent that we believe in the world states that satisfy $\alpha$. More formally, we define

$$\mathbf{Pr}(\alpha) \overset{def}{=} \sum_{\mathcal{I} \models \alpha} J(\mathcal{I}),$$

and where, as before, $\mathbf{Pr}(\alpha|\beta) = \mathbf{Pr}(\alpha \wedge \beta) \div \mathbf{Pr}(\beta)$. By this account, the degree of belief that Eric is tall given that he is male and from California is the sum of $J$ over all possible world states where Eric is tall, male, and from California divided by the sum of $J$ over all possible world states where Eric is male and from California. It is not hard to see that this definition of subjective probability satisfies the two basic postulates of probability listed in Section 12.2.

While this approach does the right thing, and tells us how to calculate any subjective probability given any evidence, there is one major problem with it: It assumes we have a joint probability distribution over all of the variables we care about. For $n$ atomic sentences, we would need to specify the values of $2^n - 1$ numbers.[2] This is unworkable for any practical application.

### 12.3.3 Belief Networks

In order to cut down on what needs to be known to reason about subjective probabilities, we will need to make some simplifying assumptions.

First, we introduce some notation. Assuming we start with atomic sentences $p_1, \ldots, p_n$, we can specify an interpretation using $\langle P_1, \ldots, P_n \rangle$, where each uppercase $P_i$ is either $p_i$ (when the sentence is true) or $\neg p_i$ (when the sentence is false). From our definition, we see that

$$J(\langle P_1, \ldots, P_n \rangle) = \mathbf{Pr}(P_1 \wedge P_2 \wedge \cdots \wedge P_n),$$

because there is a single interpretation that satisfies the conjunction of the literals.

One extreme simplification we could make is to assume that *all* of the atomic sentences are conditionally independent from each other. This amounts to assuming that

$$J(\langle P_1, \ldots, P_n \rangle) = \mathbf{Pr}(P_1) \cdot \mathbf{Pr}(P_2) \cdots \mathbf{Pr}(P_n).$$

With this assumption, we would only need to know $n$ numbers to fully specify the joint probability distribution, and therefore all other probabilities. But this independence assumption is too extreme. Typically there will be dependencies among the atomic sentences.

Here is a better idea: Let us first of all represent all the variables $p_i$ in a directed acyclic graph, which we will call a *belief network* (or Bayesian network). Intuitively, there should be an arc from $p_i$ to $p_j$ if we think of the truth of the former as directly affecting the truth of the latter. (We will see an example later.) We say in this case that $p_i$ is a *parent* of $p_j$ in the belief network.

Let us suppose that we have numbered the variables in such a way that the parents of any variable $p_j$ appear earlier in the ordering than $p_j$. We can always do this, because the graph is acyclic. Observe that by the chain rule of Section 12.2, it is the case that

$$J(\langle P_1, \ldots, P_n \rangle) =$$
$$\mathbf{Pr}(P_1) \cdot \mathbf{Pr}(P_2 | P_1) \cdot \mathbf{Pr}(P_3 | P_1 \wedge P_2) \cdots \mathbf{Pr}(P_n | P_1 \wedge \cdots \wedge P_{n-1}).$$

---

[2] This is one less than $2^n$ because we can use the constraint that the sum of all $J$ values equals 1.

We can see that formulated this way, the joint probability distribution still needs $2^n - 1$ numbers, because for each term $\mathbf{Pr}(P_{j+1}|P_1 \wedge \cdots \wedge P_j)$ there are $2^j$ conditional probabilities to specify (corresponding to the truth or falsity of $p_1, \ldots, p_j$), and $\sum 2^j = 2^n - 1$.

However, what we are willing to assume in a belief network is this:

> *Each propositional variable in the belief network is conditionally independent from the nonparent variables given the parent variables.*

More precisely, we assume that

$$\mathbf{Pr}(P_{j+1}|P_1 \wedge \cdots \wedge P_j) = \mathbf{Pr}(P_{j+1}|parents(P_{j+1})),$$

where $parents(P_{j+1})$ is the conjunction of those $P_1, \ldots, P_j$ literals that are parents of $p_{j+1}$ in the graph. With these independence assumptions, it follows that

$$J(\langle P_1, \ldots, P_n \rangle) =$$
$$\mathbf{Pr}(P_1|parents(P_1)) \cdot \mathbf{Pr}(P_2|parents(P_2)) \cdots \mathbf{Pr}(P_n|parents(P_n)).$$

The idea of belief networks, then, is to use this equation to define a joint probability distribution $J$, from which any probability we care about can be calculated.

Before looking at an example, observe that to fully specify $J$, we need to know $\mathbf{Pr}(P|parents(P))$ for each variable $p$. If $p$ has $k$ parents in the belief network, we will need to know the $2^k$ conditional probabilities, corresponding to the truth or falsity possibilities of each parent. Summing up over all variables, we will have no more than $n \cdot 2^k$ numbers to specify, where $k$ is the maximum number of parents for any node. As $n$ grows, we expect this number to be much smaller than $2^n$.

Consider the four-node belief network in Figure 12.1. This graph represents the assumption that

$$J(\langle P_1, P_2, P_3, P_4 \rangle) = \mathbf{Pr}(P_1) \cdot \mathbf{Pr}(P_2|P_1) \cdot \mathbf{Pr}(P_3|P_1) \cdot \mathbf{Pr}(P_4|P_2 \wedge P_3).$$

We can see that the full joint probability distribution is completely specified by $(1 + 2 + 2 + 4) = 9$ numbers, rather than the 15 that would be required without the independence assumptions.

## 12.3.4 An Example Network

Let us look at an example to see how we might compute using belief networks. First, we construct the graph: We assign a node to each variable in the domain and draw arrows toward each node $p$ from a select set of nodes perceived to be "direct causes" of $p$. Here is a sample problem due

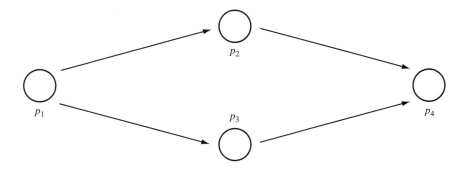

**■ FIGURE 12.1**

A Simple Belief Network

to Eugene Charniak:

> We want to do some reasoning about whether or not my family is out of the house. Imagine the family has a dog. We virtually always put the dog out (*do*) when the family is out (*fo*). We also put the dog out for substantial periods of time when it has a (fortunately, infrequent) bowel problem (*bp*). A reasonable proportion of the time when the dog is out, you can hear her barking (*hb*) when you approach the house. One last fact: we usually (but not always) leave the light on (*lo*) outside the house when the family is out.

Using this set of facts, we can construct the belief network of Figure 12.2, where the arcs can be interpreted as causal connections.

This graph represents the following assumption about the joint probability distribution:

$$J(\langle FO, LO, BP, DO, HB \rangle) =$$

$$\mathbf{Pr}(FO) \cdot \mathbf{Pr}(LO|FO) \cdot \mathbf{Pr}(BP) \cdot \mathbf{Pr}(DO|FO \wedge BP) \cdot \mathbf{Pr}(HB|DO)$$

This joint distribution is considerably simpler than the full one involving the five variables, given the independence assumptions captured in the belief network. As a result, we need only $(1 + 2 + 1 + 4 + 2) = 10$ numbers to specify the full probability distribution, as shown in the figure.

Suppose we want to use this belief network with the numbers in the figure to calculate the probability that the family is out, given that the light is on but we don't hear barking: $\mathbf{Pr}(fo|lo \wedge \neg hb)$. Using the definition of conditional probability, this translates to the following:

$$\mathbf{Pr}(fo|lo \wedge \neg hb) = \frac{\mathbf{Pr}(fo \wedge lo \wedge \neg hb)}{\mathbf{Pr}(lo \wedge \neg hb)} = \frac{\sum J(\langle fo, lo, BP, DO, \neg hb \rangle)}{\sum J(\langle FO, lo, BP, DO, \neg hb \rangle)}$$

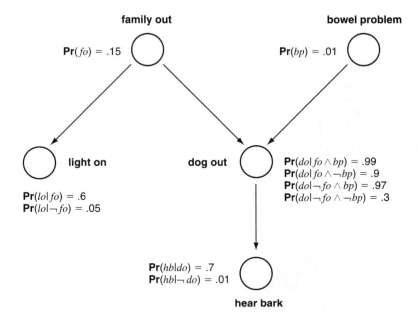

family out

**■ FIGURE 12.2**

A Belief Network Example

The sum in the numerator has four terms, and the sum in the denominator has eight terms (the four from the numerator and four others where *FO* is false). We can compute the eight needed elements of the joint distribution from the probability numbers given in the figure, as follows:

1. $J(\langle fo, lo, bp, do, \neg hb \rangle) = .15 \times .6 \times .01 \times .99 \times .3 = .0002673$,
   that is, $\mathbf{Pr}(fo) \cdot \mathbf{Pr}(lo|fo) \cdot \mathbf{Pr}(bp) \cdot \mathbf{Pr}(do|fo \wedge bp) \cdot (1 - \mathbf{Pr}(hb|do))$

2. $J(\langle fo, lo, bp, \neg do, \neg hb \rangle) = .15 \times .6 \times .01 \times .01 \times .99 = .00000891$

3. $J(\langle fo, lo, \neg bp, do, \neg hb \rangle) = .15 \times .6 \times .99 \times .9 \times .3 = .024057$

4. $J(\langle fo, lo, \neg bp, \neg do, \neg hb \rangle) = .15 \times .6 \times .99 \times .1 \times .99 = .0088209$

5. $J(\langle \neg fo, lo, bp, do, \neg hb \rangle) = .85 \times .05 \times .01 \times .97 \times .3 = .000123675$

6. $J(\langle \neg fo, lo, bp, \neg do, \neg hb \rangle) = .85 \times .05 \times .01 \times .03 \times .99 = .0000126225$

7. $J(\langle \neg fo, lo, \neg bp, do, \neg hb \rangle) = .85 \times .05 \times .99 \times .3 \times .3 = .00378675$

8. $J(\langle \neg fo, lo, \neg bp, \neg do, \neg hb \rangle) = .85 \times .05 \times .99 \times .7 \times .99 = .029157975$

Thus, $\mathbf{Pr}(fo|lo \wedge \neg hb)$ is the sum of the first four values from the previous page (.003315411) divided by the sum of all eight values (.00662369075), which is about .5.

It is sometimes possible to compute a probability value without using the full joint distribution. For example, if we wanted to know the probability of the family's being out given just that the light was on, $\mathbf{Pr}(fo|lo)$, we could first use Bayes' rule to convert $\mathbf{Pr}(fo|lo)$ to $\mathbf{Pr}(lo|fo) \times \mathbf{Pr}(fo) \div \mathbf{Pr}(lo)$. From our given probabilities, we know the first two terms, but not the value of $\mathbf{Pr}(lo)$. But we can compute that quite simply: $\mathbf{Pr}(lo) = \mathbf{Pr}(lo|fo) \times \mathbf{Pr}(fo) + \mathbf{Pr}(lo|\neg fo) \times \mathbf{Pr}(\neg fo)$. We have each of those four values available (the last one using the rule for negation), and thus we have all the information we need to compute $\mathbf{Pr}(fo|lo)$ without going through the full joint distribution.

In a sense, using the full joint probability distribution to compute a degree of belief is like using the set of all logical interpretations to compute entailment: It does the right thing, but is feasible only for small problems. While a belief network may make what needs to be known in advance practical, it does not necessarily make *reasoning* practical. Not surprisingly, calculating a degree of belief from a belief network can be shown to be NP-hard, as hard as full satisfiability. More surprisingly, determining an *approximate* value for a degree of belief can also be shown to be NP-hard. Nonetheless, specialized reasoning procedures have been developed that appear to work well on certain practical problems or on networks with restricted treelike topologies.

## 12.3.5    Influence Diagrams

Belief networks are useful for computing subjective probabilities based on independence assumptions and causal relationships, but in making decisions under uncertainty, there are usually other factors to take into account, such as the relative merit of the different outcomes and their costs. In general, these are concerns in what is usually called *decision theory* and lie outside the scope of this book. However, one simple approach to decision making is worth glancing at, because it is based on a direct extension to the belief network representation scheme we have just seen.

*Influence diagrams* attempt to extend the reasoning power of belief networks with a larger set of node-types. In Figure 12.3, which might allow us to decide what course of action to take in the face of coronary artery disease, we see four types of nodes: *Chance nodes* are drawn as circles and represent probabilistic variables as before, *deterministic nodes* are drawn as double circles and represent straightforward computations based on their inputs, *decision nodes* are drawn as rectangles and represent all-or-nothing decisions to be made by the user, and

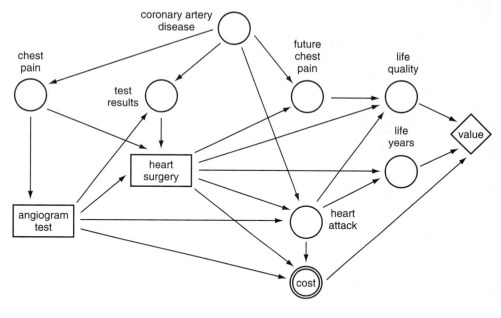

**■ FIGURE 12.3**

Influence Diagram

the *value node*—there is only one—is drawn as a diamond and represents the final decision to be made based on some valuation function. Arcs in the diagram represent the appropriate obvious influence or relevance relationships (probabilistic and deterministic) between the nodes.

The intent with diagrams like these is for a system to reason about the relationships between variables that are probabilistically determined, choice determined, and deterministically determined. This yields a powerful framework to support decision making, and a number of implemented systems reason with these sorts of representations.

## 12.3.6  Dempster–Shafer Theory

There are other techniques available for allowing a system to pool evidence and support decisions. Although we will not go into any of these in detail, it is worth mentioning one of the more prominent alternatives, often called *Dempster–Shafer theory*, after the inventors.

Consider the following example. If we flip an unbiased coin, the degree of belief would be .5 that the coin comes out heads. But now consider flipping a coin where we do not know whether or not the coin is biased. In fact, it may have tails on both sides, for all we know. In cases like this, although we have no reason to prefer heads to tails, we may not want to assign the same degree of belief of .5 to the proposition that the result is heads. Instead, due to lack of information, we may want to say only that the degree of belief lies somewhere between 0 and 1.

Instead of using a single number to represent a degree of belief, Dempster–Shafer representations use two-part measures, called *belief* and *plausibility*. These are essentially lower and upper bounds on the probability of a proposition. For a coin known to be perfectly unbiased, we have .5 belief and .5 plausibility that the result is heads; but for the mystery coin, we have 0 belief that the result is heads (meaning we have no reason to give it any credence) and 1 plausibility (meaning we have no reason to disbelieve it either). The "value" of a propositional variable is represented by a range, which we might call the *possibility distribution* of the variable.

To see where these ideas are useful, imagine we have a simple database with names of people and their believed ages. In a situation with complete knowledge, the ages would be simple values (e.g., 24). But we might not know the exact age of someone and would instead have the age field in the table filled by a range:

| Name | Age |
|---------|---------|
| Mary | [22,26] |
| Tom | [20,22] |
| Frank | [30,35] |
| Rebecca | [20,22] |
| Sue | [28,30] |

This would mean, for example, that we believed the age of Tom to lie somewhere between 20 and 22; {20, 21, 22} would be the set of possibilities for age(tom).

In this kind of setting, simple membership questions like age(x) ∈ Q are no longer applicable. It is more natural to ask about the *possibility* of Q given the possibility distribution of age(x). For example, given the table, if Q = [20, 25], it is *possible* that age(mary) ∈ Q, it is *not possible* that age(frank) ∈ Q, and it is *certain* that age(rebecca) ∈ Q.

Now consider the following question: What is the probability that the age of an individual selected at random from the table is in the range [20, 25]? We would like to say that the belief (lower bound) in this proposition is 2/5, because two of the five people in the table are of necessity in the age range from 20 to 25, and the plausibility (upper bound) in this proposition is 3/5, because at most three of the five people in the table are in the age range [.4, .6].

This calculation seems commensurate with the information provided. In fact, the Dempster–Shafer *combination rule* (more complex than we can go into here) allows us to combine multiple sources of information like these in which we have varying levels of knowledge and confidence.

## 12.4  VAGUENESS

As mentioned in Section 12.1, quite apart from considerations of frequency and degree of belief, we can consider the degree to which certain predicates are satisfied.

Let us begin with this question: Is a man tall if his height is 5 feet 9 inches? A first answer might be, compared to what? Obviously, the tallness of a man depends on whether we are comparing him to jockeys, to basketball players, or to all North American males. But suppose we fix on a reference class, so that by "tall" we really mean "tall compared to the rest of North American males." We might still want to say that this is not a clear-cut affair; people are tall *to a certain degree*, just as they are healthy, fast runners, or close to retirement to varying degrees.

Predicates like these that are intuitively thought of as holding to a degree are called *vague predicates*. In English, these correspond to adjectives that can be modified by the adverb "very," unlike, for instance, "married" or "dead." Typically, we assume that for each vague predicate there is a corresponding precise *base function* in terms of which the predicate is understood. For "tall" the base function is "height"; for "rich" it is "net worth"; for "bald" it might be something like "percentage hair cover."

We can capture the relationship between a vague predicate like Tall and its base function height using a function like the one depicted in Figure 12.4, which we call a *degree curve*. As the height of a person

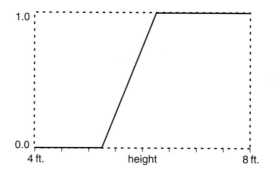

■ **FIGURE 12.4**

A Degree Curve for the Vague Predicate Tall

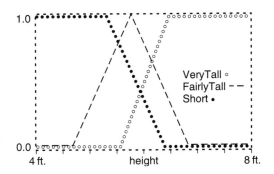

■ **FIGURE 12.5**

Degree Curves for Variants on Tall

(a North American male) varies from 4 to 8 feet, this curve shows a degree of tallness, from 0 (not at all) to .5 (middling) to 1 (totally). This definition of Tall would yield the following values for various individuals and their heights:

| Individual | Height | Degree of Tallness |
|---|---|---|
| Larry | 4'6" | 0.00 |
| Roger | 5'6" | 0.25 |
| Henry | 5'9" | 0.50 |
| Michael | 6'2" | 0.90 |
| Wilt | 7'1" | 1.00 |

Curves for Short, VeryTall, and FairlyTall, which are also based on height, are shown in Figure 12.5. The predicate Short varies in degree in a way that is complementary to Tall; VeryTall is similar to Tall but rises later; FairlyTall rises earlier but then decreases, reflecting the fact that an individual can be too tall to be considered to be only FairlyTall to a high degree. The individuals in the table would thus have the following degrees of Shortness and VeryTallness:

| Individual | Height | Degree of Shortness | Degree of VeryTallness |
|---|---|---|---|
| Larry | 4'6" | 1.00 | 0.00 |
| Roger | 5'6" | 0.75 | 0.00 |
| Henry | 5'9" | 0.50 | 0.10 |
| Michael | 6'2" | 0.10 | 0.47 |
| Wilt | 7'1" | 0.00 | 1.00 |

In a more qualitative way, given these degree curves, we might consider a man who is 5'6" pretty short (.75), and at the same time barely tall (.25). In these figures, we have drawn the degree curves as straight lines with similar slopes, but there is no reason why they cannot be smooth rounded curves or have different slopes. The crucial thing is that an object's degree of satisfaction can be nonzero for multiple predicates over the same base function, and in particular for two predicates that are normally thought of as opposites, such as Short and Tall.

### 12.4.1 Conjunction and Disjunction

As with logic and probability, we need to consider Boolean combinations of vague properties and to what degree these are taken to be satisfied. Negation poses no special problem: We take the degree to which the negation of a property is satisfied to be 1 minus the degree to which the property itself is satisfied, as with Tall and Short. In this case, reasoning with vague predicates is exactly like reasoning with probabilities, where $\mathbf{Pr}(\neg p) = 1 - \mathbf{Pr}(p)$.

Conjunctions and disjunctions, however, appear to be different. Suppose, for example, that we are looking for a candidate to train as a basketball player. We might be looking for someone who is tall, physically coordinated, strong, and so on. Imagine that we have a person who rates highly on each of these. Obviously this person should be considered a very good candidate. This suggests that the degree to which a person satisfies the conjoined criterion

$$\text{Tall} \wedge \text{Coordinated} \wedge \text{Strong} \wedge \ldots$$

should not be the product of the degrees to which he or she satisfies each individual one. If there were a total of twenty criteria, say, and all were satisfied at the very high level of .95, we would not want to say the degree of satisfaction of the conjoined criterion was only $.36 = (.95)^{20}$.

There is, consequently, a difference between the *probability* of satisfying the conjoined criterion—which, assuming independence, would be the product of the probabilities of satisfying each individual criterion—and the *degree* to which the conjoined criterion is satisfied. Arguably, the degree to which an individual is $P$ and $Q$ is the *minimum* of the degrees to which the individual is $P$ and is $Q$. Similarly, the degree to which a *disjoined* criterion is satisfied is best thought of as the *maximum* degree to which each individual criterion is satisfied.

### 12.4.2 Rules

One of the most interesting applications of vague predicates involves their use in production rules of the sort we saw in Chapter 7. In a typical application of what is sometimes called *fuzzy control*, the antecedent of a rule will concern quantities that can be measured or evaluated, and the consequent will concern some control action. Unlike standard production systems where a rule either does or does not apply, here the antecedent of a rule will apply to some degree and the control action will be affected to a commensurate degree. In that regard, these rules work less like logical implications and more like continuous mappings between sets of variables. The advantage of rules using vague predicates is that they enable inferences even when the antecedent conditions are only partially satisfied. In this kind of a system, the antecedents apply to values from the same base functions and the consequent values are taken from the same base functions. The rules are usually developed in groups and are not taken to be significant independent of one another; their main goal is to work in concert to jointly affect the output variable. Rules of this sort have been used in a number of successful engineering applications (although why they were successful remains contentious).

Let us consider an example of a set of such rules. Imagine that we are trying to decide on a tip at a restaurant based on the quality of the food and service. Assume that service and food quality can each be described by a simple number on a linear scale (e.g., a number from 0 to 10). The amount of the tip will be characterized as a percentage of the cost of the meal, where, for example, the tip might normally be around 15%. We might have the following three rules:

1. *If* the service is poor *or* the food is rancid *then* the tip is stingy.

2. *If* the service is good *then* the tip is normal.

3. *If* the service is excellent *or* the food is delicious *then* the tip is generous.

In the last rule we see vague predicates like "excellent," "delicious," and "generous," and we imagine that in most circumstances the service will be excellent to some degree, the food will be delicious to some degree, and the resulting tip should be correspondingly generous to some degree. Of course, the other two rules will also apply to some degree and could temper this generosity. We assume that for each of the eight vague predicates mentioned in the rules (like "rancid") we are given a degree curve relating the predicate to one of three base quantities: service, food quality, or tip. The problem we wish to solve is the following: Given a specific numeric rating for the service and another specific rating for the food, calculate a specific amount for the tip, subject to these rules.

One popular method used to solve this problem is as follows:

1. *transform the inputs*, that is, determine the degree to which each of the vague predicates used in the antecedents hold for each

of the inputs; in other words, use the given degree curves to determine the degree to which the predicates "poor," "rancid," "good," and so on apply for the given ratings of the inputs, service, and food.

For example, if we are given that the service rating is 3 out of 10 and the food rating is 8 out of 10, the degree curves might tell us that the service is excellent to degree 0.0 and that the food is delicious to degree 0.7.

2. *evaluate the antecedents*, that is, determine the degree to which each rule is applicable by combining the degrees of applicability of the individual predicates determined in the first step, using the appropriate combinations for the logical operators.

   For the third rule in our example, the antecedent is the disjunction of the service being excellent and the food being delicious. Using the numbers from the previous step, we conclude that the rule applies to degree 0.7 (the maximum of 0.0 and 0.7). The other two rules are similar.

3. *evaluate the consequents*, that is, determine the degree to which the predicates "stingy," "normal," and "generous" should be satisfied. The intuition is that the consequent in each rule should hold only to the degree that the rule is applicable.

   For the third rule in our example, the consequent is the predicate "generous." We need to reconsider the degree curve for this predicate to ensure that we will be generous only to the degree that this third rule is applicable. One way to do this (but not the only way) is to cut off the given degree curve at a maximum of 0.7. The other two rules can be handled similarly.

4. *aggregate the consequents*, that is, obtain a single degree curve for the tip that combines the "stingy," "normal," and "generous" ones in light of the applicability of the rules. The intuition is that each possible value for the tip should be recommended to the degree that it is supported by the rules in the previous step.

   In our example, we take the three clipped curves for "stingy," "normal," and "generous" from the previous step and we overlay them to form a composite curve whose value at any tip value is the maximum of the values given by the three individual curves. Other ways of combining these curves are possible, depending on what was done in the previous step.

5. *"defuzzify" the output*, that is, use the aggregated degree curve to generate a weighted average value for the tip.

One way to do this in our example is to take the aggregated curve from the previous step and find the center of the area under the curve. This is the tip value for which there is as much weight for lower tip values as there is for higher tip values. The result is a recommended tip of 15.8%.

The five-step process is illustrated graphically in Figure 12.6. Starting with the arrows at the bottom left-hand side, we see the two input values for service and food. Immediately above, the degree curves for "excellent" and "delicious," the antecedents of the third rule, are seen to intersect the given input values at 0.0 and 0.7. The maximum of these, 0.7, is projected to the right where it intersects the degree curve for "generous," the consequent of the third rule. Immediately to the right of this, we see this curve clipped at the value of 0.7. This clipped curve is then combined with the clipped curves for "normal" and for "cheap" just above

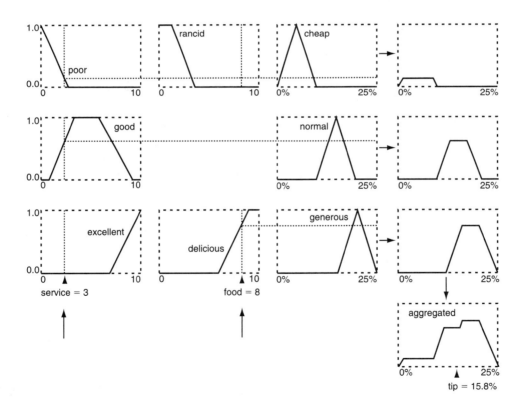

■ **FIGURE 12.6**

Fuzzy Control Example

to produce the final aggregated curve in the bottom right-hand corner. The center of the area under this final curve is the point where the tip is 15.8%, the final output. In this example, the quality of the food was sufficient to compensate for the somewhat mediocre service, yielding a slightly more generous than normal tip.

### 12.4.3 A Bayesian Reconstruction

While the procedure just described appears to work well in many applications, it is hard to motivate it from a semantic point of view, and indeed, several incompatible variants have been proposed.[3] It has been suggested that despite the conceptual differences between degrees of belief and degrees of satisfaction (noted earlier), much of the reasoning with vague predicates can be recast more transparently in terms of subjective probability.

Under a subjective probability interpretation, we treat Tall, VeryTall, FairlyTall, and so on as ordinary predicates, true of a person in some interpretations and false in others. There are no "borderline" cases: In some interpretations, a person whose height is 5'9" is tall, and in others not. Each of the base predicates, such as Tall, is associated with a base measure, such as height. We imagine that in addition to sentences like Tall(bill), we have atomic sentences like height(bill) $= n$ where $n$ is a number.

Turning now to probabilities, for each $n$, $\mathbf{Pr}(\text{height}(\text{bill}) = n)$ will be a number between 0 and 1, and the sum over all $n$ must equal to 1. As we go from $n = 4$ feet to $n = 8$ feet, say, we expect to see some sort of bell-shaped curve around a mean of, say, 5'9".

What do we expect for the curve for $\mathbf{Pr}(\text{height}(\text{bill}) = n|\text{Tall}(\text{bill}))$ as we vary $n$? We expect a bell curve again, but with a higher mean (say, 6'1") and perhaps sharper (less spread). By Bayes' rule, we know that

$$\mathbf{Pr}(\text{height}(\text{bill}) = n|\text{Tall}(\text{bill})) =$$

$$\frac{\mathbf{Pr}(\text{Tall}(\text{bill})|\text{height}(\text{bill}) = n) \times \mathbf{Pr}(\text{height}(\text{bill}) = n)}{\mathbf{Pr}(\text{Tall}(\text{bill}))}$$

What can we say about the curve for $\mathbf{Pr}(\text{Tall}(\text{bill})|\text{height}(\text{bill}) = n)$? It has to be a curve such that when you multiply it by the original bell curve and then divide by a constant (i.e., $\mathbf{Pr}(\text{Tall}(\text{bill}))$), you get the second shifted sharper bell curve. Here's the main observation: If we draw this curve, going from $n = 4$ feet to $n = 8$ feet, what we need is exactly the sort of

---

[3]Note in the restaurant example, for instance, that the impact that a degree curve has on the final tip depends on the area below that curve. A single spike at a particular value (representing a degree curve for a precise value) would have much less impact on the center-of-area calculation than a curve with a larger spread.

curve we have been calling the degree curve for tallness. In other words, the proposal in this reconstruction is to reinterpret "degree of tallness for height of $x$" as "degree of belief in tallness given a height of $x$."

What then happens to Boolean combinations of properties? Things work out as long as we are prepared to assume that

$$\mathbf{Pr}(\alpha \wedge \beta | \gamma) = min\{\mathbf{Pr}(\alpha|\gamma), \mathbf{Pr}(\beta|\gamma)\}.$$

This is allowed, provided we do not assume that $\alpha$ and $\beta$ are independent.[4] Moreover, with this assumption, we derive that

$$\mathbf{Pr}(\alpha \vee \beta | \gamma) = max\{\mathbf{Pr}(\alpha|\gamma), \mathbf{Pr}(\beta|\gamma)\}$$

by using general properties of probability.

Finally, what about the production rules? In the given restaurant example, we want to calculate an aggregate tip given the service and food rating. In subjective terms, for a food rating of $x$ and a service rating of $y$, the weighted average is defined by

$$\mathsf{AveragedTip} = \sum_{z} z \times \mathbf{Pr}((\mathsf{tip} = z) \,|\, (\mathsf{food} = x) \wedge (\mathsf{service} = y)).\ {}^{5}$$

We do not have nearly enough information to calculate the joint probabilities of all the propositions involved. However, we will sketch some reasonable assumptions that would permit a subjective value to be computed.

First, observe that for any $x$, $y$, and $z$, the value we need,

$$\mathbf{Pr}((\mathsf{tip} = z) \,|\, (\mathsf{food} = x) \wedge (\mathsf{service} = y)),$$

is equal to

$$\sum_{G,N,S} \left\{ \begin{array}{l} \mathbf{Pr}((\mathsf{tip} = z) \,|\, G \wedge N \wedge S \wedge (\mathsf{food} = x) \wedge (\mathsf{service} = y)) \times \\ \mathbf{Pr}(G \wedge N \wedge S \,|\, (\mathsf{food} = x) \wedge (\mathsf{service} = y)) \end{array} \right\}$$

where $G$ is Generous or its negation, $N$ is Normal or its negation, and $S$ is Stingy or its negation. Taking the first of these terms, we assume that the

---

[4]When $\alpha$ and $\beta$ are not independent, the only requirement on the probability of $(\alpha \wedge \beta)$ is that it be no larger than the probability of either one.
[5]We assume a countable number of possible values for the tip. Otherwise, the summations here would have to be integrals.

tip is completely determined given $G$, $N$, and $S$, so that

$$\mathbf{Pr}((\text{tip} = z) \mid G \wedge N \wedge S \wedge (\text{food} = x) \wedge (\text{service} = y)) =$$
$$\mathbf{Pr}((\text{tip} = z) \mid G \wedge N \wedge S).$$

Applying Bayes' rule, we derive that this is equal to

$$\frac{\mathbf{Pr}(G \wedge N \wedge S \mid (\text{tip} = z)) \times \mathbf{Pr}((\text{tip} = z))}{\displaystyle\sum_{u} \mathbf{Pr}(G \wedge N \wedge S \mid (\text{tip} = u)) \times \mathbf{Pr}((\text{tip} = u))}.$$

If we now assume that all tips are a priori equally likely, this is equal to

$$\frac{\mathbf{Pr}(G \wedge N \wedge S \mid (\text{tip} = z))}{\displaystyle\sum_{u} \mathbf{Pr}(G \wedge N \wedge S \mid (\text{tip} = u))}.$$

For any value of $u$, it is the case that

$$\mathbf{Pr}(G \wedge N \wedge S \mid (\text{tip} = u))$$

can be assumed to be

$$min\{\mathbf{Pr}(G \mid (\text{tip} = u)), \mathbf{Pr}(N \mid (\text{tip} = u)), \mathbf{Pr}(S \mid (\text{tip} = u))\},$$

which can be calculated from the given degree curves for Stingy, Generous, and Normal. This leaves us only with calculating

$$\mathbf{Pr}(G \wedge N \wedge S \mid (\text{food} = x) \wedge (\text{service} = y)),$$

which we can again assume to be

$$min \begin{cases} \mathbf{Pr}(G \mid (\text{food} = x) \wedge (\text{service} = y)), \\ \mathbf{Pr}(N \mid (\text{food} = x) \wedge (\text{service} = y)), \\ \mathbf{Pr}(S \mid (\text{food} = x) \wedge (\text{service} = y)). \end{cases}$$

To calculate these, we use the given production rules: We assume that the probability of a proposition like Generous is the maximum of the probability of the antecedents of all rules where it appears as a consequent. So, for example,

$$\mathbf{Pr}(\text{Generous} \mid (\text{food} = x) \wedge (\text{service} = y))$$

is assumed to be equal to

$$max \begin{cases} \textbf{Pr}(\text{Excellent} \,|\, (\text{food} = x) \wedge (\text{service} = y)), \\ \textbf{Pr}(\text{Delicious} \,|\, (\text{food} = x) \wedge (\text{service} = y)). \end{cases}$$

Taking the food quality to be independent of the service quality, this is equal to

$$max \begin{cases} \textbf{Pr}(\text{Excellent} \,|\, (\text{service} = y)), \\ \textbf{Pr}(\text{Delicious} \,|\, (\text{food} = x)), \end{cases}$$

and for these we use the remaining degree curves for Excellent, Delicious, and so on. This completes the required calculation.

## 12.5   BIBLIOGRAPHIC NOTES

The literature on probability theory is quite extensive. A recent perspective on the area is given by Jaynes [200]. For a discussion of the foundations of probability, see von Mises [415], de Finetti [90, 91], and Jeffrey [201, 202].

Bayes' rule was introduced in [25]. The postulates for probability are due to Kolmogorov [221].

An early but still comprehensive treatment of uncertain reasoning in AI is the book by Pearl [320] (see also Pearl [321]). Jensen [203] gives an introduction to belief networks (Bayesian networks). Neapolitan [302] gives an overview of the use of probability in expert systems. The complexity of reasoning with belief networks is discussed by Cooper [79], and the difficulty of doing even approximate reasoning with the networks is considered by Dagum and Luby [82].

The example in Section 12.3.4 due to Charniak is taken from [68]. Resnik [350] provides an introduction to decision theory. For a discussion of influence diagrams, see Howard and Matheson [192].

The Dempster–Shafer theory of evidence grew out of work by Dempster [101], which was subsequently extended by Shafer [376]. For recent contributions, see Yager et al. [436] and a special issue of the *International Journal of Approximate Reasoning* [4].

The description of vague predicates in the text derives from work by Zadeh on fuzzy logic [438] and fuzzy sets [437]. For a critique of fuzzy logic, see Haack [173]. See also Dubois et al. [114] for a collection of readings on fuzzy sets. Wang [420] provides an introduction to fuzzy control. The particular scheme described in Section 12.4.2 is due to Mamdani [264].

Readings on uncertain reasoning are collected in Shafer and Pearl [378]. An overview of reasoning under uncertainty is given by Paris [315]. For a treatment of uncertainty and its relationship to other areas of knowledge representation and reasoning, including some of those covered in this book, see Halpern [177].

## 12.6  EXERCISES

1. As noted in the text, one way to understand probabilities is to imagine taking a snapshot of all the entities in the domain of discourse (assuming there are only finitely many) and looking at the proportion of them having certain properties. We can then use elementary set theory to analyze the relationships among various probabilities. Under this reading, the probability of $a$ given $b$ is defined as the number of elements in both $a$ and $b$ divided by the number of elements in $b$ alone: $\mathbf{Pr}(a|b) = |a \cap b| \div |b|$. Similarly, $\mathbf{Pr}(a)$, the probability of $a$ itself, can be thought of as $\mathbf{Pr}(a|U)$, where $U$ is the entire domain of discourse. Note that according to this definition, the probability of $U$ is 1 and the probability of the empty set is 0.

Use this simple model of probability to do the following:

   (a) Prove that $\mathbf{Pr}(a \cap b \cap c) = \mathbf{Pr}(a|b \cap c) * \mathbf{Pr}(b|c) * \mathbf{Pr}(c)$.
   (b) Prove Bayes' rule: $\mathbf{Pr}(a|b) = \mathbf{Pr}(a) * \mathbf{Pr}(b|a) \div \mathbf{Pr}(b)$.
   (c) Suppose that $b_1, b_2, \ldots, b_n$ are mutually exclusive events of which one must occur. Prove that for any event $a$, it is the case that

$$\mathbf{Pr}(a) = \sum_{i=1}^{n} \mathbf{Pr}(a \cap b_i).$$

   (d) Derive (and prove correct) an expression for $\mathbf{Pr}(a \cup b)$ that does not use either disjunction or conjunction.
   (e) Recall that two statistical variables $a$ and $b$ are said to be conditionally independent if and only if $\mathbf{Pr}(a \cap b) = \mathbf{Pr}(a) * \mathbf{Pr}(b)$. However, just because $a$ and $b$ are independent, it does not follow that $\mathbf{Pr}((a \cap b)|c) = \mathbf{Pr}(a|c) * \mathbf{Pr}(b|c)$. Explain why.

2. Consider the following example:

   *Metastatic cancer is a possible cause of a brain tumor and is also an explanation for an increased total serum calcium. In turn, either of these could cause a patient to fall into an occasional coma. Severe headache could also be explained by a brain tumor.*

(a) Represent these causal links in a belief network. Let $a$ stand for "metastatic cancer," $b$ for "increased total serum calcium," $c$ for "brain tumor," $d$ for "occasional coma," and $e$ for "severe headaches."

(b) Give an example of an independence assumption that is implicit in this network.

(c) Suppose the following probabilities are given:

$\Pr(a) = .2$

$\Pr(b|a) = .8$ $\qquad$ $\Pr(b|\bar{a}) = .2$

$\Pr(c|a) = .2$ $\qquad$ $\Pr(c|\bar{a}) = .05$

$\Pr(e|c) = .8$ $\qquad$ $\Pr(e|\bar{c}) = .6$

$\Pr(d|b,c) = .8$ $\qquad$ $\Pr(d|\bar{b},c) = .8$

$\Pr(d|b,\bar{c}) = .8$ $\qquad$ $\Pr(d|\bar{b},\bar{c}) = .05$

and assume that it is also given that some patient is suffering from severe headaches but has not fallen into a coma. Calculate joint probabilities for the eight remaining possibilities (that is, according to whether $a$, $b$, and $c$ are true or false).

(d) According to the numbers given, the a priori probability that the patient has metastatic cancer is .2. Given that the patient is suffering from severe headaches but has not fallen into a coma, are we now more or less inclined to believe that the patient has cancer? Explain.

3. Consider the following example:

   *The fire alarm in a building can go off if there is a fire in the building or if the alarm is tampered with by vandals. If the fire alarm goes off, this can cause crowds to gather at the front of the building and fire trucks to arrive.*

(a) Represent these causal links in a belief network. Let $a$ stand for "alarm sounds," $c$ for "crowd gathers," $f$ for "fire exists," $t$ for "fire truck arrives," and $v$ for "vandalism exists."

(b) Give an example of an independence assumption that is implicit in this network.

(c) What are the 10 conditional probabilities that need to be specified to fully determine the joint probability distribution? Suppose that there is a crowd in front of the building one day but that no fire trucks arrive. What is the chance that there is a fire, expressed as some function of the 10 given conditional probabilities?

(d) Suppose we find out that in addition to setting off the fire alarm, vandals can cause a fire truck to arrive by phoning the Fire Department directly. How would your belief network need to be modified? Assuming all the given probabilities remain the same (including the a priori probability of vandalism), there would still not be enough information to calculate the full joint probability distribution. Would it be sufficient to be given $\mathbf{Pr}(t|v)$ and $\mathbf{Pr}(t|\bar{v})$? How about being told $\mathbf{Pr}(t|a,v)$ and $\mathbf{Pr}(t|\bar{a},\bar{v})$ instead? Explain your answers.

**4.** Consider the following example:

> *Aching elbows and aching hands may be the result of arthritis. Arthritis is also a possible cause of tennis elbow, which in turn may cause aching elbows. Dishpan hands may also cause aching hands.*

(a) Represent these facts in a belief network. Let *ar* stand for "arthritis," *ah* for "aching hands," *ae* for "aching elbow," *te* for "tennis elbow," and *dh* for "dishpan hands."

(b) Give an example of an independence assumption that is implicit in this network.

(c) Write the formula for the full joint probability distribution over all five variables.

(d) Suppose the following probabilities are given:

$$\mathbf{Pr}(ah|ar,dh) = \mathbf{Pr}(ae|ar,te) = .1$$

$$\mathbf{Pr}(ah|ar,\neg dh) = \mathbf{Pr}(ae|ar,\neg te) = .99$$

$$\mathbf{Pr}(ah|\neg ar,dh) = \mathbf{Pr}(ae|\neg ar,te) = .99$$

$$\mathbf{Pr}(ah|\neg ar,\neg dh) = \mathbf{Pr}(ae|\neg ar,\neg te) = .00001$$

$$\mathbf{Pr}(te|ar) = .0001$$

$$\mathbf{Pr}(te|\neg ar) = .01$$

$$\mathbf{Pr}(ar) = .001$$

$$\mathbf{Pr}(dh) = .01.$$

Assume that we are interested in determining whether it is more likely that a patient has arthritis, tennis elbow, or dishpan hands.

i. With no observations at all, which of the three is most likely a priori?

ii. If we observe that the patient has aching elbows, which is now the most likely?

iii. If we observe that the patient has both aching hands and elbows, which is the most likely?

iv. How would your rankings change if there were no causal connection between tennis elbow and arthritis, where, for example, $\mathbf{Pr}(te|ar) = \mathbf{Pr}(te|\neg ar) = .00999$ (instead of the two values given earlier).

Show the calculations justifying your answers.

# CHAPTER 13

# EXPLANATION AND DIAGNOSIS

■

■

■

So far in this book we have concentrated on reasoning that is primarily *deductive* in nature: Given a KB representing some explicit beliefs about the world, we try to deduce some $\alpha$, to determine if it is an implicit belief or perhaps to find a constant (or constants) $c$ such that $\alpha_c^x$ is an implicit belief. This pattern shows up not only in ordinary logical reasoning, but also in description logics and procedural systems. In fact, a variant even shows up in probabilistic and default reasoning, where extra assumptions might be added to the KB, or degrees of belief might be considered.

In this chapter, we consider a completely different sort of reasoning task. Suppose we are given a KB and an $\alpha$ that we do not believe at all, even with default assumptions. We might ask the following: Given what we already know, what would it take for us to believe that $\alpha$ was true? In other words, what else would we have to be told for $\alpha$ to become an implicit belief? One interesting aspect of this question is that the answer we are expecting will not be "yes" or "no" or the names of some individuals; instead, the answer should be a formula of the representation language.[1]

The typical pattern for deductive reasoning is as follows:

given $(p \supset q)$, from $p$, we can conclude $q$.

The corresponding pattern for what is called *abductive reasoning* is as follows:

given $(p \supset q)$, from $q$, we can posit $p$.

---

[1] In the last section of this chapter, we will see that it can be useful to have some deductive tasks that return formulas as well.

Abductive reasoning is in some sense the converse of deductive reasoning: Instead of looking for sentences entailed by $p$ given what is known, we look for sentences that would entail $q$ given what is known.[2]

Another way to look at abduction is as a way of providing an *explanation*. The typical application of these ideas is in reasoning about causes and effects. Imagine that $p$ is a cause (for example, "it is raining") and $q$ is an effect (for example, "the grass is wet"). If it rains, the grass is wet. Deductive reasoning would be used to predict the effects of rain, that is, wet grass, among others; abductive reasoning would be used to conjecture the cause of wet grass, that is, rain, among others. In this case, we are trying to find something that would be sufficient to explain a sentence's being true.

## 13.1  DIAGNOSIS

One type of reasoning about causes and effects where abductive reasoning appears especially useful is *diagnosis*. Imagine that we have a collection of causal rules in a KB of the form

$$(Disease \land \cdots \supset Symptoms)$$

where the ellipsis is a collection of hedges or qualifications. The goal of diagnosis is to find a disease (or diseases) that best explains a given set of observed symptoms.

Note that in this setting we would not expect to be able to reason deductively using diagnostic rules of the form

$$(Symptoms \land \cdots \supset Disease),$$

because facts like these are much more difficult to obtain. Typically, a disease will have a small number of well-known symptoms, but a symptom can be associated with a large number of potential diseases (e.g., fever can be caused by hundreds of afflictions). It is usually much easier to account for an effect of a given cause than to prescribe a cause of a given effect. The diagnosis we are looking for will not be an entailment of what is known; rather, it is merely a conjecture.

---

[2]The term *abduction* in this sense is due to the philosopher C. S. Peirce, who also discussed a third possible form of reasoning, *inductive reasoning*, which takes as given (a number of instances of) both $p$ and $q$, and induces that $(p \supset q)$ is true.

For example, imagine a KB containing the following (in nonquantified form, to keep things simple):

TennisElbow ⊃ SoreElbow,

TennisElbow ⊃ TennisPlayer,

Arthritis ∧ ¬Treated ⊃ SoreJoints,

SoreJoints ⊃ SoreElbow ∧ SoreHips.

Now suppose we would like to explain an observed symptom: SoreElbow. Informally, what we are after is a diagnosis like TennisElbow, which clearly accounts for the symptom, given what is known. Another equally good diagnosis would be (Arthritis ∧ ¬Treated), which also explains the symptom. So we are imagining that there will in general be multiple explanations for any given symptom, quite apart from the fact that logically equivalent formulas like (¬Treated ∧ ¬¬Arthritis) would work as well.

## 13.2 EXPLANATION

In characterizing precisely what we are after in an explanation, it is useful to think in terms of four criteria:

Given a knowledge base KB and a formula $\beta$ to be explained, we are looking for a formula $\alpha$ satisfying the following:

1. $\alpha$ is sufficient to account for $\beta$. More precisely, we want to find an $\alpha$ such that $KB \cup \{\alpha\} \models \beta$, or equivalently, $KB \models (\alpha \supset \beta)$. Any $\alpha$ that does not satisfy this property would be considered too weak to serve as an explanation for $\beta$.

2. $\alpha$ is not ruled out by the KB. More precisely, we want it to be the case that $KB \cup \{\alpha\}$ is consistent, or equivalently, that $KB \not\models \neg\alpha$. Without this, a formula like $(p \land \neg p)$, which always satisfies the first criterion, would be a reasonable explanation. Similarly, if ¬TennisPlayer were a fact in the previously described KB, then even though TennisElbow would still entail SoreElbow, it would not be an appropriate diagnosis.

3. $\alpha$ is as simple and logically parsimonious as possible. By this we mean that $\alpha$ does not mention extraneous conditions. A simple case of the kind of situation we want to avoid is when $\alpha$ is unnecessarily *strong*. In the example, a formula like

(TennisElbow ∧ ChickenPox)

satisfies the first two criteria—it implies the symptom and is consistent with the KB. But the part about chicken pox is unnecessary. Similarly (but less obviously), the $\alpha$ can be unnecessarily *weak*. If ¬Vegetarian were a fact in the KB, then a formula like

$$(\text{TennisElbow} \lor \text{Vegetarian})$$

would still satisfy the first two criteria, although the vegetarian part is unnecessary. In general, we want $\alpha$ to use as few terms as possible. In the propositional case, this means as few literals as possible.

4. $\alpha$ is in the appropriate vocabulary. Note, for example, that according to the first three criteria, SoreElbow is a formula that explains SoreElbow. We might call this the *trivial* explanation. It is also the case that SoreJoints satisfies the first three criteria. For various applications, this may or may not be suitable. Intuitively, however, in this case, because we think of SoreJoints in this KB as being almost just another name for the conjunction of SoreElbow and SoreHips, it would not really be a good explanation. Usually, we have in mind a set $\mathcal{H}$ of possible hypotheses (a set of atomic sentences), sometimes called "abducibles," in terms of which explanations are to be phrased. In the case of medical diagnoses, for instance, these would be diseases or conditions like ChickenPox or TennisElbow. In that case, SoreJoints would not be a suitable explanation.

We call any $\alpha$ that satisfies these four conditions an *abductive explanation* of $\beta$ with respect to KB.

## 13.2.1  Some Simplifications

With this definition of an explanation in hand, we will see that in the propositional case, at least, certain simplifications to the task of generating explanations are possible.

First of all, although we have considered explaining an arbitrary formula $\beta$, it is sufficient to know how to explain a single literal, or even just an atom. The reason for this is that we can choose a new atom $p$ that appears nowhere else, in which case $\alpha$ is an explanation for $\beta$ with respect to KB if and only if $\alpha$ is an explanation for $p$ with respect to $(\text{KB} \cup \{(p \equiv \beta\})$, as can be verified by considering the definition of explanation. In other words, according to the criteria in the definition, anything that is an explanation for $p$ would also be considered an explanation for $\beta$, and vice versa.

Next, while we have considered explanations that could be any sort of formula, it is sufficient to limit our attention to conjunctions of literals. To see why, imagine that some arbitrary formula $\alpha$ is an explanation for $\beta$, and assume that when $\alpha$ is converted into DNF, we get $(d_1 \vee \cdots \vee d_n)$, where each $d_i$ is a conjunction of literals. Observe that each $d_i$ entails $\beta$ and uses terms of the appropriate vocabulary. Moreover, at least one of the $d_i$ must be consistent with the KB (because otherwise $\alpha$ would not be). This $d_i$ is also as simple as $\alpha$ itself, because it has the same or a subset of the literals. So this single $d_i$ by itself can be used instead of $\alpha$ as an explanation for $\beta$.

Because a conjunction of literals is logically equivalent to the negation of a clause, it then follows that to explain a literal $\rho$ it is sufficient to look for a clause $c$ (in the desired vocabulary) with as few literals as possible that satisfies the following constraints:

1. $\mathrm{KB} \models (\neg c \supset \rho)$, or equivalently, $\mathrm{KB} \models (c \cup \{\rho\})$, and

2. $\mathrm{KB} \not\models c$.

This brings us to the topic of prime implicates.

## 13.2.2  Prime Implicates

A clause $c$ is said to be a *prime implicate* of a KB if and only if

1. $\mathrm{KB} \models c$, and

2. for every $c'$ that is a proper subset of $c$, it is not the case that $\mathrm{KB} \models c'$.

Note that for any clause $c$, if $\mathrm{KB} \models c$, then some subset of $c$ or perhaps $c$ itself must be a prime implicate of KB. For example, if we have a KB consisting of

$$\{(p \wedge q \wedge r \supset g), (\neg p \wedge q \supset g), (\neg q \wedge r \supset g)\}$$

then among the prime implicates are $(p \vee \neg q \vee g)$ and $(\neg r \vee g)$. Each of these clauses is entailed by KB, and no subset of either of them is entailed. In this KB, the tautologies $(p \vee \neg p)$, $(q \vee \neg q)$, $(r \vee \neg r)$, and so on are also prime implicates. In general, note that for any atom $\rho$, unless $\mathrm{KB} \models \rho$ or $\mathrm{KB} \models \neg \rho$, the tautology $(\rho \vee \neg \rho)$ will be a prime implicate.

Returning now to explanations for a literal $\rho$, as we said, we want to find minimal clauses $c'$ such that $\mathrm{KB} \models (c' \cup \{\rho\})$ but $\mathrm{KB} \not\models c'$. Therefore, it will be sufficient to find prime implicates $c$ containing $\rho$, in which case the negation of $(c - \rho)$ will be an explanation for $\rho$. For the earlier example KB, if we want to generate the explanations for $g$, we first generate the prime implicates of KB containing $g$, which are $(p \vee \neg q \vee g)$, $(\neg r \vee g)$, and $(g \vee \neg g)$, and then we remove the atom $g$ and negate the clauses to obtain three explanations (as conjunctions of literals): $(\neg p \wedge q)$, $r$, and $g$ itself (the negation of $\neg g$). Note that tautologous prime implicates like $(g \vee \neg g)$ will always generate trivial explanations.

## 13.2.3  Computing Explanations

Now we can derive a procedure to compute explanations for any literal $\rho$ in some vocabulary $\mathcal{H}$:

1. calculate the set of prime implicates of the KB that contain the literal $\rho$;

2. remove $\rho$ from each of the clauses;

3. return as explanations the negations of the resulting clauses, provided that the literals are in the language $\mathcal{H}$.

The only thing left to consider is how to generate prime implicates.

As it turns out, Resolution can be used directly for this: It can be shown that, in the propositional case, Resolution is complete for nontautologous prime implicates. In other words, if KB is a set of clauses, and if KB $\models c$ where $c$ is a nontautologous prime implicate, then KB $\vdash c$ (see Exercise 1). The completeness of Resolution for the empty clause, used in the Resolution chapter, is just a special case: The empty clause, if entailed, must be a prime implicate. So we can compute all prime implicates of KB containing $\rho$ by running Resolution to completion, generating all resolvents, and then keeping only the minimal ones containing $\rho$. If we want to generate trivial explanations as well, we then need to add the tautologous prime implicates to this set.

This way of handling explanations suggests that it might be a good idea to precompute all prime implicates of a KB using Resolution, and then generate explanations for a literal by consulting this set as needed. Unfortunately, this will not work in practice. Even for a KB that is a set of Horn clauses, there can be exponentially many prime implicates. For example, consider the following Horn KB over the atoms $p_i$, $q_i$, $E_i$, $O_i$ for $0 \leq i < n$, and $E_n$ and $O_n$. This example is a version of parity checking; $p_i$ means bit $i$ is on, $q_i$ means off, $E_i$ means the count up to level $i$ is even, $O_i$ means odd:

$$E_i \wedge p_i \supset O_{i+1}$$

$$E_i \wedge q_i \supset E_{i+1}$$

$$O_i \wedge p_i \supset E_{i+1}$$

$$O_i \wedge q_i \supset O_{i+1}$$

$$E_0$$

$$\neg O_0$$

This KB contains $4n + 2$ Horn clauses of size 3 or less. Nonetheless, there are $2^{n-1}$ prime implicates that contain $E_n$: Any clause of the form $[x_0, \ldots x_{n-1}, E_n]$ where $x_i$ is either $p_i$ or $q_i$ and where an even number of them are $p$s will be a prime implicate.

## 13.3  A CIRCUIT EXAMPLE

In this section, we apply these ideas to a circuit diagnosis problem. Overall, the problem is to determine which component (or components) of a Boolean circuit might have failed given certain inputs and outputs and a background KB specifying the structure of the circuit, the normal behavior of logic gates, and perhaps a fault model.

The circuit in question is the full adder shown in Figure 13.1. A full adder takes three bits as input—two addends and a carry bit from a previous adder—and produces two outputs—the sum and the next carry bit. The facts we would expect to have in a KB capturing this circuit are as follows:

■ Components, using gate predicates:

$$\forall x. \mathsf{Gate}(x) \equiv \mathsf{AndGate}(x) \vee \mathsf{OrGate}(x) \vee \mathsf{XorGate}(x);$$

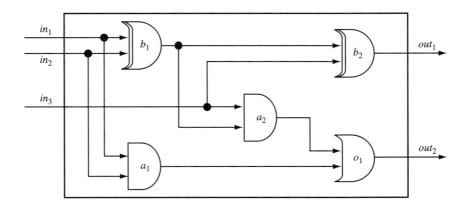

■ **FIGURE 13.1**

A Circuit for a Full Adder

AndGate($a_1$),  AndGate($a_2$),

XorGate($b_1$),  XorGate($b_2$),

OrGate($o_1$);

the whole circuit: FullAdder($f$).

- Connectivity, using functions $\text{in}_i$ for input $i$, and $\text{out}_i$ for output $i$ (where inputs and outputs are numbered from the top down in the diagram):

  $\text{in}_1(b_1) = \text{in}_1(f)$, $\text{in}_2(b_1) = \text{in}_2(f)$,

  $\text{in}_1(b_2) = \text{out}(b_1)$, $\text{in}_2(b_2) = \text{in}_3(f)$,

  $\text{in}_1(a_1) = \text{in}_1(f)$, $\text{in}_2(a_1) = \text{in}_2(f)$,

  $\text{in}_1(a_2) = \text{in}_3(f)$, $\text{in}_2(a_2) = \text{out}(b_1)$,

  $\text{in}_1(o_1) = \text{out}(a_2)$, $\text{in}_2(o_1) = \text{out}(a_1)$,

  $\text{out}_1(f) = \text{out}(b_2)$, $\text{out}_2(f) = \text{out}(o_1)$.

- Truth tables in terms of functions and, or, and xor:

  $\text{and}(0, 0) = 0$, $\text{and}(0, 1) = 0$, etc.

  $\text{or}(0, 0) = 0$, $\text{or}(0, 1) = 1$, etc.

  $\text{xor}(0, 0) = 0$, $\text{xor}(0, 1) = 1$, etc.

- The normal behavior of logic gates, using a predicate $Ab$:[3]

  $\forall x.\, \text{AndGate}(x) \wedge \neg Ab(x) \supset \text{out}(x) = \text{and}(\text{in}_1(x), \text{in}_2(x))$,

  $\forall x.\, \text{OrGate}(x) \wedge \neg Ab(x) \supset \text{out}(x) = \text{or}(\text{in}_1(x), \text{in}_2(x))$,

  $\forall x.\, \text{XorGate}(x) \wedge \neg Ab(x) \supset \text{out}(x) = \text{xor}(\text{in}_1(x), \text{in}_2(x))$.

- Finally, we may or may not wish to include some specification of possible abnormal behaviors of the circuit. This is what is usually called a *fault model*. For example, we might have the following specification:

  short circuit:

  $\forall x.\, [\text{OrGate}(x) \vee \text{XorGate}(x)] \wedge Ab(x) \supset \text{out}(x) = \text{in}_2(x)$.

In this example, nothing is specified regarding the behavior of abnormal and-gates. Of course, by leaving out parts of a fault model like this, or by

---

[3]Although this predicate was used for minimal entailment in Chapter 11, no default reasoning will be used here.

making it too weak, we run the risk that certain abnormal behaviors may be inexplicable, as we will discuss further later. Note also that abnormal behavior can be compatible with normal behavior on certain inputs (the output is the same whether or not the gate is working).

### 13.3.1 Abductive Diagnosis

The *abductive diagnosis* task is as follows: Given a KB as previously discussed, and some input *settings* of the circuit, for example,

$$in_1(f) = 1, \ in_2(f) = 0, \ in_3(f) = 1,$$

explain some output *observations* of the circuit, for example,

$$out_1(f) = 1, \ out_2(f) = 0,$$

in the language of *Ab*. What we are looking for, roughly, is a minimal conjunction $\alpha$ of ground $Ab(c)$ and $\neg Ab(c)$ terms such that

$$KB \cup Settings \cup \{\alpha\} \models Observations.$$

To do this computation, we can use the techniques described earlier, although we first have to "propositionalize" by observing, for example, that the universally quantified $x$ in the circuit example need only range over the five given gates.

To do this by hand, the easiest way is to make a table of all $2^5$ possibilities regarding which gates are normal or abnormal, seeing which of them entail the observations, and then looking for commonalities (and thus simplest possible explanations). In Figure 13.2, in each row of the table, the "entailed?" column says whether or not the conjunction of *Ab* literals (either positive or negative) together with the KB and the input settings entails the output observations. (Ignore the "consistent?" column for now.) For example, in row 5, we see that

$$Ab(b_1) \wedge Ab(b_2) \wedge \neg Ab(a_1) \wedge Ab(a_2) \wedge Ab(o_1)$$

entails the outputs; however, it is not an explanation, because

$$Ab(b_1) \wedge \neg Ab(a_1) \wedge Ab(o_1)$$

also entails the outputs (as can be verified by examining rows 5, 7, 13, and 15) and is simpler. Moreover, no subset of these literals entails the outputs. Continuing in this way, we end up with three abductive explanations:

1. $Ab(b_1) \wedge \neg Ab(a_1) \wedge Ab(o_1)$,
   gates $b_1$ and $o_1$ are defective, but $a_1$ is working;

|    | $b_1$ | $b_2$ | $a_1$ | $a_2$ | $o_1$ | entailed? | consistent? |
|----|-------|-------|-------|-------|-------|-----------|-------------|
| 1  | $Ab(b_1)$ | $Ab(b_2)$ | $Ab(a_1)$ | $Ab(a_2)$ | $Ab(o_1)$ | no | yes |
| 2  | $Ab(b_1)$ | $Ab(b_2)$ | $Ab(a_1)$ | $Ab(a_2)$ | $\neg Ab(o_1)$ | no | yes |
| 3  | $Ab(b_1)$ | $Ab(b_2)$ | $Ab(a_1)$ | $\neg Ab(a_2)$ | $Ab(o_1)$ | no | yes |
| 4  | $Ab(b_1)$ | $Ab(b_2)$ | $Ab(a_1)$ | $\neg Ab(a_2)$ | $\neg Ab(o_1)$ | no | yes |
| 5  | $Ab(b_1)$ | $Ab(b_2)$ | $\neg Ab(a_1)$ | $Ab(a_2)$ | $Ab(o_1)$ | yes | yes |
| 6  | $Ab(b_1)$ | $Ab(b_2)$ | $\neg Ab(a_1)$ | $Ab(a_2)$ | $\neg Ab(o_1)$ | no | yes |
| 7  | $Ab(b_1)$ | $Ab(b_2)$ | $\neg Ab(a_1)$ | $\neg Ab(a_2)$ | $Ab(o_1)$ | yes | yes |
| 8  | $Ab(b_1)$ | $Ab(b_2)$ | $\neg Ab(a_1)$ | $\neg Ab(a_2)$ | $\neg Ab(o_1)$ | yes | yes |
| 9  | $Ab(b_1)$ | $\neg Ab(b_2)$ | $Ab(a_1)$ | $Ab(a_2)$ | $Ab(o_1)$ | no | yes |
| 10 | $Ab(b_1)$ | $\neg Ab(b_2)$ | $Ab(a_1)$ | $Ab(a_2)$ | $\neg Ab(o_1)$ | no | yes |
| 11 | $Ab(b_1)$ | $\neg Ab(b_2)$ | $Ab(a_1)$ | $\neg Ab(a_2)$ | $Ab(o_1)$ | no | yes |
| 12 | $Ab(b_1)$ | $\neg Ab(b_2)$ | $Ab(a_1)$ | $\neg Ab(a_2)$ | $\neg Ab(o_1)$ | no | yes |
| 13 | $Ab(b_1)$ | $\neg Ab(b_2)$ | $\neg Ab(a_1)$ | $Ab(a_2)$ | $Ab(o_1)$ | yes | yes |
| 14 | $Ab(b_1)$ | $\neg Ab(b_2)$ | $\neg Ab(a_1)$ | $Ab(a_2)$ | $\neg Ab(o_1)$ | no | yes |
| 15 | $Ab(b_1)$ | $\neg Ab(b_2)$ | $\neg Ab(a_1)$ | $\neg Ab(a_2)$ | $Ab(o_1)$ | yes | yes |
| 16 | $Ab(b_1)$ | $\neg Ab(b_2)$ | $\neg Ab(a_1)$ | $\neg Ab(a_2)$ | $\neg Ab(o_1)$ | yes | yes |
| 17 | $\neg Ab(b_1)$ | $Ab(b_2)$ | $Ab(a_1)$ | $Ab(a_2)$ | $Ab(o_1)$ | no | yes |
| 18 | $\neg Ab(b_1)$ | $Ab(b_2)$ | $Ab(a_1)$ | $Ab(a_2)$ | $\neg Ab(o_1)$ | no | yes |
| 19 | $\neg Ab(b_1)$ | $Ab(b_2)$ | $Ab(a_1)$ | $\neg Ab(a_2)$ | $Ab(o_1)$ | no | yes |
| 20 | $\neg Ab(b_1)$ | $Ab(b_2)$ | $Ab(a_1)$ | $\neg Ab(a_2)$ | $\neg Ab(o_1)$ | no | no |
| 21 | $\neg Ab(b_1)$ | $Ab(b_2)$ | $\neg Ab(a_1)$ | $Ab(a_2)$ | $Ab(o_1)$ | yes | yes |
| 22 | $\neg Ab(b_1)$ | $Ab(b_2)$ | $\neg Ab(a_1)$ | $Ab(a_2)$ | $\neg Ab(o_1)$ | no | yes |
| 23 | $\neg Ab(b_1)$ | $Ab(b_2)$ | $\neg Ab(a_1)$ | $\neg Ab(a_2)$ | $Ab(o_1)$ | yes | yes |
| 24 | $\neg Ab(b_1)$ | $Ab(b_2)$ | $\neg Ab(a_1)$ | $\neg Ab(a_2)$ | $\neg Ab(o_1)$ | no | no |
| 25 | $\neg Ab(b_1)$ | $\neg Ab(b_2)$ | $Ab(a_1)$ | $Ab(a_2)$ | $Ab(o_1)$ | no | no |
| 26 | $\neg Ab(b_1)$ | $\neg Ab(b_2)$ | $Ab(a_1)$ | $Ab(a_2)$ | $\neg Ab(o_1)$ | no | no |
| 27 | $\neg Ab(b_1)$ | $\neg Ab(b_2)$ | $Ab(a_1)$ | $\neg Ab(a_2)$ | $Ab(o_1)$ | no | no |
| 28 | $\neg Ab(b_1)$ | $\neg Ab(b_2)$ | $Ab(a_1)$ | $\neg Ab(a_2)$ | $\neg Ab(o_1)$ | no | no |
| 29 | $\neg Ab(b_1)$ | $\neg Ab(b_2)$ | $\neg Ab(a_1)$ | $Ab(a_2)$ | $Ab(o_1)$ | no | no |
| 30 | $\neg Ab(b_1)$ | $\neg Ab(b_2)$ | $\neg Ab(a_1)$ | $Ab(a_2)$ | $\neg Ab(o_1)$ | no | no |
| 31 | $\neg Ab(b_1)$ | $\neg Ab(b_2)$ | $\neg Ab(a_1)$ | $\neg Ab(a_2)$ | $Ab(o_1)$ | no | no |
| 32 | $\neg Ab(b_1)$ | $\neg Ab(b_2)$ | $\neg Ab(a_1)$ | $\neg Ab(a_2)$ | $\neg Ab(o_1)$ | no | no |

▪ **FIGURE 13.2**

Diagnosis of the Full Adder

2. $Ab(b_1) \wedge \neg Ab(a_1) \wedge \neg Ab(a_2)$,
   gate $b_1$ is defective, but $a_1$ and $a_2$ are working;

3. $Ab(b_2) \wedge \neg Ab(a_1) \wedge Ab(o_1)$,
   gates $b_2$ and $o_1$ are defective, but $a_1$ is working.

Observe that not all components are mentioned in these explanations. This is because, given the settings and the fault model, we would get the same results whether or not the components were working normally. Different settings (or different fault models) could lead to different diagnoses. In fact, a key principle in this area is what is called *differential diagnosis*, that is, trying to discover tests that would distinguish between competing explanations. In the case of the circuit, this amounts to trying to find different input settings that would provide different outputs depending on what is or is not working normally. One principle of good engineering design is to make a circuit *testable*, that is, configured in such a way as to facilitate testing its (usually inaccessible) internal components.

## 13.3.2 Consistency-Based Diagnosis

One problem with the abductive form of diagnosis presented here is that it relies crucially on the presence of a fault model. Without a specification of how a circuit would behave when it is not working, certain output observations can be inexplicable, and this form of diagnosis can be much less helpful.

In many cases, however, we know how a circuit is supposed to work, but may not be able to characterize its failure modes. We would like to find out which components could be at fault when output observations conflict with this specification. Of course, with no fault model at all, we would be free to conjecture that *all* components were at fault. What we are really after, then, is a *minimal diagnosis*, that is, one that does not assume any unnecessary faults.[4]

This second version of diagnosis can be made precise as follows:

Assume KB uses the predicate *Ab* as before. (The KB may or may not include a fault model.) We want to find a set of components $D$ such that the set

$$\{Ab(c) \mid c \in D\} \cup \{\neg Ab(c) \mid c \notin D\}$$

is *consistent* with the set

KB ∪ *Settings* ∪ *Observations*

and no proper subset of $D$ is. Any such $D$ is called a *consistency-based diagnosis* of the circuit.

Thus, for consistency-based diagnosis, we look for (minimal sets of) assumptions of abnormality that are consistent with the settings and

---

[4]Note that in the earlier abductive account, we did not necessarily minimize the set of components assumed to be faulty, in that the literals $Ab(c)$ and $\neg Ab(c)$ have equal status.

observations, rather than (minimal sets of) assumptions of normality and abnormality that entail the observations.

In the case of the circuit example (with the given fault model), we can look for the diagnoses by hand by again making a table of all $2^5$ possibilities regarding which gates are normal or abnormal, seeing which of them are consistent with the settings and observations, and then looking for commonalities (and thus minimal sets of faulty components). Returning to the table in Figure 13.2, in each row of the table, the "consistent?" column says whether or not the conjunction of $Ab$ literals (either positive or negative) is consistent with the KB, together with the input settings and the output observations. (Ignore the "entailed?" column this time.) For example, in row 5, we see that

$$\{Ab(b_1), Ab(b_2), \neg Ab(a_1), Ab(a_2), Ab(o_1)\}$$

is consistent with the inputs and outputs. This does not yet give us a diagnosis, because

$$\{Ab(b_1), \neg Ab(b_2), \neg Ab(a_1), \neg Ab(a_2), \neg Ab(o_1)\}$$

is also consistent (row 16), and assumes a smaller set of abnormal components.

Continuing in this way, this time we end up with three consistency-based diagnoses: $\{b_1\}$, $\{b_2, a_2\}$, and $\{b_2, o_1\}$. Further testing on the circuit with different inputs and outputs could then be used to reduce the possibilities.

Although it is difficult to compare the two approaches to diagnosis in general terms, it is worth noting that they do behave quite differently regarding fault models. In the abductive case, with less of a fault model, there are usually fewer diagnoses involving abnormal components, because nothing follows regarding their behavior; in the consistency-based case, the opposite usually happens, because anything can be assumed regarding their behavior. For example, one of three possibilities considered in the consistency-based account is that both $b_2$ and $a_2$ are abnormal, because it is consistent that $a_2$ is producing a 0, and then that the output of $o_1$ is 0. In the abductive case, none of the explanations involve $a_2$ being abnormal, because there would then be no way to confirm that the output of $o_1$ is 0. In general, however, it is difficult to give hard and fast rules about which type of diagnosis should be used.

## 13.4  BEYOND THE BASICS

We conclude this chapter by examining some complications to the simple picture of abductive reasoning we have presented, and then finally sketching some nondiagnostic applications of abductive reasoning.

### 13.4.1  Extensions

There are a number of ways in which our account of abductive reasoning could be enlarged for more realistic applications.

**Variables and Quantification**  In the first-order case of abductive reasoning, we might need to change, at the very least, our definition of what it means for an explanation to be as simple as possible. It might also be useful to consider explaining formulas with free variables, as a way of answering certain types of *wh*-questions, in a way that goes beyond answer extraction. Imagine we have a query like $P(x)$. We might return the answer $(x = \text{john})$ using answer extraction, because this is one way of explaining how $P(x)$ could be true. But we might also return something like $Q(x)$ as the answer to the question. For example, if we ask the question, "What are yellow song birds that serve as pets?" the answer we are expecting is probably not the names of some individual birds, but rather another predicate like "canaries." Note, however, that it is not clear how to use Resolution to generate explanations in a first-order setting.

**Negative Evidence**  We have insisted that explanations entail everything to be explained. We might, however, imagine cases where missing observations need to be accounted for. For example, we might be interested in a medical diagnosis that does not entail fever, without necessarily requiring that it entail ¬fever.

**Defaults**  We have used logical entailment as the relation between an explanation $\alpha$ and what is being explained $\beta$. In a more general setting, it might be preferable to require that it be reasonable to believe $\beta$ given $\alpha$, where this belief could involve default assumptions. For example, being a bird might explain an animal being able to fly, even though it would not entail it.

**Probabilities**  We have preferred explanations and diagnoses that are as simple as possible. However, in general, not all simplest ones would be expected to be equally likely. For example, we may have two circuit diagnoses, each involving a single component, but it may be that one of them is much more likely to fail than the other. Perhaps the failure of one component makes it very likely that another will fail as well.

Moreover, the "causal laws" we have between, say, diseases and symptoms would typically have a probabilistic component: Only a certain percentage of the time would we expect a disease to manifest a symptom.

## 13.4.2  Other Applications

Finally, let us consider other applications of abductive reasoning.

**Object Recognition**  This is an application where a system is given input from a camera, say, and must determine what is being viewed. At one level, the question is this: What scene would explain the image elements being observed? Abduction is required here, because, as with diseases and symptoms, it is presumed to be easier to obtain facts that tell us what would be visible if an object were present than to obtain facts that tell us what object is present if certain patterns are visible. At a higher level, once certain properties of the object have been determined, another question to consider is this: What object(s) would explain the collection of properties discovered? Both of these tasks can be nicely formulated in abductive terms.

**Plan Recognition**  In this case, the observations are the actions of an agent, and the explanation we seek is one that relates to the high-level goals of the agent. If we observe the agent boiling water and heating a tomato sauce, we might conjecture that a pasta dish is being prepared.

**Hypothetical Reasoning**  As a final application, consider the following. Instead of asking, "What would I have to be told to believe that $\beta$ is true?" as in abductive reasoning, we ask, "What would I learn if I were told that $\alpha$ were true?" For example, we might be looking for new symptoms that would be entailed if a disease were present. This is clearly a form of deductive reasoning, but one where we are interested in returning a formula, rather than a yes/no answer or the names of some individuals. In a sense, it is the dual of explanation: We are looking for a formula $\beta$ that is entailed by $\alpha$ together with the KB, but one that is not already entailed by the KB itself, that is simple and logically parsimonious, and that is in the correct vocabulary.

Interestingly, there is a precise connection between this form of reasoning and the type of explanation we have already defined: We should learn $\beta$ on being told $\alpha$ in the sense just mentioned if and only if the formula $\neg\beta$ is an abductive explanation for $\neg\alpha$ as already defined. For instance, to go back to the tennis example at the start of the chapter, one of the new things we ought to learn on being told

$$(\text{Arthritis} \wedge \neg\text{SoreElbow})$$

would be Treated (that is, the arthritis is being treated). If we now go back to the definition of explanation, we can verify that ¬Treated is indeed an abductive explanation for

$$¬(\text{Arthritis} \wedge ¬\text{SoreElbow}),$$

because ¬Treated entails this sentence, is consistent with the KB, and is as simple as possible. The nice thing about this account is that an existing procedure for abductive reasoning could be used directly for this type of deductive reasoning.

## 13.5 BIBLIOGRAPHIC NOTES

The term *abduction* was introduced by the philosopher Charles Sanders Peirce [323, 325] (see also [324] for a selection of writings). Fann [125] discusses the development of Peirce's ideas on abduction. The volume by Eco and Sebeok [117] contains an interesting collection of essays referring to abduction. The term *inference to the best explanation* is often used to describe abduction (see, for instance, [180, 258]). As to how closely abduction captures the notion of explanation, refer to Salmon [362]. One of the things that Salmon considers is the Hempel and Oppenheim [184] *deductive-nomological* model, which is similar in many ways to abduction. One of the first papers on abduction in Artificial Intelligence was by Pople [333], who applied it to diagnosis. For a survey of abduction in AI, refer to Paul [319].

Many explanation criteria have been suggested for selecting the best abduction beyond those mentioned in this chapter. Cost-based measures, in which costs are associated with making abductive hypotheses, are given by Charniak and Shimony [69] and Stickel [402]. Ram and Leake [337] give utility-based criteria for choosing hypotheses. The procedures given for computing abduction by Pople [333] and Cox and Pietrzykowski [81] are what Stickel refers to as *most specific abductions* [402].

When it comes to computing abductive inferences, Reiter and de Kleer [349] suggest that methods can be divided into two categories: *interpreted* and *compiled* approaches. Interpreted approaches retain the knowledge base in its original form and compute abductive conclusions as required. Compiled approaches transform the knowledge base into a more convenient form for determining abductive inferences quickly and efficiently. The mechanisms proposed by Pople [333], in THEORIST [330, 331], and by Cox and Pietrzykowski [81] would be classified as interpreted. The most common form of compilation for abduction is to convert the knowledge base into prime implicates. Many methods for computing prime implicates are based on Tison's method [411]. Other methods for computing prime implicates include those of Jackson [197], Kean and Tsiknis [217], and Kean [216]. Sets of prime implicates can be viewed as a minimal CNF and contrasted with their dual, *prime implicants*, as minimal DNF. For formulas in DNF a common method of compilation is *binary decision diagrams* (BDDs) [6].

Bylander et al. [64] discuss the complexity of computing one form of abduction and find that it is NP-hard. Attardi et al. [15] discuss knowledge compilation in a first-order setting. Darwiche and Marquis [84] consider a number of knowledge compilation techniques, including prime implicates and BDDs. For an empirical assessment of knowledge compilation, see Kautz and Selman [215]. The example in the text used to show that even Horn clauses can have exponentially many prime implicates is due to McAllester [272].

The circuit example used in Section 13.3 appears in Genesereth [150], and is also considered in a paper by Reiter [346], where formal definitions of abductive diagnosis and consistency-based diagnosis are introduced. The approach developed independently by de Kleer and Williams [94, 95] is related to Reiter's consistency-based diagnosis. This work drew on earlier work in AI on model-based diagnosis [88, 178] and on truth maintenance systems [111]. These ideas were extended in the assumption-based truth maintenance systems (ATMS) considered in [349]. For the logical aspects of truth maintenance systems, see also Reinfrank [339] and Reinfrank et al. [340]. On these issues, see also Doyle [112]. Forbus and de Kleer [133] present methods for implementing truth maintenance systems.

Complementing logic-based approaches to abduction is another line of research on *set-cover*-based approaches [11, 326]. For the logic-based approaches that are the focus of this chapter, definitions are given by Console and Torasso [77]. A variant of abduction defined in terms of belief is presented by Levesque [242]. Marquis [268] considers abduction in first-order logic. Another view of abduction developed through the implementation of various systems is presented by Josephson and Josephson [205].

The THEORIST system [330, 331] uses abduction to perform default reasoning. This idea is generalized by Brewka [55]. A similar approach to THEORIST in the context of logic programming is given by Eshghi and Kowalski [120], who relate abduction and negation as failure. Such work has led to the area of abductive logic programming [207, 208]. Abduction has also been applied to diagnosis [326, 333], natural language [67, 69, 308, 402], database updates [206, 408], and scientific discovery [300].

## 13.6 EXERCISES

**1.** In Chapter 4, we saw that Resolution was logically complete for the empty clause, but not for clauses in general. Prove that Resolution is complete for prime implicates that are not tautologous. *Hint*: Assume that $c$ is a prime implicate of a set of clauses $\Sigma$. Then there is a derivation of [ ], given $\Sigma$ and the negation of $c$. Show how to modify this derivation to obtain a new Resolution derivation that ends with $c$ but uses only the clauses in $\Sigma$.

2. In this question we explore what it could mean to say that a KB "says something" about some topic. More precisely, we say that a set of propositional clauses $S$ is *relevant* to an atom $p$ if and only if $p$ appears (either positively or negatively) in a nontautologous prime implicate of $S$.

   (a) Give an example of a consistent set of clauses $S$ where an atom $p$ is mentioned but where $S$ is not relevant to $p$.

   (b) Suppose we have a clause $c \in S$ and a literal $\rho \in c$. Show that if $S \not\models c - \{\rho\}$, then $\rho$ appears in a prime implicate of $S$.

   (c) Suppose we have a clause $c \in S$ and a literal $\rho \in c$. Show that if $S \models c - \{\rho\}$, then $S$ is logically equivalent to $S'$ where $S'$ is $S$ with $c$ replaced by $c - \{\rho\}$.

   (d) Suppose $S$ is consistent. Use parts (b) and (c) to show that $S$ is relevant to $p$ if and only if there is a nontautologous clause $c \in S$ with $\rho \in c$, where $\rho = p$ or $\rho = \neg p$ such that $S \not\models c - \{\rho\}$.

   (e) Use part (d) to argue that there is a polynomial time procedure that takes a set of Horn clauses $S$ and an atom $p$ as arguments and decides whether $S$ is relevant to $p$. *Note*: the naïve way of doing this would take exponential time, because $S$ can have exponentially many prime implicates.

3. Consider the binary circuit for logical AND depicted in Figure 13.3, where $i1$, $i2$, and $i3$ are logical inverters and $o1$ is an OR gate.

   (a) Write sentences describing this circuit—its components, connectivity, and normal behavior.

   (b) Write a sentence for a fault model saying that a faulty inverter has its output the same as its input.

   (c) Assuming the fault model and that the output is 1 given inputs of 0 and 1, generate the three abductive explanations for this behavior.

   (d) Generate the three consistency-based diagnoses for this circuit under the same conditions.

   (e) Compare the abductive and consistency-based diagnoses and explain informally why they are different.

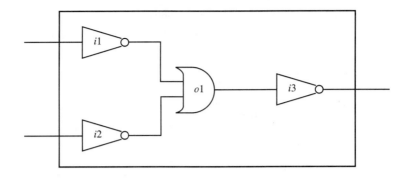

▪ **FIGURE 13.3**

A Circuit for AND

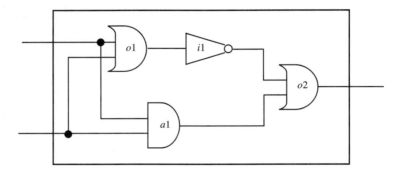

▪ **FIGURE 13.4**

A Circuit for EQUAL

4. Consider the binary circuit in Figure 13.4 that tests if its two inputs are equal, where $o1$ and $o2$ are OR gates, $i1$ is an inverter, and $a1$ is an AND gate:

(a) Write sentences describing this circuit—its components, connectivity, and normal behavior.

(b) Write a sentence for a fault model saying that a faulty OR has its output the same as its first input (the higher one in the diagram).

(c) Assuming the fault model and that the output is 1 given inputs of 0 and 1, generate the abductive explanations for this behavior.

(d) Generate the three consistency-based diagnoses for this circuit under the same conditions.

(e) Compare the abductive and consistency-based diagnoses and explain informally why they are different.

# CHAPTER 14

# ACTIONS

■

———————————————————————————————————————

■

■

The language of FOL is sometimes criticized as being an overly "static" representation formalism. Sentences of FOL are either true or false in an interpretation and stay that way. Unlike procedural representations or production systems, there is seemingly nothing in FOL corresponding to any sort of *change*.

In fact, there are two sorts of changes that we might want to consider. First, there is the idea of changing what is believed about the world. Although we will not dwell on it here, this is a very important aspect of real-world reasoning. Suppose $\alpha$ is a sentence saying that birds are the descendants of dinosaurs. At some point you might come to believe that $\alpha$ is true, perhaps by being told directly. If you had no beliefs about $\alpha$ before, this would be a straightforward process that involved adding $\alpha$ to your current KB. If you had previously thought that $\alpha$ was false, however, perhaps having concluded this from a number of other beliefs, dealing with the new information would be a much more complicated process. The study of which of your old beliefs to discard is an important area of research known as *belief revision*.

The second notion of change to consider is when the beliefs themselves are about a changing world. Instead of merely believing that John is a student, for example, you might believe that John was not a student initially, but that he became a student by enrolling at a university, and that he later graduated, and thus ceased to be a student. In this case, whereas the world you are imagining is certainly changing, the beliefs you have about John's history as a whole need not change at all.[1]

---

[1] Of course, we might also have changing beliefs about a changing world, but we will not pursue this here.

In this chapter, we will study how beliefs about a changing world of this sort can in fact be represented in a dialect of FOL called the *situation calculus*. This is not the only way to represent a changing world, but it is a simple and powerful way to do so. It also naturally lends itself to various sorts of reasoning, including planning, discussed separately in the next chapter.

## 14.1  THE SITUATION CALCULUS

One way of thinking about change is to imagine being in a certain static situation and having an action move you from that situation to a new situation. For example, you may be in the situation of standing empty-handed next to a cup of coffee, and the action of picking it up moves you into the next situation, of holding it in your hand. The situation calculus is a dialect of FOL in which such situations and actions are explicitly taken to be objects in the domain. In particular, there are two distinguished sorts of first-order terms:

- *actions*, such as jump (the act of jumping), kick($x$) (kicking object $x$), and put($r,x,y$) (robot $r$ putting object $x$ on top of object $y$). The constant and function symbols for actions are completely application dependent.

- *situations*, which denote possible world histories. A distinguished constant $S_0$ and function symbol *do* are used. $S_0$ denotes the initial situation, before any action has been performed; $do(a,s)$ denotes the new situation that results from performing action $a$ in situation $s$.

For example, the situation term $do(\text{pickup}(b_2), do(\text{pickup}(b_1), S_0))$ denotes the situation that results from first picking up object $b_1$ in $S_0$ and then picking up object $b_2$. Note that this situation is not the same as $do(\text{pickup}(b_1), do(\text{pickup}(b_2), S_0))$, because they are different histories, even though for practical purposes there may be no reason to distinguish them.

### 14.1.1  Fluents

Predicates and functions whose values may vary from situation to situation are called *fluents*, and are used to describe what holds in a situation. By convention, the last argument of a fluent is a situation. For example, the fluent Holding($r,x,s$) might stand for the relation of robot $r$ holding object $x$ in situation $s$. Thus, we can have formulas like

$$\neg\text{Holding}(r,x,s) \wedge \text{Holding}(r,x,do(\text{pickup}(r,x),s)),$$

which says that robot $r$ is not holding $x$ in some situation $s$, but is holding $x$ in the situation that results from picking it up in that situation. Note that in the situation calculus there is no distinguished "current" situation. A single formula like this can talk about many different situations, past, present, or future.

Finally, a distinguished predicate $Poss(a, s)$ is used to state that action $a$ can be performed in situation $s$. For example,

$$Poss(\mathsf{pickup}(r, x), S_0)$$

says that the robot $r$ is able to pick up object $x$ in the initial situation.

This completes the specification of the dialect of FOL that we will use to reason about actions.

## 14.1.2 Precondition and Effect Axioms

To reason about a changing world, it is necessary to have beliefs not only about what is true initially but also about how the world changes as the result of actions.

Actions typically have *preconditions*, that is, conditions that need to be true for the action to occur. For example, in a robotics setting, we might have the following:

- a robot can pick up an object if and only if it is not holding anything, the object is not too heavy, and the robot is next to the object:[2]

$$Poss(\mathsf{pickup}(r, x), s) \equiv$$
$$\forall z.\, \neg\mathsf{Holding}(r, z, s) \wedge \neg\mathsf{Heavy}(x) \wedge \mathsf{NextTo}(r, x, s);$$

- it is possible for a robot to repair an object if and only if the object is broken and there is glue available:

$$Poss(\mathsf{repair}(r, x), s) \equiv \mathsf{Broken}(x, s) \wedge \mathsf{HasGlue}(r, s).$$

Actions typically also have *effects*, that is, fluents that are changed as a result of performing the action. For example,

- dropping a fragile object causes it to break:

$$\mathsf{Fragile}(x) \supset \mathsf{Broken}(x, do(\mathsf{drop}(r, x), s));$$

- repairing an object causes it to be unbroken:

$$\neg\mathsf{Broken}(x, do(\mathsf{repair}(r, x), s)).$$

---

[2]In this chapter, free variables should be assumed to be universally quantified in the widest scope.

Formulas like these are often called *precondition axioms* and *effect axioms*, respectively.[3] Effect axioms are called *positive* if they describe when a fluent becomes true, and *negative* otherwise.

## 14.1.3   Frame Axioms

To fully capture the dynamics of a situation, we need to go beyond the preconditions and effects of actions. With what we have discussed so far, if a fluent is not mentioned in an effect axiom for an action $a$, we would not know anything at all about it in the situation $do(a, s)$. To really know how the world can change, it is also necessary to know what fluents are *unaffected* by performing an action. For example,

- dropping an object does not change its color:

$$\mathsf{Color}(x, c, s) \supset \mathsf{Color}(x, c, do(\mathsf{drop}(r, x), s));$$

- dropping an object $y$ does not break an object $x$ when $x$ is not the same as $y$ or $x$ is not fragile:

$$\neg \mathsf{Broken}(x, s) \wedge [x \neq y \vee \neg \mathsf{Fragile}(x)] \supset$$
$$\neg \mathsf{Broken}(x, do(\mathsf{drop}(r, y), s)).$$

Formulas like these are often called *frame axioms*, because they limit or frame the effects of actions. Observe that we would not normally expect them to be entailed by the precondition or effect axioms for the actions involved.

Frame axioms do present a serious problem, however, sometimes called the *frame problem*. Simply put, it will be necessary to know and reason effectively with an extremely large number of frame axioms. Indeed, for any given fluent we would expect that only a very small number of actions affect the value of that fluent; the rest leave it invariant. For instance, an object's color is unaffected by picking things up, opening a door, using the phone, making linguini, walking the dog, electing a new prime minister of Canada, and so on. All of these will require frame axioms. It seems very counterintuitive that we should need to even think about these $\approx 2 \times \mathcal{A} \times \mathcal{F}$ facts (where $\mathcal{A}$ is the number of actions and $\mathcal{F}$ the number of fluents) about what does not change when we perform an action.

What counts as a solution to this problem? Suppose the person responsible for building a KB has written down *all* the relevant effect axioms.

---

[3]These are called *axioms* for historical reasons: A KB can be thought of as the axioms of a logical theory (like number theory or set theory), with the entailed beliefs considered as theorems.

That is, for each fluent $F(\vec{x}, s)$ and action $a$ that can cause the fluent to change, we have an effect axiom of the form

$$\phi(\vec{x}, s) \supset (\neg)F(\vec{x}, do(a, s)),$$

where $\phi(\vec{x}, s)$ is some condition on situation $s$. What we would like is a systematic procedure for generating all the frame axioms from these effect axioms. Moreover, if possible, we also want a parsimonious representation for them, because in their simplest form there are too many.

Why do we want such a solution? There are at least three reasons:

- Frame axioms are necessary beliefs about a dynamic world that are not entailed by other beliefs we may have.

- Frame axioms are a convenience for the KB builder. Generating the frame axioms automatically gives us modularity, because only the effect axioms need to be given by hand. This ensures there is no inadvertent omission or error.

- Such a solution is useful for theorizing about actions. We can see what assumptions need to be made to draw conclusions about what does not change.

We will examine a simple solution to the frame problem in Section 14.2.

## 14.1.4  Using the Situation Calculus

Given a KB containing facts expressed in the situation calculus, there are various sorts of reasoning tasks we can consider. We will see in the next chapter that we can do planning. In Section 14.3, we will see that we can figure out how to execute a high-level action specification. Here we consider two basic reasoning tasks: projection and legality testing.

The *projection task* is the following: Given a sequence of actions and some initial situation, determine what would be true if those actions were performed starting in that initial situation. This can be formalized as follows:

Suppose that $\phi(s)$ is a formula with a single free variable $s$ of the situation sort, and that $\vec{a}$ is a sequence of actions $\langle a_1, \ldots, a_n \rangle$. To find out if $\phi(s)$ would be true after performing $\vec{a}$ starting in the initial situation $S_0$, we determine whether or not KB $\models \phi(do(\vec{a}, S_0))$, where $do(\vec{a}, S_0)$ is an abbreviation for $do(a_n, do(a_{n-1}, \ldots, do(a_2, do(a_1, S_0)) \ldots))$, and for $S_0$ itself when $n = 0$.

For example, using the effect and frame axioms presented in Sections 14.1.2 and 14.1.3, it follows that the fluent $\neg Broken(b_2, s)$ would hold after the sequence of actions

$$\langle \mathsf{pickup}(b_1), \mathsf{pickup}(b_2), \mathsf{drop}(b_2), \mathsf{repair}(b_2), \mathsf{drop}(b_1) \rangle.$$

In other words, the fluent holds in the situation

$$s = do(\mathsf{drop}(b_1), do(\mathsf{repair}(b_2), do(\mathsf{drop}(b_2), do(\mathsf{pickup}(b_2),$$
$$do(\mathsf{pickup}(b_1), S_0))))).$$

It is a separate matter to determine whether or not the given sequence of actions could in fact be performed starting in the initial situation. This is called the *legality testing task*. For example, a robot might not be able to pick up more than one object at a time. We call a situation term *legal* if it is either the initial situation or the result of performing an action whose preconditions are satisfied starting in a legal situation. For example, although the term

$$do(\mathsf{pickup}(b_2), do(\mathsf{pickup}(b_1), S_0))$$

is well formed, it is not a legal situation, because the precondition for picking up $b_2$ (e.g., not holding anything) will not be satisfied in a situation where $b_1$ has already been picked up. So the legality task is determining whether a sequence of actions leads to a legal situation. This can be formalized as follows:

Suppose that $\vec{a}$ is a sequence of actions $\langle a_1, \dots, a_n \rangle$. To find out if $\vec{a}$ can be legally performed starting in the initial situation $S_0$, we determine whether or not KB $\models Poss(a_i, do(\langle a_1, \dots, a_{i-1} \rangle, S_0))$ for every $i$ such that $1 \le i \le n$.

Before concluding this section on the situation calculus, it is perhaps worth noting some of the representational limitations of this language:

- *single agent*: there are no unknown or unobserved exogenous actions performed by other agents, and no unnamed events;

- *no time*: we have not talked about how long an action takes, or when it occurs;

- *no concurrency*: if a situation is the result of performing two actions, one of them is performed first and the other afterward;

- *discrete actions*: there are no continuous actions like pushing an object from one point to another or filling a bathtub with water;

- *only hypotheticals*: we cannot say that an action *has* occurred in reality, or *will* occur;

■ *only primitive actions*: there are no actions that are constructed from other actions as parts, such as iterations or conditionals.

Many of these limitations can be dealt with by refinements and extensions to the dialect of the situation calculus considered here. We will deal with the last of these in Section 14.3. First we turn to a solution to the frame problem.

## 14.2  A SIMPLE SOLUTION TO THE FRAME PROBLEM

The solution to the frame problem we will consider depends on first putting all effect axioms into a normal form. Suppose, for example, that there are two positive effect axioms for the fluent Broken:

$$\text{Fragile}(x) \supset \text{Broken}(x, do(\text{drop}(r, x), s))$$

$$\text{NextTo}(b, x, s) \supset \text{Broken}(x, do(\text{explode}(b), s)).$$

In other words, an object is broken if it is fragile and it was dropped, or something next to it exploded. Using a universally quantified action variable $a$, these can be rewritten as a single formula:

$$\exists r\{a = \text{drop}(r, x) \land \text{Fragile}(x)\} \lor$$
$$\exists b\{a = \text{explode}(b) \land \text{NextTo}(b, x, s)\} \supset$$
$$\text{Broken}(x, do(a, s)).$$

Similarly, a negative effect axiom like

$$\neg\text{Broken}(x, do(\text{repair}(r, x), s)),$$

saying that an object is not broken after it is repaired, can be rewritten as

$$\exists r\{a = \text{repair}(r, x)\} \supset \neg\text{Broken}(x, do(a, s)).$$

In general, for any fluent $F(\vec{x}, s)$, we can rewrite all of the positive effect axioms as a single formula of the form

$$\Pi_F(\vec{x}, a, s) \supset F(\vec{x}, do(a, s)), \tag{1}$$

and all the negative effect axioms as a single formula of the form

$$N_F(\vec{x}, a, s) \supset \neg F(\vec{x}, do(a, s)), \tag{2}$$

where $\Pi_F(\vec{x}, a, s)$ and $N_F(\vec{x}, a, s)$ are formulas whose free variables are among the $x_i$, $a$, and $s$.

## 14.2.1  Explanation Closure

Now imagine that we make a completeness assumption about the effect axioms we have for a fluent: Assume that formulas (1) and (2) characterize all the conditions under which an action $a$ changes the value of fluent $F$. We can in fact formalize this assumption using what are called *explanation closure axioms* as follows:

$$\neg F(\vec{x}, s) \wedge F(\vec{x}, do(a, s)) \supset \Pi_F(\vec{x}, a, s), \tag{3}$$

in other words, if $F$ were false, and made true by doing action $a$, then condition $\Pi_F$ must have been true;

$$F(\vec{x}, s) \wedge \neg F(\vec{x}, do(a, s)) \supset N_F(\vec{x}, a, s), \tag{4}$$

in other words, if $F$ were true, and made false by doing action $a$, then condition $N_F$ must have been true.

Informally, these axioms add an "only if" component to the normal form effect axioms: (1) says that $F$ is made true if $\Pi_F$ holds, whereas (3) says that $F$ is made true only if $\Pi_F$ holds.[4] In fact, by rewriting them slightly, these explanation closure axioms can be seen to be disguised versions of frame axioms:

$$\neg F(\vec{x}, s) \wedge \neg \Pi_F(\vec{x}, a, s) \supset \neg F(\vec{x}, do(a, s))$$
$$F(\vec{x}, s) \wedge \neg N_F(\vec{x}, a, s) \supset F(\vec{x}, do(a, s)).$$

In other words, $F$ remains false after doing $a$ when $\Pi_F$ is false, and $F$ remains true after doing $a$ when $N_F$ is false.

## 14.2.2  Successor State Axioms

If we are willing to make two assumptions about our KB, the formulas (1), (2), (3), and (4) can be combined in a particularly simple and elegant way. Specifically, we assume that our KB entails the following:

■ integrity of the effect axioms for every fluent $F$:

$$\neg \exists \vec{x}, a, s. \, \Pi_F(\vec{x}, a, s) \wedge N_F(\vec{x}, a, s);$$

---

[4]Note that in (3) we need to ensure that $F$ was originally false and was made true to be able to conclude that $\Pi_F$ held, and similarly for (4).

- unique names for actions:

$$A(\vec{x}) = A(\vec{y}) \supset (x_1 = y_1) \wedge \cdots \wedge (x_n = y_n)$$

$$A(\vec{x}) \neq B(\vec{y}), \text{ where } A \text{ and } B \text{ are distinct action names.}$$

The first assumption is merely that no action $a$ satisfies the condition of making the fluent $F$ both true and false. The second assumption is that the only action terms that can be equal are two identical actions with identical arguments.

With these two assumptions, it can be shown that for any fluent $F$, KB entails that (1), (2), (3), and (4) together are logically equivalent to the following formula:

$$F(\vec{x}, do(a, s)) \equiv \Pi_F(\vec{x}, a, s) \vee (F(\vec{x}, s) \wedge \neg N_F(\vec{x}, a, s)).$$

A formula of this form is called a *successor state axiom* for the fluent $F$ because it completely characterizes the value of fluent $F$ in the successor state resulting from performing action $a$ in situation $s$. Specifically, $F$ is true after doing $a$ if and only if before doing $a$, $\Pi_F$ (the positive effect condition for $F$) was true, or both $F$ and $\neg N_F$ (the negative effect condition for $F$) were true. For example, for the fluent Broken, we have the following successor state axiom:

$$
\begin{aligned}
\text{Broken}(x, do(a, s)) \equiv \\
\exists r\{a = \text{drop}(r, x) \wedge \text{Fragile}(x)\} \vee \\
\exists b\{a = \text{explode}(b) \wedge \text{NextTo}(b, x, s)\} \vee \\
\text{Broken}(x, s) \wedge \forall r\{a \neq \text{repair}(r, x)\}
\end{aligned}
$$

This says that an object $x$ is broken after doing action $a$ if and only if $a$ is a dropping action and $x$ is fragile, or $a$ is a bomb-exploding action when $x$ is near to the bomb, or $x$ was already broken and $a$ is not the action of repairing it.

Note that it follows from this axiom that dropping a fragile object will break it. Moreover, it also follows logically that talking on the phone does not affect whether or not an object is broken (assuming unique names, i.e., talking on the phone is distinct from any dropping, exploding, or repairing action). Thus, a KB containing this single axiom would entail all the necessary effect and frame axioms for the fluent in question.

## 14.2.3  Summary

We have, therefore, a simple solution to the frame problem in terms of the following axioms:

- precondition axioms, one per action,
- successor state axioms, one per fluent,
- unique name axioms for actions.

Observe that we do not get a small number of axioms at the expense of prohibitively long ones. The length of a successor state axiom is roughly proportional to the number of actions that affect the value of the fluent, and, as noted earlier, we do not expect in general that very many of the actions would change the value of any given fluent.

The conciseness and perspicuity of this solution to the frame problem clearly depends on three factors:

1. the ability to quantify over actions, so that only actions changing the fluent need to be mentioned by name;

2. the assumption that relatively few actions affect each fluent, which keeps the successor state axioms short;

3. the completeness assumption for the effects of actions, which allows us to conclude that actions that are not mentioned explicitly in effect axioms leave the fluent invariant.

The solution also depends on being able to put effect axioms in the normal form used earlier. This would not be possible, for example, if we had actions whose effects were *nondeterministic*. For example, imagine an action flipcoin whose effect is to make either the fluent Heads or the fluent Tails true. An effect axiom like

$$\text{Heads}(do(\text{flipcoin}, s)) \vee \text{Tails}(do(\text{flipcoin}, s))$$

cannot be put into the required normal form. In general, we need to assume that every action $a$ is deterministic in the sense that all the given effect axioms are of the form

$$\phi(\vec{x}, a, s) \supset (\neg)F(\vec{x}, do(a, s)).$$

How to deal in some way with nondeterministic choice and other complex actions is the topic of the next section.

## 14.3   COMPLEX ACTIONS

So far, in our treatment of the situation calculus we have assumed that there are only primitive actions, with effects and preconditions independent of each other. We have no way of handling *complex actions*, that is to say, actions that have other actions as components. Examples of these are actions like the following:

- *conditionals*: if the car is in the driveway then drive and otherwise walk;

- *iterations*: while there are blocks on the table, remove one;

- *nondeterministic choice*: pick a red block off the table and put it on the floor;

and others, as described later. What we would like to do is to *define* such actions in terms of their primitive components in such a way that we can inherit their solution to the frame problem. To do this, we need a compositional treatment of the frame problem for complex actions. This is precisely what we will provide, and we will see that it results in a novel kind of programming language.

### 14.3.1   The *Do* Formula

To handle complex actions in general, it is sufficient to show that for each complex action $A$ we care about, there is a formula of the situation calculus, which we call $Do(A, s, s')$, that says that action $A$ when started in situation $s$ can terminate legally in situation $s'$. Because complex actions can be nondeterministic, there may be more than one such $s'$. Consider, for example, the complex action

$$[\text{pickup}(b_1) \; ; \; \textit{if } \text{InRoom(kitchen)} \textit{ then } \text{putaway}(b_1) \textit{ else } \text{goto(kitchen)}].$$

For this action to start in situation $s$ and terminate legally in $s'$, the following sentence must be true:

$$
\begin{aligned}
&Poss(\text{pickup}(b_1), s) \;\wedge \\
&\quad [\,(\text{InRoom}(\text{kitchen}, do(\text{pickup}(b_1), s)) \\
&\qquad \wedge\; Poss(\text{putaway}(b_1), do(\text{pickup}(b_1), s)) \\
&\qquad \wedge\; s' = do(\text{putaway}(b_1), do(\text{pickup}(b_1), s))) \\
&\qquad\qquad\qquad \vee \\
&\quad\; (\neg\text{InRoom}(\text{kitchen}, do(\text{pickup}(b_1), s)) \\
&\qquad \wedge\; Poss(\text{goto}(\text{kitchen}), do(\text{pickup}(b_1), s)) \\
&\qquad \wedge\; s' = do(\text{goto}(\text{kitchen}), do(\text{pickup}(b_1), s)))\,]
\end{aligned}
$$

In general, we define the formula **Do** recursively on the structure of the complex action as follows:

1. For any primitive action $A$, we have

$$\mathbf{Do}(A, s, s') \overset{def}{=} Poss(A, s) \wedge s' = do(A, s).$$

2. For the sequential composition of complex actions $A$ and $B$, $[A \; ; \; B]$, we have

$$\mathbf{Do}([A \; ; \; B], s, s') \overset{def}{=} \exists s''. \; \mathbf{Do}(A, s, s'') \wedge \mathbf{Do}(B, s'', s').$$

3. For a conditional involving a test $\phi$ of the form $[if \; \phi \; then \; A \; else \; B]$, we have

$$\mathbf{Do}([if \; \phi \; then \; A \; else \; B], s, s') \overset{def}{=}$$
$$[\phi(s) \wedge \mathbf{Do}(A, s, s')] \vee [\neg\phi(s) \wedge \mathbf{Do}(B, s, s')].^{5}$$

4. For a test action, $[\phi?]$, determining if a condition $\phi$ currently holds, we have

$$\mathbf{Do}([\phi?], s, s') \overset{def}{=} \phi(s) \wedge s' = s.$$

5. For a nondeterministic branch to action $A$ or action $B$, $[A \mid B]$, we have

$$\mathbf{Do}([A \mid B], s, s') \overset{def}{=} \mathbf{Do}(A, s, s') \vee \mathbf{Do}(B, s, s').$$

6. For a nondeterministic choice of a value for variable $x$, $[\pi x. A]$, we have

$$\mathbf{Do}([\pi x. A], s, s') \overset{def}{=} \exists x. \mathbf{Do}(A, s, s').$$

7. For an iteration of the form $[while \; \phi \; do \; A]$, we have

$$\mathbf{Do}([while \; \phi \; do \; A], s, s') \overset{def}{=} \forall P\{\cdots \supset P(s, s')\}$$

where the ellipsis is an abbreviation for the conjunction of

$$\forall s_1. \; \neg\phi(s_1) \supset P(s_1, s_1)$$

$$\forall s_1, s_2, s_3. \; \phi(s_1) \wedge \mathbf{Do}(A, s_1, s_2) \wedge P(s_2, s_3) \supset P(s_1, s_3).^{6}$$

---

[5] If $\phi(s)$ is a formula of the situation calculus with a free variable $s$, then $\phi$ is that formula with the situation argument suppressed. For example, in a complex action we would use the test Broken($x$) instead of Broken($x, s$).

[6] The rule for iteration involves *second-order quantification*: The $P$ in this formula is a quantified predicate variable. The definition says that an iteration takes you from $s$ to $s'$ if and only if the smallest relation $P$ satisfying certain conditions does so. The details are not of concern here.

Similar rules can be given for recursive procedures, and even constructs involving concurrency and prioritized interrupts. The main point is that what it means to perform these complex actions can be fully specified in the language of the situation calculus. What we are giving, in effect, is a purely logical semantics for many of the constructs of traditional programming languages.

## 14.3.2  GOLOG

The formalism just presented gives us a programming language that we will call GOLOG, which generalizes conventional imperative programming languages.[7] It includes the usual imperative constructs (sequence, iteration, etc.), as well as nondeterminism and other features. The main difference, however, is that the primitive statements of GOLOG are not operations on internal states, like assignment statements or pointer updates, but rather primitive actions in the world, such as picking up a block. Moreover, what these primitive actions are supposed to do is not fixed in advance by the language designer, but is specified by the user separately by precondition and successor state axioms.

Given that the primitive actions are not fixed in advance or executed internally, it is not immediately obvious what it should mean to execute a GOLOG program $A$. There are two steps:

1. find a sequence of primitive actions $\vec{a}$ such that $\textbf{\textit{Do}}(A, S_0, do(\vec{a}, S_0))$ is entailed by the KB;

2. pass the sequence of actions $\vec{a}$ to a robot or simulator for actual execution in the world.

In other words, to execute a program we must first find a sequence of actions that would take us to a legal terminating situation for the program starting in the initial situation $S_0$, and then run that sequence.

Note that to find such a sequence it will be necessary to reason using the given precondition and effect axioms, performing both projection and legality testing. For example, suppose we have the program

$$[A \; ; \; \textit{if} \; \mathsf{Holding}(x) \; \textit{then} \; B \; \textit{else} \; C].$$

To decide between $B$ and $C$, we need to determine whether $\mathsf{Holding}(x, s)$ would be true in the situation that results from performing action $A$.

---

[7]The name comes from *Algol in logic*, after one of the original and influential programming languages.

### 14.3.3   An Example

To see how this would work, consider a simple example in a robotics domain involving three primitive actions, pickup($x$) (picking up a block), putonfloor($x$) (putting a block on the floor), and putontable($x$) (putting a block on the table), and three fluents, Holding($x,s$) (the robot is holding a block), OnFloor($x,s$) (a block is on the floor), and OnTable($x,s$) (a block is on the table).

The precondition axioms are the following:

- $Poss$(pickup($x$), $s$)  $\equiv$  $\forall z.\, \neg$Holding($z,s$);
- $Poss$(putonfloor($x$), $s$)  $\equiv$  Holding($x,s$);
- $Poss$(putontable($x$), $s$)  $\equiv$  Holding($x,s$).

The successor state axioms are the following:

- Holding($x, do(a,s)$)  $\equiv$  $a =$ pickup($x$) $\vee$
    Holding($x,s$) $\wedge\, a \neq$ putonfloor($x$) $\wedge\, a \neq$ putontable($x$);
- OnFloor($x, do(a,s)$)  $\equiv$  $a =$ putonfloor($x$) $\vee$
    OnFloor($x,s$) $\wedge\, a \neq$ pickup($x$);
- OnTable($x, do(a,s)$)  $\equiv$  $a =$ putontable($x$) $\vee$
    OnTable($x,s$) $\wedge\, a \neq$ pickup($x$).

We might also have the following facts about the initial situation:

- $\neg$Holding($x, S_0$);
- OnTable($x, S_0$)  $\equiv$  $(x = b_1) \vee (x = b_2)$.

So initially, the robot is not holding anything, and $b_1$ and $b_2$ are the only blocks on the table. Finally, we can consider two complex actions—removing a block and clearing the table:

- *proc* RemoveBlock($x$) : [pickup($x$) ; putonfloor($x$)];
- *proc* ClearTable : *while* $\exists x.$ OnTable($x$) *do*
    $\pi x$[OnTable($x$)? ; RemoveBlock($x$)].

This completes the specification of the example.

To execute the GOLOG program ClearTable, it is necessary to first find an appropriate terminating situation, $do(\vec{a}, S_0)$, which determines the actions $\vec{a}$ to perform. To find this situation, we can use Resolution theorem-proving with answer extraction for the query

$$KB \models \exists s.\ \boldsymbol{Do}(\text{ClearTable}, S_0, s).$$

We omit the details of this derivation, but the result will yield a value for $s$ like

$$s = do(\text{putonfloor}(b_2), do(\text{pickup}(b_2),$$
$$do(\text{putonfloor}(b_1), do(\text{pickup}(b_1), S_0))))$$

from which the desired sequence starting from $S_0$ is

$$\langle \text{pickup}(b_1), \text{putonfloor}(b_1), \text{pickup}(b_2), \text{putonfloor}(b_2) \rangle.$$

In a more general setting, an answer predicate could be necessary. In fact, in some cases it may not be possible to obtain a definite sequence of actions. This happens, for example, if what is known about the initial situation is that either block $b_1$ or block $b_2$ is on the table, but not which.

Observe that if what is known about the initial situation and the actions can be expressed as Horn clauses, the evaluation of GOLOG programs can be done directly in PROLOG. Instead of expanding $\boldsymbol{Do}(A, s, s')$ into a long formula of the situation calculus and then using Resolution, we write PROLOG clauses such as

```
do(A,S1,S2) :-                        /* for primitive actions */
    prim_action(A), poss(A,S1), S2=do(A,S1).
do(seq(A,B),S1,S2) :-                 /* for sequences */
    do(A,S1,S3), do(B,S3,S2).
do(while(F,A),S1,S2) :-               /* for while loops (test false) */
    not holds(F,S1), S2=S1.
do(while(F,A),S1,S2) :-               /* for while loops (test true) */
    holds(F,S1), do(seq(A,while(F,A)),S1,S2).
```

and so on. Then the PROLOG goal

```
?- do(clear_table,s0,S).
```

would return the binding for the final situation.

This idea of using Resolution with answer extraction to derive a sequence of actions to perform will be taken up again in the next chapter on planning. When the problem can be reduced to PROLOG, we get a convenient and efficient way of generating a sequence of actions. This has proven to be an effective method of providing high-level control for a robot.

## 14.4 BIBLIOGRAPHIC NOTES

The situation calculus was first introduced by McCarthy [276]. However, the variant of the situation calculus used in the text was developed by

Reiter (see [348] for a comprehensive treatment, and also Pirri and Reiter [328]). Under the McCarthy view, a situation is a complete *state* of the world at some point in time, while Reiter's view is that a situation is a *history* of actions (i.e., the sequence leading from the initial situation to the current situation). For a discussion of some of the shortcomings of the situation calculus, see Gelfond et al. [149].

The frame problem was first raised by McCarthy and Hayes [282]. Explanation closure axioms were suggested by Schubert [371] (see also [372]) following proposals by Haas [175] and Pednault [322]. The solution to the frame problem proposed by Reiter [347] extends these ideas with the introduction of successor state axioms.

For a discussion of circumscription and the situation calculus, see Baker [22, 23] (see also Kartha [210], and Kartha and Lifschitz [211]). Shanahan [379] gives a comprehensive treatment of the use of circumscription in the situation calculus and solutions to the frame problem. Frame fluents are discussed by Lifschitz [252]. Shoham [384] discusses the idea of *chronological ignorance* and minimization in reasoning about action.

In addition to the frame problem, related problems concerning reasoning about action have been investigated. The qualification problem was first discussed by McCarthy [277], and the ramification problem by Finger [131]. Recent work in this area has investigated the use of explicit notions of causality in dealing with these problems [256, 273, 274, 313, 364, 409].

The GOLOG language is introduced by Levesque et al. [246]. Reiter [348] gives an account of developments in reasoning about action leading to GOLOG and presents a number of GOLOG variants. Some important extensions of GOLOG include CONGOLOG (concurrency and interrupts) [92], INDIGOLOG (incremental deterministic) [93], STGOLOG (stochastic) [348, Chapter 12], DTGOLOG (decision theoretic) [38], and CCGOLOG (concurrent, continuous) [169]. Funge [137] introduces the Cognitive Modeling Language, which is influenced by GOLOG; he uses this language for animation and automated cinematography. GOLOG itself has been used to control mail delivery robots [237], a museum tour guide [62], and robot soccer robots [116]. LEGOLOG [245] is a system that uses GOLOG to control LEGO MINDSTORMS robots.

Alternative approaches to reasoning about action include the *event calculus* by Kowalski and Sergot [226], the $\mathcal{A}$ languages [24, 148], the features and fluents framework by Sandewall [363], and the Fluent Calculus [189] (see also Thielscher [410]).

The area of belief revision, mentioned briefly at the start of the chapter, has an extensive literature of its own. The main logic-based approach to belief revision is that developed by Alchourrón, Gärdenfors, and Makinson (commonly referred to as the AGM approach) [10, 141, 142, 144] (but see also [7, 8, 9]). A comprehensive text on this type of belief revision is Hansson [179]. The relationship between AGM belief revision and nonmonotonic reasoning is discussed in Makinson and Gärdenfors [263] and Rott [358]. Katsuno and Mendelzon [213] suggest that AGM belief revision is suited to reasoning about a static world in which a reasoning entity changes its beliefs due to mistakes or incompleteness in its beliefs. They introduce the idea of *belief update* as a distinct form of change for dynamic worlds in which the process of change is brought about due to actions that alter the world. It can be argued that AGM revision is an analogue of Bayesian conditionalization, whereas update is an analogue of Lewis's *imaging* [248]. There are various implementations of AGM belief revision systems [104, 105, 164, 424, 425]. For discussion of belief change in the situation calculus, see Shapiro et al. [380], which combines revision and update. Boutilier [37] also combines revision and update in a generalized framework (see also Friedman and Halpern [136]).

## 14.5 EXERCISES

In these exercises, and in the follow-up exercises of Chapter 15, we consider three application domains where we would like to be able to reason about action and change:

### Pots of Water

Consider a world with pots that may contain water. There is a single fluent, Contains, where Contains($p, w, s$) is intended to say that a pot $p$ contains $w$ liters of water in situation $s$. There are only two possible actions, which can always be executed: empty($p$), which discards all the water contained in the pot $p$, and transfer($p, p'$), which pours as much water as possible without spilling from pot $p$ to $p'$, with no change when $p = p'$. To simplify the formalization, we assume that the usual arithmetic constants, functions, and predicates are also available. (You may assume that axioms for these have already been provided or built in.)

### 15 Puzzle

The 15 puzzle consists of 15 consecutively numbered tiles located in a $4 \times 4$ grid. The object of the puzzle is to move the tiles within the grid so that each tile ends up at its correct location, as shown in Figure 14.1. The domain consists of *locations*, numbered 1 to 16, *tiles*, numbered 1 to 15, and, of course, actions and situations. There will be a single action move($t, l$) whose effect is to move tile $t$ to location $l$, when possible. We will also assume a single fluent, which is a function loc, where loc($t, s$) refers to the location of tile $t$ in situation $s$. The only other nonlogical terms we will use are the situation calculus predicate *Poss* and, to simplify the formalization, a predicate Adjacent($l_1, l_2$), which holds when location $l_1$ is one move away from location $l_2$. For example, location 5 is adjacent only

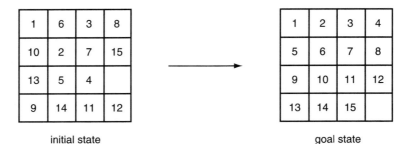

initial state                                    goal state

■ **FIGURE 14.1**

The 15 Puzzle

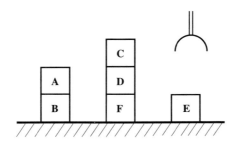

■ **FIGURE 14.2**

The Blocks World

to locations 1, 6, and 9. (You may assume that axioms for Adjacent have already been provided.)

Note that in the text we concentrated on fluents that were predicates. Here we have a fluent that is a function. Instead of writing $Loc(t, l, s)$, you will be writing $loc(t, s) = l$.

**Blocks World**

Imagine that we have a collection of blocks on a table and a robot arm that is capable of picking up blocks and putting them elsewhere, as shown in Figure 14.2.

We assume that the robot arm can hold at most one block at a time. We also assume that the robot can only pick up a block if there is no other block on top of it. Finally, we assume that a block can only support or be supported by at most one other block, but that the table surface is large enough that all blocks can be directly on the table. There are only two actions available: $puton(x, y)$, which picks up block $x$ and moves it onto block $y$, and $putonTable(x)$, which moves block $x$ onto the table. Similarly, we have only two fluents: $On(x, y, s)$, which holds when block $x$ is on block $y$, and $OnTable(x, s)$, which holds when block $x$ is on the table.

For each application, the questions are the same:

1. Write the precondition axioms for the actions.

2. Write the effect axioms for the actions.

3. Show how successor state axioms for the fluents would be derived from these effect axioms. Argue that the successor state axioms are not logically entailed by the effect axioms by briefly describing an interpretation where the effect axioms are satisfied but the successor state ones are not.

4. Show how frame axioms are logically entailed by the successor state axioms.

# CHAPTER 15

# PLANNING

■

---

■

■

When we explored reasoning about action in Chapter 14, we considered how a system could figure out what to do given a complex nondeterministic action to execute, by using what it knew about the world and the primitive actions at its disposal. In this chapter, we consider a related but more fundamental reasoning problem: how to figure out what to do to make some arbitrary condition true. This type of reasoning is usually called *planning*. The condition that we want to achieve is called the *goal*, and the sequence of actions we seek that will make the goal true is called a *plan*.

Planning is one of the most useful ways that an intelligent agent can take advantage of the knowledge it has and its ability to reason about actions and their consequences. If we think of Artificial Intelligence as the study of intelligent behavior achieved through computational means, then planning is central to this study, because it is concerned precisely with generating intelligent behavior and, in particular, with using what is known to find a course of action that will achieve some goal. The knowledge in this case involves information about the world, about how actions affect the world, about potentially complex sequences of events, and about interacting actions and entities, including other agents.

In the real world, because our actions are not totally guaranteed to have certain effects and because we simply cannot know everything there is to know about a situation, planning is usually an uncertain enterprise, and it requires attention to many of the issues we have covered in earlier chapters, such as defaults and reasoning under uncertainty. Moreover, planning in the real world involves trying to determine what future states of the world will be like, but also observing the world as plans are being executed and replanning as necessary. Nonetheless, the basic capabilities needed to begin considering planning are already available to us.

## 15.1 PLANNING IN THE SITUATION CALCULUS

Given its appropriateness for representing dynamically changing worlds, the situation calculus is an obvious candidate to support planning. We can use it to represent what is known about the current state of the world and the available actions.

The planning task can be formulated in the language of the situation calculus as follows:

Given a formula, $Goal(s)$, of the situation calculus with a single free variable, $s$, find a sequence of actions, $\vec{a} = \langle a_1, \ldots, a_n \rangle$, such that

$$\text{KB} \models Goal(do(\vec{a}, S_0)) \wedge Legal(do(\vec{a}, S_0))$$

where $do(\vec{a}, S_0)$ abbreviates $do(a_n, do(a_{n-1}, \ldots, do(a_1, S_0) \ldots))$, and $Legal(do(\vec{a}, S_0))$ abbreviates $\bigwedge_{i=1}^{n} Poss(a_i, do(\langle a_1, \ldots, a_{i-1} \rangle, S_0))$.

In other words, given a goal formula, we wish to find a sequence of actions such that it follows from what is known that

1. the goal formula will hold in the situation that results from executing the actions in sequence starting in the initial state, and

2. it is possible to execute each action in the appropriate situation (that is, each action's preconditions are satisfied).

Note that this definition says nothing about the structure of the KB, for example, whether it represents complete knowledge about the initial situation.

Having formulated the task this way, to do the planning we can use Resolution theorem-proving with answer extraction for the following query:

$$\text{KB} \models \exists s.\ Goal(s) \wedge Legal(s).$$

As with the execution of complex actions in Chapter 14, if the extracted answer is of the form $do(\vec{a}, S_0)$, then $\vec{a}$ is a correct plan. But as we will see in Section 15.4.2, there can be cases where the existential is entailed, but where the planning task is impossible because of incomplete knowledge. In other words, the goal can be achieved, but we can't find a specific way that is guaranteed to achieve it.

### 15.1.1  An Example

Let us examine how this version of planning might work in the simple world depicted in Figure 15.1. A robot can roll from room to room, possibly pushing objects through doorways between the rooms. In such a world, there are two actions: pushThru($x, d, r_1, r_2$), in which the robot pushes object $x$ through doorway $d$ from room $r_1$ to $r_2$, and goThru($d, r_1, r_2$), in which the robot rolls through doorway $d$ from room $r_1$ to $r_2$. To be able to execute either action, $d$ must be the doorway connecting $r_1$ and $r_2$, and the robot must be located in $r_1$. After successfully completing either action, the robot ends up in room $r_2$. In addition, for the action pushThru, the object $x$ must be located initially in room $r_1$, and will also end up in room $r_2$.

We can formalize these properties of the world in the situation calculus using the following two precondition axioms:

$$Poss(\text{goThru}(d, r_1, r_2), s) \equiv$$
$$\text{Connected}(d, r_1, r_2) \wedge \text{InRoom}(\text{robot}, r_1, s);$$

$$Poss(\text{pushThru}(x, d, r_1, r_2), s) \equiv$$
$$\text{Connected}(d, r_1, r_2) \wedge \text{InRoom}(\text{robot}, r_1, s) \wedge \text{InRoom}(x, r_1, s).$$

In this formulation, we use a single fluent, InRoom($x, r, s$), with the following successor state axiom:

$$\text{InRoom}(x, r, do(a, s)) \equiv$$
$$\Pi(x, a, r) \vee (\text{InRoom}(x, r, s) \wedge \neg\exists r'. \, (r \neq r') \wedge \Pi(x, a, r')),$$

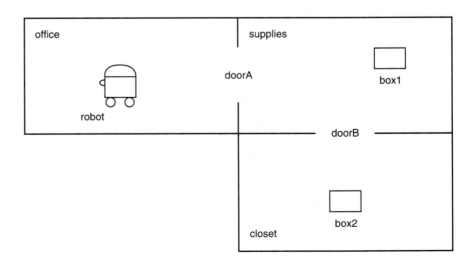

■ **FIGURE 15.1**

A Simple Robot World

where $\Pi(x,a,r)$ is the formula

$$x = \text{robot} \wedge \exists d \exists r_1.\ a = \text{goThru}(d,r_1,r)$$
$$\vee \quad x = \text{robot} \wedge \exists d \exists r_1 \exists y.\ a = \text{pushThru}(y,d,r_1,r)$$
$$\vee \quad \exists d \exists r_1.\ a = \text{pushThru}(x,d,r_1,r).$$

In other words, the robot is in room $r$ after an action if that action was either a goThru or a pushThru to $r$, or the robot was already in $r$ and the action was not a goThru or a pushThru to some other $r'$. For any other object, the object is in room $r$ after an action if that action was a pushThru to $r$ for that object, or the object was already in $r$ and the action was not a pushThru to some other $r'$ for that object.

Our KB should also contain facts about the specific initial situation depicted in Figure 15.1: There are three rooms—an office, a supply room, and a closet—two doors, two boxes, and the robot, with their locations as depicted. Finally, the KB needs to state that the robot and boxes are distinct objects and, so that the solution to the frame problem presented in Chapter 14 applies, that goThru and pushThru are distinct actions.

## 15.1.2 Using Resolution

Now suppose that we want to get some box into the office, that is, the goal we would like to achieve is

$$\exists x.\ \text{Box}(x) \wedge \text{InRoom}(x, \text{office}, s).$$

To use Resolution to find a plan to achieve this goal, we must first convert the KB to CNF. Most of this is straightforward, except for the successor state axiom, which expands to a set of clauses that includes the following (for one direction of the $\equiv$ formula only):

$$[x \neq \text{robot}, a \neq \text{goThru}(d,r_1,r_2),\ \text{InRoom}(x,r_2,do(a,s))]$$
$$[x \neq \text{robot}, a \neq \text{pushThru}(y,d,r_1,r_2),\ \text{InRoom}(x,r_2,do(a,s))]$$
$$[a \neq \text{pushThru}(x,d,r_1,r_2),\ \text{InRoom}(x,r_2,do(a,s))]$$
$$[\neg\text{InRoom}(x,r,s),\ x = \text{robot},\ a = \text{pushThru}(x,t_0,t_1,t_2),$$
$$\text{InRoom}(x,r,do(a,s))]$$
$$[\neg\text{InRoom}(x,r,s),\ a = \text{goThru}(t_3,t_4,t_5),\ a = \text{pushThru}(t_6,t_7,t_8,t_9),$$
$$\text{InRoom}(x,r,do(a,s))].$$

The $t_i$ here are Skolem terms of the form $f_i(x,r,a,s)$ arising from the existentials in the subformula $\Pi(x,a,r)$.

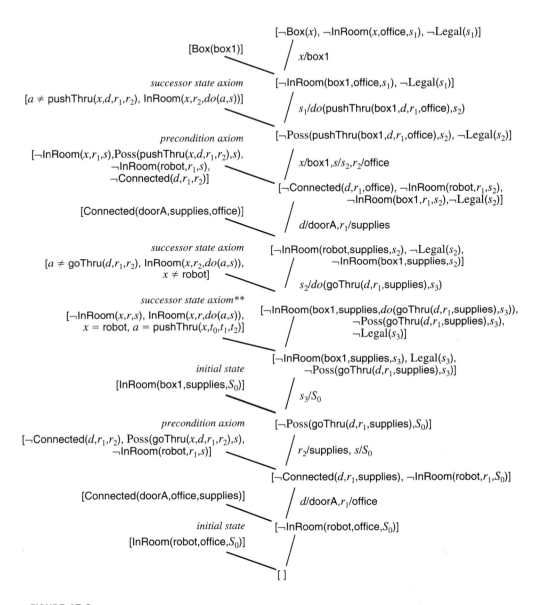

■ **FIGURE 15.2**

Planning Using Resolution

The Resolution proof tree for this planning problem is sketched in Figure 15.2. The formulas on the left are taken from the KB, and those on the right start with the negation of the formula to be proved:

$$\exists s_1 \exists x.\ \mathrm{Box}(x) \wedge \mathrm{InRoom}(x, \mathrm{office}, s_1) \wedge \mathit{Legal}(s_1).$$

Notice that whenever a *Legal* literal is derived, it is expanded to a clause containing *Poss* or to the empty clause in the case of $\neg Legal(S_0)$. For example, in the second step of the derivation, $s_1$ is replaced by a term of the form $do(\ldots, s_2)$, and so $\neg Legal(s_1)$ expands to a clause containing $\neg Poss(\ldots, s_2)$ and $\neg Legal(s_2)$. Also observe that the successor state axioms in the KB use equality, which would require some additional machinery (as explained in Chapter 4), and which we have omitted from the diagram here for simplicity.

To keep the diagram simple, we have also not included an answer predicate in this derivation. Looking at the bindings on the right side, it can be seen that the correct substitution for $s_1$ is

$$do(\mathsf{pushThru}(\mathsf{box1}, \mathsf{doorA}, \mathsf{supplies}, \mathsf{office}),$$
$$do(\mathsf{goThru}(\mathsf{doorA}, \mathsf{office}, \mathsf{supplies}), S_0)).$$

and so the plan is to first perform the goThru action and then the pushThru one.

All but one of the facts in this derivation (including a definition of *Legal*) can be expressed as Horn clauses. The final use of the successor state axiom has two positive equality literals. However, by using negation as failure to deal with the inequalities, we can use a PROLOG program directly to generate a plan, as shown in Figure 15.3. The goal would be

```
?- box(X), inRoom(X,office,S), legal(S).
```

and the result of the computation would then be

```
X = box1
S = do(pushThru(box1,doorA,supplies,office),
       do(goThru(doorA,office,supplies),s0))
```

as it was earlier. Using PROLOG in this way is very delicate, however. A small change in the ordering of clauses or literals can easily cause the depth-first search strategy to go down an infinite branch.

In fact, more generally, using Resolution theorem-proving over the situation calculus for planning is rarely practical for two principal reasons. First, we are required to explicitly draw conclusions about what is not changed by doing actions. We saw this in the derivation (in the final use of the successor state axiom, marked with ** in Figure 15.2), where we concluded that the robot moving from the office to the supply room did not change the location of the box (and so the box was still ready to be pushed into the office). In this case, there was only one action and one box to worry about; in a larger setting, we may have to reason about the properties of many objects remaining unaffected after the performance of many actions.

```
inRoom(robot,office,s0).
box(box1).   inRoom(box1,supplies,s0).
box(box2).   inRoom(box2,closet,s0).
connected(doorA,office,supplies).
connected(doorA,supplies,office).
connected(doorB,closet,supplies).
connected(doorB,supplies,closet).
poss(goThru(D,R1,R2),S) :-
    connected(D,R1,R2), inRoom(robot,R1,S).
poss(pushThru(X,D,R1,R2),S) :-
    connected(D,R1,R2), inRoom(robot,R1,S),
    inRoom(X,R1,S).
inRoom(X,R2,do(A,S)) :-
    X=robot, A=goThru(D,R1,R2).
inRoom(X,R2,do(A,S)) :-
    X=robot, A=pushThru(Y,D,R1,R2).
inRoom(X,R2,do(A,S)) :-
    A=pushThru(X,D,R1,R2).
inRoom(X,R,do(A,S)) :- inRoom(X,R,S),
    not (X=robot),
    not (A=pushThru(X,T0,T1,T2)).
inRoom(X,R,do(A,S)) :- inRoom(X,R,S),
    not (A=goThru(T3,T4,T5)),
    not (A=pushThru(T6,T7,T8,T9)).
legal(s0).
legal(do(A,S)) :- poss(A,S), legal(S).
```

■ **FIGURE 15.3**

Planning Using PROLOG

Second, and more serious, the search for a sequence of actions using Resolution (or the PROLOG variant) is completely unstructured. Notice, for example, that in the derivation, the first important choice that was made was to bind the $x$ to box1. If your goal is to get some box into the office, it is silly to first decide on a box and then search for a sequence of actions that will work for that box. Much better would be to decide on the box opportunistically based on the current situation and what else needs doing. In some cases the search should work backward from the goal; in others, it should work forward from the current state. Of course, all of this search should be quite separate from the search that is needed to reason about what does or does not hold in any given state.

In the next section, we deal with the first of these issues. We deal with searching for a plan effectively in Section 15.3.

## 15.2  THE STRIPS REPRESENTATION

STRIPS is an alternative representation to the pure situation calculus for planning. It derives from work on a mobile robot (called "Shakey") at SRI International in the 1960s. In STRIPS, we assume that the world we are trying to deal with satisfies the following criteria:

- only one action can occur at a time;

- actions are effectively instantaneous;

- nothing changes except as the result of planned actions.

In this context, this has been called the *STRIPS assumption*, but it clearly applies just as well to our version of the situation calculus. What really distinguishes STRIPS from the situation calculus is that knowledge about the initial state of the world is required to be complete, and knowledge about the effects and noneffects of actions is required to be in a specific form. In what follows, we use a very simple version of the representation, although many of the advantages we claim for it hold more generally.

In STRIPS, we do not represent histories of the world like we do in the situation calculus, but rather we deal with a single world state at a time. The world state is represented by what is called a *world model*, which is a set of ground atomic formulas, similar to a database of facts in the PLANNER system of Chapter 6 and the working memory of a production system of Chapter 7. These facts can be thought of as ground fluents (with the situation argument suppressed) under closed-world, unique-name, and domain-closure assumptions (as in Chapter 11). For the example depicted in Figure 15.1, we would have the following initial world model, $DB_0$:

InRoom(box1,supplies)        Box(box1)
InRoom(box2,closet)          Box(box2)
InRoom(robot,office)
Connected(doorA,office,supplies)    Connected(doorA,supplies,office)
Connected(doorB,closet,supplies)    Connected(doorA,supplies,closet)

In this case there is no need to distinguish between a fluent (like InRoom) and a predicate that is unaffected by any action (like Box).

Further, in STRIPS, actions are not represented explicitly as part of the world model, which means that we cannot reason about them directly. Instead, actions are thought of as *operators* that syntactically transform world models. An operator takes the world model database for some state and transforms it into a database representing the successor state. The main benefit of this way of representing and reasoning about plans is that it avoids frame axioms: An operator will change what it needs to in the database, and thereby leave the rest unaffected.

STRIPS operators are specified by pre- and postconditions. The *pre-conditions* are sets of atomic formulas of the language that need to hold before the operator can apply. The postconditions come in two parts: a *delete list*, which is a set of atomic formulas to be removed from the database, and an *add list*, which is a set of atomic formulas to be added to the database. The delete list represents properties of the world state that no longer hold after the operator is applied, and the add list represents new properties of the world state that will hold after the operator is applied. For the earlier example, we would have the following two operators:

pushThru$(x, d, r_1, r_2)$

> *Precondition*: InRoom(robot, $r_1$), InRoom($x, r_1$), Connected($d, r_1, r_2$)
>
> *Delete list*: InRoom(robot, $r_1$), InRoom($x, r_1$)
>
> *Add list*: InRoom(robot, $r_2$), InRoom($x, r_2$)

goThru$(d, r_1, r_2)$

> *Precondition*: InRoom(robot, $r_1$), Connected($d, r_1, r_2$)
>
> *Delete list*: InRoom(robot, $r_1$)
>
> *Add list*: InRoom(robot, $r_2$)

Note that the arguments of operators are variables that can appear in the pre- and postcondition formulas.[1]

A STRIPS problem, then, is represented by an initial world model database, a set of operators, and a goal formula. A solution to the problem is a set of operators that can be applied in sequence starting with the initial world model without violating any of the preconditions, and which results in a world model that satisfies the goal formula.

More precisely, a STRIPS problem is characterized by $\langle$DB$_0$, *Operators*, *Goal*$\rangle$, where DB$_0$ is a list of ground atoms, *Goal* is a list of atoms (whose free variables are understood existentially), and *Operators* is a list of operators of the form $\langle$*Act, Pre, Add, Del*$\rangle$, where *Act* is the name of the operator and *Pre*, *Add*, and *Del* are lists of atoms. A solution is a sequence

$$\langle Act_1\theta_1, \ldots, Act_n\theta_n \rangle$$

where $Act_i$ is the name of an operator in the list (with $Pre_i$, $Add_i$, and $Del_i$ as the other corresponding components) and $\theta_i$ is a substitution of constants for the variables in that operator, and where the sequence

---

[1]We use the term *operator* to describe both a generic action (with variables as arguments) and particular instances of the action (with constants as arguments).

satisfies the following:

- for all $1 \leq i \leq n$, $\mathrm{DB}_i = \mathrm{DB}_{i-1} + Add_i\theta_i - Del_i\theta_i$;
- for all $1 \leq i \leq n$, $Pre_i\theta_i \subseteq \mathrm{DB}_{i-1}$;
- for some $\theta$, $Goal\theta \subseteq \mathrm{DB}_n$.

The $+$ and $-$ in this definition refer to the union and difference of lists, respectively.

## 15.2.1   Progressive Planning

The characterization of a solution to the STRIPS planning problem immediately suggests the planning procedure shown in Figure 15.4. For simplicity, we have left out the details concerning the substitutions of variables. This type of planner is called a *progressive* planner, because it works by progressing the initial world model forward until we obtain a world model that satisfies the goal formula.

Consider once again the planning problem in Figure 15.1. If called with the initial world model ($\mathrm{DB}_0$) and the goal

$$Box(x), \; InRoom(x, office),$$

the progressive planner would first confirm that the goal is not yet satisfied and then, within the loop, eventually get to the operator goThru(doorA,office,supplies), whose precondition is satisfied in the DB.

> **input:** a world model and a goal formula
>
> **output:** a plan or fail
>
> ProgPlan[DB,*Goal*] =
>    **if** *Goal* $\subseteq$ DB **then return** the empty plan
>    **for** each operator $\langle Act, Pre, Add, Del \rangle$ such that $Pre \subseteq$ DB **do**
>       let $\mathrm{DB}' = \mathrm{DB} + Add - Del$
>       let *Plan* = ProgPlan[DB', *Goal*]
>       **if** *Plan* $\neq$ fail **then return** $Act \cdot Plan$
>    **end for**
>    **return** fail

▪ **FIGURE 15.4**

A Depth-First Progressive Planner

It then would call itself recursively with the following progressed world model:

InRoom(box1,supplies)          Box(box1)
InRoom(box2,closet)            Box(box2)
InRoom(robot,supplies)
Connected(doorA,office,supplies)    Connected(doorA,supplies,office)
Connected(doorB,closet,supplies)    Connected(doorA,supplies,closet)

The goal is still not satisfied, and the procedure then continues and gets to the operator pushThru(box1,doorA,supplies,office), whose precondition is satisfied in the progressed DB. It would then call itself recursively with a new world model:

InRoom(box1,office)            Box(box1)
InRoom(box2,closet)            Box(box2)
InRoom(robot,office)
Connected(doorA,office,supplies)    Connected(doorA,supplies,office)
Connected(doorB,closet,supplies)    Connected(doorA,supplies,closet)

At this point, the goal formula is satisfied, and the procedure unwinds successfully and produces the expected plan.

## 15.2.2 Regressive Planning

In some applications, it may be advantageous to use a planner that works backward from the goal rather than forward from the initial state. The process of working backward, repeatedly simplifying the goal until we obtain one that is satisfied in the initial state, is called *goal regression*. The planner shown in Figure 15.5 is called a *regressive* planner. In this case, the first operator we consider is the last one in the plan. This operator obviously must not delete any atomic formula that appears in the goal. Furthermore, to be able to use this operator, we must ensure that its preconditions will be satisfied; they become part of the next goal. However, the formulas in the add list of the operator we are considering will be handled by that operator, so they can be removed from the goal as we regress it.

If called with the initial world model from Figure 15.1 and the goal

$$Box(x), InRoom(x, office),$$

the regressive planner would first confirm that the goal is not satisfied and then, within the loop, eventually get to pushThru(box1,doorA,supplies,

**input:** a world model and a goal formula

**output:** a plan, or fail

RegrPlan[DB,*Goal*] =
  **if** *Goal* ⊆ DB **then return** the empty plan
  **for** each operator ⟨*Act, Pre, Add, Del*⟩ such that *Del* ∩ *Goal* = {} **do**
    let *Goal′* = *Goal* + *Pre* − *Add*
    let *Plan* = RegrPlan[DB, *Goal′*]
    **if** *Plan* ≠ fail **then return** *Plan* · *Act*
  **end for**
  **return** fail

---

▪ **FIGURE 15.5**

---

A Depth-First Regressive Planner

office), whose delete list does not intersect with the goal.[2] It then would call itself recursively with the following regressed goal:

Box(box1), InRoom(robot,supplies), InRoom(box1,supplies),
Connected(doorA,supplies,office).

The goal is still not satisfied in the initial world model, so the procedure continues and, within the loop, eventually gets to the operator goThru(doorA,office,supplies), whose delete list does not intersect with the current goal. It would then call itself recursively with a new regressed goal:

Box(box1), InRoom(robot,office), InRoom(box1,supplies),
Connected(doorA,supplies,office), Connected(doorA,office,supplies).

At this point, the goal formula is satisfied in the initial world model, and the procedure unwinds successfully and produces the expected plan.

---

## 15.3  PLANNING AS A REASONING TASK

Although the two planners just presented (or their breadth-first variants) work much better in practice than the Resolution-based planner considered earlier, neither of them works very well on large problems.

---

[2]As before, we are omitting details about variable bindings. A more realistic version would certainly leave the *x* in the goal unbound at this point, for example.

This is not too surprising, because it can be shown that the planning task is NP-hard, even for the simple version of STRIPS we have considered, and even when the STRIPS operators have no variables. It is therefore extremely unlikely that there is *any* procedure that will work well in all cases, as this would immediately lead to a corresponding procedure for satisfiability.[3]

As with deductive reasoning, there are essentially two options we can consider: We can do our best to make the search as effective as possible, especially by avoiding redundancy in the search, or we can make the planning problem easier by allowing the user to provide control information.

## 15.3.1 Avoiding Redundant Search

One major source of redundancy is the fact that actions in a plan tend to be independent and can be performed in different orders. If the goal is to get both box1 and box2 into the office, we can push box1 first or push box2 first. The problem is that when searching for a sequence of actions (either progressing a world model or regressing a goal), we consider totally ordered sequences of actions. Before we can rule out a collection of actions as inappropriate for some goal, we end up considering many permutations of those same actions.

To deal with this issue, let us consider a new type of plan, which is a finite set of actions that are only partially ordered. Because such a plan is not a linear sequence of actions, it is sometimes called a *nonlinear plan*. In searching for such a plan, we order one action before another only if we are required to do so. For getting the two boxes into the office, for example, we would want a plan with two parallel branches, one for each box. Within each branch, however, the moving actions(s) of the robot to the appropriate room would need to occur strictly before the corresponding pushing action(s).

To generate this type of plan, a *partial-order planner* is often used. In a partial-order planner, we start with an incomplete plan, consisting of the initial world model at one end and the goal at the other end. At each step, we insert new actions into the plan and new constraints on when that action needs to take place relative to the other actions in the plan, until we have filled all the gaps from one end to the other. It is worth noting, however, that the efficacy of this approach to planning is still somewhat controversial because of the amount of extra bookkeeping it appears to require.

A second source of redundancy concerns applying sequences of actions repeatedly. Consider, for example, getting a box into the office.

---

[3]One popular planning method involves encoding the task directly as a satisfiability problem and using satisfiability procedures to find a plan.

This always involves the same operators: some number of goThru actions followed by a corresponding number of pushThru actions. Furthermore, this sequence as a whole has a fixed precondition and postcondition that can be calculated once and for all from the component operators. The authors of STRIPS considered an approach to the reuse of such sequences of actions and created a set of macro-operators, or MACROPS, which were parameterized and abstracted sequences of operators. Although adding macro-operators to a planning problem means that a larger number of operators will need to be considered, if they are chosen wisely the resulting plans can be much shorter. Indeed, many of the practical planning systems work primarily by assembling precompiled plan fragments from a library of macro-operators.

## 15.3.2  Application-Dependent Control

Even with careful attention to redundancy in the search, planning remains impractical for many applications. Often the only way to make planning effective is to make the problem easier, for example, by giving the planner explicit guidance on how to search for a solution. We can think of the macro-operators, for example, as *suggesting* to the planner a sequence to use to get a box into a room. Another option is to use domain-dependent heuristic search information to rank order the possibilities in terms of estimated likelihood of success, so that we can explore the most likely candidates first.

In some cases, we can be more definite. Suppose, for example, we wish to reorganize all of the boxes in a certain distant room. We might tell the planner that it should handle this by first planning on getting to the distant room (ignoring any action dealing with the boxes) and only then planning on reorganizing the boxes (ignoring any action involving motion to other rooms). As with the procedural control of Chapter 6, constraints of this sort clearly simplify the search by ruling out various sequences of action.

In fact, we can imagine two extreme versions of this guidance. At one extreme, we let the planner search for any sequence of actions, with no constraints; at the other extreme, the guidance we give to a planner would specify a complete sequence of actions, where no search would be required at all. This idea does not require us to use STRIPS, of course, and the situation calculus, augmented with the GOLOG programming language, provides a convenient notation for expressing application-dependent search strategies.

Consider the following highly nondeterministic GOLOG program:

$$while \ \neg Goal \ do \ \{\pi a. \ a\}.$$

The body of the loop says that we should pick an action $a$ nondeterministically, and then do $a$. To execute the entire program, we need to find a sequence of actions corresponding to performing the loop body repeatedly, ending up in a final situation $s$ where $Goal(s)$ is true. But this is no more and no less than the planning task. So using GOLOG, we can represent guidance to a planner at various levels of specificity. This program provides no guidance at all. On the other hand, the deterministic program

$$\{ \quad \text{goThru}(\text{doorA}, \text{office}, \text{supplies}) \, ;$$

$$\text{pushThru}(\text{box1}, \text{doorA}, \text{supplies}, \text{office}) \, \}$$

requires no search at all. In between, however, we would like to provide some application-dependent guidance, perhaps using heuristic search information, leaving a more manageable search problem.

One convenient way to control the search process during planning is by using what is called *forward filtering*. The idea is to modify very slightly the *while* program so that not every action $a$ whose precondition is satisfied can be selected as the next action to perform in the sequence, but only those actions that also satisfy some application-dependent criterion:

$$while \ \neg Goal \ do \ \{\pi a. \ Acceptable(a)? \, ; \, a\}.$$

The intent is that the fluent $Acceptable(a, s)$ should be defined by the user to filter out actions that may be legal but are not useful at this point in the plan. For example, if we want to tell the planner that it first needs to get to the closet and only then consider moving any boxes, we might have something like the following in the KB:

$$Acceptable(a, s) \ \equiv \ \text{InRoom}(\text{robot}, \text{closet}, s) \ \wedge \ \text{BlockAction}(a)$$
$$\vee \ \neg \text{InRoom}(\text{robot}, \text{closet}, s) \ \wedge \ \text{MoveAction}(a),$$

for some suitable BlockAction and MoveAction predicates. Of course, defining an *Acceptable* properly for any particular application is not easy, and requires a deep understanding of how to solve planning problems in that application.

We can use the idea of forward filtering to define a complete progressive planner in GOLOG. The following procedure DFPlan is a recursive variant of the earlier *while* loop that takes as an argument a bound on the length of the action sequence it will consider. It then does a depth-first search for a plan of that length or shorter:

$$proc \ \text{DFPlan}(n) :$$

$$Goal? \ | \ \{(n > 0)? \, ; \, \pi a \ (Acceptable(a)? \, ; \, a) \, ; \, \text{DFPlan}(n - 1)\}.$$

Of course, the plan it finds need not be the shortest one that works. To get the shortest plan, it would be necessary to first look for plans of a certain length and only then look for longer ones:

*proc* IDPlan($n$) : IDPlan′($0, n$)

*proc* IDPlan′($m, n$) : DFPlan($m$) | {($m < n$)? ; IDPlan′($m + 1, n$)}.

The procedure IDPlan does a form of search called *iterative deepening*. It uses depth-first search (that is, DFPlan) at ever larger depths as a way of providing many of the advantages of breadth-first search.

## 15.4 BEYOND THE BASICS

In this final section, we briefly consider a small number of more advanced topics in planning.

### 15.4.1 Hierarchical Planning

The basic mechanisms of planning that we have covered so far, even including attempts to simplify the process with macro-operators, still preserve all detail needed to solve a problem all the way through the process. In reality, attention to too much detail can derail a planner to the point of uselessness. It would be much better, if possible, to first search through an *abstraction space*, where unimportant details were suppressed. Once a solution in the abstraction space were found, all we would have to do would be to account for the details of the linkup of the steps.

In an attempt to separate levels of abstraction of the problem in the planning process, the STRIPS team invented the ABSTRIPS approach. The details are not important here, but we can note a few of the elements of this approach. First, preconditions in the abstraction space have fewer literals than those in the ground space; thus they should be less taxing on the planner. For example, in the case of pushThru, at the highest level of abstraction the operator is applicable whenever an object is pushable and a door exists; without those basic conditions, the operator is not even worth considering. At a lower level of abstraction, like the one we used in our earlier example, the robot and object have to be in the same room, which must be connected by a door to the target room. At an even finer-grained level of detail, it would be important to ascertain whether the door was open (and attempt to open it if not). But that is really not relevant until we have a plan that involves going through the door with the object. Finally, in the least abstract representation, it would be important to get the robot right next to the object, and both the robot and object right next to the doorway, so that they could move through it.

## 15.4.2 Conditional Planning

In many applications, there may not be enough information available to plan a full course of action to achieve some goal. For example, in our robot domain, imagine that each box has a printed label on it that says either office or closet, and suppose our goal is to get box1 into the room printed on its label. With no further information, the full advance planning task is impossible, because we have no way of knowing where the box should end up. However, we do know that a sequence of actions exists that will achieve the goal, namely, to go into the supply room and push the box either to the office or to the closet. If we were to use Resolution with answer extraction for this example, the existential query would succeed, but we would end up with a clause with two answer literals, corresponding to the two possible sequences of action.

But now imagine that our robot is equipped with a sensor of some sort that tells it whether or not there is a box located in the same room with a label on it that says office. In this case, we would now like to say that the planning task, or a generalization of it, is possible. The plan that we expect, however, is not a linear sequence of actions, but is tree-structured, based on the outcome of sensors: Go to the supply room, and if the sensor indicates the presence of a box labeled office, then push that box into the office, and otherwise push the box into the closet. This type of branching plan is called a *conditional plan*, and a planner that can generate one is called a *conditional planner*.

There are various ways of making this notion precise, but perhaps the simplest is to extend the language of situation calculus so that instead of just having terms $S_0$ and $do(a, s)$ denoting situations, we also have terms of the form $cdo(p, s)$, where $p$ is a tree-structured conditional plan of some sort. The situation denoted by this term would depend on the outcome of the sensors involved, which of course would need to be specified. To describe, for example, the sensor from the previous paragraph, we might state something like the following:

$$\text{Fires}(\text{sensor1}, s) \equiv \exists x \exists r. \, \text{InRoom}(\text{robot}, r, s) \wedge$$
$$\text{Box}(x) \wedge \text{InRoom}(x, r, s) \wedge \text{Label}(x, \text{office}).$$

With terms like $cdo(p, s)$ in the language, we could once again use Resolution with answer extraction to do planning. How to do conditional planning *efficiently*, on the other hand, is a much more difficult question.

### 15.4.3  "Even the Best-Laid Plans …"

Situation calculus representations, and especially STRIPS, make many restrictive assumptions. As discussed in our section on complex actions, there are many aspects of action that bear investigation and may potentially impact the ability of an AI agent to reason appropriately about the world. Among the many issues in real-world planning that are currently under active investigation we find things like simultaneous interacting actions (e.g., lifting a piano, opening a doorlatch where the key and knob must be turned at the same time), external events, nondeterministic actions or those with probabilistic outcomes, noninstantaneous actions, nonstatic predicates, plans that explicitly include time, and reasoning about termination.

An even more fundamental challenge for planning is the suggestion made by some that explicit, symbolic production of formal plans is something to be avoided altogether. This is generally a reaction to the computational complexity of the underlying planning task. Some advocate instead the idea of a more "reactive" system, which observes conditions and just "reacts" by deciding—or looking up—what to do next. This one-step-at-a-time-like process is more robust in the face of unexpected changes in the environment. A reactive system could be implemented with a kind of "universal plan"—a large lookup table (or Boolean circuit) that tells you exactly what to do based on conditions. In some cases where they have been tried, reactive systems have had impressive performance on certain low-level problems like learning to walk; they have even appeared intelligent in their behavior. At the current time, though, it is unclear how far one can go with such an approach and what its intrinsic limitations are.

## 15.5  BIBLIOGRAPHIC NOTES

The classical work on planning in AI is by Green [166], who related planning to theorem-proving. An early and influential system for planning was STRIPS [128] (see also [129]), which was used in the "Shakey" robotics project [310]. For a formalization of STRIPS, see [251].

For early surveys of planning, see the review article by Georgeff [155] and the collection of readings by Allen et al. [12]. A more recent treatment is given by Dean and Wellman [97]. The computational complexity of STRIPS was considered by Bylander [63]. The complexity of planning in the popular blocks-world domain is discussed by Slaney and Thiébaux [389].

The idea of regressive planning can be traced to Waldinger [417]. Planning as satisfiability was introduced by Kautz and Selman [214], and partial-order planning by Sacerdoti [360]. For hierarchical planning and abstraction spaces, see [361]. A planning method based on graph techniques was introduced by Blum and Furst [30]. Recent approaches have introduced the use of model-checking in planning [329]. Search methods like iterative deepening, depth-first search, and breadth-first search are covered in most textbooks on AI (see the references in Chapter 1).

Wilkins's SIPE [423] was an early planner with a continuing long history of research and real-world impact. The ARPA/Rome Laboratory Planning Initiative (ARPI) [407] also led to implementations of planners used in important applications. The state of the art in planning is tested at the AIPS Planning Competition [19]. Currently, among the fastest planners are TLPLAN by Bacchus and Kabanza [20, 21], which makes use of forward filtering, and TALPLANNER [106], which is based on similar ideas.

In contrast to the more "classical" work on planning, the reactive planning approach argues against the use of representation to do any sort of lookahead (see, for example, Brooks [58]). The universal planning idea is due to Schoppers [369] (see [158] for a critique).

## 15.6 EXERCISES

These exercises are continuations of the exercises from Chapter 14. For each application, we consider a planning problem involving an initial setup and a goal.

### Pots of Water

Imagine that in the initial situation, we have two pots, a 5-liter one filled with water and an empty 2-liter one. Our goal is to obtain 1 liter of water in the 2-liter pot.

### 15 Puzzle

Assume that every tile is initially placed in its correct position, except for tile 9 in location 13, tile 13 in location 14, tile 14 in location 15, and tile 15 in location 16. The goal, of course, is to get every tile placed correctly.

### Blocks World

In the initial situation, the blocks are arranged as in Figure 14.2. The goal is to get them arranged as in Figure 15.6.

For each application, the questions are the same:

**1.** Write a sentence of the situation calculus of the form $\exists s.\, \alpha$ that asserts the existence of the final goal situation.

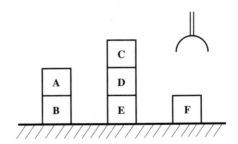

■ **FIGURE 15.6**

The Blocks-World Goal

2. Write a ground situation term $e$ (that is, a term that is either $S_0$ or of the form $do(a, e')$, where $a$ is a ground action term and $e'$ is itself a ground situation term) such that $e$ denotes the desired goal situation.

3. Explain how you could use Resolution to automatically solve the problem for any initial state: How would you generate the clauses, and assuming the process stops, how would you extract the necessary moves? (Do not attempt to write down a derivation!) Explain why you need to use the successor state axioms, and not just effect axioms.

4. Suppose we were interested in formalizing the problem using a STRIPS representation. Decide what the operators should be and then write the precondition, add list, and delete list for each operator. You may change the language as necessary.

5. Consider the database corresponding to the initial state of the problem. For each STRIPS operator and each binding of its variables such that the precondition is satisfied, state what the database progressed through this operator would be.

6. Consider the final goal state of the problem. For each STRIPS operator, describe the bindings of its variables for which the operator can be the final action of a plan, and in those cases, what the goal regressed through the operator would be.

7. Without any additional guidance, a very large amount of search is usually required to solve planning problems. There are often, however, application-dependent heuristics that can be used to reduce

the amount of search. For example,

- for the 15 puzzle, we should get the first row and first column of tiles into their correct positions (tiles 1, 2, 3, 4, 5, 9, and 13), and then recursively solve the remaining 8 puzzle without disturbing these outside tiles;
- for the blocks world, we should never move a block that is in its *final position*, where a block $x$ is considered to be in its final position if and only if either (a) $x$ is on the table and $x$ will be on the table in the goal state or (b) $x$ is on another block $y$, $x$ will be on $y$ in the goal state, and $y$ is also in its final position.

Explain how the complex actions of GOLOG from Chapter 14 can be used to define a more restricted search problem that incorporates heuristics like these. Sketch briefly what the GOLOG program would look like.

# CHAPTER 16

# THE TRADEOFF BETWEEN EXPRESSIVENESS AND TRACTABILITY

The focus of our exploration thus far has been the detailed investigation of a number of representational formalisms aimed at various uses or applications. Each had its own features, usually knit together in a cohesive whole that was justified by a particular point of view on the world (e.g., object-oriented, or procedural, or rule-based). Many of the formalisms we discussed can be viewed as extensions to a bare knowledge representation formalism based on FOL. Even features like defaults or probabilities can be thought of as additions to a basic FOL framework.

As we have proceeded through the discussion, lurking in the background has been a nagging question: Because, in the end, we would like to be able to formally represent *anything* that can be known, why not strive for a highly expressive language, one that includes *all* of the features we have seen so far? Or even more generally, why do we not attempt to define a formal knowledge representation language that is coextensive with a natural language like English?[1]

The answer is the linchpin of the art of practicing knowledge representation: Although such a highly expressive language would certainly be desirable from a *representation* standpoint, it leads to serious difficulties from a *reasoning* standpoint. If all we cared about was to formally represent knowledge in order to be able to prove occasional properties about it by hand, then perhaps we could go ahead. But if we are thinking of

---

[1] Although we will not attempt to define the expressiveness of a language precisely, we can think of it intuitively as measured by the subset of English we can properly encode.

using a mechanical reasoning procedure to manipulate the expressions of this language, especially in support of reasoning by an artificial agent, then we need to worry about what we can do with them in a reasonable amount of time. As we will see in this chapter, reasoning procedures that seem to be required to deal with more expressive representation languages do not appear to work well in practice. A fundamental fact of life is that there is a tradeoff between the expressiveness of the representation language and the computational tractability of the associated reasoning task.[2]

In this chapter, we will explore this issue in detail. We will begin with a simple description language of the sort considered in Chapter 9 and show how a very small change in its expressiveness completely changes the sort of reasoning procedure it requires. Then we will consider the idea of languages more limited than FOL and what seems to happen as they are generalized to full FOL. We will see that "reasoning by cases" in various forms is a serious concern, and that one extreme way to guarantee tractability is to limit ourselves to representation languages where only a single "case" is ever considered. Finally, we will see that there is still room to maneuver and that even limited representation languages can be augmented in various ways to make them more useful in practice. Indeed, it can be argued that much of the research that is concerned with both knowledge representation and reasoning is concerned with finding interesting points in the tradeoff between tractability and expressiveness.

It is worth noting before beginning, however, that the topic of this chapter is somewhat controversial. People, after all, are able to reason with what they know, even if much of what they know comes from hearing or reading sentences in seemingly unrestricted natural language. How is this possible? For one thing, people do not naturally explore all and only the logical consequences of what they know. This suggests that one way of dealing with the tradeoff is to allow very expressive languages, but to preserve tractability by doing a form of reasoning that is somehow less demanding. Researchers have proposed alternative logical systems with weaker notions of entailment, which might be candidates for exploration of limited reasoning with expressive representation languages. However, because the tradeoff between expressiveness and complexity is so fundamental to the understanding of knowledge representation and reasoning, we will here concentrate on that issue and leave aside the consideration of weak logics.

---

[2]Although we will not attempt to define the tractability of a reasoning task precisely, we will assume (as we have done throughout) that any reasoning task whose execution time scales exponentially with the size of the KB is intractable.

## 16.1  A DESCRIPTION LOGIC CASE STUDY

To illustrate the tradeoff between expressiveness and tractability most clearly, we begin by examining a very concrete case involving description logics and the subsumption task, as discussed in Chapter 9. We will present a new description logic language called $\mathcal{FL}$ and a subset of it called $\mathcal{FL}^-$, and show that what is needed to calculate subsumption is quite different in each case.

### 16.1.1  Two Description Logic Languages

As with $\mathcal{DL}$ in Chapter 9, the $\mathcal{FL}$ language consists of *concepts* and *roles* (but no constants) and is defined by the following grammar:

- every atomic concept is a concept;
- if $r$ is a role and $d$ is a concept, then [**ALL** $r$ $d$] is a concept;
- if $r$ is a role, then [**EXISTS** 1 $r$] is a concept;
- if $d_1 \ldots d_n$ are concepts, then [**AND** $d_1 \ldots d_n$] is a concept;
- every atomic role is a role;
- if $r$ is a role and $d$ is a concept, then [**RESTR** $r$ $d$] is a role.

There is one simple difference between $\mathcal{FL}$ and a variant that we will call $\mathcal{FL}^-$: The grammar for the $\mathcal{FL}^-$ language is the same as for $\mathcal{FL}$, but without the **RESTR** operator.

As usual, concepts can be thought of as 1-place predicates and roles as 2-place predicates. Unlike in $\mathcal{DL}$, both concepts and roles here can be either atomic (with no internal structure) or nonatomic, indicated by an operator (like **ALL** or **RESTR**) with arguments. As an aside, note that we will use [**SOME** $r$] as a shorthand for [**EXISTS** 1 $r$].

The meaning of all the operators except for **RESTR** was explained in Chapter 9. The **RESTR** operator is intended to denote a *restricted role*. For example, if :Child is a role (to be filled by a person who is a child of someone), then [**RESTR** :Child Female] is also a role (to be filled by a person who is a daughter of someone). It is important then to distinguish clearly between the following two concepts:

[**AND** Person [**ALL** :Child [**AND** Female Student]]]
[**AND** Person [**ALL** [**RESTR** :Child Female] Student]]

The first describes a person whose children are all female students; the second describes a person whose female children are all students. In the second case, nothing is said about the male children, if there are any.

Formally, the semantics for $\mathcal{FL}$ is like that of $\mathcal{DL}$. The interpretation mapping $\mathcal{I}$ is required to satisfy one additional requirement for **RESTR**:

■ $\mathcal{I}[[\mathbf{RESTR}\ r\ d]] = \{\langle x,y \rangle \in D \times D \mid \langle x,y \rangle \in \mathcal{I}[r],\ \text{and}\ y \in \mathcal{I}[d]\}.$

Thus, the set of [**RESTR** :Child Female] relationships is defined to be the set of child relationships where the child in question is female. With this definition in place, subsumption for $\mathcal{FL}$ is as before: $d_1$ subsumes $d_2$ (given an empty KB) if and only if for every interpretation $\langle \mathcal{D}, \mathcal{I} \rangle$, $\mathcal{I}[d_1]$ is a superset of $\mathcal{I}[d_2]$.

## 16.1.2   Computing Subsumption

As we have seen, the principal form of reasoning in description logics is the calculation of subsumption. We begin by considering this reasoning task for expressions in $\mathcal{FL}^-$, where we can use a procedure very similar to the one for $\mathcal{DL}$:

■ first put the expressions into an equivalent normal form,

> [**AND** $a_1, \ldots, a_n$
>      [**SOME** $r_1$], ..., [**SOME** $r_m$],
>      [**ALL** $s_1\ d_1$], ..., [**ALL** $s_k\ d_k$]]],

where $a_i$ are atomic concepts, the $r_i$ and $s_i$ are atomic roles, and the $d_i$ are themselves concept expressions in normal form;

■ to see if normal form expression $d$ subsumes normal form expression $d'$, we check that for every part of $d$ there is a matching part in $d'$:

– for every $a$, if $a \in d$, then $a \in d'$;
– for every $r$, if [**SOME** $r$] $\in d$, then [**SOME** $r$] $\in d'$;
– for every [**ALL** $s\ e$] $\in d$, there is an [**ALL** $s\ e'$] $\in d'$, such that $e$ recursively subsumes $e'$.

This procedure can be shown to be sound and complete for $\mathcal{FL}^-$: It returns with success if and only if the concept $d$ subsumes $d'$ according to the definition (with interpretations). Furthermore, it is not hard to see that the procedure runs quickly: Conversion to normal form can be done in $O(n^2)$ time, where $n$ is the length of the concept expression, and the structural matching part requires at worst scanning $d'$ for each part of $d$, and so is again $O(n^2)$.

But let us now consider subsumption for all of $\mathcal{FL}$, including the **RESTR** operator. Here we see that subsumption is not so easy. Consider, for example, the following two descriptions:

> [**ALL** [**RESTR** :Friend [**AND** Male Doctor]]
>         [**AND** Tall Rich]]

and

> [**AND** [**ALL** [**RESTR** :Friend Male]
>              [**AND** Tall Bachelor]]
>        [**ALL** [**RESTR** :Friend Doctor]
>              [**AND** Rich Surgeon]]].

It is not hard to see that the first subsumes the second: Looking at the second expression, if all your male friends are tall bachelors and all your doctor friends are rich surgeons, then it follows that all your male doctor friends are both tall and rich. On the other hand, we cannot settle the subsumption question by finding a matching part in the second concept for each part in the first. The interaction among the parts is more complicated than that. Similarly, a description like

> [**SOME** [**RESTR** $r$ [**AND** $a$ $b$]]]

subsumes one like

> [**AND** [**SOME** [**RESTR** $r$ [**AND** $c$ $d$]]]
>        [**ALL** [**RESTR** $r$ $c$] [**AND** $a$ $e$]]
>        [**ALL** [**RESTR** $r$ [**AND** $d$ $e$]] $b$]]

even though we have to work through all the parts of the second one to see why.

Because of possible interactions among the parts, the sort of reasoning that is required to handle $\mathcal{FL}$ appears to be much more complex than the structural matching sufficient for $\mathcal{FL}^-$. Is this just a failure of imagination on our part, or is $\mathcal{FL}$ truly harder to reason with? In fact, it can be *proven* that subsumption in $\mathcal{FL}$ is as difficult as proving the unsatisfiability of propositional formulas: There is a polynomial-time function $\Omega$ that maps CNF formulas into concept expressions of $\mathcal{FL}$ that has the property that for any two CNF formulas $\alpha$ and $\beta$, $(\alpha \supset \beta)$ is valid if and only if $\Omega(\alpha)$ is subsumed by $\Omega(\beta)$. Because $(\alpha \supset (p \wedge \neg p))$ is valid if and only if $\alpha$ is unsatisfiable, it follows that a procedure for $\mathcal{FL}$ subsumption could be used to check whether a CNF formula is unsatisfiable. Because it is believed that no good algorithm exists for computing unsatisfiability for CNF formulas, it follows that no good algorithm exists for $\mathcal{FL}$ expressions either.

The moral: Even small doses of expressive power—in this case adding one natural, role-forming operator—can come at a significant computational price.

This raises a number of interesting questions that are central to the knowledge representation enterprise:

1. What properties of a representation language affect or control its computational difficulty?

2. How far can expressiveness be pushed without losing the prospect of good (or at least nonexponential) algorithms?

3. When are inexpressive but tractable representation languages sufficient for the purposes of knowledge representation and reasoning?

Although these questions remain largely unanswered, some progress has been made on them. As we will see, reasoning by cases is a major source of computational intractability. As for description logics, the space of possible languages has been explored extensively, together with proofs about which combinations of operators preserve tractability.

Finally, as for making do with inexpressive languages, this is a much more controversial topic. For some researchers, anything less than "English" is a cop-out and inappropriate for AI research; others are quite content to look for inexpressive languages tailored to applications, although they might prefer to call this, "exploiting constraints in the application domain," rather than the more negative sounding, "getting by with an expressively limited language." As we will see, there is indeed significant mileage to be gained by looking for reasoning tasks that can be formulated in limited but tractable representation languages and then making efforts to extend them as necessary.

## 16.2 ▪ LIMITED LANGUAGES

The main idea in the design of useful limited languages is that there are reasoning tasks that can be easily formulated in terms of FOL entailment, that is, in terms of whether or not KB $\models \alpha$, but that can also be solved by special-purpose methods because of restrictions on the KB or on $\alpha$.

A simple example of this is Horn clause entailment. We could obviously use full Resolution to handle Horn clauses, but there is no need to, because SLD Resolution offers a much more focused search. In fact, in the propositional case, we know that there is a procedure guaranteed to run in linear time for doing the reasoning, whereas a full Resolution procedure need not and likely would not do as well.

A less obvious example of a limited language is provided by description logics in general. It is not hard to formulate subsumption in terms of FOL entailment. We can imagine introducing predicate symbols for concept expressions and writing *meaning postulates* for them in FOL. For example, for the concept

> [**AND** [**ALL** :Friend Rich]
>            [**ALL** :Child [**ALL** :Friend Happy]]],

we introduce the predicate symbol $P$ and the meaning postulate

$$\forall x.\ P(x) \equiv \forall y\, (\mathsf{Friend}(x,y) \supset \mathsf{Rich}(y)) \quad \wedge$$
$$\forall y\, (\mathsf{Child}(x,y) \supset \forall z.\, \mathsf{Friend}(y,z) \supset \mathsf{Happy}(z)).$$

This has the effect of defining $P$ to be anything that satisfies the stated property. If we have two concept descriptions and introduce two predicate symbols $P$ and $Q$, along with two meaning postulates $\mu_P$ and $\mu_Q$, it is clearly the case that the first concept is subsumed by the second if and only if

$$\{\mu_P, \mu_Q\}\ \models\ \forall x.\ P(x) \supset Q(x).$$

So if we wanted to, we could use full Resolution to calculate concept subsumption. But as we saw, for some description logic languages (like $\mathcal{FL}^-$), there are very good subsumption procedures. It would be extremely awkward to try to coax this efficient structure-matching behavior out of a general-purpose Resolution procedure.

As a third and final example, consider linear equations. Let $E$ be the usual Peano axioms of arithmetic written in FOL:

$$\forall x \forall y.\ x + y = y + x,$$
$$\forall x.\ x + 0 = x,$$

and so on. From this we can derive, for example, that

$$E \models \forall x \forall y.\ (x + 2y = 4 \wedge x - y = 1) \supset (x = 2 \wedge y = 1).$$

That is, even though we cannot formalize all of arithmetic within FOL, we can do enough of it to use Resolution (with some form of answer extraction) to solve systems of linear equations. But there is a much better way, of course: the Gauss–Jordan method with back substitution. For the example, we subtract the second equation ($x - y = 1$) from the first ($x + 2y = 4$) to derive that $3y = 3$; we divide both sides by 3 to get $y = 1$; we substitute this value of $y$ in the first equation to get $x = 2$. In general, a set of $n$ linear equations can be solved by this method in $O(n^3)$ steps, whereas the Resolution procedure can offer no such guarantee.

This idea of limited languages obviously generalizes: It will always be advantageous to use a special-purpose reasoning procedure when one exists even if a general-purpose procedure like Resolution is applicable.

## 16.3   WHAT MAKES REASONING HARD?

So when do we expect *not* to be able to use a specialized procedure to advantage? Suppose that instead of having a system of linear equations, our reasoning task started with the following formulas:[3]

$$(x + 2y = 4 \ \vee \ 3x - y = 7) \ \wedge \ x - y = 1.$$

We can still show using Resolution that this implies that $y > 0$. But if we wanted to use an efficient procedure like Gauss–Jordan to draw this conclusion, we would have to split the problem into two cases:

Given $x + 2y = 4$ and $x - y = 1$,
   we infer using Gauss–Jordan that $y = 1$, and so $y > 0$.

Given $3x - y = 7$ and $x - y = 1$,
   we infer using Gauss–Jordan that $y = 2$, and so $y > 0$.

Either way, we conclude that $y > 0$.

Reasoning this way may still be better than using Resolution. But what if we have two disjunctions to consider, $(e_1 \vee f_1) \wedge (e_2 \vee f_2)$, where the $e_i$ and $f_i$ are equations? Then we would have four cases to consider. If we had $n$ disjunctions

$$(e_1 \vee f_1) \wedge (e_2 \vee f_2) \wedge \ldots (e_n \vee f_n)$$

we would need to call the Gauss–Jordan method $2^n$ times to see what follows. For even a modestly sized formula of this type—say when $n$ is 30—this method is no longer feasible, even though the underlying Gauss–Jordan procedure is efficient. Thus, special-purpose reasoning methods will not help us if we are forced to reason by cases and invoke these procedures exponentially often.

But can we avoid this type of case analysis? Unfortunately, it seems to be demanded by languages like FOL. The constructs of FOL are ideally

---

[3]Of course, we would not expect to find a disjunction in a textbook on mathematical equations.

suited to expressing *incomplete knowledge*. Consider what we can say in FOL:

1. In(blockA, box) ∨ In(blockB, box)
   Either block A or block B is in the box.
   *But which one?*

2. ¬In(blockC, box)
   Block C is not in the box.
   *But where is it?*

3. ∃x. In(x, box)
   Something is in the box.
   *But what is it?*

4. ∀x. In(x, box) ⊃ Light(x)
   Everything in the box is light (in weight).
   *But what are the things in the box?*

5. heaviestBlock ≠ blockA
   The heaviest block is not block A.
   *But which block is the heaviest block?*

6. heaviestBlock = favorite(john)
   The heaviest block is also John's favorite.
   *But what block is this?*

In all cases, the logical operators of FOL allow us to express knowledge in a way that does not force us to answer the questions posed in italics. In fact, we can understand the expressiveness of FOL not in terms of what it allows us to say, but in terms of what it allows us to leave *unsaid*.

From a reasoning point of view, however, the problem is that if we know that block A or block B is in the box, but not which, and we want to consider what follows from this and what the world must be like, we have to somehow cover the two cases. Again, the trouble with cases is that they multiply together, and so very quickly there are too many of them to enumerate.[4] Not too surprisingly then, the limited languages we have examined (Horn clauses, description logics, linear equations) do not allow this form of incomplete knowledge to be represented.

This then suggests a general direction to pursue to avoid intractability: Restrict the contents of a KB somehow so that reasoning by cases is not required.

---

[4]This is not to suggest that we are *required* to enumerate the cases to reason correctly. Indeed, whether we need a reasoning procedure that scales with the number of cases remains open, and is perhaps the deepest open problem in computer science.

One natural question along these lines is this: Is *complete knowledge* sufficient to ensure tractability? That is, if for every sentence $\alpha$ we care about the KB entails $\alpha$ or the KB entails $\neg\alpha$, can we efficiently determine which? The answer unfortunately is *no*; a proof is beyond the scope of this book, but an informal argument is that if we have a KB like

$$\{(p \vee q), (\neg p \vee q), (\neg p \vee \neg q)\},$$

then we have a KB with complete knowledge about $p$ and $q$, because it only has one satisfying interpretation.[5] But we need to reason carefully with the entire KB to come to this conclusion and determine, for example, that $q$ is entailed.

## 16.4  VIVID KNOWLEDGE

We saw in the previous section that one way to keep reasoning tractable is to somehow avoid reasoning by cases. Unfortunately, we also saw that merely insisting on complete knowledge in a KB was not enough. In this section, we will consider an additional restriction that will be sufficient to guarantee the tractability of reasoning.

We begin with the propositional case. One property we do have for a KB with complete knowledge is that if it is satisfiable at all, then it is satisfied by a unique interpretation. To see this, suppose that KB has complete and consistent knowledge, and define the interpretation $\Im$ such that for any atom $p$, $\Im \models p$ if and only if KB $\models p$. Now consider any other interpretation $\Im'$ that satisfies KB. If KB $\models p$, it follows that $\Im' \models p$; furthermore, because KB is complete, if KB $\not\models p$, then KB $\models \neg p$, and so it follows that $\Im' \models \neg p$, and thus that, $\Im' \not\models p$. Therefore, $\Im$ and $\Im'$ agree on all atoms, and so are the same interpretation.

It follows by this argument that if a KB has complete and consistent knowledge (for some vocabulary), then there is an interpretation $\Im$ such that for any sentence $\alpha$, KB $\models \alpha$ if and only if $\Im \models \alpha$. In other words, there is a (unique) interpretation such that the entailments of the KB are nothing more than the sentences true in that interpretation. Because calculating what is true in an interpretation is such a simple matter once we are given the interpretation, we find that calculating entailments in this case will be easy too. The problem, as we saw in the previous section, is that it may be difficult to find this interpretation. The simplest way, then,

---

[5]It can be shown that finding a satisfying interpretation for a set of clauses that has at most one satisfying interpretation, although not NP-hard, is still unlikely to be solvable in polynomial time.

to ensure tractability of reasoning is to insist that a KB with complete and consistent knowledge wear this unique interpretation on its sleeve.

In the propositional case, then, we define a KB to be *vivid* if and only if it is a complete and consistent set of literals (over some vocabulary). A KB in this form exhibits the unique satisfying interpretation in a very obvious way. To answer queries with such a KB we need only use the positive literals in the KB, as we did with the CWA in Chapter 11. In fact, a vivid KB is simply one that has the CWA built in.

In the first-order case, we will do exactly the same, and base our definition on the first-order version of the CWA. We say that a first-order KB is vivid if and only if for some finite set $KB^+$ of positive function-free ground literals it is the case that

$KB = KB^+ \quad \cup$

$\{\neg p \mid p$ is atomic and $KB \not\models p\} \quad \cup$

$\{(c_i \neq c_j) \mid c_i, c_j$ are distinct constants$\} \quad \cup$

$\{\forall x [x = c_1 \lor \ldots \lor x = c_n],$ where the $c_i$ are all the constants in $KB^+\}.$

So a KB that is vivid has the CWA built in; no further assumptions are necessary. For a KB of this form, we get a simple recursive algorithm for determining whether $KB \models \alpha$, just as we did with the CWA:

1. $KB \models (\alpha \land \beta)$ iff $KB \models \alpha$ and $KB \models \beta$;

2. $KB \models (\alpha \lor \beta)$ iff $KB \models \alpha$ or $KB \models \beta$;

3. $KB \models \neg\alpha$ iff $KB \not\models \alpha$;

4. $KB \models \exists x \alpha$ iff $KB \models \alpha_c^x,$     for some $c$ appearing in KB;

5. $KB \models (a = b)$ iff $a$ and $b$ are the same constants;

6. if $\alpha$ is atomic, then $KB \models \alpha$ iff $\alpha \in KB^+$.

Notice that the algorithm for determining what is entailed by a vivid KB is just database retrieval over the $KB^+$ part. Only this part of the KB is actually needed to answer queries, and could be stored in a collection of database relations. The rest of the KB is not needed to answer questions, but is there to ensure that the recursive algorithm is correct.

## 16.4.1 Analogues, Diagrams, Models

One interesting aspect of this definition of a vivid KB is how well it accounts for what is called *analogical*, *diagrammatic*, or *model-based* reasoning.

It is often argued that a form of reasoning that is even more basic than reasoning with *sentences* representing knowledge about some world (as we consider in this book) is reasoning with *models* representing worlds directly. Instead of reasoning by asking what is entailed by a collection of sentences, we are presented with a model or a diagram of some sort and we reason by asking ourselves if a sentence is satisfied by the model or holds in the diagram.

Here is the type of example that is used to argue for this form of reasoning: Imagine the president of the United States standing directly beside the prime minister of Canada. It is observed that people have a hard time thinking about this scene without either imagining the president as being on the left or the prime minister as being on the left. In a collection of sentences representing beliefs about the scene, we could easily leave out who is on the left. But in a model or diagram of the scene, we cannot represent the leaders as being beside each other without also committing to this and other visually salient properties of the scene.

This constraint on how we seem to think about the world has led many to conclude that reasoning with models or diagrams is somehow a more basic and fundamental form of reasoning than the manipulation of sentences.

But viewed another way, it can be argued that what we are really talking about is a form of reasoning where certain kinds of properties of the world cannot be left unspecified and must be spelled out directly in the representation. A vivid KB can in fact be viewed as a model of the world in just this sense. In fact, there is clear structural correspondence between a vivid KB and the world it represents knowledge about:

- for each object of interest in the world, there is exactly one constant in $KB^+$ that stands for that object;
- for each relationship of interest in the world, there is a corresponding predicate in the KB such that the relationship holds among certain objects in the world if and only if the predicate with the constants as arguments is an element of $KB^+$.

In this sense, $KB^+$ is an *analogue* of the world it represents knowledge about.

Note that this close correspondence between the structure of a KB and the world it represents knowledge about does not hold in general. For example, if a KB consists of the sentences $\{P(a), Q(b)\}$, it might be talking about a world where there are five objects, two of which satisfy property $P$ and four of which satisfy $Q$. On the other hand, if we have a *vivid* KB where $KB^+$ is $\{P(a), Q(b)\}$, then we must be talking about a world with exactly two objects, one of which satisfies $P$ and the other of which satisfies $Q$. In the propositional case, we said that a vivid KB was uniquely satisfied; in the first-order case, a vivid KB is not uniquely satisfied, but all of the interpretations that satisfy it look the same—they are isomorphic.

The result of this close correspondence between the structure of a vivid KB and the structure of its satisfying interpretations is that many reasoning operations are much simpler on a vivid KB than they would be in a general setting. Just as, given a model of a house, we can find out how many doors the house has by *counting* them in the model, given a vivid KB, we can find out how many objects have a certain property by counting how many constants have the property. Similarly, we can represent changes to the world directly by changes to the analogue $KB^+$, adding or removing elements just as we did with the procedural representations in Chapter 6.

## 16.5 BEYOND VIVID

While vivid knowledge bases seem to provide a platform for tractable reasoning, they are quite limited as representations of knowledge. In this section, we will consider some extensions that have been proposed that appear to preserve tractability.

### 16.5.1 Sets of Literals

First, let us consider in the propositional case a KB as any finite set of literals, not necessarily complete (that is, with no CWA built in). Because such a knowledge base does not use disjunction explicitly, we might think it would be easier to reason with. It is not, however.[6] Notice that if this KB happens to be the empty set of literals, it will entail an $\alpha$ if and only if $\alpha$ is a tautology. So a good algorithm for reasoning from a set of literals would imply a good algorithm for testing for tautologies, an unlikely prospect.

However, let us now assume that the $\alpha$ in question is small in comparison with an exponentially larger KB. For example, imagine a query that uses at most 20 atoms, whereas the KB might use millions. In this case, here is what we can do: First, we can put $\alpha$ into CNF to obtain a set of clauses $c_1, c_2, \ldots, c_n$. Next, we discard tautologous clauses (containing an atom and its negation). It is then the case that KB $\models \alpha$ if and only if KB $\models c_i$ for every remaining $c_i$ (and if there are no remaining ones, then $\alpha$ was a tautology). Finally, we have this property:[7]

$$\text{KB} \models c_i \quad \text{iff} \quad (\text{KB} \cap c_i) \neq \emptyset.$$

---

[6] In fact, the presence of disjunctions is neither necessary nor sufficient for intractability.

[7] The argument is this: If the intersection of KB and $c_i$ is not empty, then clearly KB $\models c_i$; if it is empty, we can find an interpretation that makes KB true and makes $c_i$ false, and so KB $\not\models c_i$.

So under these conditions we do get tractable reasoning even in the absence of complete knowledge. However, this is for a propositional language; it is far from clear how to extend this idea to an $\alpha$ with quantifiers.

## 16.5.2   Incorporating Definitions

As a second extension, imagine that we have a vivid KB as before. Now assume that we add to it a sentence of the form $\forall \vec{x}.\ P(\vec{x}) \equiv \alpha$, where $\alpha$ is any formula that uses the predicates in the KB and $P$ is a new predicate that does not appear in the KB. For example, we might have a vivid KB that uses the predicate Parent and Female, and we could add a sentence like

$$\forall x \forall y.\ \text{Mother}(x, y) \equiv \text{Parent}(x, y) \wedge \text{Female}(x).$$

Such a sentence serves essentially to define the new predicate in terms of the old ones.

We can still reason efficiently with a vivid KB that has been extended with definitions in this way: If we have a query that contains an atom like $P(t_1, \ldots, t_n)$ where $P$ is one of the defined predicates, we can simply replace it in the query by $\alpha(t_1, \ldots, t_n)$, and continue as before. Note that this formula $\alpha$ can contain arbitrary logical operations (including disjunctions and existential quantifications), because they will end up being part of the query, not of the KB. Furthermore, it is not too hard to see that we could allow recursive definitions like

$$\forall x \forall y.\ \text{Ancestor}(x, y) \equiv \text{Parent}(x, y) \vee \exists z (\text{Parent}(x, z) \wedge \text{Ancestor}(z, y))$$

provided that we were careful about how the expansion would take place. In this case, it would be undecidable whether a sentence was entailed, but arguably, this would be a very modest and manageable form of undecidability.

This idea of a vivid KB together with definitions of unrestricted logical form has a clear connection with PROLOG. A good case can be made that in fact this, rather than Horn clauses, is the proper way to understand PROLOG from a knowledge representation point of view.

## 16.5.3   Hybrid Reasoning

Having seen various forms of limited, special-purpose reasoning algorithms, we might pose the natural question as to whether these can be combined in a single system. What we would like is a system that can use efficient procedures such as equation solvers or subsumption checkers as appropriate, but can also do general first-order reasoning (like reasoning by cases) in those perhaps rare situations where it is necessary to do so. We might have, for example, a Resolution-based reasoning system where we attempt, as much as possible, to use special-purpose reasoning procedures whenever we can, as part of the derivation process.

One proposal in this direction is what is called *semantic attachment*. The idea here is that procedures can be attached to certain function and predicate symbols. For example, in the domain of numbers, we might attach the obvious procedures to the function times and the predicate LessThan. Then, when we are dealing with a clause that has ground instances of these expressions, we attempt to *simplify* them before passing them on to Resolution. For example, the literal $P(a, \text{times}(5, 3), x)$ would simplify to $P(a, 15, x)$ using the procedure attached to times. Similarly, a clause of the form [LessThan(quotient(36, 6), 5) $\vee$ c] would simplify to c itself, once the first literal had simplified to false. Obviously this reasoning could be done without semantic attachment using Resolution and the axioms of arithmetic. However, as we argued, there is much to be gained by using special-purpose procedures.

A more general version of this idea that is not restricted to ground terms is what is called *theory resolution*. The idea here is to build a background theory into the unification process itself, the way paramodulation encodes a theory of equality. Rather than attaching procedures to functions and predicates, we imagine that the special-purpose reasoner will extend the notion of which literals are considered to be complementary. For example, suppose we have two clauses,

$$[c_1 \vee \text{LessThan}(2, x)] \quad \text{and} \quad [c_2 \vee \text{LessThan}(x, 1)].$$

Using a background theory of LessThan, we can inform Resolution that the two literals in question are complementary, exactly as if one had been $p$ and the other had been $\neg p$. In this case, we would get the theory resolution resolvent $(c_1 \vee c_2)$ in one step, using this special-purpose reasoner.

One nice application of theory resolution is the incorporation of a description logic into Resolution. Suppose that some of the predicates in a Resolution system are the names of concepts defined elsewhere in a description logic system. For example, we might have the two clauses

$$[P(x) \vee \neg \text{Male}(x)] \quad \text{and} \quad [\text{Bachelor}(\text{john}) \vee Q(y)],$$

where no Resolution steps are possible. However, if both Male and Bachelor are defined in a description logic, we can determine that the former subsumes the latter, and so the two literals are indeed complementary. Thus, we infer the clause

$$[P(\text{john}) \vee Q(y)]$$

by theory resolution. In this case, we are using a description logic procedure to quickly decide if two predicates are complementary, instead of letting Resolution work with meaning postulates, as discussed earlier.

One concern in doing this type of hybrid reasoning is making sure we do not miss any conclusions: We would like to draw exactly the same conclusions we would get if we used the axioms of a background theory. To preserve this form of completeness, it is sometimes necessary to consider literals that are "almost complementary." Consider, for example, the two clauses

$$[P(x) \lor \mathsf{Male}(x)] \quad \text{and} \quad [\neg\mathsf{Bachelor}(\mathsf{john}) \lor Q(y)].$$

There are no complementary literals here, even assuming Male and Bachelor have their normal definitions. However, there is a connection between the two literals in the clauses, in that they are contradictory unless the individual in question is married. Thus, we would say that the two clauses should resolve together to produce the clause

$$[P(\mathsf{john}) \lor Q(y) \lor \neg\mathsf{Single}(\mathsf{john})],$$

where the third literal in the clause is considered to be a *residue* of the unification. It is a simple matter in description logics to calculate such residues, and it turns out that without them, or without a significantly more complex form of Resolution, completeness would be lost.

## 16.6   BIBLIOGRAPHIC NOTES

For further discussion of expressiveness versus tractability, see [48, 243]. The review of knowledge representation by Levesque [240] examines the entire field from this perspective, arguing that much of the research can be seen as exploring useful points along the expressiveness–tractability spectrum.

In terms of research addressing the tradeoff directly, Cadoli et al. [65] show that nonmonotonic logics lead to more compact representations, but that this may be at the cost of an increase in computational complexity. Schaerf and Cadoli [365] consider approximate reasoning by looking at consequence operations that give up either soundness or completeness, resulting in a decrease in computational complexity. Logics of explicit belief (see the references in Chapter 2) explore similar ideas.

The description logics $\mathcal{FL}$ and $\mathcal{FL}^-$ are discussed by Brachman and Levesque [46]. Nebel [304] considers the computational complexity of description logics more generally. There are many papers analyzing the complexity of subsumption for description logics (see, for example,

[107, 108, 109, 303]). For the expressiveness of description logics, see Kurtonina and de Rijke [228].

The notion of a vivid KB is introduced by Levesque [241] (see also Borgida and Etherington [35] and Wagner [416]). Reasoning with analogues or models is discussed by Glasgow and a number of others in [165]. For a general reference on reasoning as a whole, viewed as the manipulation of mental models, see Johnson-Laird [204].

For a discussion of reasoning in hybrid systems, see Nebel [303]. Theory Resolution is due to Stickel [401]. The incorporation of a description logic into Resolution was achieved in the KRYPTON system [51, 52].

## 16.7 EXERCISES

1. Many of the disjunctive facts that arise in practice state that a specific individual has one property or another, where the two properties are similar. For example, we may want to represent the fact that a person is either 4 or 5 years old, that a car is either a Chevrolet or a Pontiac, or that a piece of music is either by Mozart or by Haydn. In general, to calculate the entailments of a KB containing such facts, we would need to use a mechanism that considered each case individually, such as Resolution. However, when the conditions being disjoined are sufficiently similar, a better strategy might be to try to sidestep the case analysis by finding a single property that *subsumes* the disjoined ones. For example, we might treat the original fact as if it merely said that the person is a preschooler, that the car is made by GM, or that the music is by a classical composer, none of which involve explicit disjunctions.

Imagine that you have a KB that contains among other things a *taxonomy* of one-place predicates like in Figure 16.1 that can be used

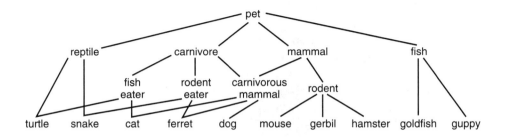

**■ FIGURE 16.1**

A Taxonomy of Pets

to find subsuming cases for disjunctions. Assume that this taxonomy is understood as exhaustive, so that, for example, it implies

$$\forall x[\text{Mammal}(x) \equiv \text{Rodent}(x) \vee \text{CarnivorousMammal}(x)].$$

(a) Given the taxonomy, what single atomic sentence could be used to replace the disjunction (Turtle(fred) ∨ Cat(fred))? Explain why no information is lost in this translation.

(b) What atomic sentence would replace the disjunction

$$(\text{Gerbil(stan)} \vee \text{Hamster(stan)})?$$

In this case, information about Stan is lost. Give an example of a sentence that follows from the original KB containing the disjunction, but that no longer follows once the disjunction is eliminated.

(c) What should happen to the disjunction

$$(\text{Dog(sam)} \vee \text{Snake(sam)} \vee \text{Rabbit(sam)})?$$

(d) Present informally a procedure that, given a taxonomy like in Figure 16.1 and a disjunction $(P_1(a) \vee \ldots \vee P_n(a))$, where the $P_i$ are predicates that may or may not appear in the taxonomy, replaces it by a disjunction containing as few cases as possible.

(e) Argue that a reasoning process that first eliminates disjunctions as we have done in parts (a) through (d) will always be *sound*.

2. In Chapter 11, we saw that under the closed-world assumption, complex queries can be broken down to queries about their parts. In particular, restricting ourselves to the propositional case, for any formulas $\alpha$ and $\beta$ it is the case that KB $\models_c (\alpha \vee \beta)$ if and only if KB $\models_c \alpha$ or KB $\models_c \beta$. This way of handling disjunction clearly does not work for regular entailment, because, for instance, $(p \vee q) \models (p \vee q)$ but $(p \vee q) \not\models p$ and $(p \vee q) \not\models q$.

(a) Prove that this way of handling disjunction *does* work for regular entailment when the KB happens to be a complete set of literals (that is, containing every atom or its negation).

(b) Show that the completeness of the KB matters here by finding a set of literals $S$ and formulas $\alpha$ and $\beta$ such that $S \models (\alpha \vee \beta)$, $S \not\models \alpha$, $S \not\models \beta$, and $\not\models (\alpha \vee \beta)$.

(c) Prove that when a KB is a set of literals (not necessarily complete) and also $\alpha$ and $\beta$ have no atoms in common, then once again KB $\models (\alpha \vee \beta)$ if and only if KB $\models \alpha$ or KB $\models \beta$.

**3.** In this question we will consider reasoning with a vivid KB and *definitions*, in a simple propositional form. Assume that a KB consists of two parts, a vivid part $V$, which is a complete and consistent set of literals over some set of atoms $A$, and for some set of atoms $\{q_1, \ldots, q_n\}$ not in $A$, a set of definitions $D = \{(q_1 \equiv \beta_1), \ldots, (q_n \equiv \beta_n)\}$, where each $\beta_i$ is an arbitrary propositional formula whose atoms are all from $A$. Intuitively, we are using $D$ to define $q_i$ as $\beta_i$. We want to examine the conditions under which we can reason efficiently with such a KB.

(a) Prove that for any propositional formula $\alpha$, $D$ entails $(\alpha \equiv \alpha')$, where $\alpha'$ is like $\alpha$ except with $q_i$ replaced by $\beta_i$. *Hint*: Show by induction on the size of $\alpha$ that any interpretation satisfying $D$ will satisfy $\alpha$ if and only if it satisfies $\alpha'$.

(b) Using part (a), prove that for any propositional formula $\alpha$, KB entails $\alpha$ if and only if $V$ entails $\alpha'$, where $\alpha'$ is as in part (a).

(c) Explain using part (b) how it is possible to determine efficiently whether KB entails an arbitrary propositional $\alpha$. State precisely what assumptions are needed regarding the sizes of the various formulas.

(d) Would this still work if $V$ were a set of propositional Horn clauses? Explain briefly.

(e) Suppose that $D$ contained "necessary but not sufficient conditions" (like we saw in description logics) of the form $(q_i \supset \beta_i)$. $D$ might contain, for example, (Dog $\supset$ Animal). For efficiency reasons, it would be nice to still replace $\alpha$ by $\alpha'$ and then use $V$, as we did earlier. Give an example showing that the resulting reasoning process would not be sound.

(f) Under the same conditions as part (e), suppose that instead of using $\alpha'$ and $V$, we use $\alpha''$, defined as follows: When $(q_i \equiv \beta_i)$ is in $D$, we replace $q_i$ in $\alpha$ by $\beta_i$ as before; but when $(q_i \supset \beta_i)$ is in $D$, we replace $q_i$ by $(\beta_i \wedge r_i)$, where $r_i$ is some new atom used nowhere else. The idea here is that we are treating $(q_i \supset \beta_i)$ as if it were $(q_i \equiv (\beta_i \wedge r_i))$ for some atom $r_i$ about which we know nothing. Show that the reasoning process is now both sound and complete. *Hint*: Repeat the argument from part (b).

**4.** Consider the following KB:

Man(sandy) $\vee$ Woman(sandy)

$\forall x[\text{Person}(x) \supset \text{Woman}(\text{mother}(x))]$

From this KB, we would like to conclude that Female(mother(sandy)), but obviously this cannot be done as is using ordinary Resolution without saying more about the predicates involved.

Imagine a version of theory resolution that works with a description logic from Chapter 9 as follows: For unary predicates, instead of requiring $P(t)$ in one clause and $\neg P(u)$ in the other (where $t$ and $u$ are unifiable), we instead allow $Q(t)$ in one clause and $\neg P(u)$ in the other, provided that $P$ subsumes $Q$. The assumption here is that some of the unary predicates in the KB will have associated definitions in the description logic. Assume we augment the KB with the following:

Man $\doteq$ [**AND** Person Male]

Woman $\doteq$ [**AND** Person Female]

where Person, Male, and Female are primitive concepts.

(a) Show using theory resolution that the conclusion now follows.

(b) Show that this derivation is *sound* by writing meaning postulates MP for the two definitions such that the conclusion is entailed by KB ∪ MP.

(c) Show that this form of theory resolution is *incomplete* by finding a sentence that is entailed by KB ∪ MP but not derivable from KB using the version of theory resolution described in this exercise.

5. We saw in Section 16.5.1 that it was possible to determine entailments efficiently when a KB was an arbitrary set of literals (not necessarily complete) and the query was small relative to the size of the KB. In this question, we will generalize this result to Horn KBs. More precisely, assume that $|KB| \geq 2^{|\alpha|}$, where KB is a set of propositional Horn clauses and $\alpha$ is an arbitrary propositional sentence. Prove that it is possible to decide whether KB entails $\alpha$ in time that is polynomial in $|KB|$. Why does this not work if $\alpha$ is the same size as the KB?

6. In this question, we will explore a different way of dealing with the computational intractability of ordinary deductive reasoning than the one we explored in the text. The idea is that instead of determining if KB $\models \alpha$, which can be too difficult in general, we determine if KB $\models^* \alpha$, where $\models^*$ is a variant of $\models$ that is easier to calculate. To define this variant, we first need two auxiliary definitions:

**DEFINITION 1** *An interpretation $\mathcal{I}$ maximally satisfies a set of (propositional) clauses S iff for every clause $c \in S$, $\mathcal{I}$ satisfies some literal in c (as usual), and falsifies at most one of the literals in c.*

(a) If a set of clauses has a maximally satisfying interpretation then it is clearly satisfiable, but the converse need not hold. Present a set of clauses (with no unit clauses) that is satisfiable but not maximally satisfiable.

(b) Let $H$ be a set of Horn clauses with no unit clauses and no empty clause. Show that $H$ is always maximally satisfiable.

(c) For any set $S$ of clauses, let $T(S) = \{[x_1, x_2] \mid$ for some $c \in S$, $x_1 \in c, x_2 \in c, x_1 \neq x_2\}$. Prove that when $S$ contains no unit clauses, $\mathcal{I}$ maximally satisfies $S$ if and only if $\mathcal{I}$ satisfies $T(S)$.

In the second definition, we eliminate unit clauses from a set of clauses:

**DEFINITION 2**    *For any set of (propositional) clauses $S$, let $BP(S)$, which is the* binary propagation *of $S$, be the set of clauses resulting from resolving away all unit clauses in $S$. More formally, for any literal $x$, such that $[x] \in S$, let $S \bullet x$ be defined as in Exercise 5 of Chapter 4. Then $BP(S)$ is the result of starting with $S$ and any unit clause $[x]$ in $S$, calculating $S \bullet x$, and then repeating this process with $S \bullet x$ (assuming it contains a unit clause) and so on, until no unit clauses remain.*

(d) What is $BP(S)$ when $S$ is

$$\{[p], [\bar{p}, s], [q, \bar{q}], [\bar{s}, \bar{r}, u, v], [\bar{q}], [r], [\bar{p}, q, t, \bar{u}]\}?$$

(e) Present an example of an unsatisfiable set of clauses $S_1$ such that $BP(S_1)$ contains the empty clause, and another unsatisfiable set $S_2$ such that $BP(S_2)$ does not contain the empty clause.

(f) Prove that $S$ is satisfiable if and only if $BP(S)$ is satisfiable. It is sufficient to prove that for any $S$ and $x$ such that $[x] \in S$, $\mathcal{I} \models S$ iff $\mathcal{I} \models S \bullet x$ and $\mathcal{I} \models x$, and the rest follows by induction.

Finally, we define $KB \models^* p$, where for simplicity, we assume that $KB$ is a set of clauses and $p$ is atomic:

**DEFINITION 3**    $KB \models^* p$ *iff $BP(KB \cup \{[\bar{p}]\})$ is not maximally satisfiable.*

(g) Present an example $KB$ and a query $p$ such that $\models^*$ does not give the same answer as $\models$. *Hint*: Use part (a). Explain whether reasoning with $\models^*$ is unsound or incomplete (or both).

(h) Prove that reasoning with $\models^*$ is both sound and complete for a $KB$ that is Horn. *Hint*: Where $H$ is Horn, consider the cases according to whether $BP(H)$ contains the empty clause, and use parts (b) and (f).

(i) Argue that for any $KB$ it is possible to determine if $KB \models^* p$ in polynomial time. You may use the fact that $BP(S)$ can be calculated in polynomial time, and that 2SAT (i.e., satisfiability restricted to clauses of length 2) can also be solved in polynomial time.

(j) Call a set of clauses *S generalized Horn* if a set of Horn clauses could be produced by inverting some of its atomic formulas, that is, by replacing all occurrences of the letter by its negation. Is $\models^*$ sound and complete for a KB that is generalized Horn? Explain.

# ■ BIBLIOGRAPHY
■
■

[1]     Special issue on ontology research. *AI Magazine*, 24(3), Fall 2003.

[2]     Special issue on knowledge representation and logic programming. *Artificial Intelligence*, 138(1–2), June 2002.

[3]     *KEE Software Development User's Manual*. IntelliCorp, Mountain View, CA, 1985.

[4]     Special issue on Dempster–Shafer theory, methodology, and applications. *International Journal of Approximate Reasoning*, 31(1–2), 2002.

[5]     Dimitris Achlioptas. Lower bounds for random 3-SAT via differential equations. *Theoretical Computer Science*, 265(1–2):159–185, 2001.

[6]     Sheldon B. Akers, Jr. Binary decision diagrams. *IEEE Transactions on Computers*, C-27(6):509–516, 1978.

[7]     Carlos E. Alchourrón and David Makinson. The logic of theory change: Contraction functions and their associated revision functions. *Theoria*, 48:14–37, 1982.

[8]     Carlos E. Alchourrón and David Makinson. On the logic of theory change: Safe contraction. *Studia Logica*, 44:405–422, 1985.

[9]     Carlos E. Alchourrón and David Makinson. Maps between some different kinds of contraction function: The finite case. *Studia Logica*, 45:187–198, 1986.

[10]    Carlos E. Alchourrón, Peter Gärdenfors, and David Makinson. On the logic of theory change: Partial meet contraction and revision functions. *Journal of Symbolic Logic*, 50(2):510–530, 1985.

[11]    Dean Allemang, Michael Tanner, Thomas Bylander, and John Josephson. Computational complexity of hypothesis assembly. In *Proceedings of the Tenth International Joint Conference on Artificial Intelligence, Milan, Italy*, pages 1112–1117. Morgan Kaufmann, San Mateo, CA, 1987.

[12]    James Allen, James Hendler, and Austin Tate, editors. *Readings in Planning*. Morgan Kaufmann, San Mateo, CA, 1990.

[13]    Grigoris Antoniou. *Nonmonotonic Reasoning*. MIT Press, Cambridge, MA, 1997.

[14]    Krystof R. Apt and Maarten H. van Emden. Contributions to the theory of logic programming. *Journal of the ACM*, 29(3):841–862, 1982.

[15]    Giuseppe Attardi, Mauro Gaspari, and Pietro Iglio. Efficient compilation of first order predicates. In *Proceedings of the Tenth European Conference on Artificial Intelligence, Vienna, Austria*, pages 440–444. John Wiley & Sons, Chichester, 1992.

[16]     Alfred Jules Ayer. *Language, Truth and Logic*, 2nd edition. V. Gollancz, London, 1962.

[17]     Franz Baader, Martin Buchheit, and Bernhard Hollunder. Cardinality restrictions on concepts. *Artificial Intelligence*, 88(1–2):195–213, 1996.

[18]     Franz Baader, Diego Calvanese, Deborah McGuinness, Daniele Nardi, and Peter Patel-Schneider, editors. *The Description Logic Handbook: Theory, Implementation, and Applications*. Cambridge University Press, Cambridge, England, 2003.

[19]     Fahiem Bacchus. The AIPS'00 planning competition. *AI Magazine*, 22(3):47–56, 2001.

[20]     Fahiem Bacchus and Froduald Kabanza. Planning for temporally extended goals. In *Proceedings of the Thirteenth National Conference on Artificial Intelligence, Portland, OR*, pages 1215–1222. AAAI Press, Menlo Park, CA, 1996.

[21]     Fahiem Bacchus and Froduald Kabanza. Using temporal logics to express search control knowledge for planning. *Artificial Intelligence*, 116(1–2):123–191, 2000.

[22]     Andrew B. Baker. A simple solution to the Yale Shooting Problem. In *Proceedings of the First International Conference on Principles of Knowledge Representation and Reasoning, Toronto*, pages 11–20. Morgan Kaufmann, Los Altos, CA, 1989.

[23]     Andrew B. Baker. Nonmonotonic reasoning in the framework of the situation calculus. *Artificial Intelligence*, 49(1–3):5–23, 1991.

[24]     Chitta Baral. *Knowledge Representation, Reasoning and Declarative Problem Solving*. Cambridge University Press, Cambridge, England, 2003.

[25]     Thomas Bayes. An essay towards solving a problem in the doctrine of chances. *Phil. Trans. Royal Society*, pages 370–418, 1763. Reprinted in *Biometrika* 45: 293–313, 1958.

[26]     John L. Bell and Moshe Machover. *A Course in Mathematical Logic*. North-Holland, Amsterdam, 1977.

[27]     Tim Berners-Lee, James Hendler, and Ora Lassila. The semantic web. *Scientific American*, 284(5):34–43, 2001.

[28]     Philippe Besnard. *An Introduction to Default Logic*. Springer-Verlag New York, Secaucus, NJ, 1990.

[29]     Wolfgang Bibel. On matrices with connections. *Journal of the ACM*, 24(4): 633–645, 1981.

[30]     Avrim L. Blum and Merrick L. Furst. Fast planning through planning graph analysis. *Artificial Intelligence*, 90(1–2):279–298, 1997.

[31]     Daniel G. Bobrow and Alan M. Collins, editors. *Representation and Understanding: Studies in Cognitive Science*. Academic Press, New York, 1975.

[32]     Daniel G. Bobrow and Terry Winograd. An overview of KRL, a knowledge representation language. *Cognitive Science*, 1(1):3–46, 1977. Reprinted in [47].

[33]     Margaret A. Boden, editor. *The Philosophy of Artificial Intelligence*. Oxford Readings in Philosophy, Oxford University Press, Oxford, 1990.

[34]  George Boolos, John P. Burgess, and Richard C. Jeffrey. *Computability and Logic*, 4th edition. Cambridge University Press, Cambridge, England, 2002.

[35]  Alex Borgida and David W. Etherington. Hierarchical knowledge bases and efficient disjunctive reasoning. In *Proceedings of the First International Conference on Principles of Knowledge Representation and Reasoning, Toronto*, pages 33–43. Morgan Kaufmann, San Mateo, CA, 1989.

[36]  Alexander Borgida, Ronald J. Brachman, Deborah L. McGuinness, and Lori Alperin Resnick. CLASSIC: A structural data model for objects. *SIGMOD Record*, 18(2):58–67, 1989.

[37]  Craig Boutilier. A unified view of qualitative belief change: A dynamical systems perspective. *Artificial Intelligence*, 98(1–2):281–316, 1998.

[38]  Craig Boutilier, Raymond Reiter, Mikhail Soutchanski, and Sebastian Thrun. Decision-theoretic, high-level agent programming in the situation calculus. In *Proceedings of the Seventeenth National Conference on Artificial Intelligence, Austin, TX*, pages 355–362. AAAI Press, Menlo Park, CA, 2000.

[39]  Robert S. Boyer and J Strother Moore. *A Computational Logic Handbook*, 2nd edition. Academic Press, London, 1998.

[40]  Ronald J. Brachman. What's in a concept: Structural foundations for semantic networks. *International Journal of Man-Machine Studies*, 9:127–152, 1977.

[41]  Ronald J. Brachman. Structured inheritance networks. In William A. Woods and Ronald J. Brachman, editors, *Research in Natural Language Understanding*, Quarterly Progress Report No. 1, BBN Report No. 3742, pages 36–78. Bolt, Beranek and Newman, Cambridge, MA, 1978.

[42]  Ronald J. Brachman. On the epistemological status of semantic networks. In Nicholas V. Findler, editor, *Associative Networks: Representation and Use of Knowledge by Computers*, pages 3–50. Academic Press, New York, 1979. Reprinted in [47].

[43]  Ronald J. Brachman. What IS-A is and isn't: An analysis of taxonomic links in semantic networks. *IEEE Computer*, 16(10):30–36, 1983.

[44]  Ronald J. Brachman. Viewing databases through a knowledge representation lens. In Kazuhiro Fuchi and Toshio Yokoi, editors, *Knowledge Building and Knowledge Sharing, Proc. KB&KS '93 Conference, Tokyo*, pages 121–124. Ohmsha, Tokyo, 1994.

[45]  Ronald J. Brachman and Hector J. Levesque. Competence in knowledge representation. In *Proceedings of the Second National Conference on Artificial Intelligence, Pittsburgh*, pages 189–192. AAAI, Menlo Park, CA, 1982.

[46]  Ronald J. Brachman and Hector J. Levesque. The tractability of subsumption in frame-based description languages. In *Proceedings of the Fourth National Conference on Artificial Intelligence (AAAI-84), Austin, TX*, pages 34–37. William Kaufmann, Los Altos, CA, 1984.

[47]  Ronald J. Brachman and Hector J. Levesque, editors. *Readings in Knowledge Representation*. Morgan Kaufmann, San Francisco, 1985.

[48]   Ronald J. Brachman and Hector J. Levesque. Expressiveness and tractability in knowledge representation and reasoning. *Computational Intelligence*, 3:78–93, 1987.

[49]   Ronald J. Brachman and James G. Schmolze. An overview of the KL-ONE knowledge representation system. *Cognitive Science*, 9(2):171–216, 1985.

[50]   Ronald J. Brachman and Brian C. Smith. *SIGART Newsletter, Special Issue on Knowledge Representation*, No. 70. ACM, New York, 1980.

[51]   Ronald J. Brachman, Richard E. Fikes, and Hector J. Levesque. KRYPTON: A functional approach to knowledge representation. *IEEE Computer*, 16(10): 67–73, 1983.

[52]   Ronald J. Brachman, Victoria P. Gilbert, and Hector J. Levesque. An essential hybrid reasoning system: Knowledge and symbol level accounts of KRYPTON. In *Proceedings of the Ninth International Joint Conference on Artificial Intelligence, Los Angeles*, pages 532–539. Morgan Kaufmann, Los Altos, CA, 1985.

[53]   Ronald J. Brachman, Deborah L. McGuinness, Peter F. Patel-Schneider, and Alex Borgida. "Reducing" CLASSIC to practice: Knowledge representation theory meets reality. *Artificial Intelligence*, 114(1–2):203–250, 1999.

[54]   Ivan Bratko. PROLOG *Programming for Artificial Intelligence*, 3rd edition. Addison-Wesley, New York, 2000.

[55]   Gerhard Brewka. Preferred subtheories: An extended logical framework for default reasoning. In *Proceedings of the Eleventh International Joint Conference on Artificial Intelligence, Detroit*, pages 1043–1048. Morgan Kaufmann, San Mateo, CA, 1989.

[56]   Gerhard Brewka. *Nonmonotonic Reasoning: Logical Foundations of Commonsense*. Cambridge University Press, Cambridge, England, 1991.

[57]   Gerhard Brewka, Jürgen Dix, and Kurt Konolige. *Nonmonotonic Reasoning: An Overview*. CSLI, Stanford, CA, 1997.

[58]   Rodney A. Brooks. A robust layered control system for a mobile robot. *IEEE Journal of Robotics and Automation*, 2:14–23, 1986.

[59]   Lee Brownston, Robert Farrell, Elaine Kant, and Nancy Martin. *Programming Expert Systems in OPS5: An Introduction to Rule-Based Programming*. Addison-Wesley, Reading, MA, 1985. Reprinted with corrections, January 1986.

[60]   Bruce G. Buchanan, Georgia L. Sutherland, and Edward A. Feigenbaum. Heuristic DENDRAL: A program for generating explanatory hypotheses in organic chemistry. In Bernard Meltzer and Donald Michie, editors, *Machine Intelligence 4*, pages 209–254. Edinburgh University Press, Edinburgh, 1969.

[61]   J. Richard Büchi. Turing machines and the entscheidungsproblem. *Mathematische Annalen*, 148:201–213, 1962.

[62]   Wolfram Burgard, Armin B. Cremers, Dieter Fox, Dirk Hahnel, Gerhard Lakemeyer, Dirk Schulz, Walter Steiner, and Sebastian Thrun. Experiences with an interactive museum tour-guide robot. *Artificial Intelligence*, 114(1–2): 3–55, 1999.

[63]    Tom Bylander. The computational complexity of propositional STRIPS planning. *Artificial Intelligence*, 69(1–2):165–204, 1994.

[64]    Tom Bylander, Dean Allemang, Michael C. Tanner, and John R. Josephson. The computational complexity of abduction. *Artificial Intelligence*, 49(1–3):25–60, 1991.

[65]    Marco Cadoli, Francesco M. Donini, and Marco Schaerf. Is intractability of non-monotonic reasoning a real drawback? *Artificial Intelligence*, 88(1–2):215–251, 1996.

[66]    Chin-Liang Chang and Richard Char-Tung Lee. *Symbolic Logic and Mechanical Theorem Proving*. Academic Press, New York, 1973.

[67]    Eugene Charniak. Motivation analysis, abductive unification, and nonmonotonic equality. *Artificial Intelligence*, 34(3):275–295, 1987.

[68]    Eugene Charniak. Bayesian networks without tears. *AI Magazine*, 12(4):50–63, 1991.

[69]    Eugene Charniak and Solomon E. Shimony. Probabilistic semantics for cost-based abduction. In *Proceedings of the Eighth National Conference on Artificial Intelligence, Boston*, pages 106–111. AAAI Press, Menlo Park, CA, 1990.

[70]    Keith L. Clark. Negation as failure. In Hervé Gallaire and Jack Minker, editors, *Logic and Databases*, pages 293–322. Plenum Press, New York, 1987.

[71]    Peter Clark and Bruce W. Porter. Building concept representations from reusable components. In *Proceedings of the Fourteenth National Conference on Artificial Intelligence, Providence, RI*, pages 369–376. AAAI Press, Menlo Park, CA, 1997.

[72]    Peter Clark and Bruce W. Porter. Using access paths to guide inference with conceptual graphs. In Dickson Lukose, Harry Delugach, Mary Keeler, Leroy Searle, and John Sowa, editors. *Conceptual Structures: Fulfilling Peirce's Dream, Proceedings of the Fifth International Conference on Conceptual Structures*, pages 521–535. Lecture Notes in Artificial Intelligence, Vol. 1257. Springer-Verlag, Berlin, 1997.

[73]    William F. Clocksin and Christopher S. Mellish. *Programming in PROLOG*, 3rd revised and extended edition. Springer-Verlag, Berlin, 1987.

[74]    Jacques Cohen. A view of the origins and development of PROLOG. *Communications of the ACM*, 31:26–36, 1988.

[75]    Alain Colmerauer, Henry Kanoui, Robert Pasero, and Philippe Roussel. Un systeme de communication homme-machine en francais. Technical report, Groupe de Recherche en Intelligence Artificielle, Université Aix-Marseille II, 1973.

[76]    Paul Compton and Bob Jansen. A philosophical basis for knowledge acquisition. *Knowledge Acquisition*, 2(3):241–257, 1990.

[77]    Luca Console and Pietro Torasso. A spectrum of logical definitions of model-based diagnosis. *Computational Intelligence*, 7:133–141, 1991.

[78]    Stephen A. Cook. The complexity of theorem-proving procedures. In *Proceedings of the Third Annual ACM Symposium on Theory of Computing, Shaker Heights, OH*, pages 151–158. Association for Computing Machinery, New York, 1971.

[79]    Gregory F. Cooper. Probabilistic inference using belief networks is NP-hard. *Artificial Intelligence*, 42(2–3):393–405, 1990.

[80]    Michael A. Covington, Donald Nute, and André Vellino. PROLOG *Programming in Depth*. Prentice Hall, Upper Saddle River, NJ, 1997.

[81]    Philip T. Cox and Tomasz Pietrzykowski. Causes for events: Their computation and applications. In *Proceedings of the Eighth Conference on Automated Deduction, Oxford*, pages 608–621. Springer, Berlin, 1986.

[82]    Paul Dagum and Michael Luby. Approximating probabilistic reasoning in Bayesian belief networks is NP-hard. *Artificial Intelligence*, 60(1):141–153, 1993.

[83]    Evgeny Dantsin, Andreas Goerdt, Edward Hirsch, Ravi Kannan, Jon Kleinberg, Christos Papadimitriou, Prabhakar Raghavan, and Uwe Schöning. A deterministic $(2 - 2/(k + 1))^n$ algorithm for k-sat based on local search. *Theoretical Computer Science*, 289(1):69–83, 2002.

[84]    Adnan Darwiche and Pierre Marquis. A knowledge compilation map. *Journal of Artificial Intelligence Research*, 17:229–264, 2002.

[85]    John Davies, Dieter Fensel, and Frank van Harmelen, editors. *On-To-Knowledge: Content-Driven Knowledge-Management through Evolving Ontologies*. John Wiley & Sons, New York, 2002.

[86]    Ernest Davis. *Representations of Commonsense Knowledge*. Morgan Kaufmann, San Francisco, 1990.

[87]    Martin Davis, George Logemann, and Donald Loveland. A machine program for theorem-proving. *Communications of the ACM*, 5(7):394–397, 1962.

[88]    Randall Davis and Walter Hamscher. Model-based reasoning: Troubleshooting. In Howard E. Shrobe, editor, *Exploring Artificial Intelligence*, pages 297–346. Morgan Kaufmann, San Mateo, CA, 1988.

[89]    Randall Davis, Howard Shrobe, and Peter Szolovits. What is a knowledge representation? *AI Magazine*, 14(1):17–33, 1993.

[90]    Bruno de Finetti. *Probability, Induction and Statistics: The Art of Guessing*. John Wiley & Sons, New York, 1972.

[91]    Bruno de Finetti. *Theory of Probability: A Critical Introductory Treatment*. John Wiley & Sons, New York, 1974.

[92]    Giuseppe De Giacomo, Yves Lespérance, and Hector J. Levesque. ConGolog, a concurrent programming language based on the situation calculus. *Artificial Intelligence*, 121(1–2):109–169, 2000.

[93]    Giuseppe De Giacomo, Yves Lespérance, Hector J. Levesque, and Sebastian Sardiña. On the semantics of deliberation in IndiGolog—from theory to implementation. In *Proceedings of the Eighth International Conference on Principles of Knowledge Representation and Reasoning*, Toulouse, France, pages 603–614. Morgan Kaufmann, San Francisco, 2002.

[94]    Johan de Kleer and Brian C. Williams. Diagnosing multiple faults. *Artificial Intelligence*, 32(1):97–130, 1987.

[95]    Johan de Kleer and Brian C. Williams. Diagnosis with behavioral modes. In *Proceedings of the Eleventh International Joint Conference on Artificial*

*Intelligence, Detroit,* pages 1324–1330. Morgan Kaufmann, San Mateo, CA, 1989.

[96]    Johan de Kleer, Jon Doyle, Charles Rich, Guy L. Steele, and Gerald J. Sussman. AMORD: A deductive procedure system. AI Memo 435, MIT, January, 1978.

[97]    Thomas L. Dean and Michael P. Wellman. *Planning and Control.* Morgan Kaufmann, San Mateo, CA, 1991.

[98]    Thomas Dean, James Allen, and John Aloimonos. *Artificial Intelligence: Theory and Practice.* Addison-Wesley, Menlo Park, CA, 1995.

[99]    Rina Dechter. *Constraint Processing.* Morgan Kaufmann, San Francisco, 2003.

[100]   James P. Delgrande. A framework for logics of explicit belief. *Computational Intelligence,* 11(1):47–88, 1995.

[101]   Arthur P. Dempster. A generalization of Bayesian inference. *Journal of the Royal Statistical Society,* 39:205–247, 1968.

[102]   Daniel C. Dennett. *The Intentional Stance.* MIT Press, Cambridge, MA, 1987.

[103]   Zoltan Dienes and Josef Perner. A theory of implicit and explicit knowledge. *Behavioral and Brain Sciences,* 22:735–755, 1999.

[104]   Simon Edmund Dixon. *Belief Revision: A Computational Approach.* Ph.D. thesis, Basser Department of Computer Science, University of Sydney, Australia, 1994.

[105]   Simon Edmund Dixon and Wayne Wobcke. The implementation of a first-order logic AGM belief revision system. In *Proceedings of the Fifth IEEE International Conference on Tools with Artificial Intelligence, Boston,* pages 40–47. IEEE, Los Alamitos, CA, 1993.

[106]   Patrick Doherty and Jonas Kvarnström. TALplanner: A temporal logic based planner. *AI Magazine,* 22(1):95–102, 2001.

[107]   Francesco M. Donini, Maurizio Lenzerini, Daniele Nardi, Werner Nutt. Tractable concept languages. In *Proceedings of the Twelfth International Joint Conference on Artificial Intelligence, Sydney, Australia,* pages 458–465. Morgan Kaufmann, San Mateo, CA, 1991.

[108]   Francesco M. Donini, Maurizio Lenzerini, Daniele Nardi, and Werner Nutt. The complexity of concept languages. In *Principles of Knowledge Representation and Reasoning: Proceedings of the Second International Conference, Cambridge, MA,* pages 151–162. Morgan Kaufmann, Los Altos, CA, 1991.

[109]   Francesco M. Donini, Maurizio Lenzerini, Daniele Nardi, and Andrea Schaerf. Reasoning in description logics. In Gerhard Brewka, editor, *Principles of Knowledge Representation,* pages 191–236. CSLI, Stanford, CA, 1996.

[110]   William F. Dowling and Jean H. Gallier. Linear-time algorithms for testing the satisfiability of propositional Horn formulae. *Journal of Logic Programming,* 1(3):267–284, 1984.

[111]   Jon Doyle. A truth maintenance system. *Artificial Intelligence,* 12(3):231–272, 1979.

[112] Jon Doyle. Reason maintenance and belief revision: Foundations versus coherence theories. In Peter Gärdenfors, editor, *Belief Revision*, pages 29–51. Cambridge University Press, Cambridge, England, 1992.

[113] Hubert Dreyfus. *What Computers Still Can't Do: A Critique of Artificial Reason.* MIT Press, Cambridge, MA, 1992.

[114] Didier Dubois, Henri Prade, and Ronald R. Yager, editors. *Readings in Fuzzy Sets for Intelligent Systems.* Morgan Kaufmann, San Mateo, CA, 1993.

[115] Richard Duda, John Gaschnig, and Peter Hart. Model design in the Prospector consultant system for mineral exploration. In Donald Michie, editor, *Expert Systems in the Microelectronic Age.* Edinburgh University Press, Edinburgh, 1979. Reprinted in Bonnie L. Webber and Nils J. Nilsson, editors, *Readings in Artificial Intelligence*, pages 334–348. Tioga, Los Altos, CA, 1981.

[116] Frank Dylla, Alexander Ferrein, and Gerhard Lakemeyer. Acting and deliberating using GOLOG in robotic soccer: A hybrid architecture. In *Proceedings of the Third International Cognitive Robotics Workshop, Edmonton, Alberta*, pages 29–36. AAAI Press, Menlo Park, CA, 2002.

[117] Umberto Eco and Thomas A. Sebeok, editors. *The Sign of Three — Dupin, Holmes, Peirce.* Indiana University Press, Bloomington, 1988.

[118] Paul Edwards, editor. *The Encyclopedia of Philosophy.* Macmillan, New York, 1967.

[119] Herbert B. Enderton. *A Mathematical Introduction to Logic.* Academic Press, New York, 1972.

[120] Kave Eshghi and Robert A. Kowalski. Abduction compared with negation by failure. In *Proceedings of the Sixth International Conference on Logic Programming, Lisbon, Portugal*, pages 234–254. MIT Press, Cambridge, MA, 1989.

[121] John Etchemendy. *The Concept of Logical Consequence.* Harvard University Press, Cambridge, MA, 1990.

[122] David W. Etherington and Raymond Reiter. On inheritance hierarchies with exceptions. In *Proceedings of the Third National Conference on Artificial Intelligence (AAAI-83), Washington, DC*, pages 104–108. William Kaufmann, Los Altos, CA, 1983. Reprinted in [47].

[123] Ronald Fagin and Joseph Y. Halpern. Belief, awareness and limited reasoning. *Artificial Intelligence*, 34(1):39–76, 1987.

[124] Scott E. Fahlman. NETL: *A System for Representing and Using Real-World Knowledge.* MIT Press, Cambridge, MA, 1979.

[125] Kuang T. Fann. *Peirce's Theory of Abduction.* Martinus Nijhoff, The Hague, The Netherlands, 1970.

[126] Dieter Fensel, Ian Horrocks, Frank van Harmelen, Stefan Decker, Michael Erdmann, and Michel C. A. Klein. OIL in a nutshell. In Rose Dieng and Olivier Corby, editors, *Knowledge Engineering and Knowledge Management Methods, Models, and Tools: Twelfth International Conference, EKAW 2000*, pages 1–16. Lecture Notes in Computer Science, Vol. 1937. Springer-Verlag, Heidelberg, 2000.

[127]   Richard E. Fikes and Tom Kehler. The role of frame-based representation in reasoning. *Communications of the ACM*, 28(9):904–920, 1985.

[128]   Richard E. Fikes and Nils J. Nilsson. STRIPS: A new approach to the application of theorem proving to problem solving. *Artificial Intelligence*, 2(3–4):189–208, 1971.

[129]   Richard E. Fikes and Nils J. Nilsson. STRIPS, a retrospective. *Artificial Intelligence*, 59(1–2):227–232, 1993.

[130]   Nicholas V. Findler, editor. *Associative Networks: Representation and Use of Knowledge by Computer*. Academic Press, New York, 1979.

[131]   J. Jeffrey Finger. *Exploiting Constraints in Design Synthesis*. Ph.D. thesis, Stanford University, 1987.

[132]   Melvin Fitting. *First-Order Logic and Automated Theorem Proving*, 2nd edition. Springer-Verlag, New York, 1996.

[133]   Kenneth D. Forbus and Johan de Kleer. *Building Problem Solvers*. MIT Press, Cambridge, MA, 1993.

[134]   Charles L. Forgy. Rete: A fast algorithm for the many patterns/many objects match problem. *Artificial Intelligence*, 19(1):17–37, 1982.

[135]   Gottlob Frege. *Begriffsschrift, eine der arithmetischen nachgebildete Formelsprache des reinen Denkens*. Halle, Berlin, 1879. English translation in Jean van Heijenoort, editor, *From Frege to Gödel: A Source Book in Mathematical Logic, 1879–1931*, pages 1–82. Harvard University Press, Cambridge, MA, 1967.

[136]   Nir Friedman and Joseph Y. Halpern. A knowledge-based framework for belief change, Part II: Revision and update. In *Proceedings of the Fifth International Conference on Principles of Knowledge Representation and Reasoning, Bonn, Germany*, pages 190–201. Morgan Kaufmann, San Francisco, 1994.

[137]   John D. Funge. *AI for Games and Animation: A Cognitive Modeling Approach*. A. K. Peters, Natick, MA, 1999.

[138]   Dov M. Gabbay and Franz Guenthner, editors. *Handbook of Philosophical Logic*, 2nd edition. 9 volumes (18 volumes expected). Kluwer, Dordrecht, The Netherlands, 2001–2002.

[139]   Dov M. Gabbay, Christopher John Hogger, and John Alan Robinson, editors. *Handbook of Logic in Artificial Intelligence and Logic Programming: Vols. I–V*. Oxford University Press, Oxford, 1993–1998.

[140]   Hervé Gallaire, Jack Minker, and Jean-Marie Nicolas. Logic and databases: A deductive approach. *ACM Computing Surveys*, 16(2):153–185, 1985.

[141]   Peter Gärdenfors. *Knowledge in Flux: Modeling the Dynamics of Epistemic States*. Bradford Books, MIT Press, Cambridge, MA, 1988.

[142]   Peter Gärdenfors. The dynamics of belief systems: Foundations vs. coherence theories. *Revue Internationale de Philosophie*, 44:24–46, 1990.

[143]   Peter Gärdenfors and David Makinson. Revisions of knowledge systems using epistemic entrenchment. In *Proceedings of the Second Conference on Theoretical Aspect of Reasoning about Knowledge, Pacific Grove, CA*, pages 83–96. Morgan Kaufmann, San Mateo, CA, 1988.

[144]    Peter Gärdenfors and Hans Rott. Belief revision. In Dov M. Gabbay, Christopher John Hogger, and John Alan Robinson, editors, *Handbook of Logic in Artificial Intelligence and Logic Programming*. Vol. IV: *Epistemic and Temporal Reasoning*, pages 35–132. Oxford University Press, Oxford, 1995.

[145]    Michael R. Garey and David S. Johnson. *Computers and Intractability: A Guide to the Theory of NP-Completeness*, 2nd printing with update edition. W. H. Freeman, San Francisco, 1980.

[146]    Allen Van Gelder, Kenneth A. Ross, and John S. Schlipf. The well-founded semantics for general logic programs. *Journal of the ACM*, 38(3):620–650, 1991.

[147]    Michael Gelfond and Vladimir Lifschitz. Classical negation in logic programs and disjunctive databases. *New Generation Computing*, 9(3–4):365–385, 1991.

[148]    Michael Gelfond and Vladimir Lifschitz. Action languages. *Electronic Transactions on AI*, 3(16):193–210, 1998.

[149]    Michael Gelfond, Vladimir Lifschitz, and Arkady Rabinov. What are the limitations of the situation calculus? In Robert S. Boyer, editor, *Automated Reasoning: Essays in Honor of Woody Bledsoe*, pages 167–179. Kluwer, Dordrecht, The Netherlands, 1991.

[150]    Michael R. Genesereth. The use of design descriptions in automated diagnosis. *Artificial Intelligence*, 24(1–3):411–436, 1984.

[151]    Michael R. Genesereth. Knowledge Interchange Format. In *Principles of Knowledge Representation and Reasoning: Proceedings of the Second International Conference, Cambridge, MA*, pages 599–600. Morgan Kaufmann, Los Altos, CA, 1991.

[152]    Michael R. Genesereth and Richard E. Fikes. *Knowledge Interchange Format*, version 3.0 reference manual. Technical Report Logic-92-1, Stanford University, Stanford, CA, 1992.

[153]    Michael R. Genesereth and Nils J. Nilsson. *Logical Foundations of Artificial Intelligence*. Morgan Kaufmann, Los Altos, CA, 1987.

[154]    Gerhard Gentzen. Untersuchungen über das logische Schliessen. *Mathematische Zeitschrift*, 39:176–210, 405–431, 1934. Translated as Investigations into logical deduction, in M. E. Szabo, editor and translator, *The Collected Papers of Gerhard Gentzen*, pages 68–131. North-Holland, Amsterdam, 1969.

[155]    Michael P. Georgeff. Planning. *Annual Review of Computer Science*, 2:359–400, 1987.

[156]    Edmund L. Gettier. Is justified true belief knowledge? *Analysis*, 23:121–123, 1963. Reprinted in [168].

[157]    Matthew L. Ginsberg, editor. *Readings in Nonmonotonic Reasoning*. Morgan Kaufmann, Los Altos, CA, 1987.

[158]    Matthew L. Ginsberg. Universal planning: An (almost) universally bad idea. *AI Magazine*, 10(4):40–44, 1989.

[159]    Matthew L. Ginsberg. Knowledge interchange format: The KIF of death. *AI Magazine*, 12(3):57–63, 1991.

[160]    Matthew L. Ginsberg. *Essentials of Artificial Intelligence*. Morgan Kaufmann, San Francisco, 1993.

[161]    Kurt Gödel. *Über die Vollständigkeit des Logikkalküls.* Ph.D. thesis, University of Vienna, 1930.

[162]    Kurt Gödel. Über formal unentscheidbare Sätze der Principia Mathematica und verwandter System I. *Monatshefte für Mathematik und Physik*, 38:173–198, 1931.

[163]    Kurt Gödel. *On Formally Undecidable Propositions of Principia Mathematica and Related Systems.* Basic Books, New York, 1962. Translated by Bernard Meltzer. Reprinted by Dover, New York, 1992. Original appears in [162].

[164]    Nikos Gorogiannis and Mark D. Ryan. Implementation of belief change operators using BDDs. *Studia Logica*, 70(1):131–156, 2002.

[165]    Janice I. Glasgow, editor. Taking issue forum on imagery and AI. *Computational Intelligence*, 9(4):309–333, 1993.

[166]    Cordell Green. Applications of theorem proving to problem solving. In *Proceedings of the First International Joint Conference on Artificial Intelligence, Washington, DC*, pages 219–239. Morgan Kaufmann, Los Altos, CA, 1969.

[167]    Cordell Green. Theorem-proving by resolution as a basis for question-answering systems. In Bernard Meltzer and Donald Michie, editors, *Machine Intelligence 4*, pages 183–205. Edinburgh University Press, Edinburgh, 1969.

[168]    A. Phillips Griffiths, editor. *Knowledge and Belief.* Oxford University Press, London, 1967.

[169]    Henrik Grosskreutz and Gerhard Lakemeyer. Turning high-level plans into robot programs in uncertain domains. In *Proceedings of the Fourteenth European Conference on Artificial Intelligence, Berlin*, pages 548–552. IOS Press, Amsterdam, 2000.

[170]    Adam Grove. Two modellings for theory change. *Journal of Philosophical Logic*, 17:157–170, 1988.

[171]    Thomas Gruber. Toward principles for the design of ontologies used for knowledge sharing. *International Journal of Human–Computer Studies*, 43(5–6): 907–928, 1995.

[172]    Susan Haack. *Philosophy of Logics.* Cambridge University Press, Cambridge, England, 1978.

[173]    Susan Haack. Do we need fuzzy logic? *International Journal of Man–Machine Studies*, 11:437–445, 1979. Reprinted in [174].

[174]    Susan Haack. *Deviant Logic, Fuzzy Logic: Beyond the Formalism.* University of Chicago Press, Chicago, 1996. Revised edition of *Deviant Logic*, Cambridge University Press, Cambridge, England, 1974.

[175]    Andrew R. Haas. The case for domain-specific frame axioms. In *Proceedings of the 1987 Workshop on the Frame Problem in Artificial Intelligence*, pages 343–348. Morgan Kaufmann, Los Altos, CA, 1987.

[176]    Armin Haken. The intractability of Resolution. *Theoretical Computer Science*, 39:297–308, 1985.

[177]    Joseph Y. Halpern. *Reasoning about Uncertainty.* MIT Press, Cambridge, MA, 2003.

[178]    Walter Hamscher, Luca Console, and Johan de Kleer, editors. *Readings in Model-Based Diagnosis*. Morgan Kaufmann, San Mateo, CA, 1992.

[179]    Sven Ove Hansson. *A Textbook of Belief Dynamics: Theory Change and Database Updating*. Kluwer, Dordrecht, The Netherlands, 1999.

[180]    Gilbert H. Harman. Inference to the best explanation. *Philosophical Review*, 74:88–95, 1965.

[181]    Patrick J. Hayes. In defense of logic. In *Proceedings of the Fifth International Joint Conference on Artificial Intelligence, Cambridge, MA*, pages 559–565. Morgan Kaufmann, Los Altos, CA, 1977. Reprinted in [47].

[182]    Patrick J. Hayes. The logic of frames. In Dieter Metzing, editor, *Frame Conceptions and Text Understanding*, pages 46–61. Walter de Gruyter, Berlin, 1979.

[183]    Frederick Hayes-Roth, Donald A. Waterman, and Douglas B. Lenat, editors. *Building Expert Systems*. Addison-Wesley, Reading, MA, 1983.

[184]    Carl G. Hempel and Paul Oppenheim. Studies in the logic of explanation. *Philosophy of Science*, 15:135–175, 1965.

[185]    James Hendler and Deborah L. McGuinness. The DARPA agent markup language. *IEEE Intelligent Systems*, 15(6):67–73, 2000.

[186]    Carl Hewitt. PLANNER: A language for proving theorems in robots. In *Proceedings of the First International Joint Conference on Artificial Intelligence, Washington, DC*, pages 295–301. Morgan Kaufmann, Los Altos, CA, 1969.

[187]    Wilfred Hodges. *Logic*. Penguin Books, Harmondsworth, Middlesex, UK, 1977.

[188]    Christopher John Hogger. *Introduction to Logic Programming*. Academic Press, London, 1984.

[189]    Steffen Hölldobler and Josef Schneeberger. A new deductive approach to planning. *New Generation Computing*, 8(3):225–244, 1990.

[190]    Alfred Horn. On sentences which are true of direct unions of algebras. *Journal of Symbolic Logic*, 16:14–21, 1951.

[191]    Ian Horrocks and Peter F. Patel-Schneider. Reducing OWL entailment to description logic satisfiability. In *Proceedings of International Semantic Web Conference (ISWC2003)*, pages 17–29, Sundial Resort, Florida, October 2003. Lecture Notes in Computer Science, Vol. 2870. Springer-Verlag, Heidelberg, 2003.

[192]    Ronald A. Howard and James E. Matheson. Influence diagrams. In Ronald A. Howard and James E. Matheson, editors, *Readings on the Principles and Applications of Decision Analysis*, Vol. 2, pages 721–762. Strategic Decisions Group, Menlo Park, CA, 1984.

[193]    Michael N. Huhns and Munindar Singh, editors. *Readings in Agents*. Morgan Kaufmann, San Francisco, 1997.

[194]    Michael Huth and Mark D. Ryan. *Logic in Computer Science: Modelling and Reasoning about Systems*. Cambridge University Press, Cambridge, England, 2000.

[195]    David J. Israel. The role of logic in knowledge representation. *IEEE Computer*, 16(10):37–42, 1983.

[196]    Peter Jackson. *Introduction to Expert Systems*. Addison-Wesley, Reading, MA, 1990.

[197]    Peter Jackson. Computing prime implicates incrementally. In *Proceedings of the Eleventh Conference on Automated Deduction, Saratoga Springs, New York*, pages 253–267. Lecture Notes in Artificial Intelligence, Vol. 607. Springer-Verlag, Heidelberg, 1992.

[198]    Joxan Jaffar and Jean-Louis Lassez. Constraint logic programming. In *Conference Record of the Fourteenth Annual ACM Symposium on Principles of Programming Languages, Munich, Germany*, pages 111–119. Association for Computing Machinery, New York, 1987.

[199]    Joxan Jaffar, Spiro Michaylov, Peter J. Stuckey, and Roland H. C. Yap. The CLP(R) language and system. *ACM Transactions on Programming Languages and Systems*, 14(3):339–395, 1992.

[200]    Edwin T. Jaynes. *Probability Theory: The Logic of Science*. Cambridge University Press, Cambridge, England, 2003.

[201]    Richard Jeffrey. *The Logic of Decision*. McGraw-Hill, New York, 1965.

[202]    Richard Jeffrey. *Probability and the Art of Judgment*. Cambridge Studies in Probability, Induction, and Decision Theory. Cambridge University Press, Cambridge, England, 1992.

[203]    Finn V. Jensen. *An Introduction to Bayesian Networks*. University College London Press, London, 1996.

[204]    Philip N. Johnson-Laird. *Mental Models*. Harvard University Press, Cambridge, MA, 1983.

[205]    John R. Josephson and Susan G. Josephson, editors. *Abductive Inference: Computation, Philosophy, Technology*. Cambridge University Press, Cambridge, England, 1994.

[206]    Antonis C. Kakas and Paolo Mancarella. Database updates through abduction. In *Proceedings of the Sixteenth Conference on Very Large Databases, Brisbane, Australia*, pages 650–661. Morgan Kaufmann, San Mateo, CA, 1990.

[207]    Antonis C. Kakas, Robert A. Kowalski, and Francesca Toni. Abductive logic programming. *Journal of Logic and Computation*, 2(6):719–770, 1993.

[208]    Antonis C. Kakas, Robert A. Kowalski, and Francesca Toni. The role of abduction in logic programming. In Dov M. Gabbay, editor, *Handbook of Logic in Artificial Intelligence and Logic Programming*, Vol. 5, pages 235–324. Oxford University Press, Oxford, 1995. An updated version of [207].

[209]    Byeong H. Kang, Paul Compton, and Phillip Preston. Multiple classification ripple down rules: Evaluation and possibilities. In *Proceedings of the Ninth Knowledge Acquisition for Knowledge Based Systems Workshop*, Banff, Alberta, Canada, pages 17.1–17.20. 1995.

[210]    G. Neelakantan Kartha. Two counterexamples related to Baker's approach to the frame problem. *Artificial Intelligence*, 69(1–2):379–391, 1994.

[211]   G. Neelakantan Kartha and Vladimir Lifschitz. A simple formalization of actions using circumscription. In *Proceedings of the Fourteenth International Joint Conference on Artificial Intelligence, Montreal*, pages 1970–1977. Morgan Kaufmann, San Mateo, CA, 1995.

[212]   Hirofumi Katsuno and Alberto O. Mendelzon. On the difference between updating a knowledge base and revising it. In *Principles of Knowledge Representation and Reasoning: Proceedings of the Second International Conference, Cambridge, MA*, pages 387–394. Morgan Kaufmann, Los Altos, CA, 1991.

[213]   Hirofumi Katsuno and Alberto O. Mendelzon. On the difference between updating a knowledge base and revising it. In Peter Gärdenfors, editor, *Belief Revision*, pages 183–203. Cambridge University Press, Cambridge, England, 1992. This paper extends [212].

[214]   Henry Kautz and Bart Selman. Planning as satisfiability. In *Proceedings of the Tenth European Conference on Artificial Intelligence, Vienna, Austria*, pages 359–363. John Wiley & Sons, Chichester, 1992.

[215]   Henry Kautz and Bart Selman. An empirical evaluation of knowledge compilation by theory approximation. In *Proceedings of the Twelfth National Conference on Artificial Intelligence, Seattle*, pages 155–161. AAAI Press, Menlo Park, CA, 1994.

[216]   Alex Kean. A formal characterisation of a domain independent abductive reasoning system. Technical Report HKUST-CS93-4, Department of Computer Science, Hong Kong University of Science and Technology, March 1993.

[217]   Alex Kean and George Tsiknis. An incremental method for generating prime implicants/implicates. *Journal of Symbolic Computation*, 9(2):185–206, 1990.

[218]   William Calvert Kneale and Martha Kneale. *The Development of Logic*. Clarendon Press, Oxford, 1964.

[219]   Donald E. Knuth and Peter B. Bendix. Simple word problems in universal algebra. In John Leech, editor, *Computational Problems in Abstract Algebra*, pages 263–267. Pergamon Press, Oxford, 1970.

[220]   Teuvo Kohonen. *Self-Organization and Associative Memory*, 3rd edition. Springer-Verlag, Berlin, 1989.

[221]   Andrei N. Kolmogorov. *Foundations of the Theory of Probability*. Chelsea, New York, 1950.

[222]   Kurt Konolige. On the relation between default logic and autoepistemic logic. *Artificial Intelligence*, 35(3):343–382, 1988.

[223]   Robert A. Kowalski. Predicate logic as a programming language. *Information Processing*, 74:569–574, 1974.

[224]   Robert A. Kowalski. *Logic for Problem Solving*. Elsevier Science, New York, 1979.

[225]   Robert A. Kowalski. The early years of logic programming. *Communications of the ACM*, 31:38–43, 1988.

[226]   Robert A. Kowalski and Mark J. Sergot. A logic-based calculus of events. *New Generation Computing*, 4:67–95, 1986.

[227]    Sarit Kraus, Daniel Lehmann, and Menachem Magidor. Nonmonotonic reasoning, preferential models and cumulative logics. *Artificial Intelligence*, 44(1): 167–207, 1990.

[228]    Natasha Kurtonina and Maarten de Rijke. Expressiveness of concept expressions in first-order description logics. *Artificial Intelligence*, 107(2):303–330, 1999.

[229]    Yannis Labrou. *Semantics for an Agent Communication Language*. Ph.D. thesis, Department of Computer Science and Electrical Engineering, University of Maryland, Baltimore County, 1996.

[230]    Yannis Labrou and Tim Finin. Semantics and conversations for an agent communication language. In *Proceedings of the Fifteenth International Joint Conference on Artificial Intelligence, Nagoya*, pages 584–591. Morgan Kaufmann, San Francisco, 1997. Reprinted in [193].

[231]    John E. Laird, Allen Newell, and Paul S. Rosenbloom. SOAR: An architecture for general intelligence. *Artificial Intelligence*, 33(1):1–64, 1987.

[232]    Fritz Lehmann and Ervin Y. Rodin, editors. *Semantic Networks in Artificial Intelligence*. Pergamon Press, Oxford, 1992.

[233]    Alexander Leitsch. *The Resolution Calculus*. Texts in Theoretical Computer Science. Springer-Verlag, Berlin, 1997.

[234]    Edward John Lemmon. *Beginning Logic*. Nelson, London, 1967.

[235]    Douglas B. Lenat and Ramanathan V. Guha. *Building Large Knowledge-Based Systems: Representation and Inference in the CYC Project*. Addison-Wesley, Reading, MA, 1990.

[236]    Maurizio Lenzerini, Daniele Nardi, and Maria Simi, editors. *Inheritance Hierarchies in Knowledge Representation and Programming Languages*. John Wiley & Sons, Chichester, 1991.

[237]    Yves Lespérance, Hector J. Levesque, Fangzhen Lin, Daniel Marcu, Raymond Reiter, and Richard Scherl. A logical approach to high-level robot programming: A progress report. In *Control of the Physical World by Intelligent Systems, Working Notes of the 1994 AAAI Fall Symposium*, pages 79–85. AAAI Press, Menlo Park, CA, 1994.

[238]    Hector J. Levesque. Foundations of a functional approach to knowledge representation. *Artificial Intelligence*, 23(2):155–212, 1984.

[239]    Hector J. Levesque. A logic of implicit and explicit belief. In *Proceedings of the Fourth National Conference on Artificial Intelligence (AAAI-84), Austin, TX*, pages 198–202. William Kaufmann, Los Altos, CA, 1984.

[240]    Hector J. Levesque. Knowledge representation and reasoning. *Annual Review of Computer Science*, 1:255–288, 1986.

[241]    Hector J. Levesque. Making believers out of computers. *Artificial Intelligence*, 30(1):81–108, 1986.

[242]    Hector J. Levesque. A knowledge-level account of abduction. In *Proceedings of the Eleventh International Joint Conference on Artificial Intelligence, Detroit*, pages 1061–1067. Morgan Kaufmann, San Mateo, CA, 1989.

[243]   Hector J. Levesque and Ronald J. Brachman. A fundamental tradeoff in knowledge representation and reasoning (revised version). In Ronald J. Brachman and Hector J. Levesque, editors, *Readings in Knowledge Representation*, pages 41–70. Morgan Kaufmann, San Francisco, 1985.

[244]   Hector J. Levesque and Gerhard Lakemeyer. *The Logic of Knowledge Bases*. MIT Press, Cambridge, 2000.

[245]   Hector J. Levesque and Maurice Pagnucco. LEGOLOG: Inexpensive experiments in cognitive robotics. In *Proceedings of the Second International Cognitive Robotics Workshop*, pages 104–109. ECAI, Berlin, 2000.

[246]   Hector J. Levesque, Raymond Reiter, Yves Lespérance, Fangzhen Lin, and Richard Scherl. GOLOG: A logic programming language for dynamic domains. *Journal of Logic Programming*, 31:59–84, 1997.

[247]   David Lewis. *Counterfactuals*. Harvard University Press, Cambridge, MA, 1973. Reprinted with corrections, 1986.

[248]   David Lewis. Probabilities of conditionals and conditional probabilities. *The Philosophical Review*, 85:297–315, 1976.

[249]   Vladimir Lifschitz. Computing circumscription. In *Proceedings of the Ninth International Joint Conference on Artificial Intelligence, Los Angeles*, pages 121–127. Morgan Kaufmann, Los Altos, CA, 1985.

[250]   Vladimir Lifschitz. Pointwise circumscription. In *Proceedings of the Fifth National Conference on Artificial Intelligence (AAAI-86), Philadelphia*, pages 406–410. Morgan Kaufmann, Los Altos, CA, 1986.

[251]   Vladimir Lifschitz. On the semantics of STRIPS. In *Proceedings of the 1986 Workshop on Reasoning about Actions and Plans, Timberline Lodge, OR*, pages 1–9. Morgan Kaufmann, Los Altos, CA, 1987.

[252]   Vladimir Lifschitz. Frames in the space of situations. *Artificial Intelligence*, 46(3):365–376, 1990.

[253]   Vladimir Lifschitz. Circumscription. In Dov M. Gabbay, Christopher John Hogger, and John Alan Robinson, editors, *Handbook of Logic in Artificial Intelligence and Logic Programming*, Vol. 3, pages 298–352. Oxford University Press, Oxford, 1994.

[254]   Vladimir Lifschitz, editor. *Formalizing Common Sense: Papers by John McCarthy*. Intellect, Exeter, England, 1998.

[255]   James Lighthill. Artificial Intelligence: A general survey. In J. Lighthill, N. S. Sutherland, R. M. Needham, H. C. Longuet-Higgins, and D. Michie, editors, *Artificial Intelligence: A Paper Symposium*. Science Research Council of Great Britain, London, 1973.

[256]   Fangzhen Lin. Embracing causality in specifying the indirect effects of actions. In *Proceedings of the Fourteenth International Joint Conference on Artificial Intelligence, Montreal*, pages 1985–1991. Morgan Kaufmann, San Mateo, CA, 1995.

[257]   Robert K. Lindsay, Bruce G. Buchanan, Edward A. Feigenbaum, and Joshua Lederberg. *Applications of Artificial Intelligence for Organic Chemistry: The DENDRAL Project*. McGraw-Hill, New York, 1980.

[258]    Peter Lipton. *Inference to the Best Explanation*. Routledge, London, 1991.

[259]    John W. Lloyd. *Foundations of Logic Programming*, 2nd, extended edition. Springer-Verlag, Berlin, 1987.

[260]    George F. Luger. *Artificial Intelligence: Structures and Strategies for Complex Problem Solving*, 4th edition. Addison-Wesley, London, 2002.

[261]    Witold Łukaszewicz. *Non-Monotonic Reasoning: Formalization of Commonsense Reasoning*. Ellis Horwood, New York, 1990.

[262]    David Makinson. Bridges between classical and nonmonotonic logic. *Logic Journal of the IGPL*, 11(1):69–96, 2003.

[263]    David Makinson and Peter Gärdenfors. Relations between the logic of theory change and nonmonotonic logic. In Andre Fuhrmann and Michael Morreau, editors, *The Logic of Theory Change*, pages 185–205. Lecture Notes in Artificial Intelligence, Vol. 465. Springer-Verlag, Berlin, 1990.

[264]    Ebrahim H. Mamdani. Advances in the linguistic synthesis of fuzzy controllers. *International Journal of Man–Machine Studies*, 8:669–678, 1976.

[265]    Zohar Manna and Richard Waldinger. *The Logical Basis for Computer Programming*. Vol. 1: *Deductive Reasoning*. Addison-Wesley, Reading, MA, 1985.

[266]    V. Wiktor Marek and Miroslaw Truszczyński. Relating autoepistemic and default logics. In *Proceedings of the First International Conference on Principles of Knowledge Representation and Reasoning, Toronto*, pages 276–288. Morgan Kaufmann, Los Altos, CA, 1989.

[267]    V. Wiktor Marek and Miroslaw Truszczyński. *Nonmonotonic Logic: Context Dependent Reasoning*. Springer-Verlag, Berlin, 1993.

[268]    Pierre Marquis. Extending abduction from propositional to first-order logic. In *Proceedings of the International Workshop on Fundamentals of Artificial Intelligence*, pages 141–155. Lecture Notes in Computer Science, Vol. 535. Springer-Verlag, Berlin, 1991.

[269]    Kim Marriott and Peter J. Stuckey. *Programming with Constraints: An Introduction*. MIT Press, Cambridge, MA, 1998.

[270]    João P. Martins and Stuart C. Shapiro. A model for belief revision. *Artificial Intelligence*, 35(1):25–79, 1988.

[271]    Marta Cialdea Mayer and Fiora Pirri. Propositional abduction in modal logic. *Journal of the Interest Group on Pure and Applied Logics*, 3(6):907–919, 1995.

[272]    David McAllester. A widely used truth-maintenance system. AI Memo, MIT, Cambridge, MA, 1985.

[273]    Norman McCain and Hudson Turner. A causal theory of ramifications and qualifications. In *Proceedings of the Fourteenth International Joint Conference on Artificial Intelligence, Montreal*, pages 1978–1984. Morgan Kaufmann, San Mateo, CA, 1995.

[274]    Norman McCain and Hudson Turner. Causal theories of action and change. In *Proceedings of the Fourteenth National Conference on Artificial Intelligence, Providence, RI*, pages 460–465. AAAI Press, Menlo Park, CA, 1997.

[275]   John McCarthy. Programs with common sense. In *Mechanization of Thought Processes*, Vol. 1, Proc. Symposium, National Physical Laboratory, London, pages 77–84, November 1958. Reprinted in Marvin Minsky, editor, *Semantic Information Processing*, pages 216–270. MIT Press, Cambridge, MA, 1968. Reprinted in [47].

[276]   John McCarthy. Situations, actions, and causal laws. Technical report, Stanford University Artificial Intelligence Project, 1963.

[277]   John McCarthy. Epistemological problems in artificial intelligence. In *Proceedings of the Fifth International Joint Conference on Artificial Intelligence, Cambridge, MA*, pages 1038–1044. Morgan Kaufmann, Los Altos, CA, 1977. Reprinted in [47] and [254].

[278]   John McCarthy. Circumscription: A form of non-monotonic reasoning. *Artificial Intelligence*, 13(1–2):27–39, 1980. Reprinted in [254].

[279]   John McCarthy. Applications of circumscription to formalizing commonsense knowledge. *Artificial Intelligence*, 28(1):89–116, 1986. Reprinted in [254].

[280]   John McCarthy. History of circumscription. *Artificial Intelligence*, 59(1–2):23–26, 1993.

[281]   John McCarthy. Modality, si! modal logic, no! *Studia Logica*, 59(1):29–32, 1997.

[282]   John McCarthy and Patrick Hayes. Some philosophical problems from the standpoint of artificial intelligence. In Donald Michie and Bernard Meltzer, editors, *Machine Intelligence 4*, pages 463–502. Edinburgh University Press, Edinburgh, 1969. Reprinted in [254].

[283]   John McDermott. R1: An expert in the computer systems domain. In *Proceedings of the First National Conference on Artificial Intelligence, Stanford, CA*, pages 269–271. AAAI, Menlo Park, CA, 1980.

[284]   John McDermott. R1: The formative years. *AI Magazine*, 2(2):21–29, 1981.

[285]   John McDermott. R1: A rule-based configurer of computer systems. *Artificial Intelligence*, 19(1):39–88, 1982.

[286]   Deborah L. McGuinness and Frank van Harmelen, editors. OWL web ontology language overview. Technical report, World Wide Web Consortium, 2003.

[287]   Karl Meinke and John V. Tucker, editors. *Many-Sorted Logic and Its Applications*, John Wiley & Sons, Chichester, 1993.

[288]   Elliot Mendelson. *Introduction to Mathematical Logic*, 4th edition. Chapman and Hall, London, 1997.

[289]   Marc Mezard, Giorgio Parisi, and Riccardo Zecchina. Analytic and algorithmic solution of random satisfiability problems. *Science*, 297:812–815, 2002.

[290]   Jack Minker. On indefinite databases and the closed-world assumption. Lecture Notes in Computer Science, Vol. 138, pages 292–308. Springer-Verlag, Berlin, 1982.

[291]   Jack Minker. Logic and databases: A 20 year perspective—updated in honor of Ray Reiter. In Hector J. Levesque and Fiora Pirri, editors, *Logical Foundations for Cognitive Agents: Contributions in Honor of Ray Reiter*, pages 234–299. Springer, Berlin, 1999.

[292]  Marvin Minsky. A framework for representing knowledge. In John Haugeland, editor, *Mind Design*, pages 95–128. MIT Press, Cambridge, MA, 1981. Reprinted in [47].

[293]  David Mitchell, Bart Selman, and Hector J. Levesque. Hard and easy distributions of SAT problems. In *Proceedings of the Tenth National Conference on Artificial Intelligence, San Jose, CA*, pages 459–465. AAAI Press, Menlo Park, CA, 1992.

[294]  Robert C. Moore. The role of logic in knowledge representation and common-sense reasoning. In *Proceedings of the Second National Conference on Artificial Intelligence, Pittsburgh*, pages 428–433. AAAI, Menlo Park, CA, 1982. Reprinted in [299].

[295]  Robert C. Moore. Possible-world semantics for autoepistemic logic. In *Proceedings of the Non-Monotonic Reasoning Workshop, New Paltz, NY*, pages 344–354. AAAI, Menlo Park, CA, 1984. Reprinted in [299].

[296]  Robert C. Moore. Semantical considerations on nonmonotonic logic. *Artificial Intelligence*, 25(1):75–94, 1985. Reprinted in [299].

[297]  Robert C. Moore. The role of logic in artificial intelligence. In I. Benson, editor, *Intelligent Machinery: Theory and Practice*. Cambridge University Press, Cambridge, England, 1986. Reprinted in [299].

[298]  Robert C. Moore. Autoepistemic logic revisited. *Artificial Intelligence*, 59(1–2): 27–30, 1993. Reprinted in [299].

[299]  Robert C. Moore. *Logic and Representation*. CSLI Lecture Notes, Vol. 39. CSLI, Stanford, CA, 1995.

[300]  Steven Morris and Paul O'Rorke. An approach to theory revision using abduction. In *Working Notes of the 1990 Spring Symposium on Automated Abduction*, pages 33–37. Technical Report 90-32. University of California, Irvine, 1990.

[301]  Ernest Nagel and James R. Newman. *Gödel's Proof*. New York University Press, New York, 1958. Revised edition, cowritten with Douglas R. Hofstadter, 2002.

[302]  Richard E. Neapolitan. *Probabilistic Reasoning in Expert Systems: Theory and Algorithms*. John Wiley & Sons, New York, 1990.

[303]  Bernhard Nebel. *Reasoning and Revision in Hybrid Systems*. Lecture Notes in Artificial Intelligence, Vol. 422, Springer-Verlag, Berlin, 1990.

[304]  Bernhard Nebel. Terminological reasoning is inherently intractable. *Artificial Intelligence*, 43(2):235–249, 1990.

[305]  Allen Newell. The knowledge level. *Artificial Intelligence*, 18(1):87–127, 1982.

[306]  Allen Newell and Herbert A. Simon. GPS, a program that simulates thought. In Edward A. Feigenbaum and Julian Feldman, editors, *Computers and Thought*, McGraw-Hill, New York, 1963. Republished by AAAI Press/MIT Press, Menlo Park, CA/Cambridge, MA, 1995.

[307]  Allen Newell and Herbert A. Simon. *Human Problem Solving*, Prentice Hall, Englewood Cliffs, NJ, 1972.

[308]  Hwee Tou Ng and Raymond J. Mooney. On the role of coherence in abductive explanation. In *Proceedings of the Eighth National Conference on Artificial Intelligence, Boston*, pages 337–342. AAAI Press, Menlo Park, CA, 1990.

[309]     Nils J. Nilsson. *Problem Solving Methods in Artificial Intelligence.* McGraw-Hill, Toronto, 1971.

[310]     Nils J. Nilsson. Shakey the robot. Technical report, SRI, 1984.

[311]     Nils J. Nilsson. *Artificial Intelligence: A New Synthesis.* Morgan Kaufmann, San Francisco, 1998.

[312]     Ulf Nilsson and Jan Maluszynski. *Logic, Programming and* PROLOG. John Wiley & Sons, Chichester, 1995.

[313]     Maurice Pagnucco and Pavlos Peppas. Causality and minimal change demystified. In *Proceedings of the Seventeenth International Joint Conference on Artificial Intelligence, Seattle,* pages 125–130. Morgan Kaufmann, San Francisco, 2001.

[314]     George S. Pappas and Marshall Swain, editors. *Essays on Knowledge and Justification.* Cornell University Press, Ithaca, NY, 1978.

[315]     Jeff B. Paris. *The Uncertain Reasoner's Companion: A Mathematical Perspective.* Cambridge Tracts in Theoretical Computer Science 39. Cambridge University Press, Cambridge, England, 1994.

[316]     Peter F. Patel-Schneider. Small can be beautiful in knowledge representation. In *Proceedings of the IEEE Workshop on Principles of Knowledge-Based Systems, Denver,* pages 11–16. IEEE Press, Los Alamitos, CA, 1984.

[317]     Peter F. Patel-Schneider. A four-valued semantics for terminological logics. *Artificial Intelligence,* 38(3):319–351, 1989.

[318]     Peter F. Patel-Schneider, Ronald J. Brachman, and Hector J. Levesque. ARGON: Knowledge representation meets information retrieval. In *Proceedings of the First Conference on Artificial Intelligence Applications, Denver,* pages 280–286. IEEE Computer Society Press, Silver Spring, MD, 1984.

[319]     Gabrielle Paul. Approaches to abductive reasoning: An overview. *Artificial Intelligence Review,* 7:109–152, 1993.

[320]     Judea Pearl. *Probabilistic Reasoning in Intelligent Systems: Networks of Plausible Inference,* 2nd revised printing. Morgan Kaufmann, San Francisco, 1988.

[321]     Judea Pearl. Belief networks revisited. *Artificial Intelligence,* 59(1–2):49–56, 1993.

[322]     Edwin P. D. Pednault. ADL: Exploring the middle ground between STRIPS and the situation calculus. In *Proceedings of the First International Conference on Principles of Knowledge Representation and Reasoning, Toronto,* pages 324–332. Morgan Kaufmann, Los Altos, CA, 1989.

[323]     Charles Sanders Peirce. *Collected Papers of Charles Sanders Peirce.* Vols. 1–8, edited by Charles Hartshorne, Paul Weiss, and Arthur W. Burks. Harvard University Press, Cambridge, MA, 1931–1958.

[324]     Charles Sanders Peirce. *Philosophical Writings of Peirce.* Selected and edited with an introduction by Justus Buchler. Dover, New York, 1955. Unaltered republication of book published in 1940 by Routledge and Kegan Paul.

[325]     Charles Sanders Peirce. *Reasoning and the Logic of Things.* Edited by Kenneth Laine Ketner, with an introduction by Kenneth Laine Ketner and Hilary Putnam. Harvard University Press, Cambridge, MA, 1992.

[326]   Yun Peng and James A. Reggia. *Abductive Inference Models for Diagnostic Problem-Solving.* Springer-Verlag, New York, 1990.

[327]   Roger Penrose. *The Emperor's New Mind: Concerning Computers, Minds, and the Laws of Physics.* Vintage, London, 1990.

[328]   Fiora Pirri and Raymond Reiter. Some contributions to the metatheory of the situation calculus. *Journal of the ACM,* 46(3):261–325, 1999.

[329]   Marco Pistore and Paolo Traverso. Planning as model checking for extended goals in non-deterministic domains. In *Proceedings of the Seventeenth International Joint Conference on Artificial Intelligence, Seattle,* pages 479–486. Morgan Kaufmann, San Francisco, 2001.

[330]   David Poole. A logical framework for default reasoning. *Artificial Intelligence,* 36(1):27–47, 1988.

[331]   David Poole, Randy Goebel, and Romas Aleliunas. THEORIST: A logical reasoning system for defaults and diagnosis. In Nick Cercone and Gordon McCalla, editors, *The Knowledge Frontier: Essays in the Representation of Knowledge,* pages 331–352. Springer-Verlag, New York, 1987.

[332]   David Poole, Alan Mackworth, and Randy Goebel. *Computational Intelligence: A Logical Approach.* Oxford University Press, New York, 1998.

[333]   Harry E. Pople Jr. On the mechanization of abductive logic. In *Proceedings of the Third International Joint Conference on Artificial Intelligence, Stanford, CA,* pages 147–152. Morgan Kaufmann, Los Altos, CA, 1973.

[334]   Zenon Pylyshyn. *Computation and Cognition: Toward a Foundation for Cognitive Science.* MIT Press, Cambridge, MA, 1984.

[335]   M. Ross Quillian. *Semantic Memory.* Ph.D. thesis, Carnegie Institute of Technology, 1966.

[336]   M. Ross Quillian. Semantic memory. In Marvin Minsky, editor, *Semantic Information Processing,* pages 216–270. MIT Press, Cambridge, MA, 1968.

[337]   Ashwin Ram and David Leake. Evaluation of explanatory hypotheses. In *Proceedings of the Thirteenth Annual Conference of the Cognitive Science Society, Chicago,* pages 867–871. Lawrence Erlbaum Associates, Hillsdale, NJ, 1991.

[338]   Han Reichgelt. *Knowledge Representation: An AI Perspective.* Ablex, Norwood, NJ, 1991.

[339]   Michael Reinfrank. *Fundamentals and Logical Foundations of Truth Maintenance.* Ph.D. thesis, Department of Computer and Information Science, University of Linköping, 1989.

[340]   Michael Reinfrank, Oskar Dessler, and Gerhard Brewka. On the relation between truth maintenance and autoepistemic logic. In *Proceedings of the Eleventh International Joint Conference on Artificial Intelligence, Detroit,* pages 1206–1212. Morgan Kaufmann, San Mateo, CA, 1989.

[341]   Raymond Reiter. Equality and domain closure in first-order databases. *Journal of the Association for Computing Machinery,* 27(2):235–249, 1980.

[342]   Raymond Reiter. A logic for default reasoning. *Artificial Intelligence,* 13(1–2): 81–132, 1980.

[343]   Raymond Reiter. On interacting defaults. In *Proceedings of the Seventh International Joint Conference on Artificial Intelligence, Vancouver*, pages 270–276. AAAI, Menlo Park, CA, 1981.

[344]   Raymond Reiter. Nonmonotonic reasoning. *Annual Review of Computer Science*, 2:147–186, 1987.

[345]   Raymond Reiter. On closed world data bases. In Hervé Gallaire and Jack Minker, editors, *Logic and Databases*, pages 55–76. Plenum Press, New York, 1987.

[346]   Raymond Reiter. A theory of diagnosis from first principles. *Artificial Intelligence*, 32(1):57–95, 1987.

[347]   Raymond Reiter. The frame problem in the situation calculus: A simple solution (sometimes) and a completeness result for goal regression. In *Artificial Intelligence and Mathematical Theory of Computation: Papers in Honor of John McCarthy*, pages 359–380. Academic Press, New York, 1991.

[348]   Raymond Reiter. *Knowledge in Action: Logical Foundations for Specifying and Implementing Dynamical Systems*. MIT Press, Cambridge, MA, 2001.

[349]   Raymond Reiter and Johan de Kleer. Foundations of assumption-based truth maintenance systems: Preliminary report. In *Proceedings of the Sixth National Conference on Artificial Intelligence (AAAI-87), Seattle*, pages 183–188. Morgan Kaufmann, Los Altos, CA, 1987.

[350]   Michael D. Resnik. *Choices: An Introduction to Decision Theory*. University of Minnesota Press, Minneapolis, 1987.

[351]   Peter Revesz. *Introduction to Constraint Databases*. Springer-Verlag, New York, 2002.

[352]   Elaine Rich and Kevin Knight. *Artificial Intelligence*, 2nd edition. McGraw-Hill, New York, 1990.

[353]   Tom Richards. *Clausal Form Logic: An Introduction to the Logic of Computer Reasoning*. Addison-Wesley, Boston, 1989.

[354]   Gordon A. Ringland and David A. Duce, editors. *Approaches to Knowledge Representation: An Introduction*. Research Studies Press, Letchworth, Hertfordshire, England, 1988.

[355]   Don D. Roberts. *The Existential Graphs of Charles S. Peirce*. Mouton de Gruyter, The Hague, 1973.

[356]   R. Bruce Roberts and Ira P. Goldstein. *The FRL primer*. AI Memo 408, Artificial Intelligence Laboratory. MIT, Cambridge, MA, 1977.

[357]   John Alan Robinson. A machine-oriented logic based on the Resolution principle. *Journal of the Association for Computing Machinery*, 12(1):23–41, 1965.

[358]   Hans Rott. *Change, Choice and Inference: A Study of Belief Revision and Nonmonotonic Reasoning*. Oxford University Press, Oxford, 2001.

[359]   Stuart J. Russell and Peter Norvig. *Artificial Intelligence: A Modern Approach*, 2nd edition. Prentice Hall, Upper Saddle River, NJ, 2002.

[360]   Earl Sacerdoti. The nonlinear nature of plans. In *Proceedings of the Fourth International Joint Conference on Artificial Intelligence, Tbilisi, Georgia*, pages 206–214. Morgan Kaufmann, Los Altos, CA, 1975.

[361] Earl Sacerdoti. Planning in a hierarchy of abstraction spaces. *Artificial Intelligence*, 5(2):231–272, 1974.

[362] Wesley C. Salmon. *Four Decades of Scientific Explanation*. University of Minnesota Press, Minneapolis, 1989.

[363] Erik Sandewall. *Features and Fluents: The Representation of Knowledge about Dynamical Systems*. Vol. 1. Oxford University Press, Oxford, 1995.

[364] Erik Sandewall. Underlying semantics for action and change with ramification. *Linköping Electronic Articles in Computer and Information Science*, 3:307–329, 1998.

[365] Marco Schaerf and Marco Cadoli. Tractable reasoning via approximation. *Artificial Intelligence*, 74(2):249–310, 1995.

[366] Roger C. Schank and Robert P. Abelson. *Scripts, Plans, Goals, and Understanding: An Inquiry into Human Knowledge Structures*. Lawrence Erlbaum Associates, Hillsdale, NJ, 1977.

[367] Karl Schlecta. *Nonmonotonic Logics: Basic Concepts, Results, and Techniques*. Lecture Notes in Artificial Intelligence, Vol. 1187. Springer-Verlag, Berlin, 1997.

[368] James G. Schmolze and Thomas A. Lipkis. Classification in the KL-ONE knowledge representation system. In *Proceedings of the Ninth International Joint Conference on Artificial Intelligence, Karlsruhe, Germany*, pages 330–332. William Kaufmann, Los Altos, CA, 1983.

[369] Marcel J. Schoppers. Universal plans for reactive robots in unpredictable domains. In *Proceedings of the Tenth International Joint Conference on Artificial Intelligence, Milan, Italy*, pages 1039–1046. Morgan Kaufmann, San Mateo, CA, 1987.

[370] Marcel J. Schoppers. *Representation and Automatic Synthesis of Reaction Plans*. Ph.D. thesis, University of Illinois at Urbana-Champaign, 1989.

[371] Lenhart K. Schubert. Monotonic solution of the frame problem in the situation calculus: An efficient method for worlds with fully specified actions. In Henry E. Kyburg, Ronald P. Loui, and Greg N. Carlson, editors, *Knowledge Representation and Defeasible Reasoning*, pages 23–67. Kluwer, Dordrecht, The Netherlands, 1990.

[372] Lenhart K. Schubert. Explanation closure, action closure and the Sandewall test suite for reasoning about change. *Journal of Logic and Computation*, 4(5):679–900, 1994.

[373] John Searle. Minds, brains, and programs. *Behavioral and Brain Sciences*, 3(3):417–457, 1980.

[374] John Searle. *Minds, Brains and Science: The 1984 Reith Lectures*. Penguin Books, London, 1984.

[375] Bart Selman, Hector J. Levesque, and David Mitchell. A new method for solving hard instances of satisfiability. In *Proceedings of the Tenth National Conference on Artificial Intelligence, San Jose, CA*, pages 440–446. AAAI Press, Menlo Park, CA, 1992.

[376]   Glenn Shafer. *A Mathematical Theory of Evidence*. Princeton University Press, Princeton, NJ, 1976.

[377]   Glenn Shafer. *The Art of Causal Conjecture*. MIT Press, Cambridge, 1996.

[378]   Glenn Shafer and Judea Pearl, editors. *Readings in Uncertain Reasoning*. Morgan Kaufmann, San Francisco, 1990.

[379]   Murray Shanahan. *Solving the Frame Problem: A Mathematical Investigation of the Common Sense Law of Inertia*. MIT Press, Cambridge, MA, 1997.

[380]   Steven Shapiro, Maurice Pagnucco, Yves Lespérance, and Hector J. Levesque. Iterated belief change in the situation calculus. In *Proceedings of the Seventh International Conference on Principles of Knowledge Representation and Reasoning, Breckenridge, CO*, pages 527–538. Morgan Kaufmann, San Francisco, 2000.

[381]   Stuart C. Shapiro. The SNePS semantic network processing systems. In Nicholas V. Findler, editor, *Associative Networks: Representation and Use of Knowledge by Computers*, pages 179–203. Academic Press, New York, 1979. Reprinted in [47].

[382]   Stuart C. Shapiro. An introduction to SNePS 3. In Bernhard Ganter and Guy W. Mineau, editors, *Conceptual Structures: Logical, Linguistic, and Computational Issues*, pages 510–524. Lecture Notes in Artificial Intelligence, Vol. 1867, Springer-Verlag, Berlin, 2000.

[383]   Stuart C. Shapiro and Frances L. Johnson. Automatic belief revision in SNePS. In *Proceedings of the Eighth International Workshop on Nonmonotonic Reasoning, Breckenridge, CO*, 2000.

[384]   Yoav Shoham. *Reasoning about Change*. MIT Press, Cambridge, MA, 1988.

[385]   Yoav Shoham. *Artificial Intelligence Techniques in* PROLOG. Morgan Kaufmann, San Francisco, 1994.

[386]   Edward H. Shortliffe. *Computer-Based Medical Consultations:* MYCIN. Elsevier, New York, 1976.

[387]   Thoralf A. Skolem. Logisch-kombinatorische untersuchungen über die erfüllbarkeit oder beweisbarkeit mathematischer sätze nebst einem theoreme über die dichte mengen. *Videnskapsakademiets Skrifter I. Matematisk-naturvidenskabelig klasse*, 4:1–36, 1920. Also appears in Jens E. Fenstad, editor, *Th. Skolem: Selected Works in Logic*, pages 103–136. Universitetsforlag, Oslo, 1970.

[388]   Thoralf A. Skolem. Über die mathematische logik. *Norsk Matematisk Tidsskrift*, 10:125–142, 1928.

[389]   John Slaney and Sylvie Thiébaux. Blocks world revisited. *Artificial Intelligence*, 125(1–2):119–153, 2001.

[390]   Brian Cantwell Smith. *Reflection and Semantics in a Procedural Language*. Ph.D. thesis, Massachusetts Institute of Technology, Cambridge, MA, 1982. Also appears as Technical Report MIT/LCS/TR-272, MIT.

[391]   Paul Smolensky. On the proper treatment of connectionism. *Behavioral and Brain Sciences*, 2:1–74, 1988.

[392]   John F. Sowa. *Conceptual Structures: Information Processing in Mind and Machine*. Addison-Wesley, Reading, MA, 1984.

[393]    John F. Sowa, editor. *Principles of Semantic Networks: Explorations in the Representation of Knowledge.* Morgan Kaufmann, San Mateo, CA, 1991.

[394]    John F. Sowa. *Knowledge Representation: Logical, Philosophical, and Computational Foundations.* Brooks Cole, Pacific Grove, CA, 2000.

[395]    Richard M. Stallman and Gerald J. Sussman. Forward reasoning and dependency-directed backtracking in a system for computer-aided circuit analysis. *Artificial Intelligence,* 9(2):135–196, 1977.

[396]    Lynn Andrea Stein. Skeptical inheritance: Computing the intersection of credulous extensions. In *Proceedings of the Eleventh International Joint Conference on Artificial Intelligence, Detroit,* pages 1153–1158. Morgan Kaufmann, San Mateo, CA, 1989.

[397]    Lynn Andrea Stein. Computing skeptical inheritance. In Maurizio Lenzerini, Daniele Nardi, and Maria Simi, editors, *Inheritance Hierarchies in Knowledge Representation and Programming Languages,* pages 69–81. John Wiley & Sons, Chichester, 1991.

[398]    Lynn Andrea Stein. Resolving ambiguity in nonmonotonic inheritance hierarchies. *Artificial Intelligence,* 55(2–3):259–310, 1992.

[399]    Leon Sterling and Ehud Shapiro. *The Art of* PROLOG. MIT Press, Cambridge, MA, 1986.

[400]    Mark E. Stickel. A nonclausal connection-graph resolution theorem-proving program. In *Proceedings of the Second National Conference on Artificial Intelligence, Pittsburgh,* pages 229–233, AAAI, Menlo Park, CA, 1982.

[401]    Mark E. Stickel. Automated deduction by theory resolution. *Journal of Automated Reasoning,* 1(4):333–355, 1985.

[402]    Mark E. Stickel. A PROLOG-like inference system for computing minimal-cost abductive explanations in natural-language interpretation. *Annals of Mathematics and Artificial Intelligence,* 4:89–106, 1991.

[403]    Gerald J. Sussman and Drew McDermott. Why conniving is better than planning. AI Memo 255A, MIT, Cambridge, MA, 1972.

[404]    Gerald J. Sussman and Terry Winograd. MICRO-PLANNER reference manual. Technical report, Artificial Intelligence Laboratory, MIT, Cambridge, MA, 1970.

[405]    Alfred Tarski. Über den Begriff der logischen Folgerung. *Actes du Congrés International de Philosophie Scientifique,* 7:1–11, 1936. Translated in [406].

[406]    Alfred Tarski. *Logic, Semantics, Mathematics.* Clarendon Press, Oxford, 1956.

[407]    Austin Tate. *Advanced Planning Technology: Technological Achievements of the ARPA/Rome Laboratory Planning Initiative.* AAAI Press, Menlo Park, CA, 1996.

[408]    Ernest Teniente. An abductive framework to handle consistency-preserving updates in deductive databases. In *Proceedings of the ICLP'95 Joint Workshop on Deductive Databases and Logic Programming and Abduction in Deductive Databases and Knowledge-Based Systems,* pages 111–125. GMD-Studien No. 266, GMD, Sankt Augustin, Germany, 1995.

[409]    Michael Thielscher. Ramification and causality. *Artificial Intelligence,* 89(1–2): 317–364, 1997.

[410]   Michael Thielscher. Introduction to the fluent calculus. *Linköping Electronic Articles in Computer and Information Science*, 3(14):179–192, 1998.

[411]   Pierre Tison. Generalization of consensus theory and application to the minimization of boolean functions. *IEEE Transactions on Electronic Computers*, 4:446–456, 1967.

[412]   David S. Touretzky. *The Mathematics of Inheritance Systems*. Morgan Kaufmann, Los Altos, CA, 1986.

[413]   David S. Touretzky, John F. Horty, and Richmond H. Thomason. A clash of intuitions: The current state of nonmonotonic multiple inheritance systems. In *Proceedings of the Tenth International Joint Conference on Artificial Intelligence, Milan, Italy*, pages 476–482. Morgan Kaufmann, San Mateo, CA, 1987.

[414]   Maarten H. van Emden. Red and green cuts. *Logic Programming Newsletter*, 2, 1982.

[415]   Richard von Mises. *Probability, Statistics and Truth*, 2nd revised English edition prepared by Hilda Geiringer. Allen & Unwin, London, 1957. Republished by Dover, New York, 1981. Translation of the third German edition, 1951.

[416]   Gerd Wagner. *Vivid Logic: Knowledge-Based Reasoning with Two Kinds of Negation*. Lecture Notes in Artificial Intelligence, Vol. 764. Springer-Verlag, Berlin, 1994.

[417]   Richard Waldinger. Achieving several goals simultaneously. In Edward W. Elcock and Donald Michie, editors, *Machine Intelligence 8*, pages 94–136. Ellis Horwood, Chichester, 1975. Reprinted in Bonnie L. Webber and Nils J. Nilsson, editors, *Readings in Artificial Intelligence*, pages 250–271. Tioga, Los Altos, CA, 1981.

[418]   R. J. Walker. An enumerative technique for a class of combinatorial problems. In Richard E. Bellman and Marshall Hall Jr., editors, *Combinatorial Analysis: Proceedings of the Symposium on Applied Mathematics*. Vol. X, pages 91–94. American Mathematical Society, Providence, 1960.

[419]   Hao Wang. Toward mechanical mathematics. *IBM Journal of Research and Development*, 4:2–22, 1960. Reprinted in Hao Wang, *Logic, Computers, and Sets*, Science Press, Peking, 1962; Hao Wang, *A Survey of Mathematical Logic*, North-Holland, Amsterdam, 1964; Hao Wang, *Logic, Computers, and Sets*, Chelsea, New York, 1970.

[420]   Li-Xin Wang. *A Course in Fuzzy Systems and Control*. Prentice Hall, Upper Saddle River, NJ, 1997.

[421]   Donald A. Waterman. *A Guide to Expert Systems*. Addison-Wesley, Reading, MA, 1986.

[422]   Alfred North Whitehead and Bertrand Russell. *Principia Mathematica*, 2nd edition. Cambridge University Press, Cambridge, England, 1927.

[423]   David E. Wilkins. *Practical Planning: Extending the Classical AI Planning Paradigm*. Morgan Kaufmann, San Mateo, CA, 1988.

[424]   Mary-Anne Williams. Iterated theory base change: A computational model. In *Proceedings of the Fourteenth International Joint Conference on Artificial Intelligence, Montreal*, pages 1541–1550. Morgan Kaufmann, San Mateo, CA, 1995.

[425]   Mary-Anne Williams. Towards a practical approach to belief revision: Reason-based change. In *Proceedings of the Fifth International Conference on Principles of Knowledge Representation and Reasoning, Cambridge, MA,* pages 412–421. Morgan Kaufmann, San Francisco, 1996.

[426]   Terry Winograd. Frame representations and the declarative/procedural controversy. In Daniel G. Bobrow and Allan M. Collins, editors, *Representation and Understanding: Studies in Cognitive Science,* pages 185–210. Academic Press, New York, 1975.

[427]   Patrick Henry Winston. Learning structural descriptions from examples. In Patrick Henry Winston, editor, *Psychology of Computer Vision,* pages 157–209. McGraw-Hill, New York, 1975. Reprinted in [47].

[428]   Patrick Henry Winston. *Artificial Intelligence,* 3rd edition. Addison-Wesley, Reading, MA, 1992.

[429]   Ludwig Wittgenstein. *Tractatus logico-philosophicus.* Routledge and Kegan Paul, London, 1974. Originally published in German in *Annalen der Naturphilosophie,* 1921, as *Logisch-Philosophische Abhandlung.*

[430]   William A. Woods. What's in a link: Foundations for semantic networks. In Daniel G. Bobrow and Allan M. Collins, editors, *Representation and Understanding: Studies in Cognitive Science,* pages 35–82. Academic Press, New York, 1975. Reprinted in [47].

[431]   Larry Wos. *The Automation of Reasoning: An Experimenter's Notebook with* OTTER *Tutorial.* Academic Press, San Diego, 1996.

[432]   Larry Wos and George A. Robinson. Paramodulation and set of support. In *Proceedings of the IRIA Symposium on Automatic Demonstration, Versailles,* pages 276–310. Springer-Verlag, Berlin, 1968.

[433]   Larry Wos, George A. Robinson, and Daniel F. Carson. Efficiency and completeness of the set of support strategy in theorem proving. *Journal of the Association of Computing Machinery,* 12(4):536–541, 1965.

[434]   Jon R. Wright, Elia S. Weixelbaum, Karen E. Brown, Gregg T. Vesonder, Stephen R. Palmer, Jay I. Berman, and Harry H. Moore. A knowledge-based configurator that supports sales, engineering, and manufacturing at AT&T Network Systems. In *Proceedings of the Innovative Applications of Artificial Intelligence Conference, Washington, DC,* pages 183–193. AAAI Press, Menlo Park, CA, 1993.

[435]   Robert M. Wygant. CLIPS: A powerful development and delivery expert system tool. *Computers and Industrial Engineering,* 17:546–549, 1989.

[436]   Ronald R. Yager, Mario Fedrizzi, and Janus Kacprzyk. *Advances in the Dempster-Shafer Theory of Evidence.* John Wiley & Sons, New York, 1994.

[437]   Lotfi A. Zadeh. Fuzzy sets. *Information and Control,* 8:338–353, 1965.

[438]   Lotfi A. Zadeh. Fuzzy logic and approximate reasoning. *Synthese,* 30:407–425, 1975.

# ■ INDEX
■
■

The following is a list of all the important concepts presented in the text.
The page number indicates where the concept is first introduced or defined.